Psychosocial Factors Affecting Health

Psychosocial Factors Affecting Health

Edited by

MACK LIPKIN, JR.
KAREL KUPKA

PRAEGER SPECIAL STUDIES • PRAEGER SCIENTIFIC

Library of Congress Cataloging in Publication Data
Main entry under title:

Psychosocial factors affecting health.

    Bibliography: p.
    Includes index.
    1. Medicine and psychology—Congresses.
2. Social medicine—Congresses. 3. Nosology—
Congresses. I. Lipkin, Mack. II. Kupka,
Karel, M.D. [DNLM: 1. Disease—Classification.
2. Psychosocial deprivation. 3. Socioeconomic
factors. 4. Sociology, Medical—Classification.
WM 31 P974]
R726.5.P795 1982   362.1   82-11249
ISBN 0-03-061964-5

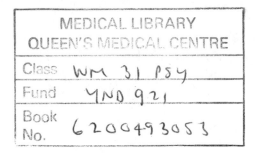
Published in 1982 by Praeger Publishers
CBS Educational and Professional Publishing
a Division of CBS Inc.
521 Fifth Avenue, New York, New York 10175 U.S.A.

Foreword

Generally speaking, books that are born of conferences do not make the best reading. As reviewers often point out, they lack cohesion in subject matter, let alone style, and their purpose is sometimes mysterious. I believe that this book can escape criticism concerning its purpose. The conferences from which it arose were not intended to give scholars an opportunity to display their wares. The 1979 meeting in Bellagio and subsequent meetings were working conferences inspired by a desire, widely shared internationally, to create a better method for documenting human ill health.

The constitution of the World Health Organization defines *health* in terms of physical, mental, and social well-being. Although this definition has been cited on innumerable occasions, it has yet to be implemented in the recording and classification of the departures from health that lead people to seek care. As a consequence, our illness records are unidimensional. They reduce the ills of humankind to the physical axis, concealing the mental anguish and the social distress that so often cause or aggravate a physical complaint.

As long as the unidimensional accounting of illness continues, both the care of patients and the formulation of policy will be too limited in scope to bring about the higher level of health for which humankind has reason to hope.

The chapters of this book reflect a concerted effort to develop a theoretical framework for the triaxial classification of illness and to devise a practical means of implementing such a classification. Whatever the outcome, this will be a historic document. If the endeavor is successful, the book will provide a faithful record of the early stages. If it is unsuccessful, a careful reading of this book will allow future workers to avoid failure by learning from our mistakes.

—CAROL BUCK
PRESIDENT
INTERNATIONAL EPIDEMIOLOGICAL ASSOCIATION

Contents

Classification of Psychosocial Factors Affecting Health

MACK LIPKIN, JR.

In his *Brown Book,* the celebrated philosopher Wittgenstein wrote, "one may object to the description which we give of the language of a tribe, that in the specimens we give of their language we let them speak English, thereby already presupposing the whole background of the English language, that is, our usual meanings of the words. . . . Now what characterizes an order as such, or a description as such, or a question as such, etc., is—as we have said —the role which the utterance of these signs plays in the whole practice of the language" (1).

Medicine and its related disciplines are today struggling with the issues presented in such condensed fashion by Wittgenstein. The question of the "role which the utterance" of the medical person plays is a subject of enormous controversy. In addition to the criticisms about medicalization, excessive use of jargon, inaccessibility, and other complaints about medicine's aggrandizing tendencies and its communication barriers to normal people, there are more fundamental criticisms. An enormous body of research and experience, presented from almost every conceivable point of view, suggests that deficiencies exist in the dominant languages or paradigms of modern biotechnical medicine. One major deficiency in the dominant language set in medicine is the subject of this book. This book attempts to show why there is a deficiency, to indicate what it is, and to suggest an approach to creating some improvement. The deficiency it addresses is the systematic bias in medical classifications toward the biological and anatomical and away from the psychological and social aspects of illness and care. By *classifications* are meant formalized embodiments of medical language, such as the *International Classification of Diseases (ICD)* (2). This classification is the most significant both because of its history and its functions. It is international—accepted by the World Health

Organization (WHO), which is responsible for its maintenance and improvement—and it functions as the basis of medical recording. It is the medium of much of the world's health statistics. These in turn underlie planning and remuneration. The case presented in this book, through a variety of approaches and perspectives, rests on the fundamental notion that the central language of the profession significantly influences and reflects the whole practice of the profession. It is for this reason that attention to classification is of fundamental importance.

The history of the classifications presently adopted (there are always classifications of disease in every culture) and sanctioned by WHO and most of the world's official medical groups has central relevance to their present structure. *ICD* traces its roots to the origins of vital statistics in England in the late eighteenth century. The initial motivation for collection for vital statistics was in part curiosity and in part the need to plan for deaths. Planning for deaths was needed because bodies had to be carted away, plots created for burial, persons paid to perform these functions, and so forth. Thus, even in its origins, our classification was centrally related to planning. Being curious and needing to make better plans, the persons responsible for the initial function of counting dead bodies—essentially, counting the number of people in one pile—became interested in sorting the bodies out by cause of death. Thus the initial mortality count spread into an accounting of causes of death. At first these were gross and primitive. Then in the mid-nineteenth century, with the onset of gross pathology and then of microscopic pathology, expanding understanding of the causes of death permitted more and more "piles," each containing fewer and fewer bodies. Now there are about 53,000 entries in the *ICD* English index.

By 1854, numbers and varieties of classifications of death had proliferated. International comparisons were being made about causes of death. It was felt finally that it was time to ask qualified individuals—in this case, William Farr of England and Mare d'Espine of Geneva—to create an internationally acceptable classification of diseases. It may be noted that *diseases* was already the term used when *causes of death* was meant. The first *ICD* was finally ratified in 1893. It was then revised approximately every ten years; the ninth was agreed on in 1975. During this time, the ratification process became more and more officially sanctioned. In 1946, WHO became responsible for the international classification through its *ICD* division.

Of interest in this early history are three factors. First, both initial and subsequent attention was given primarily to causes of death. This meant that the categories and organization derived from mortality data and findings, from gross and then microscopic pathology, and from their descendants. This orientation is both understandable and justifiable. The initial motivation was interest in causes of death. It was more easily organized on the basis of gross and microscopic pathology, which consisted of readily available data conveniently derived after the patient had died. It was objectively based on things people could see, touch, measure, and keep in formalin jars or slide boxes as long as proof was necessary. But a problem was discovered in this orientation toward fatal diseases and toward increasingly tiny units of sources of data, from the anatomical to the microscopic to the biochemical and now even to the submolecular. The problem was first brought into clear formal display by the British after World War II. Studies of the Royal College of General Practitioners showed that up to 40% of the visits to general practitioners could not be classified under *ICD* rubrics. The reason for this was simple. The classification started with the end of the illness process and with the extreme result in cases. They looked at the final causes, not at the whole of the illness experience. It did not correspond readily to what people as patients go through. It introduced a new language and hence a new world view, in Wittgenstein's sense, into the set of medical experiences previously talked about in plainer language by doctors and their patients.

It was, again, an interest in planning coupled with plain curiosity about medical processes that led to the development of a new approach to classification, which focuses on what is actually said and done in the practitioner's office with the practitioner's live patients. This process-oriented empirical approach to classification led to a series of classifications beginning with the so-called "E book" and ending with the recent publication of the *International Classification of Health Problems in Primary Care,* second revision (*ICHPPC*-2) (3). This is a thoroughly field-tested, empirically derived classification of problems in primary care; while having many fewer rubrics than *ICD* (371 in contrast to 53,000), it accounts for more than 90% of the problems encountered in primary care as field-tested around the world.

The last decade in classification in medicine has been distinguished by the development of *ICHPPC*-2 and the growing collaboration between the creators of *ICHPPC* and those responsible for *ICD*. The outcome of this is that *ICHPPC*-2 was made compatible with *ICD* in its various modifications through adoption of compatible numeric codes.

The second noteworthy feature of the early *ICD* was that it focused on single entities that tended to be physical in nature. That is, it was a unidimensional classification: If a person was classified as having one problem, the person did not have all the rest. Each visit, episode, or problem was expected to have a single rubric to explain it. How realistic is that? Because our instruments are unidimensional, we do not know definitively how realistic this is. Many of the data presented in this book suggest that health is multideterminate and that illness is multideterminate. A classification that is unidimensional must leave out important issues, factors, and relationships between these determinants.

The third noteworthy feature of the early history again derived from the focus on causes of death. This led to the relative exclusion of problems and issues that did not often cause physical death. Thus, in particular, psychological and social factors tended not to be recorded.

In short, the history of classification is that, as it has tremendously organized and simplified an enormous body of knowledge, it has imposed on that body of knowledge a specific world view. Because it essentially derived from the tools and techniques of pathology, it has tended to omit a whole range of relevant phenomena, with serious effects on the language of medicine and hence on its perceptions of its subject.

It also has seriously affected the perception of the importance and place of general practice. This bias, because it is so pervasive in health statistics, has affected planning and remuneration as well. When not counted, the omitted problems do not count. When not counted, they are not paid for. When they are not paid for, they are less valued. When they are less attractive to practitioners, the incentive to note them and deal with them then rests on purely humanitarian grounds, and their chances of recognition are diminished.

As well, education about the nature of medicine must share the same biases as the language of medicine in which it is taught. Thus medical education presently deals at much greater length with much less prevalent and important problems than it does with highly prevalent and significant psychological and social aspects of care. For example, although most medical residents know how to detect and to care for nonketotic hyperosmolar diabetic coma, a relatively rare event, few know how to detect or care for patients at high suicidal risk from depression. While the former condition is very uncommon, yet widely taught about, the latter is the leading nontraumatic cause of death in the second and third decades of life in industrial societies. Yet it is fair to say that most physicians are not prepared to detect or to treat it. That is one small example of the effects of these biases.

This book represents one small preliminary effort to initiate dialogue toward correction of these problems. In October 1979, a small group of scholars interested in the classifications of problems in primary care or in psychosocial aspects of care met in Washington, D.C., in the offices of the Division of Epidemiology of the National Institute of Mental Health. Using the existing classifications, they attempted to craft a new basis for classification of problems in primary care. The main features of the new classification (presented in detail in Chapter 11) are three:

- It is very simple, so that it can be used for international comparisons, be widely usable, and remain reliable. It was felt that until experience tells us which categories should be added and which omitted, it is best to be simple.
- It proposes that classifications of episodes of illness be in three dimensions, not just one. That is, in addition to the physical dimension present-

ly used and represented in *ICD,* it suggests the use of a psychological axis and a social axis.

• The classification attempts to use already existing categories based on preexisting classifications whenever possible.

The group meeting in Washington proposed a new classification of psychological and social factors—that is, to add to *ICD* and *ICHPPC*-2 a second and third axis and to create thereby a triaxial classification of problems in primary care. This proposed classification was presented to a larger group of scholars and practitioners in a five-day meeting at the Villa Serbelloni in Bellagio, Italy, in November 1979. At that conference, papers were presented and discussed to support and to dispute the arguments for new classifications. The first group of papers addressed the underlying argument about the structure of medicine and whether it is uni- or multideterminate. Arguments were heard from epidemiological, psychophysiological, and sociological perspectives that medicine is multideterminate. Hence its classifications must be multideterminate as well.

Once this broad view was accepted, the authors turned a finer focus on primary care. One author examined the phenomenology found when a simple classification of psychological issues was used. A second used the sociological concept of humanization as a sample theme to probe the complex ways in which such themes enter the fabric of care. A third looked at specific research about a specific sociological concept, *values deficiency.* This was both illuminating and disturbing, because it showed the complexity of the issues to be enormous. The finding that there may be many intermediate variables between illness events and psychological and social events suggests how difficult it will be to find the right factors to use in our classifications. The relatively elementary understanding presently available in this field, despite the elegance of some of its basic research (4), should not discourage us. We are more advanced than the earliest statisticians were in England when they began to count bodies and only had one pile. We at least have several "piles." But we are still not able convincingly to resolve the issues involved in William James's question: "Does a man cry because he is sad, or he is sad because he cries?"

Given, however, that primary care is multideterminate and requires a multideterminate model of classification, how ought we to classify the multiple determinants of problems occurring in primary care? Our initial approach to this was to review the existing classifications in detail. As well, the need for a psychosocial classification system was reviewed epidemiologically.

Then a proposed classification was presented, together with a special look at the issues of the mental health and social problems of children. Some alternative classifications were also discussed.

Finally, proposed applications of the new classifications were explored. The problem of cross-cultural applications was examined in detail. The use and utility of the triaxial classification in primary care settings was studied by examination of some examples of successful uses of modified classifications. Finally, the educational program necessary to permit adoption of a new classification was discussed. This is an important issue, because true acceptance of the new classification requires a change in language and hence a shift in the paradigms of the speaker.

The results of the 1979 Bellagio conference were several. First, a set of recommendations was made by the conferees to WHO. These are included in this volume as Chapter 21. The primary recommendation was that a triaxial classification of health problems in primary care be field-tested as soon as possible. In response to this, two more conferences were held, and these have resulted in plans for a field trial using seven international primary care centers. The initial phases of the trial are under way under the auspices of WHO. It is anticipated that the field trial's preliminary results will be available in 1983. On the basis of the field trial, further revision of the classification should be feasible in time for consideration for inclusion in the tenth revision of *ICD*.

The true impetus for these efforts derives from the nature of health care itself. Our knowledge of this is reflected in data about health care such as that presented here. However, certain individuals and institutions are playing important roles in bringing about this historic shift. Notable has been the Mental Health Division of WHO under the leadership of Norman Sartorius. They have carried the administrative weight of this project. Much of the initiative derives as well from the epidemiological branch of the National Institute of Mental Health in the United States. Its leader is Darrel A. Regier. The Rockefeller Foundation has contributed both through the support of its Deputy Director for Health Sciences, Kerr L. White, and through the use of its offices and the Villa Serbelloni at Bellagio, Italy.

The production of this book has been significantly helped by the editors' staffs, especially at The Rockefeller Foundation. Michael Kaufman added greatly. Carol Buck played an important role in chairing the first conference. Michael Shepperd has been of enormous help as participant, through his inspiring life's work, and as an administrative troubleshooter from time to time. Maurice Wood has been indefatigable as an author, a planner, and the representative of the World Organization of National Colleges, Academies, and Academic Associations of General Practitioners/Family Physicians (WONCA). The editors are grateful to all of these people.

This book reflects several sorts of contributions. First, it contains the paper prepared after the initial meeting of the small group in Washington, D.C., in October 1979, as well as the papers prepared as background material for the larger conference held in Bellagio, Italy, in November 1979. These papers have been substantially revised and cross-referenced. The book also contains other papers prepared for the two subsequent conferences. Finally, it includes as Chapter 22 the second revision of the proposed classification. This revision was undertaken at the conference held in February 1981 in Bellagio, at which the six-center international field trial of the classification was also planned.

The discussions held at the three conferences were extensive and detailed. Although detailed notes and rapporteurial summaries were made of these, there has been no attempt to record them here. Rather, the editors have attempted to distill the essence of the issues in the brief introductory or concluding sections in each major part of the book.

REFERENCES

1. L. Wittgenstein, *The Blue and Brown Books* (New York: Harper & Row, 1965, p. 102).

2. World Health Organization, *Manual of the International Statistical Classification of Diseases, Injuries, and Causes of Death,* 9th revision (Geneva: Author, 1977).

3. World Organization of National Colleges, Academies, and Academic Associations of General Practitioners/Family Physicians, *International Classification of Health Problems in Primary Care,* 2nd revision (London: Oxford University Press, 1979).

4. See, for example, H. Weiner, *Psychobiology and Human Disease* (New York: Elsevier, 1977).

Psychosocial Factors Affecting Health

I

Multidimensional Determinants of Health

Each of the authors in Part I uses a different conceptual and experiential frame: Buck adduces epidemiological data, Hongvivatana uses primarily psychophysiological data, Bonifacio draws heavily on sociological concepts and data, and Westerholm brings these together in the context of the Western medical systems of Sweden. Yet these authors, despite different backgrounds, argue similarly. The complexity of health and illness, however seen, requires complex models that include the social and psychological as well as the physical. None of the authors attempts to be exhaustive. Each argues by example and is intentionally impressionistic. But the individual cases are enhanced by the collective force of the arguments. Taken together, their presentations are convincing.

Several commonalities are of particular note. They make the issue more forceful today than it was, say, 25 years ago when the great blossoming of biotechnical Western medicine was in its upslope. First, each author alludes to the phenomenon of the expanding expectations from the health system. The Director General of the World Health Organization (WHO) is quoted to the effect that health is necessary for socioeconomic progress. The converse is true as well: Socioeconomic progress creates a healthier population. Spectacular successes of science in general and medicine in particular, such as the availability of penicillin and its derivatives and the eradication of smallpox, have lead to generalization of expectation for high-technology miracles. The medical profession has supported this belief both for realistic and politi-

1

cal reasons. WHO, both in its constitution and in the Alma Ata declaration of the goal of "Health for All by the Year 2000," promotes raised expectations.

Simultaneous with expanding definitions of the role and responsibility of health professionals has been increasing knowledge of the scope of medicine and of its interrelatedness with other social and psychological life. Each author cites numerous studies that demonstrate a critical role for psychological and social factors in the causes of and predisposition to disease. Thus preventive work must take these factors into account. Each author shows that psychological and social factors are critical in determining how and when persons become patients. Psychological and social factors are shown to affect the times when people seek care and to determine when sort of care they seek. Without knowing how these things work, without knowledge of the determinants of illness and illness behavior, it is impossible to plan care systems effectively. Without the specific knowledge of these factors, it is impossible for a health care professional to plan an adequate care and preventive regimen for a specific patient.

Psychological and social factors also enter into the determination of compliance with care regimens. Therefore they contribute to the effectiveness or failure of care. They interact in the patients' healing processes both through placebo and Hawthorne effects and through less direct effects on healing.

Most of the authors in this section point to a need for further information. Such need is well documented in works such as those by Houpt and colleagues (1) and Williams and Clare (2). Most of the studies cited are indirect with respect to primary health care and psychosocial components. They either look at selected subsets of illness phenomenology or use epidemiological and population-sampling methods rather than direct surveys of large populations of defined nature. We are still in a relatively primitive state of knowledge concerning the elementary phenomenology of primary illness experience. Our knowledge needs in this area are further discussed in Part II.

REFERENCES

1. J. L. Houpt, C. S. Orleans, L. K. George, and H. K. H. Brody, *The Importance of Mental Health Services to General Health Care* (Cambridge, Mass.: Ballinger, 1979).

2. P. Williams and A. Clare, *Psychosocial Disorders in General Practice.* New York: Grune & Stratton, 1979.

1

Determinants of Health: People, Situations, and Social Systems

CAROL BUCK

INTRODUCTION

During this century, medicine has become a highly technical field from which miracles are expected by a society that has almost unlimited faith in the power of science and technology to relieve human hardship. There is a widespread belief that all ill health will ultimately be curable by drugs or surgery.

It is true that modern medicine has provided preventive and curative measures that would have been regarded as miraculous in an earlier era. But it is also true that human behavior, individually and collectively, creates health problems that defy purely medical solutions.

Scientific and technical discoveries made it possible to control malaria. In countries where these discoveries were applied, there was a risk of replacing death from malaria with death from malnutrition if the reproductive behavior of human beings and the organization of agriculture could not deal with the increased longevity suddenly brought about by the disappearance of a killing disease (1).

The purpose of this chapter is to show the extent to which health is influenced by all aspects of human society. Until we understand this and form our policies accordingly, it is unlikely that we will be able to make substantial improvements in the well-being of mankind.

These issues are discussed by proceeding up the hierarchy from people, to situations, to social systems.

PEOPLE

This section examines factors that operate at the personal and family level to cause ill health or to make it difficult for sick people to find and use appropriate care for their illnesses.

3

What Makes People Sick?

Genetic Causes

At the most basic level are the genetic determinants of disease. In some diseases, such as hemophilia and muscular dystrophy, the genetic component is all-determining and requires little contribution from the individual's environment. Fortunately, such diseases are rare. Far more common are genetic influences on bodily or mental function that make the individual more susceptible to causal factors in the environment. The contribution of salt intake to hypertension is one example. It appears that the effect of salt may be particularly important in a person genetically predisposed to hypertension (2).

Because of common genetic predispositions, members of a family will tend to suffer similar illnesses, a fact that can be usefully exploited in the early detection of remediable diseases. But genes do not by any means explain all the familial clustering of disease that one observes.

Other Familial Causes

Members of a family share a common physical and psychological environment, either of which can have a negative influence upon health.

The material deprivations of poverty may affect the food, shelter, and clothing available to the family, thereby increasing the susceptibility of its members to diseases caused by nutritional deficiency, overcrowding, dampness, and cold, and elevating the risk of accidents from fires and other hazards associated with poor housing. Although there has been little systematic investigation of the contribution of each of these specific concomitants of poverty, the relationship between poverty and disease has been repeatedly documented. Damon and his colleagues in Boston have made an important contribution to the study of the effects of the residential environment on health and have indicated the lines along which further research should proceed (3).

Psychological deprivations, although greatly increased by the circumstances of poverty, can occur in affluent families. Parents who are psychologically unsuited to the rearing of children can inflict emotional damage upon their children even if they satisfy their material needs.

General Environmental Causes

Beyond the immediate environments of the family, there are many factors that can affect health. Most obvious are those in the physical environment, such as noise, air and water pollution, unsafe working conditions, and traffic hazards. But also important are circumstances in the psychological and social environment, such as insecurity of employment, isolation, racial discrimination, and other forms of harassment.

Personal Behavior

Health is directly affected by a variety of personal habits, particularly diet, exercise, and the use of tobacco and alcohol. It is important to recognize that such habits can be strongly influenced by genetic, familial, and general environmental factors. Although alcohol consumption, for example, appears to be a matter of personal choice, the freedom of choice actually available to an individual can be constrained by genetic predisposition, familial example, and the habits of associates at work and in the neighborhood.

Operation of Causal Factors

In this brief space it is impossible to discuss the mechanisms by which all these causal factors operate. Some operate in a very direct and specific manner, as in the case of deafness caused by noise-induced injury to the ear. More often, and particularly with the social and psychological factors, the causal mechanisms are exceedingly complex, although the final common pathway is through the nervous and endocrine systems of the individual. For a masterly review of the evidence, the reader is directed to the Wade Hampton Frost Lecture given by the late John Cassell in 1976 (4).

What Makes It Difficult for People to Find and Use Appropriate Care for Illness?

Lack of information is one reason people do not find and use appropriate care. If a person does not understand the significance of a symptom and persists for long in self-treatment, care may be dangerously delayed. Even if the person understands that a symptom may be dangerous he or she may not know where to go for further treatment.

Fear of the consequences of illness may lead an individual to deny symptoms, a phenomenon that has frequently been observed among cancer patients.

Medical care can be inaccessible for a variety of reasons. The person may not be able to afford the direct cost of care or the indirect costs associated with loss of earnings while under treatment. The source of care may be too distant in relation to available transportation, or it may be open only during hours when the person is tied down by a job or by the care of dependents.

Even if appropriate care has been sought, compliance with treatment may not occur. The reasons for noncompliance are many and have been reviewed in depth by Haynes and colleagues (5). Inability to afford prescribed drugs, lack of understanding of the purpose of treatment or the schedule of medication, and discouragement by the patient's family or peers are frequently encountered causes by noncompliance. In some instances there is a more subtle factor at work; the patient may not wish to recover, because the illness brings psychological and social gains that are greater than its discomforts.

SITUATIONS

This section deals with a wider constellation of factors that cause or promote ill health. Some degree of overlap with the previous section is impossible to avoid, however, since "situations" are created by "people."

Psychological and Social Stressors

Poverty, rejection, bereavement, marital breakdown, and cultural dislocation are all known to be associated with illness (6). Their effects can be found in children as well as in adults, as the recent work of Beaglehole has shown (7). Beaglehole and his colleagues studied blood pressure among families migrating from the Tokelau Islands to New Zealand. When longitudinal measurements were made on the same children before and after migration, it was found that their blood pressure rose following the move to New Zealand. An increase in weight associated with the change to a Western diet only partially accounted for the elevation of blood pressure; thus it is likely that psychological as well as physical concomitants of migration were involved.

Sometimes, as Cassell has pointed out (8), it is difficult to know whether a social stressor is a cause of illness or whether it and the illness are both produced by an underlying psychological problem. The difficulty is perhaps most evident with marital breakdown, where personality factors are very likely to have been operative before the breakdown occurred. Such an alternative explantion of the effects of social situations, although possible, must not be generalized to the point of denying that situations can lead directly to illness. The design of the New Zealand study of blood pressure eliminated the possibility that children predisposed to hypertension were the ones most likely to leave the Tokelau Islands. Similarly, Cobb's study of the health of men who became unemployed after their factory had closed was freed from the possibility that illness caused unemployment, rather than the reverse (9).

Lack of Social Support

Social support refers to the mutual esteem and help of a person's network of family, friends, and colleagues. When social support is lacking, the effect of social stressors upon health is greatly increased; whereas in the presence of strong social support, people can emerge relatively unscathed from highly stressful situations. The evidence from a variety of studies of this phenomenon has been reviewed by Cobb (10).

It is possible that many of the ill effects of industrialization and migration are due to the loss of the individual's social supports when his or her familiar environment is disrupted or left behind. Social support affects more than the occurrence of ill health. It may also affect the outcome of illness by influencing compliance with treatment. The social support of one's family is likely to be particularly important in fostering compliance.

Unhealthy Physical Environment

The most obvious situational cause of ill health, and the one most responsible for the severe health problems of the developing countries is an unhealthy physical environment. Scanty and impure water supplies, perpetual shortage of food, and exposure to arthropod vectors of infectious disease are potent causes of death and disability.

SOCIAL SYSTEMS

It is easy, but probably incorrect, to believe that the health care system is the social system most related to health. Before we consider health care, we must realize that the political and economic characteristics of a country may be a major, indeed *the* major, determinant of health. If the general political system is one that allows unhealthy circumstances, we cannot expect much benefit from improvements in the health care system. Some of the systems and policies that affect health are now discussed.

The Economic System and the Economic Policy

Brenner has produced substantial evidence that wide fluctuations in the business cycle have an adverse effect upon the health of people, especially upon the health of those who are most vulnerable to unemployment and redundancy (11). If the economic system puts productivity and growth as ends in themselves, rather than as means for improving the quality of life, it is unlikely that measures will be developed to dampen the fluctuations in the business cycle or to cushion people from their effects.

In addition to the adverse effects of economic instability, there is the equally important issue of income distribution. Policies concerning minimum wages, social insurance, and income tax all have a bearing upon the prevalence of poverty, and thus ultimately upon the occurrence of ill health.

On a global level, economic policies encourage the development of pollution havens, as well as of tax havens. If legislation in a developed country prohibits or requires stringent controls over highly polluting industrial processes, economic policies encourage the transfer of such industries to developing countries, which are happy to risk environmental pollution in return for the jobs that are provided. The multinational corporate structure of modern industry makes it just as easy to find pollution havens as to find tax havens. Often the tax haven and the pollution haven are one and the same.

Certain specific economic policies are also of relevance to health. As McKeown points out, it is strange that we tolerate artifically high prices for goods that are deemed to be healthful (12). For example, in the Western world, whole-grain bread is now more expensive than bread made from refined flour. According to McKeown, it was not more expensive prior to the accumulation of evidence that dietary fiber might have a protective effect against cardiovascular disease. The converse, equally bad, is an economic system that depends for a substantial portion of revenue upon the taxes levied against unhealthful goods (tobacco and alcohol). Under such circumstances, the official discouragement of consumption lacks sincerity.

Some economic policies put technological achievements above the welfare of the worker and the consumer. In many countries, profitable industrial technologies are introduced without regard to the potential harmful effects upon their employees or consumers. Compounding this problem are generally inadequate systems of social and health statistics, which make it difficult even to discover the adverse effects upon health of industrial processes. In Canada, for example, a Royal Commission was appointed to examine the health and safety of mine workers in the province of Ontario. Its report included recommendations concerning the need for adequate recording and regular review of data on potentially hazardous exposures and on the mortality of those exposed (13). It is amazing that such recommendations are necessary in the second half of the twentieth century.

The Social System and Social Policy

Social policies can induce psychosocial stress and reduce the network of support available to the individual. Immigration policies in many Western countries, for example, favor the individual immigrant over the family; thus they may force families to leave behind a mentally or physically ill member. It would be fair to say that the present health restrictions imposed upon immigrants to North America work in the direction of improving the health of the *recipient* country. In some parts of the world, immigrants are encouraged to come on a cyclical or temporary basis so that social insurance payments need not be made on their behalf.

Another aspect of the social system that has an effect upon health is the manner in which goods are promoted and marketed. The difficulties in prohibiting the advertising of alcohol and tobacco are well known. Less obvious is the toleration of advertising strategies that encourage the downward drift of unhealthy practices from the upper to the lower social classes. Marmot and his colleagues in Great Britain have evidence to suggest that by the time the upper classes had reduced their smoking and altered their diets in what is believed to be a prudent direction, the lower classes had changed their habits in the opposite direction (14). In a plutocratic social system, it is acceptable to advertise in a manner that encourages the poor to emulate the rich, even if the underlying motive is to maintain a market for goods that the rich have come to recognize as harmful. A more global manifestation of this phenomenon is the aggressive sale of high-tar cigarettes to the developing countries of the world.

Social policy determines the importance accorded to town planning, through which the beauty, cohesiveness, quiet, and safety of a neighborhood can be enhanced. Although there is no evidence to prove that beautiful surroundings have a favorable effect on health, it is most likely that they do. Many cities have destroyed old neighborhoods, moving the displaced population to high-rise dwellings in inconvenient and isolated settings where a social support system is unlikely to develop.

Social policy influences the nature of education and thus affects the degree to which children are correctly informed about factors affecting health. This includes education about diet, exercise, safety, and other aspects of physical health, as well as education about human sexuality, marriage, and child rearing.

Social policy can encourage substitutes for natural support systems in urbanized areas where neighborhood systems are weak. Some examples are Alcoholics Anonymous, Big Brother programs for children in mother-headed families, John Howard Societies in Canada for the rehabilitation of criminal offenders and the support of their families, and community programs that offer elderly people an opportunity to engage in the daytime care of preschool children. The last example is particularly important, because the benefits are reciprocal and thus reproduce most faithfully the characteristics of natural social support systems.

The Health Care System and Health Policies

In most of the developed countries, the health care system encourages the diagnosis and treatment of the acute phase of illness and discourages prevention, follow-up, and long-term care. More unfortunately, this policy is being copied by the developing countries, where it is even less suited to the needs of the people. Why do we follow such a policy?

The underlying reason is mentioned in the opening paragraph of this chapter. Acute care requires the greatest application of technology. Society is in love with medical technology, partly because of a belief in its supremacy, and partly because it is an exciting and dramatic aspect of health care. When it comes to thrills, immunization and day hospitals for the senile are at the bottom of the list; heart transplants are at the top.

In recent years, the health care system has been concerned with an alleged reform in the dismantling of long-stay institutions and the transfer of patients from these institutions back to their communities. The idea is sound, but the predominantly money-saving motive behind it tends to make it unsound in practice. The necessary investment in community services is seldom made; consequently, the patients and their families are thrown upon their own resources to a degree that exhausts their natural support systems. The short-term economic benefits of such a policy may appear substantial, but it is likely that the longterm social and economic consequences are bad.

The social system and the health care system may work together in a manner that favors upper- and middle-class patients. The best known example is in psychiatry, where it has been shown that drugs are the predominant therapies for lower-class patients, psychotherapy being reserved for patients whose social background is sufficiently akin to that of the therapist that rapport is easily established. This problem could be tackled by teaching health professionals to adapt their psychotherapeutic techniques to patients with limited verbal skills. In doing so, the professionals might develop new therapeutic insights (15).

An obvious flaw of many health care systems is the financial deterrent that prevails in the absence of comprehensive health insurance. It is justified on the grounds that people would bring trivial ailments for care unless a financial barrier discouraged them from doing so. The evidence in support of this view is meager and largely anecdotal. It is far more likely that a financial deterrent discourages the poor, whose health is generally worse than that of the rich, and has little effect upon the health care behavior of the middle- and upper-income groups. A deterrent payment deters only those who cannot afford it.

If we wish to promote self-care, we should do it directly by making the necessary information available, rather than allowing self-care to occur by default among people whose economic position forces them to avoid professional care. It is likely that self-care is performed better by the well educated; the folly of a health care system that indirectly encourages self-care among those least able to carry it out should be amply evident.

REFERENCES

1. J. E. Meade, "Population Explosion, the Standard of Living, and Social Conflict," *The Economic Journal* 77 (1967):223.

2. G. Mimura et al., "A Study on Twins with Hypertension and Cerebrovascular

Disease in Japan," in *Prophylactic Approach to Hypertensive Diseases,* ed. Y. Yamori et al. (New York: Raven Press, 1979).

3. A. Damon, "The Residential Environment, Health, and Behavior," in *The Effect of the Man-Made Environment on Health and Behavior,* ed. L. E. Hinkle and W. C. Loring (Atlanta: U.S. Department of Health, Education and Welfare, 1977).

4. J. Cassell, "The Contribution of the Social Environment to Host Resistance," *American Journal of Epidemiology* 104 (1976):107.

5. R. D. Haynes et al., eds., *Compliance in Health Care* (Baltimore: Johns Hopkins University Press, 1979).

6. A. R. Kagan and L. L. Levi, *Health and Environment—Psychosocial Stimuli— A Review* (Stockholm: Karolinska Institut, 1971).

7. R. Beaglehole et al., "Blood Pressure in Tokelauan Children in Two Contrasting Environments," *American Journal of Epidemiology* 108 (1978):283.

8. J. Cassell, "Factors Involving Sociocultural Incongruity and Change," *Milbank Memorial Fund Quarterly* 45 (1967):41.

9. S. Cobb, "Physiological Changes in Men Whose Jobs Were Abolished," *Journal of Psychosomatic Research* 18 (1974):245.

10. S. Cobb, "Social Support as a Moderator of Life Stress," *Psychosomatic Medicine* 38 (1976):300.

11. M. H. Brenner, "Mortality and the National Economy," *Lancet* 2 (1979):568.

12. T. McKeown, *The Role of Medicine* (Oxford: Blackwell Scientific Publications, 1979).

13. *The Royal Commission on the Health and Safety of Workers in Mines.* (Ottawa: Government of Ontario, 1976).

14. M. G. Marmot et al., "Changing Social Class Distribution of Heart Disease," *British Medical Journal* 2 (1978):1109.

15. F. Riessman et al., eds., *The Mental Health of the Poor* (Glencoe, N.Y.: Free Press, 1964).

2

The Need for and Scope of Assessing Psychosocial Factors Affecting Health in Developing Countries

THAVITONG HONGVIVATANA

Health, as defined by the constitution of the World Health Organization (WHO) in 1946, is a state of complete physical, mental, and social well-being, and not merely the absence of disease and infirmity. Yet the individual and biological conception of health and illness has been dominating medical thinking and practice, to the neglect of the social context. This dominance has prevailed despite the age-old recognition of social causation of diseases.

Many great medical practitioners in history were conscious about the social component of health. The Hippocratic humoral theory of medicine is a classic example of the relation between the environments—physical and social—and the prevalence and severity of various diseases (1). During the Industrial Revolution, Rudoff Virchow, a prominent German social philosopher and medical writer, argued that poverty bred disease; he even asserted that it was the responsibility of physicians to support social reforms to reconstruct society according to a pattern favorable to the health of human beings (2). In addition, the fact that the mind acts upon the body and can produce physical disorders has been an important part of medical knowledge since the days of Galen (3,4). Yet these social conceptions of disease play no role in current medical thinking and practice.

The impacts of social environment or ecology on health have been well established in psychosomatic, anthropological, and sociological studies today. Ambiguities still prevail, however, and operational programs along this line are almost nonexistent. Most authorities in medicine and public health are too pragmatic to accept and help enforce the concept of health defined by WHO. They consider the definition to have virtually no operational or practical significance. Some even prefer to ignore the definition problem altogether (5).

The definition problem is not trivial; it surely has significant implications for health care research, planning, and provision. Ideal depictions could serve as guidelines for concrete actions if real efforts, not lip service or benign neglect, are put forward. In this regard the program on psychosocial factors affecting health, announced at the 29th WHO Assembly, seems to be the first official systematic inquiry and operation in the area of the social component of health (6).

In Western countries, the role of social and psychological factors in health has been made clear by a large number of psychosomatic, sociological, and psychological studies. In developing countries, however, social and psychological components of health rarely receive attention from medical practitioners and social scientists. This chapter is thus designed to indicate the need for assessing the negative impact of psychosocial problems in developing countries. It is divided into three parts. First, a brief conceptual review is made. Second, the need in the context of developing societies is justified in detail. The third part outlines the scope of assessment and other relevant research topics.

A BRIEF CONCEPTUAL OVERVIEW
OF THE HEALTH-RELATED PSYCHOSOCIAL MODEL

Recently in industrialized countries it was found that some major diseases— that is, hypertension, cancer, and coronary heart disease—have no single establishable organic cause. Therefore, there has been growing interest in finding out whether certain psychosocial factors are etiologically related to the onset and course of such diseases.

The Stress Concept and Psychosocial Factors

Psychosocial factors in the context of health, as defined by WHO, are those factors affecting personal health, health care, and community well-being, stemming from the psychosocial makeup of individuals and conditioned by the wider social and cultural environment (6). Empirical studies of health and illness employing psychosocial approaches usually revolve around the concept of *stress*. Yet it is widely acknowledged that there are semantic as well as conceptual difficulties associated with the stress concept (7,8,9). The semantic difficulty is eased by distinguishing between *stress state* and *stressor* (7). *Stressors* are situations in social and cultural milieus that act as noxious stimuli to individuals (e.g., life crises, intense competition, rapid social and cultural change, mobility, and migration). *Stress state* is the resultant adverse psychological state of tensions, anxiety, fear, depression, and the like, residing in the individual. Stress state, in turn, may have pathological effects on the body.

Conceptual debate focuses mainly on whether the pathological effect of stressors is invariable, affecting all people in similar manner, or idiosyncratic, affecting each person differently depending on his or her personality, interpretation of the situation, and so forth (8,10). The former view is best represented by the development of the Social Readjustment Rating Scale in stress research (11). The scale is a list of life change events, weighted by scores indicating the relative level of expected adjustment required by each event. Thus it is unique in its emphasis on events requiring readjustments of the individual, irrespective of whether they are perceived as comfortable or unpleasant. The latter view holds that it is not an objective stress situation per se or its associated readjustments that impinge on the individual, but that his or her negative perception of such a stressor is etiologically related to the onset of disease (12). King, in his review of social-psychological studies on health, suggests that the idiosyncratic approach seems to be more relevant to the question of "who will become ill," while the invariant scheme is more relevant to the "type of illness" that will ensue (13). To the present author, the debate also reflects a difference in emphasis on stressor and stress state between the two approaches. It also reveals the difficulty of establishing the relationship between stressor and stress state. Supposedly, the adverse psychological effect of a social situation must not be assumed but empirically tested.

Psychosocial Stress as Disease Etiology

Psychosocial studies of health and illness could be classified into two related perspectives: etiology and illness response (13). The first approach considers psychosocial factors in causal relationship with the onset of specific diseases or general pathogenic conditions. The study of illness response takes illness as a source of stress affecting psychodynamic balance and interpersonal relations of the sick, which may have aggravated the disease process. Another variant of the second approach emphasizes the situation in which psychosocial stress unrealted to a condition interacts with the illness, resulting in a constellation of chronic disability that is difficult to tackle medically (8). Since the emphasis of this chapter is on the need for assessing the impact of psychosocial factors on health, the conceptual review here is confined to the etiological role of psychosocial factors.

The psychosocial perspective on disease etiology is based on the observation that illness is not solely a biological or physical phenomenon. An illness episode is also an event that occurs in a social context, with its networks of social and interpersonal relationships, culture, and values defining the nature of social relationships, goals, means, and aspirations of individuals. The social environment in its dynamic state could be a source of supports as well as threats to individuals. A social environment threat, given a person's perception of it and his or her coping or adaptive capacity, could manifest itself in an adverse psychological state that precipitates the onset of illness. Social situations may act directly on the body, as in the case of accident, alcoholism, and psychosomatic diseases; or they may act indirectly by putting the individual in a situation of increased vulnerability to disease agents (i.e., social values, custom, food habits, etc.) or making him or her biologically more susceptible to disease agents (i.e., hypertension, coronary heart disease, etc.). Expressing it another way, in epidemiological terms, social stress induces a psychological state of anxiety, depression, and so forth, which in turn upsets the homeostasis in the body and increases the susceptibility of the organism to disease agents through neuroendocrine and psychoimmunological mechanisms. In other words, the stress state caused by a threatening social environment upsets the balance between the host and disease agents, and this results in the decrease of host resistance (7). This is so because ubiquitous disease agents could persist symbiotically in the human body without causing obvious harm.

The questions facing health-related social-psychological inquiry, then, is this: What are the psychosocial factors capable of adversely affecting the psychological state of individuals, thus making them susceptible to what diseases?

Existing empirical studies of the so-called psychosocial etiology of the disease process could be classified into two groups according to sources of stress: society-focused and individual-focused. For the former group, society at large is the source of stress; the approach is exemplified by studies of relationships between drastic social and cultural change and the onset of specific diseases, such as elevated blood pressure and coronary heart disease. For example, it has been reported that South American cities that were growing more rapidly than other cities (implying more rapid social change) had been suffering from a higher rate of mortality from hypertension (14). The individual-focused group is rather micro-oriented in emphasizing personal situations as main sources of stress. Among important personal stressful situations are geographic movement, life style change, life events or crises, status inconsistency, and personality conflicts (15). It has been demonstrated, for example, that mobility and migration are related to various illnesses, including cardiovascular diseases and mental disorders (16,17).

The impact of social stress on the onset of essential hypertension has attracted wide attention in industrialized Western countries, especially the United States. Many studies have established a significant relationship between social stress and elevated blood pressure (18). According to a large number of authorities, modern society is characterized by many stressful features—for instance, disruption of traditional cohesive social organization, migration, family instability, relative deprivation, status incongruity, intense competition, social alienation, job pressure, and so forth (18,19,20). These features have uprooted people from familiar and warm social environments, values, and expected modes of behavior and adjustment. This results in a widespread condition of stress and anxiety that is conducive to pathogenesis in vulnerable individuals.

Identification of Psychosocial Factors

There are two important conceptual problems that concern the identification and measurement of the social component of health.

First, most empirical psychosocial studies to date rarely give a clear operational definition of *psychosocial factor*. The definition given by WHO, mentioned earlier, does not do much to clarify the concept. Supposedly, the psychosocial process is related to the concept of stress, in which *stressor* has to be distinguished from *stress state* for conceptual clarity. By the same token, as a basis for understanding the psychosocial process, it is important first to differentiate psychological from social variables. Yet the genesis of the "psychosocial" concept is the causal relationship between social (stresssor) and psychological (stress state) variables. Theoretically, a psychosocial factor could be considered either as a psychological symptom rooted in a specific social environment, or as a social problem and its resulting adverse psychological state in individuals.

In practice, however, psychosocial studies usually focus on stressful social problems. Yet exhaustive identification of areas of stress structured by the social order seems difficult, although not impossible. This is so because it is difficult to establish relationships between specific social problems and their psychological correlates. Many authors have indicated that a particular situation is stressful or not, depending on how individuals perceive it; this perception in turn is dependent on social values. More importantly, it should be obvious that the impact of psychosocial factors on health cannot be direct, but is mediated through various coping and stress-reducing mechanisms in the society, which are culture-bound.

Although society is the major source of stress, it also provides social support and other stress-reducing and coping mechanisms for vulnerable members. The extent of this varies, however, from society to society. This is clearly illustrated by the fact that, despite living in almost the same stressful urban industrial environment, the Japanese suffers less from coronary heart disease than the Japanese-American who lives in continental America does (21,22). This is because the in-group work community, unique to Japanese society, acts as an effective stress-reducing mechanism (22).

The above discussion implies that an "ideal" list of social stress areas affecting health should be flexible enough to be cross-culturally modified and adapted.

The second problem is reflected in the unresolved dispute on the nature of the psychosocial etiology—whether it is specific or nonspecific. Cassell, in reviewing studies in this area, concludes that the weight of evidence does not support the notion of etiological specificity (7). Mechanic has reported that discomforting psychological states play an important role in at least some kinds of disease, and may possibly have some role in all disease processes (8). The issue of specific versus nonspecific etiology would be problematic to the formulation of public health programs aimed at modification of psychosocial factors.

THE NEED FOR ASSESSING HEALTH IMPACTS OF PSYCHOSOCIAL FACTORS IN DEVELOPING COUNTRIES

Some Pitfalls of Western Medicine

If the mechanistic concept of disease, which has originated in the Western world, has led to the neglect of the social component of health in industrialized countries, a similar phenomenon must have occurred in developing societies as well. This is because Western scientific medicine, with its education, professionalism, and ideology, has been internationalized and exported to developing countries in almost exact form and substance (23,24,25).

Apart from the major criticism that modeling medical education and health service systems after the Western ideal leads to enormous unmet health needs of the population in developing societies, the limits of scientific medicine also lie in its culture-bound nature. There is no doubt that diseases like hypertension, heart disease, cancer and tuberculosis, which are prevalent in Western societies and cannot be explained solely by the biological etiology-specific medical theory, can be found (though on a smaller scale) in developing countries as well. However, what is more important is that health cultures in underdeveloped areas are variant and alien to Western medicine; this fact makes things more complicated for modern medical practitioners. According to this perspective, illnesses are likely to be culture-bound or rooted in culturally determined psychosocial stresses in which mechanistic medical interventions may prove to be failures. Two examples may be mentioned here. There seems to be an agreement that conventional scientific medicine alone is unable to deal with the Latin American *susto,* a malaise known locally as caused by fright and resulting in "soul loss," the symptoms of which are nervousness, insomnia, loss of appetite, inability to urinate, depression, and introversion. Anthropological studies have established that *susto* is a product of a complex interaction of biological, environmental, cultural, and psychological factors (26,27). *Falling out* (seizure-like episodes with no evidence of organicity), found exclusively among black Americans, Bahamians, and Haitians, is another problem requiring therapeutic approaches that are both transdisciplinary (social science/medicine) and transcultural (28).

In most developing countries where Western medicine has achieved a legally dominant status in the health system, the position of traditional medicine has deteriorated. Yet the new ruling medical profession does not possess, and seems reluctant to acquire, the traditional healing attitude of viewing and treating the patient as a "whole person"—the attitude that is psychologically valued most by patients. Thus it is often reported that modern or cosmopolitan medicine coexists in developing countries with traditional healing—that is, that a pluralistic medical system has arisen. An inherent feature of this phenomenon is that a large number of patients, if they do not feel better upon initial contact with cosmopolitan medicine, subsequently resort to traditional healers who are more socially accessible and more responsive to their psychological needs. In rural Thailand, it is reported that patients with complex but well-known psychosomatic problems—stomach ulcers, chronic colitis, high blood pressure, migraines, and the whole host of "nervous" complaints—go untreated, and the doctors do not have any concern for them (29). Many of these patients turn to traditional healers and quacks for further care. A survey of the utilization of traditional medicine in Malaysia reveals that a large proportion of patients, regardless of the nature of complaints (physical or psychological), believe that cosmopolitan medicine is a partial healing system that neglects the social, psychological, and spiritual aspects of healing (30).

As a matter of fact, the persistence of traditional medicine and its viability, despite the official dominant status of Western medicine in developing coun tries, should be evidence to modern medical practitioners that there is a need to broaden and modify their orthodox approach.

Development and Psychosocial Process

Developing countries, as the term implies, have been attempting a complex and multifaceted economic and sociocultural transformation. This means a process of drastic physical, cultural, and behavioral changes, which may have unintended adverse effects on the health of the populace. That the physical change inherent in the development process upsets the ecological balance and fosters diseases is well illustrated by Dubos and others (31,32). However, psychosocial stresses resulting from development efforts in these countries do not receive enough attention, possibly because of their elusive nature and deliberate negligence on the part of development planners.

Yet on the basis that many socially induced diseases have increased and been brought to attention in developed industrialized countries, it seems logical to expect that the same phenomenon emerges in developing societies as well. After all, most of these countries have been taking the same route to development as that followed in the West. Because development in emerging countries has been deliberately and consciously planned since the end of World War II, changes are relatively more intensive. Further, due to the short period of attempted development, the traditional cohesive social order is still alive in the memory of most natives. Seen from these perspectives, the rate of social, cultural, and behavioral changes would be perceptibly high. The adverse psychosocial effect of development, as expected, must surely be traumatic and pathogenic. Along with progress comes the disease of progress.

It is fair to say that decades of development in most Third World countries have hardly resulted in significant alleviation of poverty and suffering for the underprivileged majority. The development process in most of these countries is rather uneven. Poverty, malnutrition, and low standards of living are still widespread, while only a handful of privileged people reap most of the fruits of development. Even for the health sector, the maldistribution of health resources, typical in developing societies, is also a manifestation of this phenomenon (33). Certainly poverty breeds diseases—directly, through lack of necessary means of living (e.g., poor houses, poor sanitation), and indirectly, by way of psychosocial processes (e.g., unemployment, relative deprivation, alienation). The new social structure and relations are themselves reservoirs of stress for many individuals. One study reveals that the penetration of commercial and exchange relations into the countryside breaks down the cohesive rural society and contributes to high morbidity among the populace (34). Other studies report a strong correlation between extent of industrialization and higher rate of mental disorder among developing countries (35,36).

The few empirical studies on the process of urbanization, an essential component of so-called modernization of developing countries, consistently indicate urbanization correlates of increasing psychological stress and widespread mental health problems (37,38). Migrations from rural to urban areas provoke massive demographic and behavioral changes of leaving the rural village, the land, and domestic responsibilities to women, children, and old men. The urban environment, in which individuals interact with strangers instead of family and friends, causes identity crises and widespread social alienation or anomie. Job pressures in industrial factories go hand in hand with occupational disease. Contacts with Western goods and civilization lead to rising expectations and relative deprivation. Unemployment adds to the list of stressful situations. Meanwhile, some segments of the urban population become more and more Westernized in their culture and life styles; and this, according to Murphy (39), is also a cause of increased mental illness.

Indeed, the magnitude of mental health problems in developing countries is alarming. WHO has reported that in all developing countries more than 40 million people are suffering from serious untreated mental disorders. Although the extent of mild mental disorders (psychoneuroses, emotional disorder, personality problems) is much more difficult to ascertain, surveys have shown that they may affect as many as 10% of the total population (40). Recently the WHO Coordinated Project on Monitoring Mental Health Needs carried out in Thailand (41) has given prevalence rate of 2.9 per 1,000 for mental illness in a study area on the basis of inpatient and unnotified outpatient census. However, using the notified outpatient census figure—that is, the figure if the residents in the area are informed about the presence of a psychiatric team—the rate jumps to 15.3 per 1,000.

Etiological studies using a psychosocial analysis are rare in developing countries. Yet the ones available consistently point to the important role played by psychosocial variables in precipitating certain diseases. Scotch, in his study of elevated blood pressure in rural and urban Zulu communities, reported higher blood pressure in urban areas, and the sociocultural variables significant in predicting high blood pressure were indicative of nonadaptive patterns for urban living, which induced psychological stress (42). A more recent study involved the Pacific islanders who migrated to Samoa and New Zealand (43). On the basis of prospective research design, the study concluded that the migrants to New Zealand had significantly higher blood pressure. Controlling for other factors, it was found that those who adopted the European way of life were more subject to high blood pressure than were the ones who restricted themselves mostly to native social life.

Despite a vast array of potential stressful social situations in the developing countries, systematic investigation of the operation of psychosocial factors has remained an underdeveloped area.

Response to Illness

In developing countries, the need for psychosocial assessment also exists in the area of response to illness. Especially important are the psychological factors influencing the seeking of health care, the provision of government health services, and the doctor-patient relationship.

The need for psychosocial assessment is justified by the fact that despite the shortage and maldistribution of all types of resources, particularly health resources, the paradoxical phenomenon of underutilization of available health services is widespread in developing countries (44). This creates an enormous waste of health resources in the midst of inadequacy. In the variegated medical system of Thailand, the problem of underutilization of government health services, particularly at the primary care level (health centers), is obvious and probably critical (45,46,47,48,49,50). For example, in 1970 a nationwide survey of health service utilization in Thailand by the Ministry of Public Health showed that only 17% of the population survey used the public health facilities yearly, although the average Thai got sick twice a year (50). This occurs despite the fact that in Thailand, especially in the countryside, the public sector is the major provider of health services. Bryant reported that a Thai physician responsible for 100,000 people saw five or ten outpatients a day and did little else (48). Another study (46) showed that a secondary health center in a rural area had only three outpatient visits on an average working day; the figure increased to 5.5 visits if provision of preventive care was accounted for.

The underutilization of rural health services is surely not unique to Thailand. The same phenomenon has been reported in Colombia: Even in the rural areas around Cali, only 40% of the population used the health center (48). Another study, in Trinidad and Tobago, showed that only 13% of the sampled rural mothers resorted to modern doctors for treatment of infant and child-hood illnesses (51). A joint UNICEF/WHO study strongly asserts that the phenomenon of underutilization of available rural health facilities is wide-spread in most developing countries (44).

Why people do not use health services when they are physically accessible is a crucial question of medical care in developing countries. Yet systematic documentations and analyses of this problem are few and inadequate. More importantly, the reasons for this phenomenon are not well understood.

Some factors have been cited as reasons for this underutilization. Geo-graphic location of health centers may be incongruent with the pattern of population distribution. Hence distance coupled with transportation prob-lems acts as a barrier to utilization. Inadequate service quality at the health center may result in "bypassing," which leads to underutilization of health centers and at the same time overburdens services such as hospitals. Folk con-ception of disease etiology is indicated by various studies as the reason for preference for traditional rather than cosmopolitan medicine among the pop-ulation (52,53).

All these factors are only partial explanations for the underuse of public health facilities in rural areas. A complete account of this phenomenon must include psychological variables as potential inhibiting factors. For instance, "social distance" is emphasized by various authors as a deterrent factor in underutilization of government rural health services in Thailand (45,47). Pa-tients visiting government health units have to pay the psychic costs, in addi-tion to the monetary costs, associated with inferior-superior class relations or patron-client relations; all these costs may dissuade them from future con-tacts. In Colombia, "social distance" between users and providers of health services is also one of the important causes of underutilization (48).

In developing societies, especially in rural areas, it has often been indicated that doctor-patient relationships and communication are rather poor (29,54). This may be attributed to social distance, as discussed above, and the reluc-tance of health personnel themselves to go beyond purely "medical" aspects of the patient. To the patient, however, the illness has both physical and psy-chosocial dimensions. Therefore, professional consultation only partially meets the patient's need and may not result in recovery at all. A more illumi-nating case of consultation that often ends up with the patient's dissatisfac-tion with and underutilization of service is consultation for chronic illness re-sulting from the interaction of psychosocial stress and illness in the individual. Due to the scientific medical practitioners' attitude of negligence toward and blindness to the patient's social and psychological problems, treatments of-fered appear inadequate, and the patient prefers to see traditional healers. Various anthropological studies of the utilization of traditional medicine by the population in developing countries consistently indicate that patients with chronic illness prefer to see traditional healers rather than modern doctors (30,55).

On the whole, it is likely that illness behavior influenced by sociocultural and psychological factors is important in explaining the phenomenon of underutilization in developing societies. The whole area of responses to illness needs to be assessed in detail.

SCOPE OF ASSESSMENT

Broadening the conception of health and illness to include psychological and social considerations is a rather difficult task. This is the case even in Western countries, where numerous psychosomatic, anthopological, and sociological empirical inquiries have confirmed the effect of psychosocial stresses on health and illness. In developing societies, where the masses are poor and the limited health resources available are severely maldistributed, the prospect of a broader approach to health and medicine is even gloomier. However, a "countervailing force" must now be initiated. A promising beginning step is to convince medical practitioners that psychosocial factors have negative impacts on health and interfere in the healing process. For this to be achieved, a thorough assessment of the impact of psychosocial factors and further relevant research are necessary.

It is important to empirically test the relationship between psychosocial factors and the health of various population groups. Priority should be given to groups that are at high risk for psychosocial stress, particularly factory workers, migrants, and other deprived groups. Efforts should be directed at assessment of psychosocial problems in rural areas, in which the majority of the Third World population resides. With their limited resources, the health sectors of developing countries cannot afford a narrow, expensive, wasteful, orthodox approach to medical care provision. It may be hoped that information about the psychosocial component of illness will serve as a basis for developing an effective integrated approach to rural health services.

Specific etiological study of the psychosocial process should also be initiated. Prevalence of high blood pressure and heart disease is on the increase in urban areas. Thus it will be interesting to prove whether this increase is related to psychosocial stresses. Mental disorder and psychosomatic problems have also become more prevalent in developing societies. The question, again, is this: How they are related to social problems?

It is the present author's belief that the area of illness response and behavior needs rigorous investigations. Important are (1) study of the characteristic reactions of patients and their families to illness, disability, and other stress-producing environmental factors; (2) study of folk medical beliefs, culture, and practices; (3) study of relation and communication between health personnel and patients; (4) study of patients' attitudes toward government health services and compliance with these services. Further, there is an urgent need for analytical studies of the health service underutilization problem in rural areas, and corrective measures should be planned and implemented without delay.

Lastly, further thought must be put into different methods of organizing health care and social services to deal effectively with psychosocial stresses.

REFERENCES

1. R. Dubos, *Mirage of Health* (New York: Harper & Row, 1971).

2. N. Poynter, *Medicine and Man* (Harmondsworth, England: Penguin, 1973).

3. G. Rosen, "The Evolution of Social Medicine," in *Handbook of Medical Sociology,* ed. H. E. Freeman, S. Levine, and L. G. Reeder (Englewood Cliffs, N.J.: Prentice-Hall, 1979).

4. LeShan points out that Galen, employing the humoral theory of medicine, believed that "melancholic" women were more prone to cancer than those of "sanguine" temperament. L. LeShan, "Psychological Status as a Factor in the Development of Malignant Disease: A Critical Review," *Journal of the National Cancer Institute* (1959):21.

5. S. Kelman, "The Social Nature of the Definition Problem in Health," *International Journal of Health Services* 5(1975):625–40.

6. "Psychosocial Factors and Health," *WHO Chronicle* 30(1976):337–39.

7. J. Cassell, "The Contribution of the Social Environment to Host Resistance," *American Journal of Epidemiology* 104(1976):107–11

8. D. Mechanic, *Medical Sociology* (New York: Free Press, 1978).

9. H. B. Kaplan, "Social Psychology of Diseases," in *Handbood of Medical Sociology,* ed. H. E. Freeman, S. Levine, and L. G. Reeder (Englewood Cliffs, N.J.: Prentice-Hall, 1979).

10. L. E. Hinkle et al., "Studies in Human Ecology," *American Journal of Psychiatry* 114(1957):212–20.

11. T. H. Holmes and R. H. Rahe, "The Social Readjustment Rating Scale," *Journal of Psychosomatic Research* 11(1967):213–18.

12. L. E. Hinkle, Jr., and H. G. Wolff, "Ecologic Investigation of the Relationship between Illness, Life Experience, and the Social Environment," *Annals of Internal Medicine* 49(1958):1370–73.

13. S. H. King, "Social-Psychological Factors in Illness," in *Handbook of Medical Sociology,* ed. H. E. Freeman, S. Levine, and L. G. Reeder (Englewood Cliffs, N.J.: Prentice-Hall, 1979).

14. J. Henry and J. C. Cassell, "Psychosocial Factors in Essential Hypertension: Recent Epidemiologic and Animal Experimental Evidence," *American Journal of Epidemiology* 90(1969):171–200.

15. S. Graham and L. G. Reeder, "Social Factors in the Chronic Illnesses," in

Handbook of Social Medicine, 2nd ed., ed. H. E. Freeman, S. Levine, and L. G. Reeder (Englewood Cliffs, N.J.: Prentice-Hall, 1972).

16. J. Smith and J. Cassell, "Factors Involving Sociocultural Incongruity and Change," *Milbank Memorial Fund Quarterly* 45(1967):21–49.

17. M. Kantor, ed., *Mobility and Mental Health* (Springfield, Ill.: Charles C Thomas, 1965).

18. J. Ever, "Hypertension as a Disease of Modern Society," *International Journal of Health Services* 5(1975):539–58.

19. C. C. Hughes and J. M. Hunter, "Development and Disease," in *Social Organization of Health,* ed. H. P. Dreitzel (New York: Macmillan, 1971).

20. A. Kiev, "The Study of Folk Psychiatry," in *Magic, Faith, and Healing,* ed. A. Kiev (New York: Macmillan, 1974).

21. Y. S. Matsumoto, "Social Stress and Coronary Heart Disease in Japan: A Hypothesis," *Milbank Memorial Fund Quarterly* 48(1970):9–36.

22. C. G. Mermot and S. L. Syme, "Acculturation and Coronary Heart Disease in Japanese-Americans," *American Journal of Epidemiology* 104(1976):225–47.

23. P. J. Donaldson, "Foreign Intervention in Medical Education: A Case Study of the Rockefeller Foundation's Intervention in a Thai Medical School," *International Journal of Health Services* (1976):251–71.

24. M. S. Goldstein and P. J. Donaldson, "Exporting Professionalism: A Case Study of Medical Education," *Journal of Health and Social Behavior* 20(1979):322–27.

25. E. R. Brown, "Exporting Medical Education: Professionalism, Modernization, and Imperialism," *Social Science and Medicine* 13A(1979):585–96.

26. J. Klein, "*Susto:* The Anthropological Study of Diseases of Adaptation," *Social Science and Medicine* 12B(1978):23–28.

27. A. J. Rubel, "The Epidemiology of a Folk Illness: *Susto* in Hispanic America," in *Culture, Disease, and Healing,* ed. D. Landy (New York: Macmillan, 1977).

28. H. H. Weidman, " 'Falling Out': A Diagnostic and Treatment Problem Viewed from a Transcultural Perspective," *Social Science and Medicine* 13B(1978):95–113.

29. E. E. Boesch, *Communication between Doctors and Patients in Thailand* (West Germany: Socio-Psychological Research Centre on Development Planning, University of the Saar, 1972).

30. H. K. Heggenhougen, "The Utilization of Traditional Medicine: A Malaysian Example," *Social Science and Medicine* 14B(1980):39–44.

31. R. Dubos, *Men, Medicine, and Environment* (Harmondsworth, England: Penguin, 1970).

32. C. C. Hughes and J. M. Hunter, "Disease and Development in Africa," in *Social Organization of Health,* ed. H. P. Dreitzel (New York: Macmillan, 1971).

33. V. Navarro, "The Underdevelopment of Health or the Health of Underdevelopment: An Analysis of the Distribution of Health Resources in Latin America," *International Journal of Health Services* 4(1974):5–28.

34. A. C. Laurell et al., "Disease and Rural Development: A Sociological Analysis of Morbidity in Two Mexican Villages," *International Journal of Health Services* 7(1977):401–23.

35. E. B. Brody, "Psychiatric Implications of Industrialization and Rapid Social

Change," *Journal of Nervous and Mental Disorders* 156(1973):295–96.

36. G. Mustafar, "Society in Relation to Mental Health in Kenya," *Journal of Nervous and Mental Disorders* 156(1973):300–5.

37. S. Kellert et al., "Cultural Change and Stress in Rural Peru," *Milbank Memorial Fund Quarterly* 45(1967):391–415.

38. V. Zigas and J. van Delden, "New Guinea: Studies Relating the Medical and Behavioral Sciences, Part I," *Social Science and Medicine* 6(1972):681–87.

39. M. B. Murphy, "Social Change and Mental Illness," in *Causes of Mental Disorder: A Review of Epidemiological Knowledge* (New York: Milbank Memorial Fund, 1961).

40. *Organization of Mental Health Services in Developing Countries,* WHO Technical Report Series no. 564 (Geneva: World Health Organization, 1975).

41. Division of Mental Health, World Health Organization, "WHO Project on Monitoring Mental Health Needs" (Bangkok: Ministry of Public Health, Thailand, 1979, mimeographed).

42. N. Scotch, "Sociocultural Factors in the Epidemiology of Zulu Hypertension," *American Journal of Public Health* 53(1967):1205–13.

43. "Down with High Blood Pressure," *WHO Chronicle* 32(1978):136–37.

44. V. Djukanovic and E. P. Mach, *Alternative Approaches to Meeting Basic Health Needs in Developing Countries* (Geneva: World Health Organization, 1975).

45. J. N. Riley and S. Sermsri, *The Variegated Thai Medical System as a Context for Birth Control Services* (Bangkok: Institute of Population and Social Research, Mahidol University, 1974).

46. D. Muangman, "Thailand: Country Report," in *Health Aspects of Community Development in Southeast Asia,* ed. M. T. Maruchi (Tokyo: Southeast Asian Medical Information Centre, 1977).

47. C. Cunningham, "Thai Injection Doctors: Antibiotic Mediators," *Social Science and Medicine* 4(1970):1–24.

48. J. Bryant, *Health and the Developing World* (Ithaca, N.Y.: Cornell University Press, 1969).

49. F. A. Day and B. Leoprapai, *Patterns of Health Utilization in Upcountry Thailand* (Bangkok: Institute of Population and Social Research, Mahidol University, 1977).

50. P. O. Woolley, *Syncrisis: The Dynamic of Health,* vol. 12, *Thailand,* DHEW no. (os)74-50008 (Washington, D.C.: Government Printing Office, 1974).

51. W. R. Aho and K. Minott, "Creole and Doctor Medicine: Folk Beliefs, Practices, and Orientations to Modern Medicine in Rural and Industrial Suburban Settings in Trinidad and Tobago, the West Indies," *Social Science and Medicine* 11(1977): 349–55.

52. A. C. Colson, "The Differential Use of Medical Resources in Developing Countries," *Journal of Health and Social Behavior* 12(1972):226–37.

53. L. R. Schwartz, "The Hierarchy of Resort in Curative Practices: The Admiralty Islands, Melanesia," *Journal of Health and Social Behavior* 10(1969):201–9.

54. M. Greyhton, "Communication between Peasants and Doctors in Tunisia," *Social Science and Medicine* 11(1977):319–24.

55. M. A. Gould, "The Implication of Technological Change for Folk and Scientific Medicine," *American Anthropologist* 59(1957):507–13.

3

The Disease Model as a Determinant of the Health Care Organization Model

MANUEL FLORES BONIFACIO

One of the most important challenges that confronts humanity in the contemporary world is to discover ways to improve the quality of life. In attempting to tackle multidimensional human problems, various types of expertise are being harnessed. One central problem that has been given full attention by international experts is health. While it is true that doctors have been able to combat and eradicate some major health problems like smallpox, others have remained. At the same time, new types of health problems are emerging because of the many changes in the human environment, such as the diseases brought about by the very drugs that are also beneficial to humans. Given the inherent vulnerability of human beings to many disorders, there appears to be no final solution to their health problems. The basic vulnerability of humanity to disorders will always be with us. Perhaps the best to which humans can aspire is to find ways of protecting themselves against the effects of certain diseases.

Recognizing the significance of health to the improvement of human well-being, it becomes important to ask what is meant by *health*, or more specifically, by *being healthy?* One of the most comprehensive statements on the meaning of *health* is found in Declaration 1 of Alma Ata, which states that "health, which is a state of complete physical, mental, and social well-being, and not merely the absence of disease or infirmity, is a fundamental human right and that attainment of the highest possible level of health is a most important worldwide social goal whose realization requires the action of many other social and economic sectors in addition to the health sector" (World Health Organization 1978, p. 2).

This definition is comprehensive in the sense that it cuts across the various dimensions of human well-being. It emphasizes the need for always considering humans as physical, mental, and social beings; the interrelationship among these major components is an active one. Thus, health has three basic

27

components—namely, physical, mental, and social ones. If only one of these components is confronted in approaching health problems, then whatever that solution may be, it will certainly be inadequate. In addressing the problem of health, therefore, one must take into serious consideration all three components. The definition of *health* as well-being demands that the type of health care organization model be integrated to incorporate each of the components we have identified. Why?

One way of answering this question is to examine the nature of a disease model and show its effects on the nature and type of health care organization. A *disease state* "is one that is recognized as involving a near certainty of temporary disability, a danger of permanent impairment, or a risk of premature death" (Feldstein, Piot, and Sundaresan 1973, p. 12). This definition identifies a disease by its three possible consequences for human well-being: temporary disability, permanent impairment, and risk of premature death. Perhaps it is in consideration of the risk of premature death that health programs are forced to address themselves to curative and preventive services. When a disease strikes a person, the process of intervention is to relieve the person of the disorder. When others are in danger of being affected, other health resources are mobilized, for a disease not only affects a single person but may also affect others. In some critical instances, removal of the person from the community may be necessary so that more health services can be utilized, thereby increasing the person's chances of survival. While the removal of the sick person from the community may be necessary, this is not the ultimate solution to the problem. Many times, such an approach is complemented by an expanded treatment program together with some preventive programs aimed at checking the further spread of the disease and the establishment of provision for the care of the relatives of the sick. In addition to this, health education may be undertaken so that the community will be able to protect itself by mobilizing community action.

While an uncontrolled disease state may impair the social functioning of the person and thereby reduce his or her opportunity to be a productive member of society, being healthy does not necessarily imply that a person will be productive. There are numerous cases of unhealthy individuals who are still very productive. However, it is the awareness of impairment that has led practitioners to emphasize the physical aspects of health care. The general pattern of intervention is to cure persons of their illnesses and return them to a healthy state. It is a known fact, however, that this intervention is an ideal situation and cannot be extended to the general population, due to limitations in health resources and in the effectiveness of medical treatment. We know that while health services should reach everyone, they seldom do. An understanding of the conditions that bring this about can change our conception of the disease state and of health care organizations. For instance, while medical services may be given free by the health service program of the government, not everyone has direct access to such services. Even if they have access, at times people do not take advantage of the services offered because of the potential cost of the medicine that will be prescribed to them and, worse, the possibility of being hospitalized. Hospitalization will not only take them away from their families, but, more importantly, from their work, thereby jeopardizing the welfare of their families. Thus, "whether a person decides to seek help, and the form of help he seeks, depends on the availability of treatment resources, their physical proximity, and the psychological and monetary costs of seeking assistance" (Mechanic 1971, p. 209). It is clear, therefore, that the actual access of a given person to health and related resources is related to his or her socioeconomic situation.

> Indirectly, socioeconomic level is an important variable in accounting for response to illness because in a very gross way differences in socioeconomic level encompass differences in health values, understanding and information concerning disease, future and preventive planning, cultural expectations concerning health services, feeling of social distance between oneself and health practitioners, and so on. Thus, impoverished persons tend to know less about disease than more affluent members of our society, and they engage less in preventive planning, accept discomfort more routinely, and feel less at ease in medical setting. (Mechanic 1971, pp. 192–93)

In other words, while disease states have few class boundaries, access to services has many. Because society is stratified and one of its bases is income, not everyone enjoys the same opportunities; thus access to health services cannot be enjoyed by everyone. While some have complete access to sophisticated services, others are totally deprived of access to any service. Many of the deprived develop their own manner of coping with disease, either by using lay services or by denying the disease completely. "For people at subsistence levels the expenditures of money to ward off disease or check on symptoms that are not disabling may be a luxury which must be foregone in preference to providing food, clothing, and shelter" (Rosenstock 1969, p. 186). In other words, "most ailments are treated at home. Some parents bring their children to the *herbolario* (folk healer) first before they go to the doctor. The main reason given by some mothers is that they do not have money for medicine, as well as for the doctor's fee" (Jocano 1973, p. 83). We may infer from the foregoing that because of the actual and perceived cost of medical services that many poor families cannot afford, they may refer the illness to some traditional causes requiring the assistance of a traditional healer rather than a doctor.

When folk medicine fails, the poor are likely to take at least two options. The first is that they may pool their kinship resources and other resources to bring the patient to Western services. When too few resources can be mobilized, continued use of folk medicine and invoking the assistance of the spirits remains in order. For instance,

> in the rural areas many people believe in "bad air," God's will, and witchcraft as the causes of sickness. "Bad air" is said to be ordinary air which is used by evil spirits as a medium of their power in doing harm to man. 77 percent of the household heads believe in its existence. Preventive measures for these possible causes of sickness are: (1) amulet attached to a string which is tied around the waist—the amulet is said to contain bits of articles which could repel evil spirits; and (2) memorized verses which are said to be in Latin (and not understood by anyone). The chanted verses are believed to drive away the evil spirits. (Paul 1976, p. 190)

Given this situation, some illnesses become so advanced that even the best of medical services can no longer save the patient from death or disability.

Most people when affected by a disease acknowledge that they need medical attention, but because of deprivation and limited resources, they would generally turn to people other than the doctor. This situation is perhaps best illustrated in the rural area.

> The rural people are used to the services of traditional "doctors." These services are personalized; the practitioner makes the sick and his relatives understand that he (the traditional "doctor") is "only an instrument of God." There are several psychological assurances which the patient and his household derive from the services of the traditional "doctor." But it is doubtful if most of the herbs which are boiled for the patient to drink, and the oil which is rubbed on the patient, have curative effects in terms of strengthening the body or weakening the germs. Many professional physicians have time and again alleged that in many cases "pains have been made worse" by traditional remedial measures, or persons "had been hastened to death instead of being saved from death" because of the use of traditional measures of curing the sick. (Paul 1976, p. 192)

A comparative study of urban and rural doctors regarding their perception of patients revealed that patients would come and consult a physician during the more advanced state of the disease. The most important reason given for delay is the cost of medicine and medical services (Bonifacio 1979, p. 114).

Poverty generates ill health, and ill health generates further poverty.

> A low level of health is often directly linked to poverty, which in turn stems from unequal distribution of wealth and resources. In rural areas, the low productivity and weak purchasing power of most families tend to be perpetuated or aggravated by such problems as inequitable land tenure or ownership; limited availability of water for irrigation; lack of economic incentives, markets, and credit; and wasteful agricultural practices. Some of these inequities are deeply rooted in the traditional power structures of the countries concerned, and most

of them are of formidable magnitude. In urban slums, poverty—and hence poor health—is aggravated by rural migrants flooding into the cities at rates well beyond the capacity of industry and other employers to provide jobs or other means of livelihood. Better health for all, therefore, cannot be separated from a more just socioeconomic development, of which it is at once a cause and consequence, a means and an end. (Donoso 1978, p. 102)

In other words, better health for everyone cannot be attained, because

access to . . . essential resources (material resources in terms of food, shelter, medical care, etc., as well as symbolic goods in the form of status, self-esteem, and power) are dependent on the breadwinner's position in the occupational structure and on his capacities to compete for occupational achievement. Opportunities for upward mobility and the capacity to exploit such opportunities are influenced, however, not only by native endowment; they are also influenced by factors over which the individual has little or no control, such as accidents of birth related to complications of pregnancy associated with poverty, and lack of adequate prenatal care. In addition, the family into which the child is born and the capacities of the parents to play the parental roles are related to [the] social class position of the family and its access to resources of income, housing, medical care, and education. Racial and ethnic membership and community attitudes toward minorities are additional factors influencing individual's life chances. Most important, perhaps, is the opportunity structure itself, that is, the roles available to individuals and the societal supports and resources to enable the individual to participate in society. (Romanyshyn 1971, p. 38)

In short, therefore, the access of a person to various opportunities and resources is always limited by his or her location in the social stratification, and a more just socioeconomic development cannot be achieved without opening up some of the closed avenues to more people in society.

The ideals of equal opportunity cannot be completely realized in a society where the poor are not given the chance to have more access to opportunities; because of our very high emphasis on advanced technology, the capabilities needed are those of advanced education. In view of this, the poor will remain poor and thus will have no access to opportunities, especially those that relate to health.

The most consistent and abundant finding in the literature of illness behavior is that lower-class persons have less information and knowledge about disease, and have different cultural assumptions, beliefs, and understandings concerning symptoms and disease processes. Lower-class people are less likely than persons in higher social strata to recognize the signs of major illnesses, to understand body functioning, to use preventive health services, but are more likely to hold irrational ideas about illness, rely on folk medicine and fringe practitioners, and delay seeking medical treatment. (Mechanic 1971, p. 207)

From the foregoing, it is very clear that we cannot simply consider the nature and consequence of the disease state only from a physical point of view. Both psychological and sociological conditions will have to be taken into consideration for a more adequate health care system to be developed. While it is true that as a general rule health services are being extended to the general population, such services must be based on extensive knowledge of those who are going to receive such services. There is a need to know a people's concept of health and illness—especially their own concept of illness. This is important, since their degree of impairment is very much related to their concept of illness.

> Severe illness is always a psychological crisis for the individual and a social crisis for his family. All cultures anticipate such contingencies by furnishing criteria for weighing the severity of the crisis and specifying the steps to be taken when an event is identified as a crisis. Whether or not to call in a specialist, which type of specialist to summon, how to behave in his presence, how to utilize his advice, all depend on how the illness is classified. The category itself is determined as much by cultural definition as by the intrinsic nature of the ailment. With any community the methods and assumptions of the specialist tend to be attuned to the beliefs of those who use his services, since both parties are subject to the same system of expectation and the same cultural environment. To each, the behavior of the other is "natural." (Paul 1976, p. 6)

What must be considered, therefore, is the assessment of their knowledge of the various components of ill health, most specially in terms of its severity. The issue of severity may be the least attended to, since many people are not fully aware of the possible complications of what they are suffering from.

> The need for health workers to understand how beliefs and practices function in meeting the medical needs of the people in any community, more especially in the rural areas, is also indicated. Health workers, while maintaining their skills and competence in medical matters, should also maintain a high level of interest in the person and his family problems. The approach should not only be mainly physiologic assessment but also, and perhaps to a greater extent, a sociologic and anthropologic assessment of the patient needing help. It further indicates that health workers, to be acceptable and effective in their delivery of care to people, must bear in mind that the individual's ideas and practices relating to health and illness are for the most part inseparable from the kinship system, family structure, economic organization, and religious institution of the community. (Kuan 1977, pp. 67–72)

The significance of the foregoing can best be seen in terms of recognizing that the entire range of human feelings, whether good or bad, is organized in terms of a series of cultural definitions. These definitions provide individuals with a system of conceptualizing their feelings, which makes these feelings understandable to themselves and therefore communicable to others. The extent to which others will understand their feelings is also based on the others' being part of the entire network of cultural definitions. This applies to illness behavior, which, too, is sociocultural.

Thus, we can see two factors affecting people's perception of health and illness. One is their set of attitudes, and the other is their location in the social structure. These two factors are interrelated, since a person's attitude structure is generally influenced by his or her location in the social stratification. Finally, we have to account for people's health values and the general values of their social life. We have to know their values and beliefs as these relate to themselves, their families, friends, neighbors, community, and country. For example, do they have fatalistic beliefs regarding health and illness? Do they feel that ill health is something that will inevitably affect people and that they cannot do anything about it? Or do they feel that illness is something that can be prevented by doing something with the self and the environment? A fatalistic view of illness is indeed very difficult to overcome, since it implies that an individual is not in a position to solve it. In contrast, if the individual believes that a problem can be overcome, then facilitating health intervention will not be a very difficult task. Both views are to a large extent a function of cultural orientation. A person who is generally denied many opportunities in social life copes with such denial in terms of fate, and this fatalistic orientation becomes his or her basic source of therapy since it will soften the impact of frustration due to poverty. On the other hand, a person with access to opportunity is likely to adopt a posture of trust and confidence, leading to a strong sense of "becoming." Such a person is one who will not accept the conditions of his or her life as fate, but as that which can be overcome. While such a conceptualization is not reflected in the available data, the following is suggestive:

> The full extent of the disadvantaged status of the poor becomes visible when we examine the manipulative actions that people take to remove illness and resolve morbid episodes. Manipulation as a rule implies that the patient uses the help of other people—lay as well as professional—and attempts to interact with them in an ordered way to regain health. But the possibility of interaction available to any person depends on social power, mastery, and other privileges which vary in accordance with social class. Thus, the interaction pattern available to the poor is restricted when compared to that of the better-off classes; it is weaker, less efficient, and less conforming with the requirements of the professional standards. (Kosa, Zola, and Antonovsky 1969, p. 323)

In a similar context, we find that "if those of low income who experience symptoms are less likely to go to the physician than to friends and family, and will enter into the professional referral system only when they have exhausted lay remedies, they must be even more reluctant to enter the professional referral system when the feel reasonably well'' (Rosenstock 1969, pp. 187–88).

On the basis of the foregoing discussion, therefore, the disease model cannot simply attend only to the physical manifestations of the illness. The model has to confront the health problem from a multidimensional perspective that includes physical, cultural, structural, and psychological conditions of the patient. In other words, there is a need to situate the problems of illness within a social psychological framework, because illness is always defined not only by the professional medical practitioner, but also by the patient's values, beliefs, and location in the social stratification. There is always a need to harmonize the cultural and medical definition of illness; otherwise, there will be conflict between the medical practitioner and the patient. The conflict is often difficult to resolve. One of the most important means by which it can be resolved is to take into full consideration the social-psychological framework of illness.

> The principle that health programs should ''start with people as they are and the community as it is'' applies both at home and abroad. It is equally applicable whether the goal is to persuade Peruvian housewives to boil their drinking water or to convince the citizens of Seattle to accept floridation. The principle itself is no longer novel; its validity is generally acknowledged by professional workers in the fields of public health and preventive medicine. The problem is how to implement the principle. The real challenge is to discover just where particular groups of people stand; a willingness to meet them must be matched by a knowledge of the meeting place. (Paul 1976, pp. 476–77)

If the multidimensional perspective is accepted, then what should be the nature of the health care organization model? If such a perspective is adopted, the model should be organized along physical, cultural, structural, and psychological dimensions. The basic thrust of the model should be the transformation of human beings themselves into the instruments for the improvement of their well-being. The three basic health strategies of curative, preventive, and developmental treatment will be more effective and efficient when such a multidimensional perspective is adopted. These three strategies are, in fact, interconnected, and it is a mistake to view them as separate strategies.

While it is true that many times our point of entry into the health care delivery system is through the curative procedures, this is never an end in itself, since the need to cure is always accompanied by the need to prevent. This should likewise be seen not in terms of the isolated case of the patient, but in the proper social-psychological framework. In addition, these twin processes must also be combined with a developmental orientation, since cure and prevention should always be done in terms of developing human capabilities and potentials, so that in the final analysis the improvement of the community itself becomes the basis for both a direct and indirect program of cure and prevention. The centrality of the concept of development in a multidimensional model of health care delivery system is inescapable, since we are always interested in improving human capabilities and potentials so that in the long run social inequities can be reduced and access to opportunities maximized. We find in Declaration 21 of Alma Ata that

> ways of solving health problems vary from one country and community to another according to different stages of development, but should provide promotive, preventive, curative, rehabilitative, and emergency care appropriate to meet the main health problems in the community, with special attention to vulnerable groups, and be responsive to the needs and capacities of the people. The Conference reaffirmed the importance of establishing and further developing a comprehensive national health system of which primary health care is an integral part, encouraging the full participation of the population in all health-related activities. (World Health Organization 1978, p. 18)

Regarding the recommendation of community participation in primary health care, we find that

> the Conference, considering that national and community self-reliance and social awareness are among the key factors in human development, and acknowledging that people have the right to participate in the process for the improvement and maintenance of their health, recommends that government encourage and ensure full community participation through the effective propagation of relevant information, increased literacy, and the development of the necessary institutional arrangements through which individuals, families, and communities can assume responsibility for their health and well-being. (World Health Organization 1978, p. 23)

From the foregoing, we find three basic goals of primary health care: social participation, self-determination, and self-reliance. Cutting across these goals is the idea of the development of humanity. Human beings cannot attain an improved quality of life if they are not given the opportunity to participate and become real partners in such a process. In the true spirit of development, vigorous efforts must be exerted in order to remove historical vestiges of social exploitation and replace these with new structures that would give people more access to various opportunities. The idea of the development of humanity takes cognizance of the full capabilities of human beings and the many untapped potentials that have never been developed due to exploitation. Thus by designing health programs with the total commitment and participation of the people, new health consciousness will emerge, thereby improving the capabilities of people for making use of preventive health programs. While these goals are of central importance to the improvement of the health status of any given community, one nagging question that must be raised is this: How can we achieve them? Can the idea of development be assumed in the various goals?

The idea of development must not be assumed but must be stated explicitly, because a careful delineation of the concept has certain implications in the delivery of health and related services. There is a need to separate conceptually the notion of *development* from *change*. Very simply, *development* means the actual processes of improving some social elements in order to enhance the delivery of health services. The basic assumption is that activities that can serve as points of entry in the delivery of health services exist in the community. For instance, in many communities, health needs are being met by traditional healers. As a developmental strategy, it will be necessary to win the healers to the side of health personnel so that they become allies of the health workers. Through their interaction, the traditional healers learn new ideas about health and illness, and the health workers, in turn, learn about folk medicine and how to work with the people in the community. In this way health workers will no longer be considered as a threat, but as associates interested in the promotion of health in the community through the efforts of the people themselves. Through their joint efforts, untapped potentials in the community can be identified and developed so that these become involved in the partnership of delivering health service.

With regard to *change,* the primary emphasis is on literally changing or replacing conditions working against the improvement of health status. For instance, wrong health habits can bring about many negative consequences on the health status of the community, and, in view of this, there is a need to change such habits. Although development and change are separate conceptually, they often go together in the actual process of transforming a community.

Thus, if the health care organization model is determined by a macro perspective, its thrust must be transformative in nature. How is this to be accomplished? Mahler, the Director-General of WHO, answers:

> There is now a much clearer understanding that little if any real development, that is, socioeconomic development and not merely economic growth, will be achieved *without man himself being the focus for it.* Productive manpower with proper qualifications in the sine qua non for such socioeconomic development. But if people are to be productive they must enjoy a satisfactory level of health; only then will they be able to improve their work capacity and help to create the conditions required for improving their own well-being and that of society of which they are members. Health is essential for the generation of the critical mass of human energy required to raise production and to break out of the poverty equilibrium. (Mahler 1979, p. 319; italics added)

This is indeed very important, since it emphasizes that ultimately any development program, including one for health, must take human beings as the focus.

What does it mean to argue that the transformative nature of the health care model must be focused on human beings? There is a need to know the inner organization of all human behavior—sources of strength and weaknesses, motivations, values, beliefs, attitudes, aspirations, and so on. All these components of human personality, social system, and culture must be taken into serious consideration, since, without a full knowledge of them, the development and change of human health habits will be difficult to accomplish. Let us once more examine the situation of the poor with regard to health consciousness and the difficulties of changing their health-related behavior. "The values for knowledge and for health exhibited by the poor, their tendency to use shorter time horizons as a framework for planning, their reluctance to use professional referral and service systems, perhaps guided by a general feeling of powerlessness in the face of a hostile environment, all suggest that the problem of altering their behavior will prove to be highly complex and not susceptible of simple remedies" (Rosenstock 1969, p. 188). In view of this, the strategy is not only to understand a patient's personality, but also to use such knowledge to tap the many potentials that up to now have remained untapped. For instance, we know that while farmers in the rural areas may not be knowledgeable of the complex disease cycle in humans, they are fully knowledgeable of the disease cycle in plants. This type of knowledge should not be ignored, but instead should be utilized in developing a new health consciousness by extending their current knowledge of the disease cycle in plants to that of humans. It seems that at times because of our eagerness to transfer new knowledge to people, we forget that they have very rich and varied historical experiences that should serve as a basis and foundation for generating other levels of consciousness, particularly health consciousness.

We cannot simply say that human behavior must be organized around the notion of self-determination, self-reliance, and social participation. In order to do this, there is a need to understand people's self-conception and self-esteem. As has been pointed out earlier, if an individual's self-conception revolves around the idea of fatalism, then certainly training him or her to be self-reliant will be very difficult.

The same can be said regarding social participation. While the importance of social participation is beyond dispute, its achievement is not without problems. In order to facilitate the general social participation of people, there is an urgent need to understand their location in the social stratification and their network of relationship. There is need to know how the various social roles are related to the power structure and to the decision-making processes in the community. A good example of these major structural dimensions can perhaps be found in the family structure. For instance, who wields power in the family? How are decisions made? In general, who makes the decisions? Such knowledge has an important bearing on our understanding of many other structural relationships in society.

Finally, there is a need to know and understand the premises underlying both the psychological and structural organizations of behavior and how these organizations in turn generate values. For instance, suppose we find in a society that the basic value orientation of the people is personalistic in nature—that intimacy, sharing, and total involvement are most valued. When we inquire why such a society holds on to such a value orientation, we have to examine the structural relationships in society and try to find out the dynamics of opportunity and access to resources. Upon a closer look into the dynamics of social stratification, we find that many people are deprived and do not have access to resources; in order to be able to augment the little that they have, they must value intimacy, sharing, and total involvement. They know they cannot survive alone and will often require the assistance of others in the community. Thus there is always a need to keep in mind the dynamic relationship between values and structures in order to be able to have a deeper understanding of human behavior.

By adopting the multidimensional perspective in organizing health care, policy making in health can be coordinated with the policies of other development programs designed to enhance human well-being. These agencies must develop an integrated conceptual framework focused on total health as a basis for achieving human well-being. In this manner, physical, cultural, structural, and psychological conditions will be the basis of the concept of total health. Program planning should be based both on interagency collaboration and program complementation. By complementing the strengths and weaknesses of agencies, program overlap can be minimized. For instance, while there can be several points of entry in community health education campaigns, schools and parent-teacher associations are natural points of entry. Hence, instead of several agencies doing exactly the same campaign, major responsibility can be given to the ministry of education. In this manner we can readily cut down training duplication and community disgust from too much exposure to the same information. What the ministry of health can do in this regard is to see to it that health education programs in education are based on the goals that the ministry of health is trying to accomplish. Similar complementation can be undertaken with agriculture, transportation and communication, and so forth.

With complementarity as a basis for planning agency programs, priority setting will involve both independent agency activity and interagency collaboration. When various agencies sit down together to discuss their own priorities and the basis for them, they will be able to thresh out how realistic their targets are and how these targets can dovetail with the priorities of other agencies. In this manner interagency politics can be minimized, and other vested interests can be checked and perhaps turned around for more effective programming to hasten the achievement of development goals and the promotion of human wellbeing.

The multidimensional perspective and the complementarity approaches in terms of total health will facilitate personnel training in terms of a "Gestalt" concept, thereby making development workers cognizant of their professional and community roles, not only in behalf of their "own" agencies but more in terms of interagency relationship and collaboration. While it is true that agency personnel still have to be trained by their own agencies, ways can be devised so that interagency training can be realized. In this way, both human and material resources can also be planned and utilized on a complementary basis, thereby using them to the maximum. This is most urgent in those developing countries that do not have enough resources to meet the growing demands of their individual programs. By complementing resources, duplication and inadequacies can be minimized, and effective programming can be achieved through the full utilization of interagency resources. One major implication of this is that agencies will no longer talk in terms of "their" own resources. Rather, a sense of collective consciousness will probably emerge. Through this approach, budgeting can be rationalized, waste of resources can be controlled, and resource underutilization can be reduced. In working together, they will be able to realize the real meaning of participation, which they need to understand through practice before they can teach others to participate. In other words, before they can transform others, they themselves will have to be transformed.

Finally, in generating community participation, providing the community with a broad perspective will make its involvement more meaningful. This will be greatly enhanced by its perception of concerted efforts being extended by all agencies involved in development. These agencies will be armed with a comprehensive understanding of the multidimensional perspectives of the community, and will start their programs where the people are. They will use the strength and potentials of the people not only to generate participation, but in the long run to transform them into self-reliant communities—concerned, committed, and responsible for their own development.

REFERENCES

Bonifacio, M. F. 1978. "Family Physician: The Sociological Aspect of His Community Role." In *Proceedings of the First Seminar-Workshop on Developing Standards in Family Medicine: An Overview*. Manila: The Philippine Academy of Family Physicians.

Bonifacio, M. F. 1979. "Rural-Urban Doctors in Some Southern Tagalog Areas: A Social-Psychological Comparison." Mimeographed research report.

Donoso, G. 1978. "Health Care and Community Action." *WHO Chronicle* 32:102–5.

Feldstein, M., S. M. A. Piot, and T. K. Sundaresan. 1973. *Resource Allocation Model for Public Health Planning: A Case Study of Tuberculosis Control.* Geneva: World Health Organization.

Jocano, F. L. 1973. *Folk Medicine in a Philippine Municipality.* Manila: National Museum.

Kosa, J., I. K. Zola, and A. Antonovsky. 1969. "Health and Poverty Reconsidered." In *Poverty and Health: A Sociological Analysis,* edited by J. Kosa, A. Antonovsky, and I. K. Zola. Cambridge, Mass.: Harvard University Press.

Kuan, L. G. 1977. "Concepts of Illness and Health Care Intervention in an Urban Community." *Graduate Seminar Journal* 1:61-72.

Mahler, H. 1979. "The Role of Health in Socioeconomic Development: WHO's Director General Makes an Appeal to the ECOSOC." *WHO Chronicle* 33:315-21.

Mechanic, D. 1971. "Response Factors in Illness: The Study of Illness Behaviors." In *Patients, Physicians, and Illness,* edited by E. G. Jaco. New York: Free Press.

Paul, B., ed. 1976. *Health, Culture, and Community: Case Studies of Public Reaction to Health Programmes.* New York: Russell Sage Foundation.

Romanyshyn, J. M. 1971. *Social Welfare: Charity to Justice.* New York: Random House.

Rosenstock, 1969. "Prevention of Illness and Maintenance of Health." In *Poverty and Health: A Sociological Analysis,* edited by J. Kosa, A. Antonovsky, and I. K. Zola. Cambridge, Mass.: Harvard University Press.

World Health Organization. 1978. *Primary Health Care: Report of the International Conference on Primary Health Care, Alma Ata, USSR, 6-12 September, 1978.* Geneva: Author.

4

The Need for Assessing Psychosocial Factors Affecting Health in Developed Countries

PETER WESTERHOLM

The scope of the problems of definition and classification of psychosocial factors in the environment is related to the objectives of defining and classifying. Lack of clear-cut objectives is a serious deficiency in any program with ambitions to be put into practical use. If it is accepted that we aim at disease prevention with our activities, it is appropriate to emphasize the three classical strategies of the preventive approach. These are as follows (1):

- Decreasing vulnerability and increasing resistance in persons and groups. Immunization, improved nutrition and hygiene, and informational and educational procedures fall under this heading.
- Making early identification of high risk individuals or groups who are offered preventive therapy or change of environment.
- Eliminating or protecting against noxious environmental agents such as toxic chemicals, radiation, and others.

Any discussion of the scope of psychosocial factors in health is, in this author's opinion, best conducted in the perspective of these three strategies.

In this chapter some general aspects of the problem of psychosocial factors are discussed in an attempt to give a bird's-eye view. Then the rather more restricted scope of the working environment, which is a more defined sector of the environment, is treated, offering a keyhole perspective.

DEFINITIONS AND CONCEPTS

Psychosocial factors arise from social and technical arrangements mediated through perception and experience. They include structures and processes in the total environment that can lead to pathogenic or, conversely, to health-promoting effects. Their perception is subject to individual and group determinants such as customs, attitudes, and personality (1).

Starting from this rather general view, the common denominators in psychosocially induced health disturbances tend to crystallize as follows:

• Discrepancy between human needs and possibilities for their satisfaction.
• Discrepancy between human capacity and environmental demands.
• Discrepancy between human expectations and the perceived situation.

As to the mechanisms of disease causation, they may for the purpose of this discussion be described in a rather simple model. Generalized, this would mean that the combined effect of the individual's characteristics—sometimes called the personal psychobiological program—and the psychosocial stimuli determines the psychological, behavioral, and physiological responses of each individual. These responses may be called *stress,* according to the definition of this concept given by Selye (2). The reactions may be of many kinds (anxiety, depression, abuse of alcohol or drugs, disturbances in lipid or cathecol amine metabolism). The reactions may be regarded as potential precursors of disease or indeed disease manifestations in themselves, or impaired quality of life. The reaction may be modified by a number of interacting factors such as economy, physical environment, nutrition, and so on.

It should not be forgotten that there are also protective factors in the environment. The interacting variables with protective effects have been classified by Kagan and Levi (3) according to three categories:

1. Mental processes: habituating; adapting; coping; substituting (learning) other ways of satisfying need); increasing tolerance of ambiguity; learning; critical period (imprinting); reinforcing by painful association; conditioning.

2. Psychosocial factors: membership in a group; available acceptable substitute activities; access to advice; availability of someone to talk to about personal troubles; education.

3. Physiosocial factors: nutrition; clothing; housing; health services.

A heightened level of information and education is generally accompanied by increased awareness and expectations. It may also contribute to an improved ability to cope with stressful events. Thus, it may act both ways. The relative importance of these main factors modifying causes and effects varies within wide limits, and the whole question naturally is a matter of much controversy.

On the effect side, it is similarly difficult to tell at which point the reactions should be regarded as precursors of disease or disease itself. Many of the reactions exist below the level of consciousness. Furthermore, the manifestations of these states and the incentive they provide to seek professional advice for them depend to a great extent on the interpretation and attitudes of the affected person. We cannot tell when the feeling of anxiety or depression, as it is perceived by the individual, is to be regarded as disease or a precursor to it. Nor can we tell with accuracy at which level the arterial blood pressure or urinary catechol amine excretion passes the boundaries of what is to be regarded as indicative of predisease or disease.

In a discussion of psychosocial factors in the environment, some essential elements in our lives with rather broad implications cannot be disregarded. They include such things as population growth; urbanization; uneven distribution of resources; and shortages of food, income, and housing for millions of people in the world. Some people may like to add political structures to this list. They are part of the psychosocial reality.

A few words about high-risk groups are appropriate here. Important such groups include the following:

- Groups subjected to uprooting.
- Children and older people.
- Handicapped persons.

The term *uprooting* covers a wide range of issues. Depriving individuals and groups of experience, sociocultural and emotional support, material means, or a sense of belonging and purpose in life all fall under this rubric. *Uprooting* in this wide sense may affect many persons and groups in a modern society. Divorced persons, redundant workers, and migrant groups are examples of groups subjected to uprooting. There are many others.

Childhood and old age are generally accompanied by increased vulnerability to noxious stimuli in the environment. In the young, moving away from the family, entering an occupation, and coming into new social settings may be accompanied by psychosocial stressors. At the other end of the spectrum, there are the elderly. They may suffer from social isolation, grief over loss of relatives and friends, fears over illness and death.

The handicapped group is difficult to define. The environmental setting varies and determines to some extent what is and what is not to be regarded as a handicap. Among the handicapped are the blind, deaf, mentally retarded and ill, drug addicts, and alcoholics, to mention a few important examples.

The causal relationships between exposure to psychosocial stressors and subsequent disease is supported by numerous experimental studies. In 1975, the World Health Organization (WHO) drew attention to the following points:

- Low socioeconomic status is in many communities associated with shorter life expectancy, increased risk for mental disorders, and higher rates of infant mortality and cervical cancer.
- Overall morbidity and mortality rates for lung cancer and hypertension

increase for first-generation migrants from rural to urban areas. The on-set of tuberculosis, myocardial infarction, and depressive illness is pre-ceded by an excessive number of meaningful life events, such as death of a relative, marriage, or change of occupation.
- Recovery or failure to recover from disease is also related to psychosocial influences. Attitudes, beliefs, and behavior in society at large are im-portant contributory factors to the disability caused by mental disorders.

THE WORKPLACE: FACTORS AT WORK IN ONE SECTOR OF THE ENVIRONMENT

Of the 24 hours in a day, we spend roughly 8 hours at work. Why should we then pay so much attention to the working environment? In the Western world, work constitutes a large and important part of a person's sense of identity and self-esteem. Our own sense of the worth of the contributions we make colors the image we have of ourselves and of our lives as a whole.

There are in fact a number of studies indicating that the work situation may function as a place of social learning, not least as regards relations of power and influence. The work situation may be regarded as the micro so-ciety where every person has a position—of favor or disfavor—concerning his or her degree of influence and role in making decisions on matters of or-ganization, salary, and the nature of tasks (4).

No wonder, then, that the working environment has become both a battle-field and an experimental field in the power game involving a great number of interested parties. An important part of the evolution of democracy in the Scandinavian countries is taking place in the scenario provided by the work-ing environment. There is an increasing awareness of the importance of work content in terms of its scope for variation, influence, autonomy, and decison making. People are demanding that their work provide opportunities for the development of their knowledge and skills, creativity, independence, and re-sponsibility. Deficiencies in these respects have negative repercussions for the individual. The quality of life—in a broad sense—deteriorates.

Earlier, preventive work in the working environment has emphasized physical factors. This view has now been broadened with inclusion of the social and psychological climate of the workplace and its influence on health and quality of life.

The elements of the social working environment can broadly be described as follows:

- Work content.
- Work organization: (1) technology; (2) leadership.
- Forms of cooperation within a given and defined organization, including human interrelations.

Work content subsumes, by and large, the following items:

- Meaningfulness of work.
- Opportunities to participate in planning and execution.
- Self-development.

The making of shoes can serve as an illustration of this model. In former times, the shoemaker made shoes from materials that he had purchased himself. He took the measurements, decided on style together with the customer, produced a shoe, and got paid for it. He also was told whether his work was good or bad and whether his services were in demand. A modern shoe factory that meets society's demands for efficient production has fragmented these functions and dispersed them in a large number of specialized units. It may be easy to forget that the individual employee, in spite of this, has the same fundamental needs as before to know whether his work is good or bad and whether it is appreciated (5).

The term *technology* is usually seen to embrace the technical equipment, the wage system, and the working schedule. It also includes psychological and social effects of physical factors. Noise, for instance, causes bad communications, which in themselves are an important part of the psychosocial environment; chemical hazards may cause anxiety; and so forth.

Leadership is an important ingredient in the psychosocial climate. A working organization entails division of roles. This design may be decisive for the possibilities of the individual to function satisfactorily, as well as for his or her work satisfaction. The setting of communications is very much part of the leadership role. This is important for the possibilities for employees to influence their own situation. It should also be observed that in many organizations there may exist powerful informal leadership systems beside the formal organization. This means that there are persons who function in practice as leaders and have just as much influence on the emotional climate and group performance as the formal leader does, if not more. Informal leadership and control systems are, of course, related to all the complex issues of group dynamics.

A few words about social relations are in order here. The human being is a social animal and needs the company of others. Our relations to our fellow humans are of the greatest importance for our identity and self-esteem. This is true in the work setting as well. We have some ideas about which factors are important. They include size, group dynamics, division of power, competition, and social support.

The size of the group is important in determining how the communications' process develop. Large groups entail risks for hidden communications, rumors and intrigues, and formation of unknown and informal groups inside and outside the intended organization. This may create emotional tensions and have a negative influence on the security and well-being of the group.

Group dynamics is the interplay between the members of the group in joint activities. Awareness of these processes is essential for the group as a whole to achieve its objectives. There is no need to rate on the subjects of competition and social support, as these are largely self-explanatory.

A double perspective has been used here with the intention of illustrating the wide range of factors available to explain environmentally induced mental illness. The list is by no means complete. My intention has only been to show that we are confronted with different sets of factors, depending on whether we are operating on a general level or focusing on some limited sector of the total environment. The working environment has been selected here to exemplify a limited sector. There are of course others. The list of factors thus can be made very long. There are certainly also many between-country and within-country differences.

PROBLEMS OF CLASSIFICATION

This discussion has some bearing on the problems of classification. If one wishes to develop an etiological axis in a disease classification—and there have been many attempts to do this—this means in practice that a selection of putative causes has to be made from a long list. It is very difficult to achieve this in a reproducible and standardized way. The difficulty is naturally of superhuman dimensions if the ambition is to select *one* cause among several possible.

The reason for this difficulty is the simple fact that we know so little about disease etiology and pathogenesis in the domain of psychiatry. An accurate classification of cause requires reasonably solid knowledge about which causal mechanisms have been operating in each individual case. It should be recognized that very much of both clinical science and clinical practice is not oriented toward disease etiology. It is a well-known part of everyday practice in psychiatry that patients are dealt with and treated without knowledge of what has caused their illness or disease. This practice, of course, is by no means unique to psychiatry. How many doctors do really treat disease etiology when dealing with a case of coronary occlusion? It is difficult to pick out the causative factor in a disease with multifactorial etiology. Even in the hands of an expert, this practically always boils down to guesswork.

I think we must accept that statements on disease causation are uncertain and may indeed be seriously wrong. In the present state of medical knowledge, they are by nature opinions and theories. They reflect schools of thought and attitudes of clinics or individual doctors. The history of medicine has taught us that these opinions may be subject to change. We do not really know which of our current concepts will be laughed at in the future and which views will hold the field by that time. Not too many years ago it was seriously thought that masturbation was an important cause of mental disease, just to mention one example.

In practice, this means that an axis of etiology in psychiatry can be regarded as a tool for describing patients and disease states, but also with equal justification as a tool for describing doctors, clinics, and medical schools.

In any discussion of a system of classification based on disease cause, the remarks made by Essen-Möller on classification systems in 1961 are appropriate:

> By *divergency* is here meant the basic differences in views and schooling which pervade psychiatry. Here the task cannot possibly be one of achieving agreement or compromise. On the contrary, since divergencies of view must be considered essentially fruitful, it would seem appropriate to look out for a system of classification which admits of this type of disagreement, and even makes the differences stand out more clearly. In fact, this is exactly what happens when a system of double classification is consistently used. This is because the controversial points are mainly confined only to one of the two classifications, namely that of etiology, while syndromes are recognized more or less in the same way by different schools (even when identical terms are not always used).

It is important to recognize that the scientist and the clinician have differing requirements regarding accuracy of information. The clinician formulates a hypothesis concerning a model for disease causation. This hypothesis is modified and perhaps exchanged for a new one as time goes on. With increasing knowledge about the patient, it may be necessary to bring in a new concept of a patient's disease and to consider new sets of causative factors. This should be kept in mind when considering a classification system for use in clinical practice. Data that are collected as part of good clinical practice in the individual case of a doctor-patient relationship do not guarantee success when used for research purposes. It is perfectly sound clinical practice to select one cause as a working hypothesis in dealing with an individual patient and to modify the hypothesis as new knowledge is acquired. If, however, these data are used for research purposes, the scientist should be aware of the mechanisms for their generation. If data on disease cause are aggregated from several hospital units, researchers should be aware that they will probably consist of a number of added-up guesses.

To restore the balance after this negative criticism, it must be emphasized that it is undeniably important to find out more about disease causation in psychiatry. This calls for clinical research. It is also a truism to say that it is important to treat the cause of disease when this is known. The point here is only that to construct an axis of etiology in disease classification is beset with most awkward difficulties. Of course, other kinds of axes are not equally difficult. The difficulties in constructing an etiological axis arise from the present state of medical knowledge about disease causation.

Clinicians, research workers, and statisticians have differing demands on an axis of etiology. Its usefulness then probably will very much depend on what it is intended to be used for. Ottosson and Perris in 1973 presented a system for multidimensional classification for use in psychiatry(7).

To conclude this two-sided attempt to highlight some of the complex issues involved, we now return to the point of origin. The question is this: Why should we wish to define and classify psychosocial factors relevant to health? The simple answer would then be to improve knowledge in this field. The basis for such improvement is correct, relevant, and sufficient definition of all the concepts involved. This applies equally for the phenomena we observe on the effect side—that is, disease and ill health—and for those on the exposure side—that is, the factors we wish to invoke as causal, contributory, or effect-modifying.

We may wish to improve our understanding with proper epidemiological studies or simply to get a better organization of our own patient files. There are several optional levels of ambition. If we wish to use the classification for epidemiological purposes, it must be emphasized that our interest cannot be one-sidedly directed to the cases of disease we observe. If we aim at prevention, we must turn our attention to the distribution of disease-producing factors in the populations at risk from which the cases have been drawn. This, of course, is difficult, but there is no way around it. For primary prevention, we must know more about the environment and not only about the cases that come to our attention. If, however, we wish the classification to improve the care of the individual patient this is a different matter altogether. We can then focus more on the observations we make on the individual and try to systematize them for the purpose. The improvement of individual care is another objective for a system of classification; it deserves to be explored more.

To sum up, then, classifications are good as tools for improving and systematizing knowledge. They cannot replace knowledge which does not exist. They should be discussed in the light of operational objectives and yields.

REFERENCES

1. L. Levi, "Psychosocial Factors in Preventive Medicine," in *Report to the Surgeon General on Health Promotion and Disease Prevention* (Washington, D. C.: National Academy of Sciences, 1979).

2. H. Selye, "The Evolution of the Stress Concept: Stress and Cardiovascular Disease," in *Society, Stress, and Disease,* vol. 1, *The Psychosocial Environment and Psychosomatic Diseases,* ed. L. Levi (London: Oxford University Press, 1971), pp. 299–311.

3. A. R. Kagan and L. Levi, "Health and Environment-Psychosocial Stimuli: A Review," in *Society, Stress, and Disease,* vol. 2, *Childhood and Adolescence,* ed. L. Levi (London: Oxford University Press, 1975), pp. 241–60.

4. G. Westlander, *Summaries of Three Research Reports about Relations between Working Conditions, Life Situation, and Quality of Life* (Stockholm: The Swedish Council of Personnel Administration, 1977).

5. C-G. Sandberg and G. Nerell, "The Psychosocial Working Environment: An Integrated View of Man and His Environment" (educational lecture material, Swedish Joint Industrial Safety Council, November 1979).

6. E. Essen-Möller, "On Classification of Mental Disorders," *Acta Psychiatrica Scandinavica* 37(1961):119–26.

7. J-O. Ottosson and C. Perris, "Multidimensional Classification of Mental Disorders," *Psychological Medicine* 3(1973):238–43.

II

Multidimensional Models in Primary Care

Part I illustrates epidemiological, sociological, psychophysiological, and health systems approaches to arguments about the complexity of health care. Determinants of health care cannot be understood, conceptualized, quantified, or planned for without taking into account the psychological and social aspects of the persons involved. Because health and illness are multideterminant, so must models of care be. Part II of this book looks at the multideterminant aspects of *primary* care through three different lenses.

The first author, Lamberts, looks at the phenomenology found in a primary care practice in the Netherlands. He presents, as a model, a classification of illness and *problem behavior* and then examines data derived from use of the model. He is able thereby to demonstrate the high prevalence of problem behavior in his practice population and to illustrate how such data informs one's understanding of the nature of practice. The implications of this for education and health systems planning are obvious.

Deliege uses a different approach by examining a specific social concept in care: *humanization*. She shows the degee to which such concepts pervade and influence the entire fabric of care. They determine not only who is admitted and the manner in which the person is treated, but also many aspects of healing. Her analysis illustrates another multideterminant view of primary care. She then goes on to illustrate potential strategies for change and effects that change might create. The value of the illustration, aside from the intrinsic importance of humanization, is that it shows how awareness of social factors in this case can alter one's views of the system.

Hankiss and his colleagues create an altogether different perspective on similar problems. They report on the role of values and value deficiencies in health care recording systems. Whereas Lamberts is primarily concerned with phenomenology and Deliege with a change in a specific concept, Hankiss shows the difficulty of studying factors like values. Many of their effects are indirect, as in the example of *values deficiencies.* Values deficiencies occur when a person perceives that a situation lacks something of value that it should not lack, such as status or support. This then is associated with a variety of illness outcomes. Simple classification schemes or diagnostic approaches may miss critical connections between life events and illness or disease phenomena if they are unable to detect such indirect effects. The subtlety of the interconnections among factors that Hankiss illustrates suggests there may be factors in the primary care area that have relevance for care but are not immediately appreciated or recorded by practitioners. Because they are not appreciated or recorded, they do not enter classifications schemes of health statistics; they do not enter planning; and they do not become the basis for education, reimbursement, or treatment approaches.

Hankiss and his colleagues focus on the possibility that intervening variables such as values deficiencies, when low or absent, can lead to an internal state such as insecurity that in turn leads to illness onset through psychophysiological steps. This model is similar to Cassell's who postulates on epidemiological grounds that loss of social stability, through many means, leads to increased host susceptibility to many, if not all, types of disease (1). It is similar to the sophisticated models of authors such as Weiner (2), who summarizes the data for six different models of transduction of psychological or social phenomena into disease causation or predisposition. These six models have as common features an initial event in the outside world, reception or perception of the event in the organism, psychological and physiological changes that are variously associated, pathophysiological change that results, and bodily perception of illness and illness behavior (3). Psychological and social facts are relevant in these models to disease causation or predisposition. But they also determine, influence, and color each of the subsequent events and each of their interconnections. This complexity renders the usual biochemical models and thinking of a clinician dangerous when misapplied. Such models—usually short, simple, and algebraic in their form, and typically looking like an algorithm—are necessary for day-to-day clinical practice; however, they may leave out important determinants of outcome. Unless such determinants enter into the thinking of the totality of health care, such thinking will not be able to cover the range of phenomena.

REFERENCES

1. J. Cassell, "The Contribution of the Social Environment to Host Resistance," *American Journal of Epidemiology* 104(1976):107–23.

2. H. Weiner, *Psychobiology and Human Disease* (New York: Elsevier, 1977).

3. M. Lipkin, Jr., "Disease and Illness as Processes: The Lessons of the Couvade Example for a Notion of Appropriate Medical Care," in *Use and Abuse of Medicine,* ed. M. de Vries, R. L. Berg, and M. Lipkin, Jr. (New York: Praeger, 1982).

5

Psychosocial Problems and the Disease Model: Two Major Determinants of Primary Health Care Delivery

HENK LAMBERTS

A disease model provides the conceptual basis for every health care system. It has a strong cohesive power. It provides an essential incentive for differentiation. But it also forms a source for growing skepticism. The justification for criticizing the disease model may be salient in many instances. However, other models—such as the psychosocial models—meet serious problems when trying to balance the zeal of their adherents with the elaboration of valid, quantitative, and not overly biased information, meant to sustain the new paradigms.

As in many other places, the interest of the primary health care team in Rotterdam-Ommoord is focused on the role of psychosocial problems. The team considers the concept of *problem behavior* a standard example of a psychosocial, nondisease model. Problem behavior implies a different point of view from the disease model. The disease model indicates people's complaints, symptoms and ailments in the terminology of well-defined, nosologically aligned diseases, existing within the context of the same person. A psychosocial model is in contrast with this, although a range of definitions is possible, varying from major emphasis on the social circumstances and the political context to an exclusively individually oriented approach. The notion of a disease is principally excluded or placed in a broader context.

DEFINITION

At the Rotterdam-Ommoord center, *problem behavior* is defined as the behavior of the patient in contact with a family physician (or other primary care provider), where it is clear to both of them that a life problem is being discussed; this is differentiated from *illness behavior*. It is well known that not all people with an illness or feeling of illness show "illness behavior." *Illness behavior* relates to those occasions where someone, assuming that he or she is suffering from an illness and requires professional help, adopts the role of patient and seeks help from a professional. It is common knowledge that an impressive amount of illness behavior cannot be explained on the basis of detectable disease. Figure 5.1 shows the overlap among the concepts of illness, illness feeling, illness behavior, and problem behavior.

Within the limitations of this approach, a number of practical experiences have been gathered in Ommoord during the past decade, and these have recently been summarized (9). This chapter is not a general overview, an attempt to convert the nonbeliever, or an effort to persuade those who doubt the validity of a psychosocial approach in primary health care. Internationally, a widely accepted change in attitude as to the content of health care and also as to the reasons for people entering the health care system can be seen (reference 15 and Part I of this volume deal with that). Rather, this chapter aims at providing information that supports the following assertions:

Figure 5.1. Diagram showing relationship among illness, illness feeling, illness behavior, and problem behavior: (1) Illness behavior that is also problem behavior; (2) Illness behavior on the basis of illness, no problem behavior; (3) Illness behavior without illness; no problem behavior; (4) Problem behavior but no illness behavior; (5) Illness and feeling ill, but not showing illness behavior; (6) Illness without illness feeling and without illness behavior.

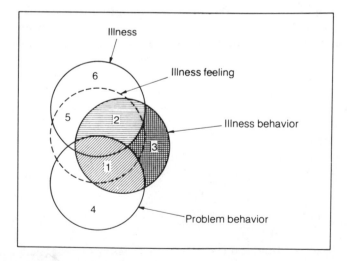

Source: Compiled by the author.

1. When the daily work of family physicians/general practitioners is analyzed, with the practical and explicit inclusion of a classification of psychological and social problems, it is in most instances apparent that every year 10–20% of a defined practice population presents psychological and social problems, accounting for 30–50% of all patient-doctor contacts.

2. Recognizing problem behavior and differentiating it from illness behavior are feasible for any family physician (or other primary care provider) who wishes to do so.

3. Problem behavior provides the strongest single predictor of primary care utilization available (3).

4. The recognition of problem behavior and its differentiation from illness behavior can decrease the utilization of specialist care.

5. The classification of psychosocial problems in the primary care setting is served by a biaxial system, with psychological problems (the form of a psychosocial problem) being distinguished from social problems (the content of a psychosocial problem).

6. The classification of psychosocial problems provides primary health care with a variety of semantic, cultural, methodological, and conceptual difficulties, which are, however, not essentially different nor more complicated than those met when classifying diseases.

7. The *International Classification of Health Problems in Primary Care,* second edition (*ICHPPC*-2) (6) offers the best compromise now available. It essentially provides the framework for a triaxial classification of problems, taking into account somatic, psychological, and social aspects. However, it lacks satisfactory possibilities to classify the reasons why people seek care. The recently proposed *Reasons for Contact* classification (15) illustrates this.

8. Primary health care has a cultural function, forming the more or less well-lubricated joint between the national health care system and society. By establishing its interrelations, it can provide a medium for promoting concepts such as teamwork, consumer participation, deprofessionalization, and auditing. Primary health care can be a powerful instrument to fight the medicalization of society and the damaging aspects of labeling people with a medical diagnosis; it can enhance self-care, diminish the use of specialist care, and support the formulation of a less disease-oriented health care policy.

PRACTICAL EXPERIENCES

Some results from two major research projects in the Ommoord Health Center, Netherlands, are presented here. Both the 1972 morbidity analysis (8) and the monitoring project begun in May 1979 (10) have a number of advantages:

1. The denominator problem in its classical form—how to define a population—is in Ommoord's case well solved when compared with the situation in the United States and many other countries. Every Dutch inhabitant has his or her "own" general practitioner, and this relationship is officially acknowledged not only by the national insurance (with a capitation-fee system, mainly for workers below a certain level of income and for old-age pensioners), but also for private patients (who pay their doctor on a fee-for-service basis). Neither group of patients can gain access to specialist care without referrals by their general practitioners. This is important for the estimation of incidences and prevalences of certain complaints, problems, and diseases, since the active practice population is exactly known at any moment.

2. The accuracy of the results is relatively good. All patient-doctor contacts are continuously recorded by general practitioners trained in coding, recording, and classifying. Also, the recording system allows for easy modification of diagnoses whenever an initial problem classification proves to be incorrect.

3. The number of contacts and of problems available for analysis is relatively large. In the 1972 morbidity analysis, four general practitioners with stabilized and closed practice lists recorded 29,900 contacts (mean 2.7, standard deviation 3.1) with 10,894 patients. Thus 27,700 (mean 2.6, standard deviation 2.7) different problems were classified. Of all patients on the list, 73% had at least one contact with their doctor in 1972.

The monitoring project was begun May 1, 1979, with the help of 12 general practitioners (10). Together they care for approximately 21,000 patients. They record the content of every encounter with the help of a specially designed problem-oriented family record, adapted to easy coding. A minicomputer is used for the analysis and monitoring of the continuous flow of information.

The monitoring project is focused on the collection, analysis, and monitoring of continuous information of all contacts between general practitioners and their patients during two years. The central aim is to investigate the professional behavior of general practitioners, with special emphasis on changing this behavior in certain well-described and desired directions. These changes are meant to be facilitated by feedback information to the patient. A second goal of the monitoring project is to analyze morbidity and utilization patterns in a well-defined (denominator know) population with an emphasis on the reliability of coding, classification, and registration.

The results of the first year present renewed support for the importance of psychosocial problems in family practice. In Figure 5.2, results from the first year are presented in order to give an impression of the content of Dutch general practice as far as this is represented by the members of the monitoring group. The age/sex distribution of the active population is represented in Figure 5.3.

In Figure 5.2, it appears that the majority of the classifications were coded "sure" (83%). The percentage of changed diagnoses (4%) is accordingly limited.

Figure 5.4 lists the percentages of the population presenting in the first year with at least one psychological or social problem and those suffering from at least one chronic disease. According to this, 14% of the population presented with a psychological problem, 11.2% with a social problem, and 9.1% were suffering from a chronic disease likely to influence daily life. This implies that every year approximately 11% of the population consults the

Figure 5.2. Summary of results (all encounters during one year—active population). $n = 20,330$

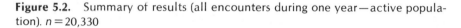

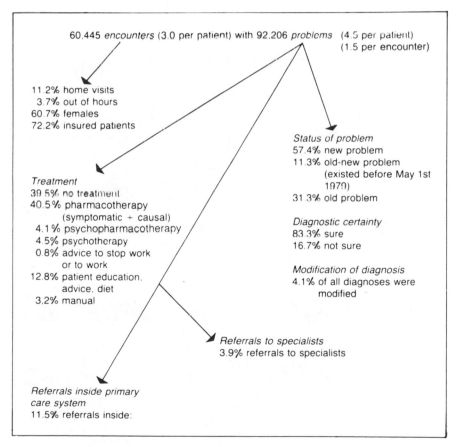

60.445 *encounters* (3.0 per patient) with 92.206 *problems* (4.5 per patient)
(1.5 per encounter)

11.2% home visits
3.7% out of hours
60.7% females
72.2% insured patients

Status of problem
57.4% new problem
11.3% old-new problem
(existed before May 1st 1979)
31.3% old problem

Treatment
39.5% no treatment
40.5% pharmacotherapy
(symptomatic + causal)
4.1% psychopharmacotherapy
4.5% psychotherapy
0.8% advice to stop work
or to work
12.8% patient education,
advice, diet
3.2% manual

Diagnostic certainty
83.3% sure
16.7% not sure

Modification of diagnosis
4.1% of all diagnoses were
modified

Referrals to specialists
3.9% referrals to specialists

Referrals inside primary care system
11.5% referrals inside:

Source: Compiled by the author.

Figure 5.3.   Age-sex distribution of active patient population as of January 7, 1980.

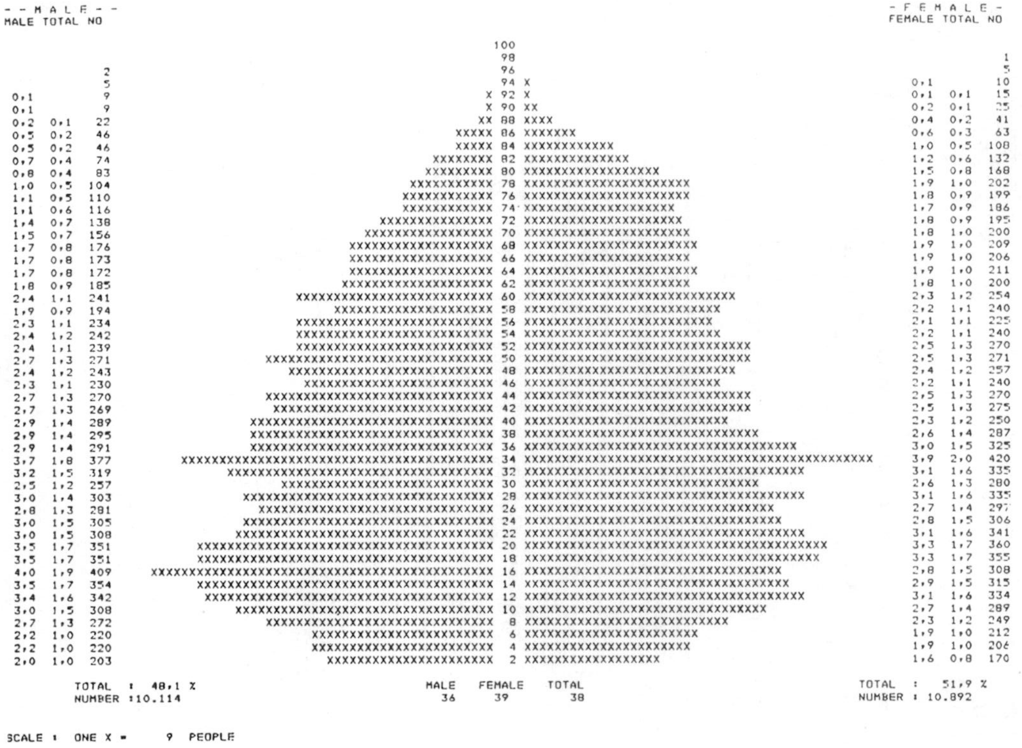

- M A L E -
MALE TOTAL NO

- F E M A L E -
FEMALE TOTAL NO

SCALE = ONE X = 9 PEOPLE

	MALE	FEMALE	TOTAL
	36	39	38

TOTAL : 48.1 %   NUMBER :10,114

TOTAL : 51.9 %   NUMBER : 10,892

Source: Compiled by the author.

Figure 5.4. Existence of psychological and social problems and of chronic diseases during the first year. $n = 20,330$

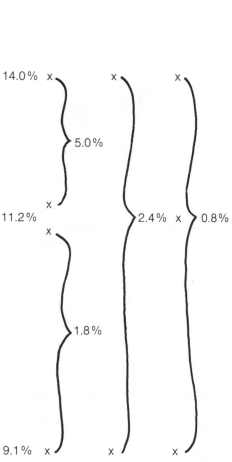

Psychological problems
—anxiety, hypochondriac disorder, depressive disorder, surmenage or neurasthenia, "neurosis," transient situational disturbance, other psychological problems, stammering and stuttering, tics, suicide attempt.

Social problems
—alcohol abuse, economic problem, housing problem, person-with-disease problem, marital problem with or without sex problem, parent-and-child problem, parent or in-law problem, family disruption, other family problems, educational problem, social maladjustment, occupational problem, phase-of-life problem, legal problem, homosexuality problem.

Chronic disease
—malignancy, diabetes, perniciosa, schizophrenia, organic psychosis, affective psychosis, multiple sclerosis, parkinsonism, senile dementia, epilepsy, blindness, rheumatic heart disease, myocardial ischemia or infarction, heart failure, pulmonary heart disease, cerebrovascular disease, arteriosclerosis excluding heart and brain, chronic bronchitis, bronchiectasis, emphysema and COPD, asthma, chronic enteritis, ulcerative colitis, rheumatoid arthritis.

14.0%   5.0%

11.2%   2.4%   0.8%

1.8%

9.1%

Source: Compiled by the author.

general practitioner with a social problem (one classified in the last chapter of the *ICHPPC*-2) and approximately 14% with a psychological problem (mainly those classified in Chapter 5 of the *ICHPPC*-2).

PREVALENCE OF PSYCHOLOGICAL AND SOCIAL PROBLEMS

The above-mentioned results are not surprising. Psychological and social problems form an essential part of the content of primary health care. Both the 1972 morbidity analysis and the first results of the 1979 monitoring project are consistent with a number of publications that are summarized in Tables 5.1–5.4.

In further support of the importance of psychological and mental problems, Regier, Goldberg, and Taube (16) convincingly argue that every year at least 15% of the U.S. population suffers from a "mental disorder." However, a striking contrast occurs in the important Virginia morbidity study (13), where only 5% of the diagnoses belong to Chapter 5 of the *ICHPPC*-2 (mental disorders) and less than 1% to Chapter 20 of the *ICHPPC*-2 (social problems). The authors mention the possibility of underreporting by the classifying doctors as an explanation for these low percentages. The reason for underreporting appears to be the lack of awareness of psychosocial problems.

Metcalfe (14) and Stewart, McWhinney, and Buck (18) also point out the considerable importance of psychosocial problems in primary care. Both demonstrate that general practitioners are often unaware of these problems, so they do not establish and record problem behavior in the contact with the patient. Interdoctor variation is found to be considerable in this respect. Some reasons for this are known; many more stay unclear or unknown.

In summary, it appears to be a safe and even rather conservative estimation that every year 10–20% of any practice population present psychological and/or social problems to their family physicians, provided that conditions enhancing the responsiveness of both doctor and patient ("open contact") and the practical means to classify these problems (such as *ICHPPC*-2) are present.

PSYCHOSOCIAL PROBLEMS AND UTILIZATION OF PRIMARY HEALTH CARE

An important question is whether explicit attention to problem behavior produces sufficient advantages to warrant digression from the disease model. Is the patient better off? Is there benefit for the doctor? Does it help to imple-

Table 5.1.   Prevalence of Psychosocial Problems in Primary Medical Care

	Men	Women	Total	Remarks
Lamberts, 1974, 1975 (Ommoord Netherlands)			18	All ages, entire practice population
Cooper et al., 1973 (UK)	6	17		15 years and older
Hodgkin, 1973 (UK)			10	All ages, entire practice population
Johnstone and Goldberg, 1976 (UK)			32	Adults in waiting room
Martin et al., 1957 (UK)			4	All ages, entire practice population
Morbidity Survey (RCGP et al., 1974) (UK)			11	All ages, entire practice population
Oliemans, 1969 (Netherlands)			7	All ages, entire practice population
Stewart et al., 1975 (USA)		22		Adult women
Wolfe and Badgley, 1972 (Canada)			20	Only patients with at least one contact

Source: H. Lamberts, "Problem Behaviour in Primary Health Care," *Journal of the Royal College of General Practitioners* 29(1979):331–35.

ment health care policies? Analysis of the utilization of primary health care is relevant to this issue. In Table 5.5, some results from the 1972 morbidity analysis are summarized, as produced in a joint project with the Economic Institute of Leiden University (3,17).

The method used to compute the figures in Table 5.5 is complicated, so those interested are referred to the original publications (3,8,17). It is well known that the yearly number of patient-doctor encounters varies. This variation can partially be explained with the help of additional information. In

Table 5.2. Comparison of Prevalences

	Prevalence per 1,000 persons per year		
	Ommoord 1972	Netherlands 1967	England 1971
Types of reaction	173	72	83
Life problems	183	5	±8
Problems about young children	33	—	—
'Psychosomatic'	144	101	133
'Functional disorders'	305	188	152
'True' psychiatry	7	5	8

Source: H. Lamberts, "Problem Behaviour in Primary Health Care," *Journal of the Royal College of General Practitioners* 29(1979):331–35.

Table 5.3. 30,000 Classifications of Problems in Primary Health Care in 1972 (*n* = 10,794)

	Percentages
Clear, somatic diagnosis	*41*
Chronic impairment of daily life activities	*5*
Problem behaviour and psychological reactions	*31*
Reaction forms	*6*
Psychosomatic diseases	*6*
Clear problems of life	*7*
Functional complaints	*11*
Procedural	*10*
Vague, unclear	*18*

Source: H. Lamberts, "Problem Behaviour in Primary Health Care," *Journal of the Royal College of General Practitioners* 29(1979):331–35.

Table 5.4. Differentiation of Life Problems (per 1,000 Patients per Year) (*n* = 10,794)

Relationship problem	
'Man/wife' (not sexual)	33
Other family members (parents, parents in law)	7
'Man/wife' (sexual)	21
In the family (children/parents)	24
Work problem	31
School, emancipation, education	8
Crisis situations	17
Phase of life	8
Other well defined problems	30

Source: H. Lamberts, "Problem Behaviour in Primary Health Care," *Journal of the Royal College of General Practitioners* 29(1979):331–35.

Table 5.5. Maximum Influence on Primary Care Utilization of Each Variable, with the Other Variables Fixed on the Population Mean

Variable	Percentage
Sex (female)	57
Social class (high)	13
Insurance (nationally insured)	13
Housing (apartment building)	14
Interdoctor variation	14
Existence of serious disease	112
Existence of problem behavior	140
Existence of problem behavior in family	10

this case it is evident, for example, that women have 57% more contacts with their general practitioner than men, when the influence of all other variables (such as age, social class, insurance, the existence of a serious disease or of problem behavior, etc.) is excluded.

Problem behavior appears to be the strongest single predictor of the yearly number of encounters. The relevance of these sometimes impressively high figures, however, is limited. Generally, the total amount of variation in utilization that can be explained is very limited (in this case, maximally 24%). Also, the existence of both a serious somatic disease (a chronic disease interfering with the daily life of the patient) and problem behavior has an inherent influence of utilization. Seriously ill people need their doctors often, while the definition of *problem behavior* requires at least one contact.

In several other utilization studies, the importance of introducing a variable describing some aspect of problem or illness behavior has been demonstrated further. Kohn and White (7) are disappointed by the limited percentage of variance in utilization that they can explain. This disappointment is commonly shared in the literature, notwithstanding the fact that most authors do indicate significant relations between some independent variables and utilization (1,2,4,5). The amount of utilization that can be explained with demographic information in the monitoring project approximates 15%, while a rather steep climb to 24% occurs when problem behavior is added to the equations. This finding is compatible with the studies by Hershey, Luft, and Gianaris (5), and by Tessler, Mechanic, and Dimond (19). Roughly, the results of all the above-mentioned studies indicate that 10–15% of variation in utilization can be explained with the help of a variety of demographic variables, and that this percentage climbs to 20–25% when some information about the existence of psychosocial problems is added.

The first experiences with the 1979 monitoring project sustain this strong quantitative association between utilization and the presentation of social psychological problems, but also a connection between utilization and chronic diseases. The percentage of each utilization group (Figure 5.5, Table 5.6) presenting some aspect of problem behavior during the first year of the project grows linearly with the number of encounters.

INFLUENCE OF PSYCHOSOCIAL PROBLEMS ON REFERRALS TO SPECIALISTS

Rutten and van der Gaag (17) used the 1972 morbidity analysis to estimate the influence of certain variables on referrals to specialists. The total variance in the number of referrals that could be explained with age and with the variables in Table 5.5 remained very limited (4% of all referrals).

An interesting element, however, is the negative correlation of problem behavior with referrals, independent of the number of patient-doctor contacts. It was calculated that problem behavior had a maximal negative influence of − 34% (keeping all other variables on their population mean) on referrals, given the number of patient-doctor contacts.

This suggests that once psychological and social problems are recognized, the general practitioner is less willing to refer the patient to a specialist.

CLASSIFICATION OF PSYCHOSOCIAL PROBLEMS

Any classification formalizes reality and at the same time reduces it. Medical diagnoses have many limitations. Labeling the patient's problem with a diagnosis—choosing whether to call it being a disease or a psychosocial problem—introduces a new reality both for the patient and for the care provider, because the label in many instances is synonymous with a certain action or a certain expectation.

ICHPPC-2 forms a compromise between the resistance of some to the introduction of psychosocial problems in a medical classification and the strong demand of others for a nationally accepted classification for family physicians. The Classification Committee of the World Organization of National Colleges, Academies, and Academic Associations of General Practitioners/Family Physicians (WONCA) is very much aware of the need for a compromise, as is the working group responsible for the proposed *Reasons for Contact* classification (15). For both classifications, numerous semantic, conceptual, and methodological problems have been acknowledged. The

Figure 5.5. Percentage of the population with psychological or social problems or a chronic disease during one year for several utilization rates in the same year.

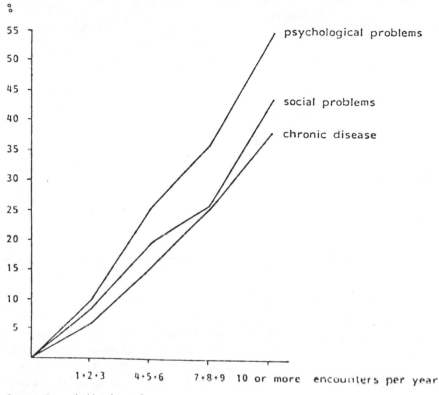

%

55
50
45
40
35
30
25
20
15
10
5

psychological problems

social problems

chronic disease

1·2·3   4·5·6   7·8·9   10 or more   encounters per year

Source: Compiled by the author.

lack of definitions for the rubrics used in *ICHPPC*-2, the lack of specificity, and the ambiguous position of psychosocial problems in an essentially disease-oriented classification are evident.

While *ICHPPC*-1 (the first edition of *ICHPPC*) can be seen as a landmark in the emancipation of international family medicine, *ICHPPC*-2 can be characterized as a *mariage de raison* between a better developed frame of reference for primary care and the ninth edition of the *International Classification of Diseases* (ICD-9), with the outspoken hope that this coupling will give birth to a prodigious child. The *Reasons for Contact* classification possibly indicates the direction in which such a child could develop.

While developing *ICHPPC*-2, it was evident to the members of the Classification Committee that the lack of definitions for the majority of the rubrics frustrates its practical use. It was decided, therefore, to develop an appendix

Table 5.6.   Percentage of Each Utilization Group with At Least One Psychological or At Least One Social Problem during Nine Months

Number of Contacts	Percentage with Psychological Problems	Percentage with Social Problems	Percentage without Psychological or Social Problems
1	5.5	3.5	91.6
2	10.6	7.4	83.9
3	17.5	12.2	74.6
4	24.3	14.4	68.5
5	25.5	17.2	64.8
6	30.5	19.9	59.4
7	35.1	19.8	55.1
8	40.4	28.5	48.3
9	48.4	26.4	42.3
≥10	52.8	33.4	35.5

to *ICHPPC*-2, consisting of definitions of most rubrics. A first round was based on definitions of approximately 150 codes of *ICHPPC*-2, produced by all members of the Committee. A second round, consisting of proposed new definitions emanating from the first round, was decided upon in London in October 1979, and will be published as an aid for those working with *ICHPPC*-2. The Classification Committee subjected some of the definitions of the first round to a closer look, trying to discern patterns in the large variation of definitions for each rubric. Of course, this is a rather arbitrary exercise. The members of the Classification Committee do not necessarily represent a general or national point of view. The subjective manner in which the members tried to describe 10 separate elements in the variation between definitions (Figure 5.6) can easily be criticized.

To facilitate the overview, a grid was used, allowing the location of each definition for each of the ten elements described in Figure 5.6 on a 5-point scale, taking all definitions for a rubric into account. (In Figure 5.7, two examples are presented.) The ten selected elements proved to be neither exhaustive nor independent. *ICHPPC*-2 is apparently very heterogeneous. This is a basic problem that coincides with the fact that the content of primary health care is essentially heterogeneous. Apart from this conclusion, the Classification Committee found no indications that the definability of psychological or social rubrics is more complicated or less clear than that of disease-oriented rubrics. This conclusion is supported by the 1972 morbidity analysis and the 1979 monitoring project.

TRAINING IN THE USE OF THE
CLASSIFICATION AND CODING SYSTEM

It is essential for the use of *ICHPPC*-2 or any other coding system that all group members agree on the way it should be applied. In our case, repeated and detailed group discussions were a major training for reaching agreement.

Apart from this, 50 fictional patient-doctor encounters were prepared on paper. All group members were requested to code each vignette on an encounter form. The cases were designed so as to overrepresent the complexities and difficulties that can arise with the complicated system used. The group discussed all cases and decided on the correct solution for each case. This im-

Figure 5.6.   Description of ten elements in the variation of definitions.

1. *Exclusion of other diagnoses*—inclusion in a rubric is determined by ruling out alternative or related diagnoses. Therefore, what is not included in the rubric becomes as important as what is included. For instance, pulmonary heart disease does not include conditions due to a primary heart disease.

2. *Objective signs or evidence present*—inclusion in the rubric depends on identification of specific clinical investigative signs which are considered more or less pathognomonic for the disorder. For instance, auscultating, X-ray, or respirometric evidence are required for a diagnosis of chronic bronchitis.

3. *Patient's opinion*—inclusion in the rubric depends on the subjectively defined complaint or symptomatic presentation of the patient regardless of objective clinical or investigative evidence and of course checked for communicative accuracy anamnestically by the doctor; for instance, headache, abdominal pain.

4. *Anatomical elements*—specific structures or locations in the human body are an essential part of the definition; for instance, hemorrhoids.

5. *Use of health or illness metaphor*—inclusion in the rubric requires that an essentially social or psychological problem is seen by the doctor or patient or both as a problem affecting the health or producing illness in the patient.

6. *Cultural value*—inclusion in the rubric is dependent to a significant degree on the definition containing an important element based on a particular cultural setting or bias.

7. *Doctor's opinion*—inclusion in the rubric depends on the doctor's judgment apart from the patient's subjective claims or objective evidence.

8. *Proof of other nature (Epidemiologic History)*—where epidemiologic factors, family history or other such supportive diagnostic indications are important to inclusion in the rubric. For instance, intestinal disease—presumed infectious or viral when there is a cluster of similar cases in the community.

9. *Discrete entity diagnosis*—when the diagnosis in question rests on identification of specific etiological agents (measles) or failing this, a simple pathophysiologic disturbance (excess wax in the ear canals).

10. *Big, essential intercoder (interdoctor) variation*—when there are numerous or important divergences between the authors of the definitions in their use of or omission of the above themes and/or in terms of other disagreements.

Source: Compiled by the author.

Figure 5.7. (a) Educational problem; (b) Hemorrhoids.

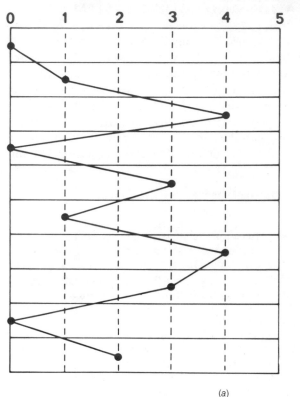

1. Exclusion of other diagnoses
2. Objective signs and/or evidence must be present
3. Patient's opinion
4. Anatomical elements
5. Use of health or illness metaphor
6. Cultural value
7. Doctor's opinion
8. Proof of other nature (epidemiologic, history, etc.)
9. Discrete entity diagnosis
10. Big intercoder-variation

(a)

Source: Compiled by the author.

plied in many instances that not one but several answers were considered correct, while a more differentiated classification was accepted in some cases. An example of the cases used is given by the following:

During the fourth encounter with Mr. C., it appears that physiotherapy did not help him very much. Mr. C. is anxious and feels he might suffer from a slipped disc. Repeated physical examination—in full agreement with the X-rays—shows no sign of this. Mr. C. is not satisfied, and he is referred to an orthopedic surgeon. Apart from this, he now complains about his working conditions and vague precordial pain. He is afraid of a myocardial infarction. The physical examination confirms the suspicion that intercostal myalgia is the reason for the pain. Nevertheless an ECG is ordered. The problems at work are briefly discussed. While leaving the consultation room, Mr. C. informs his doctor that his wife is now on national insurance and no longer a private patient.

Figure 5.7. (*continued*)

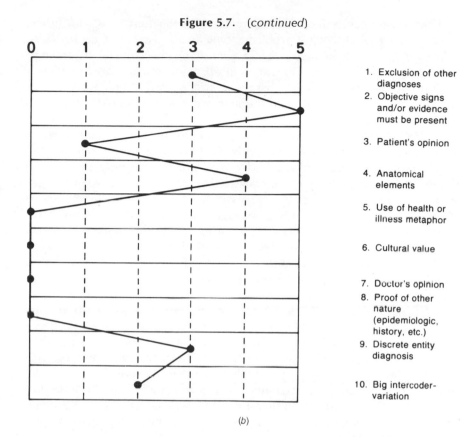

1. Exclusion of other diagnoses
2. Objective signs and/or evidence must be present
3. Patient's opinion
4. Anatomical elements
5. Use of health or illness metaphor
6. Cultural value
7. Doctor's opinion
8. Proof of other nature (epidemiologic, history, etc.)
9. Discrete entity diagnosis
10. Big intercoder-variation

(*b*)

With these 50 cases, a minimum of 420 codes and classifications were introduced, with 124 additional variations. The average number of mistakes made was 49.5 (SD 13.7). Half these mistakes (4.6%) were "real" mistakes (e.g., wrong classifications), the other half (4.5%) were missing diagnoses. Comparison of the results in the first 25 with those in the second 25 cases revealed no systematic improvement. It is realistic to estimate the error rate at less than 4.5%, while underreporting can explain the missing of another 4.5% or less.

In both categories, the psychosocial classifications were not overrepresented. It also appeared that during the project the amount of certain classifications is relatively high (± 98%) in the chapter with social problems. There proved to be more doubt when using the classifications for psychological problems (± 88% "sure").

Doctors sometimes label inconsistently with themselves or with others when labeling psychological problems. One doctor used the label *neurosis,* while another preferred *neurasthenic reaction* or *anxiety.* The influence of psychosocial problems on cooperation in a team of primary care providers is very strong (11,12). The social workers, district nurses, and physiotherapists all consider care for patients with problem behavior as essential to their professional role.

ICHPPC appears to be a relatively useful tool for team communication when psychosocial problems are involved. *ICHPPC*-1 was presented to all members of the Ommoord team who were not general practitioners (12) (eight district nurses, four physiotherapists, two social workers, two midwives), with the question to what extent every rubric was professionally relevant to them. ("When a patient has this problem, do you—as a nurse, a physiotherapist, a midwife, a social worker—think you can contribute to its solution in a professional way?") The general practitioners did the same, considering the professional contribution of the "other" disciplines when a patient had a problem, classifiable by the 371 rubrics of *ICHPPC*-1.

The average score for each rubric (maximally three points) was calculated for all the disciplines. In Table 5.7, some of the results are summarized. Theoretically, 1,123 points could be awarded. The nurses claimed the largest part of *ICHPPC* as professionally relevant, the social workers the smallest.

Psychological and social problems provided practically no disagreement between the doctors and the other team members. In most instances two, three, or even all four other disciplines claimed psychosocial problems as professionally relevant, and the general practitioners agreed. Table 5.8 represents our experiences with the role of several team members regarding psychosocial problems (9,11).

THE CULTURAL FUNCTION OF PRIMARY CARE

Conceptual or "idealistic" reasons make it worthwhile to distinguish undifferentiated illness behavior from behavior where a disease can be established and from behavior where a nonmedical problem clearly is the main reason for seeking care. Between the extremes of clearly medical and clearly nonmedical problems, one finds a large number of hazily defined ailments (vague complaints, alibi functions, social constraints for other solutions).

When one wishes to withstand the medicalization of society, one of the things that can be done least is the restriction of illness behavior. Doing this, however, is primarily based on a value judgment and not on proven effectiveness. When a general practitioner decides psychosocial problems are important, he or she probably will meet and classify those problems more frequently than might someone for whom psychosocial problems are essentially non-

Table 5.7. Claims for the Professional Relevance of *ICHPPC* (371 Classifications — Maximum Possible Score 1,123 Points)

Care-Giving Group	Score
General practitioners	489
Nurses	414
Physiotherapists	245
Midwives	109
Social workers	67

medical problems, not belonging to the disease-oriented frame of reference of the primary care provider. Some people will interpret this as a self-fulfilling prophecy. Others, however, consider it a part of the cultural function of primary care to modify its content actively and to provide the community with appropriate indications for care models that are not simply disease-oriented. A self-fulfilling prophecy in the form of a nondisease model is acceptable in a cultural context.

The cultural function of primary care is not limited to the differentiation of several forms of behavior (see Figure 5.8). A shift in the goals for primary care, for example, by introducing a different concept of health can be equally relevant. A more appropriate working definition of *health,* based on the experiences of individuals themselves, seems to be that health is that state of being experienced by individuals where they feel well and where their bodies are no great concern to them. In this state they are physically fit and able to live in

Table 5.8. Estimate of Psychotherapeutic Relations per 1,000 Patients of the Practice Population per Year among Several Providers

Estimate of psychotherapeutic relationship per 1,000 patients of the practice population per year between several providers.	
General practitioner	180
Physiotherapists	50
Nurses — well baby clinics	20
— home care	15
Social worker	9
Mental health agencies, psychiatrists, mental hospitals	16

Figure 5.8.   The cultural functions of primary care.

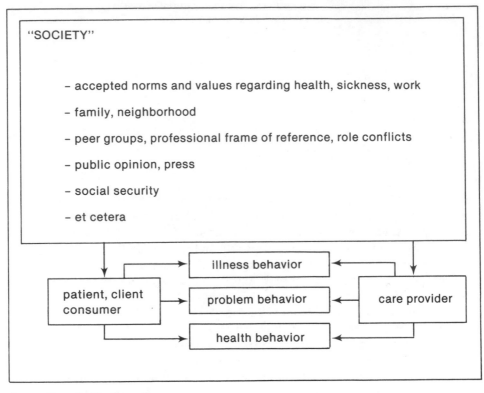

Source: Compiled by the author.

such a way that this is satisfying for themselves, taking into account the limitations presented by the difficult situations, common for human existence.

We become aware of the impact of certain diagnoses or labels on medical care utilization and on the "health" of the patient. Not only in the domain of problem behavior, but also in that of illness, new realities are constituted both with the application or with the denial of certain labels or diagnoses. It is questionable whether people with problems of life should be channeled into the (primary) health care setting in the first place. It is certain that people should not be lured into illness behavior when no medical problem exists.

Primary care essentially does not have the power to change this, putting aside the question of whether the professional group is really willing to use such influence. It is inconceivable, however, that a major change in the relation between society and the medical care system would occur without a drastic decrease in clinical facilities. Primary care has abundant facilities at its disposal to influence the values and norms both of society and of the health care system. Psychosocial problems can form a major catalyst in this respect.

REFERENCES

1. J. G. Anderson, "Demographic Factors Affecting Health Utilization," *Medical Care* 11(1973):104.

2. M. H. Banks et al., "Factors Influencing Demand for Primary Medical Care in Women Aged 20–44 Years: A Preliminary Report," *International Journal of Epidemiology* 4(1975):189.

3. J. van der Gaag and W. van der Ven, "The Demand for Primary Health Care," *Medical Care* 16(1978):299–312.

4. R. Geertsen et al., "A Reexamination of Suchman's Views on Social Factors in Health Care Utilization," *Journal of Health and Social Behaviour* 16(1975):226.

5. J. C. Hershey, H. S. Luft, and J. M. Gianaris, "Making Sense Out of Utilization Data," *Medical Care* 13(1975):838.

6. World Organization of National Colleges, Academies, and Academic Associations of General Practitioners/Family Physicians, *International Classification of Health Problems in Primary Care,* 2nd ed. (London: Oxford University Press, 1979).

7. R. Kohn and K. L. White, *Health Care: An International Study* (London: Oxford University Press, 1976).

8. H. Lamberts, "De morbiditeitsanalyse—1972 door de groepspraktijk Ommoord; een nieuwe ordening van ziekte—en probleemgedrag voor de huisartsgeneeskunde," *Huisarts en Wetenschap* 17(1974):445–73, 18(1975):7–39, 61–73.

9. H. Lamberts, "Problem Behaviour in Primary Health Care," *Journal of the Royal College of General Practitioners* 29(1979):331–35.

10. H. Lamberts, "Primary Health Care Monitoring Project: A Year of Practical Experience with a Computerized Information System," *Huisarts en Wetenschap* 23(1980):293–304.

11. H. Lamberts and F. E. Riphagen, "Working Together in a Team for Primary Health Care: A Guide to Dangerous Country," *Journal of the Royal College of General Practitioners* 25(1975):745–52.

12. H. Lamberts and E. Sloot, "Multidisciplinaire probleemclassificatie," *Huisarts en Wetenschap* 21(1978):53–59.

13. D. W. Marsland, M. Wood, and F. Mayo, "Content of Family Practice," *Journal of Family Practice* 3(1976):37–68.

14. D. H. H. Metcalfe, "The Recognition of Family and Social Problems by General Practitioners: Toward Developing a Taxonomy," *Journal of the Royal College of General Practitioners* 28(1978):46–52.

15. *Reasons for Contact with Primary Care Services: A Model Classification* (Geneva: WHO Working Group, 1979).

16. D. A. Regier, I. D. Goldberg, and C. A. Taube, "The De Facto U.S. Mental Health Services System," *Archives of General Psychiatry* 35(1978):685–93.

17. F. F. H. Rutten and J. van der Gaag, "Referrals and Demand for Specialist Care in the Netherlands," *Health Services Research* 12(1977):233–49.

18. M. A. Stewart, I. R. McWhinney, and C. W. Buck, "The Doctor/Patient Relationship and Its Effect upon Outcome," *Journal of the Royal College of General Practitioners* 29(1979):77–82.

19. R. Tessler, D. Mechanic, and M. Dimond, "The Effect of Psychosocial Distress on Physician Utilization: A Prospective Study," *Journal of Health and Social Behaviour* 17(1976):353.

6

Humanization of Health Care: Rationale, Means, and Strategies

DENISE DELIEGE

INTRODUCTION

The way care is provided to patients is an important social factor affecting health. If proper attention is paid to the overall context of care, and not merely to its technical aspects, patients will be more likely to cooperate in the care process and to derive greater benefit from it. This assessment is shared by many with experience in this field, and there are numerous examples in the literature which provide evidence. Nevertheless, more systematic surveys in this area would be useful.

The social aspects of hospitals deserve special attention. These involve a complexity of forces that can, on the one hand, hinder personal care and relationships between doctors and patients, and, on the other hand, provide the necessary infrastructure for adequate care.

The attention devoted to social aspects of hospital health care often stems from a more global context: a process of "humanization" of care. Some may wonder about the need for such an endeavor in an institution designed precisely to provide care for human beings. Thus, the first section of this chapter is devoted to explaining the reasons favoring the effort in this direction.

Those who wish to promote humanization within hospitals may wonder how best to organize their efforts. There have been many experiences throughout the world; they are worth reviewing. The second section thus outlines the main fields of possible action.

Even if many obstacles remain, paths for achievement exist. Both aspects are briefly outlined in the third section.

This chapter, while newly written, draws heavily on the ideas in a book by Denise Deliege and Xavier Leroy, *Humanisons les hopitaux* (Paris: Maloine, 1978), sponsored by the Sandoz Institute for Health and Socioeconomic Studies. The summary partly uses the comment written by I. Roberts in *World Hospitals*, 15(1979). Full documentation and references can be found in these sources.

REASONS FOR PROMOTING
HUMANIZATION OF HOSPITAL CARE

The hospital is a special type of enterprise, oriented toward the "patients' health." But efforts to achieve this goal can be hampered or helped by certain aspects of hospital life that the institution shares with any other enterprise:

- It is a community of people.
- It is bound by economic constraints.
- It produces services for "clients."

As a result, although the official jargon states that "patients come first," another sociological reality exists, one made up of a variety of concepts that stem from divergent points of view and produce conflicts of interest.

The humanization process can be seen as a means of reconciliation, favoring the mutual acceptance of necessary compromises.

Globally speaking, the humanization process will help to do the following:

- Sustain the therapeutic process.
- Attain higher efficiency.
- Improve the outlook of both those who work and those who reside in the hospital.

Humanization is thus an attempt to meet various needs stemming from the complexity of the institution, which is at one and the same time a place to care and to cure, an economic enterprise, and a community of people. Table 6.1 shows how these internal structures each have their own limited objectives and leitmotives. Most advanced care for all and the finest technical facilities ("a place to care and to cure"); management and marketing ("an economic enterprise"); and individual satisfaction, quality of life, and cohesion of the group ("community of people").

Table 6.1.   Humanization: The Attempt to Meet Various Needs Originating in the Complexity of the Hospital as an Institution

Internal Structure	Objectives	Underlying Leitmotives and Means
Place to care and cure	"Most advanced care for all"	Technical facilities
Economic enterprise	Efficiency	Management marketing
Community of people	Individual satisfaction	Quality and cohesion of the group

The pole of convergence may be found around the concept of *global health,* as Figure 6.1 indicates. Borrowing some concepts from epidemiology, this may be seen as an attempt within a given environment to bring better health to the patients (the "hosts") through the vector "personnel," using socioeconomic techniques as "agents."

Let us now consider each structure separately and discuss why humanization can help each reach its own specific goal while global health acts as a point of convergence.

The Hospital as an Institution Providing Care

Adequate care implies that modern technical facilities are provided and that the patient is considered as a whole person, taking into account those psychosocial factors that can aggravate or even cause the disease, or those that hamper the therapeutic process.

The duality of global and reduced action is a daily problem in many contexts—for example, the difficulty of passing the stage of *"in vitro* experience" to apply new techniques *in vivo.*

Examples can also be drawn from hospital life. For one thing, common sense shows that some patients bring special problems while others do not. But are patients treated differently according to the potential risk or problems? For example, are certain behaviors encouraged in order to cope with various characteristics or pathologies? Or are young patients who are traumatized by a sudden accident treated differently from the chronically ill who return regularly?

To give another example, are hospitals and hospital employees aware of the trials besetting patients, and do they really try to palliate these trials? Patients are expected to be spartan about their experience, but how can they escape from the frequent turmoil, unpleasantness, and distress around them? They find themselves deeply dependent on others, even for the most trifling of needs. They are in the dark about what is or is not being done for them; they resent having doctors talking about them over their heads. They are asked to give blind obedience. But is this the best way to enlist the full powers of healing?

Patients' fears can lead the staff to become defensive, and they, in turn, may become more apprehensive. They lose his customary status and freedom of action and, surrounded by restrictions and a wall of silence, do not know where to turn. Separated from their own familiar world, they are made all too well aware that nobody is indispensable. If this continues for long, they become more and more socially isolated, and the hospital seems indifferent to their plight.

Pitchforked into a strange world with its own rules, they are expected to fit in and be "good patients." Some manage to do so; others do not, and regress

Figure 6.1. Pole of convergence: Global health.

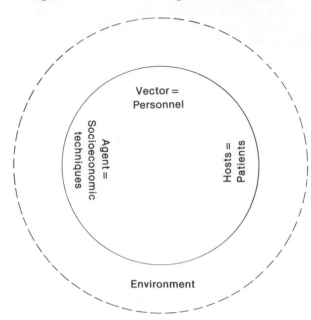

into childish or aggressive behavior or apathy. Some fit in all too well, cling-ing to their lives in the hospital by displaying fresh symptoms of illness.

Life is led at the behest, sometimes even at the whims, of the staff. This is particularly true in psychiatric hospitals, where things are constantly charac-terized as either "normal" or "deviant." To crown it all, there is the element of boredom, which is known to have physiological effects and to produce ag-gression and even suicide.

In relation to all this, we need only be reminded that human beings have various kinds of needs, which they do not shed on becoming hospital pa-tients. These economic, social, and psychological needs are reflected in such problems as being short of money, not knowing what services are available, or coming to terms with illness and the steps needed to return to normal life.

While this may seem too one-sided a picture, almost everyone could point to some telling examples of how distressing it can be, even for those who work in hospitals, to be admitted as patients. (At the same time, none of this con-tradicts the other aspect of the hospital, equally true and recognized by grate-ful patients: its wonderful ability to save lives and to provide for the basic care that is so dramatically needed when a person becomes disabled.)

Another point stems in part from the above discussion: Surveys have shown that hospitalized patients often have a large number of psychological symptoms. While these should be detected and cared for during the hospital stay, in most cases they are not. Studies tend to show that only about 25–40% percent of actual needs seem to be met.

Finally, common sense indicates that a patient's attitude plays an important role in treatment. Professionals know that very sick people in a hospital may just give up and die when they feel abandoned; that anorexia can stem from a lack of motivation toward life; that boredom (widespread in hospitals) can induce aggressive behavior and even suicide; and that lack of social stimuli may lead to apathy and degeneration.

On the other hand, there are many examples to show that people confronted with the threat of death (lost travelers, concentration camp and war victims, etc.) can produce unexpected reserves of energy in order to survive. One can thus assume that large resources of brain, will, and love are broadly underused in the process of care. Indeed, do hospitals and health care workers really call upon patients' will to live, their understanding of expectations, their pride, their love for their relatives? How much effort is put into attempts to enlist those powers of healing?

The Hospital as an Economic Enterprise

Humanization can also be a useful management tool for the hospital administration. Just as it increases the satisfaction of patients, it also tends to improve the outlook of hospital personnel. Having satisfied personnel is thought to increase overall efficiency because it lowers turnover and absenteeism. Efficiency is also increased because a more motivated employee will be more inclined to be concerned, to help, and to participate; the result will be "better care" for the patients.

Satisfied patients can also be a powerful "marketing" tool, since they can propagate the reputation of the hospital and thus act as a factor to attract future patients.

The Hospital as a Community of People

The hospital is also a community of people living together (the patients) or working together (the personnel). Is it a meaningful objective to see that they are satisfied?

While some would consider this a feature of a "spoiled" society, others regard it as part of the "quality of life," a valuable objective, a modern application of traditional altruism.

The discussion in the previous sections, however, shows that the expected outcome is even more significant, since both the management of the institution and the therapeutic process can benefit from it: Happy nurses will be more likely to help patients, and motivated patients will be more cooperative in getting well.

MEANS TO PROMOTE HUMANIZATION
OF HOSPITAL CARE

Two types of strategies can be carried out in order to draw the full potential of energies inside the hospital toward improving "global" health: either scattered actions, often acting as palliatives, without lasting effect; or a deliberate policy aimed at enlisting all material staff resources to achieve comprehensive care of the patient in three dimensions—physical, mental, and social.

A deliberate global policy should focus on patients and their health, in every sense of the term, by means of teamwork and with the active participation of the patient.

In order to achieve these goals, actions should be taken on various fronts: to improve the environment, to mobilize the personnel, and to enlist patient participation.

Action to Improve the Environment

One way of saving patients from the hazards of hospital life is to avoid taking them to the hospital. This is already done to a certain extent by using such alternative means as day care units, night care units, home care, and "hospitals at home." But these facilities do not replace existing ones and, in fact, might even increase the global costs if the existing facilities remain used by other clients.

In order to decrease hospitalization rates and costs, some incentives should be offered to doctors. Sidney Lee has proposed innovative measures in this direction: doctors should be involved in setting performance goals that reduce overall costs and, at the same time, are compatible with good medical care and even increase the global output of health. For example, prepaid group practices in the United States have shown that large population groups can benefit from medical care at a hospitalization rate about half the average (even after standardization for age and sex distribution). Allowing for extra days that may be necessary for socioeconomic reasons (if the population of the prepaid group practice is better off than those who do not receive its benefits), targets could be set for hospitalization rates or days per inhabitant, and financial incentives would encourage doctors to aim toward the chosen target.

Measures could be taken to make hospital settings more hospitable and to improve some organizational aspects of services.

Making the Hospital Hospitable

Hospitality within the hospital can be a target even prior to admission. Later, attention should be paid to admission, which is a crucial moment for the patient, and to various aspects of the stay, in order to make it more pleasant.

Before Admission. Open days for the public, lectures for clubs of elderly, and preadmission visits (especially for children and psychiatric patients) can all contribute to reducing people's fear of large hospital buildings.

Before or upon Admission. Information leaflets can be useful either beforehand or upon admission. They should not, however, be considered a substitute for personal contact. Human warmth, smiles, gentle attention to the fears and needs of the patient, are all essential. Secretaries assigned to the admissions desk should be properly trained in this respect. While a hostess can be helpful, volunteers' associations can do a wonderful job of guiding patients to their room and making the link with the staff on the ward.

During the Stay. Patients will appreciate such amenities as a telephone, TV, games, books, and a shop for small odds and ends. Nevertheless, the quality of the human environment will still be more important—roommates who are compatible; relatives allowed to visit at their convenience, or even to stay with him or at a nearby inexpensive hostel.

These proposals are but first steps. It is more important to probe more deeply to meet the patients' inner sufferings and anxieties. A major component of this human environment is the support provided by the staff itself, and the quality of the overall "therapeutic climate" of the hospital. For this, a few basic attitudes are vital: to listen to the patients, to talk gently, to inform the patients of and to explain the reasons for treatment, and to give support to the dying.

• To listen to patients is essential in order to increase the possibilities of successful treatment, since medical advice can be made more precise and effective when related to what the patients themselves have to say.

• Gentleness is warmly and gratefully appreciated; even such factors as tone of voice have their impact for good or ill. Furthermore, patients tend to respond according to what they imagine the staff thinks of them. (Similarly, the medical and other staff members often play the parts they think are expected of them, parts in which their own prestige seems to loom large.) The psychology of all this can be turned to the advantage of both patients and staff when the staff is aware of the different roles it can play.

• People today are more accustomed to being well *informed* about what is going on. Patients and their families are eager to know more about the diagnosis, the results of tests, treatment, the expected outcome, the likely length of stay, and so on. Faced with this, doctors may be tempted to justify the traditional reticence of their profession by suggesting that patients are not yet in a fit state to understand, leaving the patients to rely on snatches of conversation among the staff and hearsay from other patients. But patients are entitled to at least a minimum of information without being fobbed off with evasive or patronizing answers. This varies with the individual and the illness. In the case of terminal patients, skill is necessary; such patients can best be enlightened step by step, and only if they really ask for the truth and are thought to be able to bear it.

• The process of *explaining* to patients *why* things are happening might help to enlist their full cooperation. Practice may vary as to who should provide the information and explanations. Having a patient's family doctor do it, for example, gives the advantage of enabling the doctor to participate in the patient's stay in the hospital in a way that is not contrived. Nurses are also in a good position to interpret medical language for the benefit of patients.

• The ethos of scientific medicine seems to regard death as the loathed foe, and doctors can be tempted to keep patients "officially alive." One of the dangers in this complex issue is that patients might appear to be put on the scrap heap once they are beyond the effect of therapy. If, on the other hand, patients find that they can still turn to their doctors to the last, they are saved from the fear that nothing more will be done for them. Families, too, have a crucial part to play in saving patients from isolation at the end of his life. This is well recognized at the hospices that have come into being for terminal care, notably St. Christopher's Hospice in London. Where family support is lacking, the staff strives to achieve the same effect.

Improving Some Organizational Aspects of Services

The desire to provide a humane service should show itself in the way the clinical units are organized. Apart from chaplains and volunteers, there are other ways to enhance the effect of the clinical units, such as by seconding to them staff from the supporting services. Continuity of care is important, and this, as well as greater satisfaction in the work, is one of the advantages of "integrated care," by teams of nurses assigned to the same patient for the whole of their stay. Teamwork also helps in achieving "systematic care"—that is, in identifying the basic causes of a patient's illness by working together from as many different points of view as possible. Formal communications are of vital importance for the benefit of the patient. However, the two main channels, the ward round and the medical record, have their limitations as means of eliciting all the relevant information. During rounds the patient is likely to be overawed, and much of value is likely to be omitted from the record, even when notes by nurses are included. (These communications should include observations from *all* members of the staff dealing with the patient.) Formal meetings of the whole staff speed up and improve the circulation of information.

Another source of help for the clinician is medical psychology, which sheds light on the effect of the personal relationships between patient and staff, or among members of the staff, and this subject should be part of the doctor's education.

Finally, there is the element of conviviality. The idea of a "therapeutic community" based on an absence of hierarchy (if not quite on anarchy) is fraught with danger and is probably out of place in any but some small hospitals. This, however, does not rule out the value of a "happy ship" as a means of achieving a good result.

For some patients there is the question of psychiatric help, if the mental aspect of the illness is found to loom large enough. For these cases, it may be useful to have psychiatric units in general hospitals or, even better, to have psychiatrists helping their colleagues to cope with those patients throughout the various departments. An example of a close accord between psychiatric and general care is the hospital at Lausanne, Switzerland, where the patient is seen by the physician and the psychiatrist at the same time.

Personnel Policy

One of the main ways for creating the desired climate of opinion is to have a personnel policy, with a chief to direct it and to monitor each individual's progress. The aim should be to implement techniques already adopted in efficient enterprises that are directed toward better care of patients and to the satisfaction and motivation of the personnel. Among such techniques are the following:

- The induction of staff—for example, through information period or leaflet.
- Good working conditions—for instance, convenient working hours and different weekly working periods, meals at work, housing and babysitting near the hospital.
- Integrating each member of the staff in the organization—for example, by matching employees and nurses working together, distributing information (e.g., through a bulletin), or setting up an employee assistance program.
- Methodical recruitment—namely, through selection tests.
- Promotion—through a yearly review, taking into account relationships with patients.
- Further training, either on the ward or in the framework of the hospital at large (e.g., within specific professional groups), or outside the institution with special groups or schools.
- Participation in the management, either at the top level or at the shop level (concentration on the ward, management by group objectives).

The Patients' Participation

What about the patients themselves and their part in all this? Their instinct of self-preservation is a source of energy still largely untapped, and the powers of their will, intelligence, and affection are all underestimated. As noted earlier, much evidence can be put forward to support this assumption:

- The wonders people manage to accomplish when their lives are threatened: for example, survival of accidents in the jungle, mountains, or desert; survival in concentration camps.
- Self-control of pain by special techniques, such as the Oriental methods.
- The degeneration observed in people deprived of adequate stimuli.

In Western civilization, illness is perceived as something extraneous, not at all something from within persons themselves, and so it is all too often assumed that treatment can go ahead successfully without sick persons' active participation. Such a concept probably leads to a vast waste of energy; many doctors miss their objectives, while potential help from the patients and their families is overlooked. A policy aimed at enlisting this assistance would be welcome and could also benefit from the positive actions of former patients.

Participation of patients can be said to begin with their leading healthy lives, and the corollary of this for the hospital is to play its part in health education.

When the question of treating illnesses arises, the patients must surely have a say, especially nowadays, when people are demanding more of a say in the decisions that affect their lives. This leads to the necessity to request the patients' agreement whenever important choices have to be made, especially when they induce different consequences on the patients' future lives. This is often the case when there is a choice, say, between surgery and another, long-term, form of treatment. In order to be able to make a meaningful choice, such a patient should be duly informed and counseled beforehand. Above all, patients should be aware of what to expect ("normal" pain, for instance), and also of what is expected of them. This adult form of cooperation induces a much more peaceful state of mind for patients and a much more positive approach to their treatment, especially when they have to endure surgery and postsurgical pain. The written word can often be used to good effect for this purpose, as in the information sheet provided to patients at the Centre de Cardiologie de Lyon (France).

Moreover, patients should be involved in a "feedback" process, a common technique for measuring the efficiency of actions taken and the performance of management. Thus patients should be more systematically offered the opportunity to inform the hospital authorities of what they really think. This is not to say that patients should be regarded as infallible or unbiased—only that their voices should be heard. This is, in any case, no more than what is commonly expected nowadays by consumers.

There are many ways to solicit feedback and to put it to good use. These include the conventional suggestion box or its present-day equivalent, the telephone; invitations to former patients to return for discussion, to serve on permanent boards, or to stay at the hospital for several days; or appointment of a special staff, an ombudsman, or an "ombudsteam" to gather and meet complaints. All these can be useful, but they also tend to be highly biased, reflecting only the complaints of those who are dissatisfied. A more systematic review, based on a standardized questionnaire and random sampling, is the only way to obtain an overview of the general opinion. This is the best approach for any manager willing to improve conditions according to the wishes of his or her overall "clientele." However, if the review is to be of practical use and accomplish more than to confirm a few cliches, it must be carefully prepared and sufficiently detailed.

OBSTACLES AND PATHS TO ACHIEVEMENT

Obviously there are obstacles to all these suggestions, particularly the lack of material resources and what might be called the "psychosociological" barriers. In response to the first, it should be noted that many of these proposals bring their own rewards by making better use of resources, both in material and staff, thus making it possible to find the time for the humanization process. For those measures that require extra funding, various sources can be suggested: government funds, local communities, research grants, hospital shops, private sponsors, and charities.

Several of the psychosociological barriers are probably harder to tackle. There is the preponderance of prestige enjoyed by the medical profession, compared with that of the economic and behavioral sciences from which many of the recommendations are drawn. There is the defensive shell that many members of the hospital staff who are responsible for patient care build around themselves; understandably, they believe they can take on the care but not the "cares" of patients. Another obstacle involves the rivalries and conflicts of interest among groups and individuals, partly as a result of the need for specialization. This is unavoidable to some extent, but it is also a force that can sometimes be harnessed for good. Finally, there is once more the patients' situation as they see it themselves, perhaps dazzled by the marvels of medicine and its trappings, and fortunate if they are not bewildered by it all.

There is no simple and perfectly efficient method of overcoming these obstacles with a 100% rate of success. By adopting the measures described, the personnel could also more successfully adopt an attitude of "detached concern," which is useful in coping with the heavy requirements mentioned. In addition, many of the techniques advocated could lead to an improvement in the "quality of life" in the hospital.

No dramatic improvement is to be expected overnight; it is a matter of years rather than months. How is the prescription to be administered? It is a question of persuading those concerned, and especially hospital medical staff members on whom success or failure usually depends, to adopt these combined findings of sociology, psychology, and management.

Since a policy of this kind is likely to call for considerable changes in the hospital, ways for facilitating the "mechanisms of transition" should be thoroughly imagined and should be carefully put into action as follows:

A committee of all the professions involved will direct the policy. Working groups will freely examine specific problems and report to the committee, which then decides on an order of priorities and launches pilot projects in selected units, especially those involving a long stay or prolonged attendance, such as rehabilitation. In diagnosing the state of the hospital, the committee could also turn to help from the kind of consultants who make studies and advise management in industry. The process is strengthened by the appointment of a coordinator to keep up the momentum, and by an independent observer who will make comparative studies, preferably both before and after action has been taken.

The overall message might be roughly summed up in two phrases: "Techniques alone are not enough," and "No man is an island."

In fact, the problem of internal cooperation is not new. As far back as 1860, Florence Nightingale found herself writing, "But above all, I am anxious . . . in particular . . . for their sake [the sick] let us be most careful to carry the 'Doctor' with us."

Though there are times when even the most convincing techniques of sociology and management theory can prove to be not quite the philosopher's stone, that is no reason for not trying. What is needed now is not so much an undue refinement of research, but a selective and sustained effort to put good ideas into practice—selective, to match the strengths and weaknesses of a given hospital; sustained, to keep up the standard of care.

7

The Role of Values and Value Deficiencies in Primary Health Care Recording Systems

ELEMER HANKISS
ROBERT MANCHIN
LASZLO FUSTOS

THE MISSING LINK

The psychosocial program of the World Health Organization (WHO) promoting "a more comprehensive understanding of health with the full recognition of its psychosocial components" (1) seems to be an important step in improving health care provision. The extension of the primary health care recording and reporting system to include "psychosocial problems," as proposed in this volume, may have three important results:

1. Taking psychosocial factors into consideration may improve primary health care services.
2. It may help to coordinate the activities of health services and those of other social agencies and, in the long run, may relieve the former of at least part of the burden imposed on them by the patients contacting them only with psychosocial or so-called "life" problems.
3. It may provide the basis for improved health statistics, health planning, and resource allocation.

The question is now whether the "multiaxial recording system" proposed by a working team at the National Institute of Mental Health, Rockville, Maryland, in October 1979 (referred to hereafter as Regier et al.—see Chapter 11, this volume) and accepted by the 1979 Bellagio conference with certain modifications would fulfill the hopes attached to it in the course of the field testing. In this chapter, this question is discussed from the *outside,* from the aspect of sociological research.

The proposed classification presupposes the interaction among the different factors concerning health shown in Figure 7.1. The present discussion does not deal with problems relating to the left side of the model—namely, to the fact that there is a complex and multilateral relationship among various "disorders" and "symptoms." For example, somatic symptoms could belong not only to somatic disorders but to mental and psychological disorders as well; somatic disorders could also have psychiatric and psychological symptoms; and so forth. The exploration of such cross-connections has always been an important part of medical diagnostic work; this work could certainly be effectively helped by a clear and systematic recording of symptoms and disorders.

This chapter deals with the system of connections indicated at the right side of the model—that is, it examines how the so-called "social problems" are related to health, and, specifically, to somatic, mental, and psychological disorders. In the present authors' opinion, the above model presupposes a too direct connection between social problems and disorders. This does not mean that there is no direct contact between the two groups of factors. Inadequate housing and food may be a direct cause for tuberculosis. In certain cases, "marital discord" may directly cause different injuries of the body, and an unhealthy working place may cause a variety of chronic diseases. But in most cases the social problems listed by Regier et al. (see Table 11.1, this volume) and other social problems of this sort have only an *indirect* effect on

Figure 7.1.   Interaction among factors affecting health (the Regier et al. model).

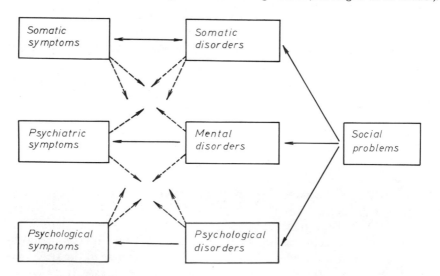

Source: Compiled by the authors.

human health. There is an intermediate link that is not taken into consideration in Chapter 11 and in other chapters of this volume. It would be important, however, to consider this link in the field of both diagnostic and therapeutic work. In order to explain what is meant here by this missing link, a short detour into the field of quality-of-life research is necessary.

The detour is all the less arbitrary because quality-of-life researchers would be willing to accept as the definition of *good life quality* the paragraph of the constitution of WHO, adopted in 1946, according to which "health is a state of complete physical, mental, and social well-being" (2). There is a certain degree of overlapping between the fields of health and value sociology, and their explorations, terminologies, and specific ways of seeing problems are likely to be of mutual help to each other.

It may prove useful to include two basic concepts used in quality-of-life research in the above-mentioned recording and reporting system. One is *value* or *life value;* the other is *value vehicle.* The concept of *value* is used here in a different sense from that used in axiology. Its meaning is much closer to the concept of *use value* as used in economic theory, although in quality-of-life research a much wider range of factors is regarded as values. All those physical, mental, and emotional events or states that constitute the experience of well-being are considered values. *Value vehicles,* on the other hand, are those physiological, economic, social, and environmental factors (such as nutrition, comfortable home, satisfactory job, human rights, friendship, etc.) that convey these values to people and make it possible for them to experience or assimilate these values (3).

"Social problems" arise—and here an attempt is made to mesh the terminology of the WHO program and that of quality-of-life research—when one of the value vehicles breaks down and is not able to provide those concerned with the necessary values. Quality-of-life researchers usually integrate value vehicles into *domains* (called *domains of life, subsystems, content areas, environments,* etc.). If a closer look is taken at these domains, it turns out that they are basically identical with the "Classification of Social Problems" in Table 11.1. For instance, in the Quality-of Life Research Project of the Hungarian Academy of Sciences, the following domains are used (4) (the numbers of Regier et al. are indicated in brackets):

Health

Food [III]

Shelter [I]

Financial situation, standard of
    living [III]

Conjugal problems, sex [IV]

Family life [V, VI, VII]

Human relations [IX]

Leisure

Social environment, change in social environment [II, XIII, XIV]

Political environment [XIII, XIV]

Cultural environment, cultural change

Physical environment

Education [XI]   Cycle-of-life issue [IX]
Occupation [XII]   Social roles (e.g., gender, race),
                                               role conflict, etc.

Let us now take a look at the values themselves. In the course of quality-of-life research, the following values have proved important from the aspect of ensuring a good life quality (there are certain overlappings between the values to be listed, but various considerations make it necessary to handle certain subcategories separately):

Physical well-being   Opportunity to attain one's goals
  Feeling of comfort   Getting ahead
  Lack of pain   Mobility, growth
  Vitality   Success, achievement
Feeling of security   Sense of efficiency
  Absence of anxiety   Creative activity
Lack of stress   Challenging tasks
Identity   Perspectives
Self-esteem   Positive expectations
  Dignity   Independence, freedom
Having a role   Power, control over one's life
  Sense of status, prestige   Meaningful norms
Consideration, respect   Knowledge
  Being accepted and appreciated   Being informed of one's situation
    by others   in the world
Love, loyalty   Sound balance between continuity
Togetherness   and change
  Sense of community   Maturity
  Integration   Inner harmony
Meaningful goals
  Life has meaning

Does Chapter 11 take these or similar values into consideration? It does not, at least not systematically. In the "Proposed Classification of Psychological Symptoms" (Table 11.2), there are certain values, or, more exactly, there are some *value deficiencies* ("tension," "anxiety," "hopelessness," "low self-esteem," "guilt," "identity problems," etc.), but these are mixed in under "Disorders" in the main headings, and under "Symptoms" listed below the main headings. Most of the above-listed values or value deficiencies are not indicated in this classification.

It is important, however, to take into consideration values or the lack of such values and to record them separately, since they are neither symptoms nor disorders, but rather their causes. There is a causal relationship between them. "Self-esteem," for instance, is an important value, a significant source of health or of good life quality. Its lack is likely to lead to a deterioration of health or life quality to some extent, and to various psychological (and, indirectly, to different psychiatric and somatic) disorders, as Figure 7.2 indicates. (The disorders in Figures 7.2–7.3 are taken from Table 11.2.).

Another example is "lack of security," which would cause the disorders illustrated in Figure 7.3, among others.

Since adequate therapy presupposes the elimination of the cause, it would be important to explore and record these value deficiencies with great care—in the proposed classification, as they are the missing link between social problems and psychological (and, to a lesser extent, somatic and mental) disorders. In the majority of cases, social problems do not directly result in different disorders; they usually work indirectly, when people are deprived of certain values of basic necessity. As a consequence, the immediate cause of a disorder or a disease is not the social problem itself, but the value deficiency created by the social problem. Therefore, the system of interactions among factors concerning health, as shown in Figure 7.1, should be modified as shown in Figure 7.4.

The inclusion of this intermediate factor is justified mainly with respect to

Figure 7.2.   Relationship between low self-esteem as a value deficiency and some psychological disorders that may be triggered by it.

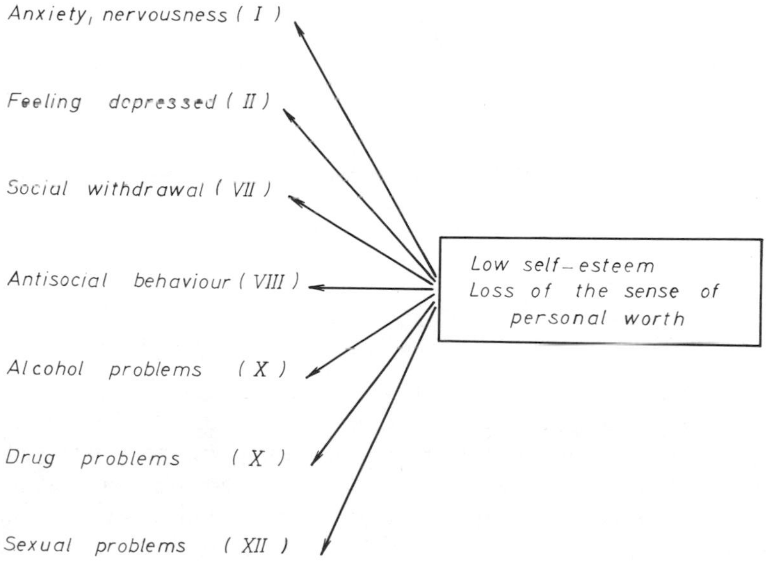

Source: Compiled by the authors.

Figure 7.3. Relationship between feeling of insecurity as a value deficiency and some psychological disorders that may be triggered by it.

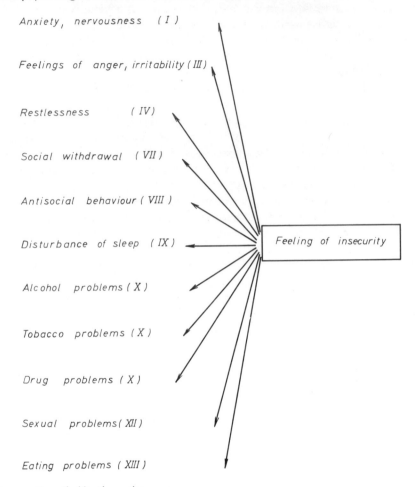

Source: Compiled by the authors.

psychological disorders. But in some cases, it could also prove important as far as psychiatric disorders are concerned; as is well known, the chronic lack of one or another value of basic necessity in early childhood may generate mental diseases. Such value deficiencies are routinely dealt with in analytic and psychotherapeutic practice. In the case of somatic disorders, the examination of the direct effect generated by value deficiencies may be mostly disregarded because recording them (e.g., diminished vitality) would not tell us more, perhaps even less, than recording the social problem itself (e.g., poverty, malnutrition) would.

The relationship between *social problems and value deficiencies* is not as simple and unambiguous as the arrow seems to indicate in Figure 7.4. Just as the same value deficiency can lead to more than one psychological disorder (see Figures 7.2 and 7.3), it can itself be generated by several social problems. This system of bilateral interaction is outlined in Figure 7.5 (the "Disorders" numbers are from Table 11.2, those of "Social Problems" from Table 11.1).

If we add to this that every value deficiency may be brought about by several social problems and that each of them may lead to various disorders, we arrive at a rather complicated system of interactions. Furthermore, deficiencies also interact and may amplify or offset one another's impact. Stress, for instance, is in itself a value deficiency, but several other value deficiencies, too, may be among its sources (e.g., physical pain, insecurity, loss of identity, role conflict, lack of opportunity to attain one's goals, failure, feeling of inefficiency, etc.).

From here on, this chapter examines only one of the two dimensions of the above system of interactions in greater detail. It does *not* deal with the prob-

Figure 7.4. Interaction among factors affecting health (the proposed model).

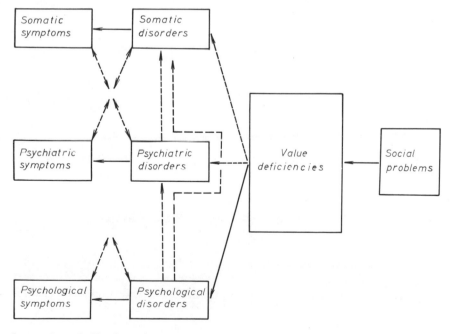

Source: Compiled by the authors.

Figure 7.5. Interaction between social problems and health disorders mediated by a value deficiency.

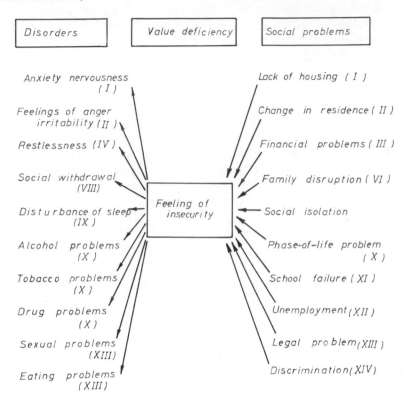

Source: Compiled by the authors.

lem of what kind of disorders are brought on by the various value deficiencies:

Disorders ⟵⟶ Value deficiency

It is the task of physicians, psychiatrists, and psychologists to explore these interconnections. The analysis of the other dimension—that is, to examine what kinds of value deficiencies are brought on by various social problems—

Value deficiency ⟵⟶ Social problems

is mainly a task for sociologists and sociopsychologists. The rest of this chapter is devoted to an analysis of this dimension and an attempt to show that the interrelationships between social problems and value deficiencies can be, and are, worth exploring.

THE ROLE OF SOCIAL PROBLEMS IN GENERATING VALUE DEFICIENCIES

How and to what extent do social problems have an effect on the progress of the generation of values and value deficiencies? Let us first look at standard of living as a social factor affecting health and life quality. The question is, to what extent does it depend on the level of a country's economic development, and especially on the living standard of the population as a whole, that the people be provided with the values necessary for a good life or, using the WHO terminology, for a state of complete health? As a first step, let us not discuss values separately, but assess their aggregated impact on people's well-being. Sociologists usually measure this overall perceived life quality with the help of various "happiness" and "satisfaction" scales. Hadley Cantril, for instance, conducted a survey in 13 countries during the early 1960s, comparing the level of economic development of the different countries with the average happiness or satisfaction level of people (5). Respondents had to rate themselves on a 9-point "self-anchoring" scale, and they were to decide where they stood between the two extremes of "best possible life" and "worst possible life."

Figure 7.6 shows that economic development (or standard of living) *is* a social problem, since a lower level of development generates a relative value deficiency, leading to a lower level of satisfaction. But the figure shows also that economic development explains only a part of the variation in satisfaction. Other factors—political, social, cultural, and psychological—have to be taken into consideration if one wants to have a fuller knowledge of the latent processes of the generation of values and value deficiencies. Figure 7.7 illustrates that the same social problem may have different impact on the generation of various values.

The relation beween social problems and values generated turns out to be even more intricate if it is analyzed in a time perspective—that is, if we examine how economic growth within a country affects changes in the perceived quality of life. This kind of longitudinal data is available only for the United States.

Figure 7.8 shows that while per capita income increased by 40% between 1951 and 1965, the number of people considering themselves "highly" or "fairly" happy shows a decrease of 30%. Although a whole line of hypothetical reasons could be listed here (e.g., the gradual worsening of the polit-

Figure 7.6. Relationship between (a) socioeconomic development and (b) national average levels of self-ratings on a happiness scale (1960).

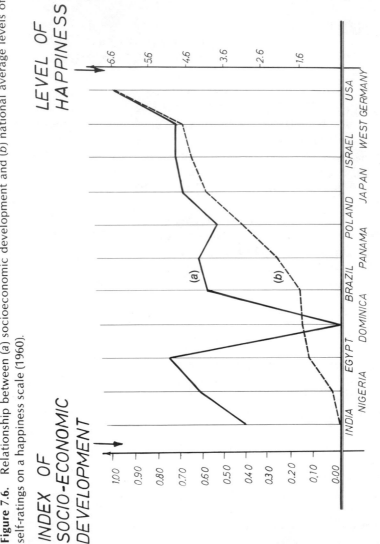

INDEX OF
SOCIO-ECONOMIC
DEVELOPMENT

LEVEL OF
HAPPINESS

COUNTRIES ⟶

Source: Adapted from Table XII/1 of reference 5.

Figure 7.7. Satisfaction with one's level of living (and some other factors) according to income brackets in Hungary, 1977–78.

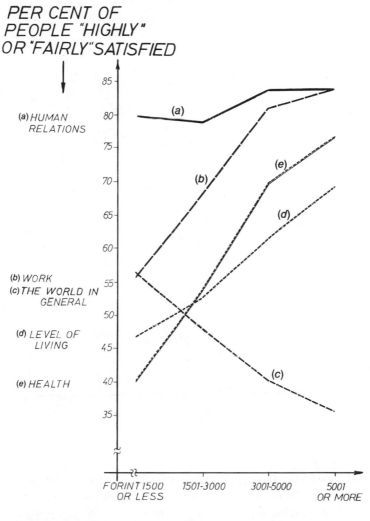

Figure 7.8.   Interrelationship between a rising level of living and changes in the average level of self-ratings of Americans on a happiness scale.

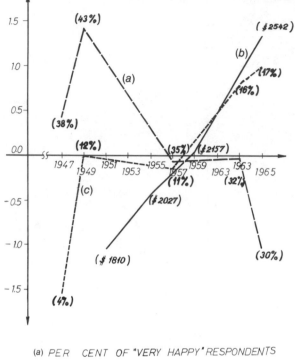

(a) *PER CENT OF "VERY HAPPY" RESPONDENTS*

(b) *PER CAPITA   PERSONAL   INCOME*

(c)*PER CENT OF "NOT HAPPY" RESPONDENTS*

Source: Adapted from Tables 3 and 7 of reference 7.

ical climate since the early 1950s—the Cold War, McCarthyism, increasing ethnic and social tensions, the Vietnam war, etc.), a factor of a different kind may also be mentioned here—namely, the so-called "aspiration explosion." During the years after World War II, a rise in people's expectations was triggered all over the world, and in some countries this rise sooner or later took an almost exponential course. Economic development could certainly not keep pace, and since satisfaction with one's standard of living depends to a significant extent upon the distance between one's aspirations and one's given living standard, the greater the distance, the lower the level of satisfaction. This interdependency can be illustrated in a simplified form, as Figure 7.9 demonstrates.

In the Hungarian survey, certain questions were posed in two different ways. In one, the framework of reference was not defined, thus letting subjects measure themselves primarily against their own levels of aspiration; respondents were simply asked how they were satisfied with various aspects of their lives. In other cases, the framework of reference within which respondents were asked to measure themselves was clearly defined, and thus the influence of aspirations was controlled—at least to a certain extent. These were the so-called "self-assessment" questions, in which the subjects were asked to rank themselves on a 9-point scale, where the top rank was always occupied by people in most favorable positions ("the richest," "the most useful," "the most educated," "those with the most power") and the lowest rank by people in the least favorable situations ("the poorest," "the least useful," "the least educated," etc.). Figure 7.10 shows the variation in satisfaction levels, and Figure 7.11 shows the variation in self-assessment levels by

Figure 7.9.   Supposed interrelationship between aspiration levels and satisfaction levels in the Hungarian study.

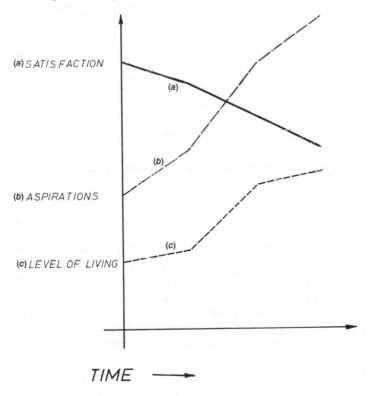

Source: HQOLS 1977–78, interim reports—see reference 6.

age. Here we are already analyzing the impact of another social problem—that of life cycle—on generation of values and value deficiencies.

The first thing that attracts attention in these two figures is the contrary motion of the satisfaction and self-assessment graphs. While the majority of satisfaction levels are rising, the vast majority of self-assessment levels are decreasing with age. As regards first the satisfaction levels, there are certain values where the increase in satisfaction parallels the objective increase in the amount of the value in question. Social status, for instance, increases during the first three or four decades of one's life, just as the accompanying satisfaction increases, as indicated by the respective graph; the standard of living follows approximately the same course, as indicated by its respective satisfaction graph. In other cases, objective circumstances do not account for the rise in the levels of satisfaction. In these cases, a decrease in the level of expectations may be responsible for the rising satisfaction levels.

The self-assessment graphs follow an opposite pattern. With advancing age, people rate themselves lower and lower in the various value hierarchies. The question arises whether they judge their situation more objectively here than when measuring themselves against their aspirations. This is not necessarily the case. The graph that stands for satisfaction with one's level of living, for instance, follows the objective pattern more closely than the relative self-assessment graph does. On the average, people in Hungary reach their highest income level in the 45–55 age bracket, and not at the beginning of their careers, as shown in Figure 7.11. In the same way, the graph of satisfaction with social status follows the objective situation better than the graph of self-assessment concerning power does. The contrary is the case with educational levels; here self-ratings are closer to the truth.

There are many more noteworthy details that indicate just how complex the relationship between objective circumstance (social problems) and values or value deficiencies (which may lead to psychological disorders) may be. It can be seen, for instance, that satisfaction with family life and satisfaction with one's personal relationships remains virtually unchanged throughout one's life. This may be further evidence supporting the hypothesis frequently formulated in sociology that these factors play a stabilizing role. The state of one's health, however, can have a destabilizing role in one's life, as is indicated by the steep decline with age of the satisfaction graph. This destabilization of human life due to deteriorating health is so fast and dramatic that it may play a part in prompting people to unconsciously increase their level of satisfaction through other factors in their lives, even despite objective facts. It is possible, then, that the odd phenomenon of satisfaction levels' rising with age, observed in Figure 7.10, carries a compensating function: Though unconscious, these arbitrary rises may counterbalance to a certain extent the negative impact that the growing lack of the value of health may have on people's psychological health status.

Figure 7.10. Satisfaction with various life domains and life values according to age in Hungary, 1977–78.

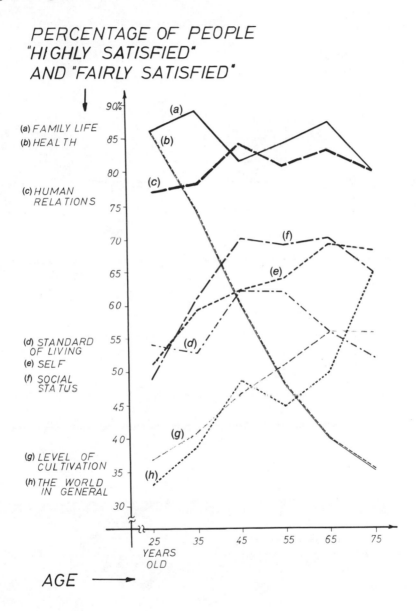

PERCENTAGE OF PEOPLE
"HIGHLY SATISFIED"
AND "FAIRLY SATISFIED"

(a) FAMILY LIFE
(b) HEALTH

(c) HUMAN RELATIONS

(d) STANDARD OF LIVING
(e) SELF
(f) SOCIAL STATUS

(g) LEVEL OF CULTIVATION
(h) THE WORLD IN GENERAL

AGE ⟶

25 YEARS OLD

Source: HQOLS 1977–78, cross-tabulations—see reference 6.

Figure 7.11. Self-ratings of Hungarians on various value scales in 1977–78.

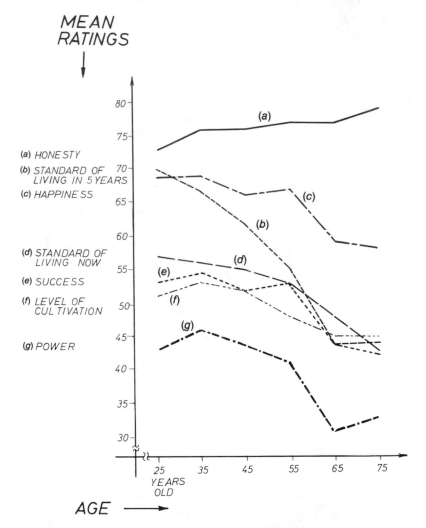

Source: HQOLS 1977–78, cross-tabulations—see reference 6.

Self-ratings concerning honesty may also have such a compensating function. As they grow older, people rate themselves lower and lower in every other dimension of social space; yet perceived honesty retains its high position throughout their lifetimes, or climbs even a bit higher. Self-ratings in honesty play such a compensating or counterbalancing role in connection with almost all the social problems analyzed (income, employment, education, sex, etc.).

The above discussion indicates that many factors must be taken into consideration when one wants to explore the relationship between social problems, values or value deficiencies, and psychological disorders. Instead of a mere listing of these three factors, only a careful analysis of these interrelationships can help us detect and understand the disease-generating role of social problems. General practitioners, of course, have wide experience in identifying these interrelationships; sociologists can learn a great deal from them. But, on the other hand, quality-of-life research, too, might have some lessons for primary health care experts. It may even be suggested that in the course of the field testing of the 1979 Bellagio proposals, the possibility of cooperation between primary health care *experts* and quality-of-life researchers should also be tested. Sociological surveys can locate social problems with a fair degree of accuracy, and—as this chapter has tried to show—they can also locate and measure value deficiencies. It would be important to see if these findings would complement the information gathered by general practitioners in the course of consultations with patients. And, though sociological indexes are computed only for and characterize only groups of people and not individuals, one could control on an experimental basis whether serious individual deviations from average community rates on various value scales could be considered as indications of the possible presence or imminence of a psychological disorder.

But if sociological indexes and averages cannot be used on the individual level, they could certainly be used on the community level as elements of an "early warning system" that would make broader preventive efforts possible.

PERCEIVED HEALTH AS A VALUE
VERSUS HEALTH AS A SOCIAL PROBLEM

Perceived health (physical well-being, absence of pain, vitality, sense of comfort) is one of the most important life values; it is a basic criterion of good life quality. People's objective health status, on the other hand, is among the most important social concerns; it generates and destroys a multitude of values in every society. Both of these aspects of health have been analyzed in the Hungarian survey. In what follows, first, a few examples show how social problems affect perceived health as a basic value; and a demonstration of the effect of health as a social problem on some important life values concludes the chapter.

In the survey, an attempt was made to estimate the level of perceived health with the help of satisfaction scales and lists of "symptoms" or "complaints of ill health." The latter listed common problems or symptoms concerning health and requested subjects to indicate how often they have such problems ("daily," "several times a week," "once a week," "several times a month," "once or so a month," "less frequently," "never"). Various indexes were constructed during the analysis of the data and compared with the most significant demographic and socioeconomic factors. In other words, the survey examined how the different social problems generated in various life domains affect the perceived health of the individuals—that is, how and to what extent they deprive them of this basic value. A few of the results are now given. The frequency of "complaints of ill health" shows changes according to age, as Figure 7.12 demonstrates.

It should be noted that before the next survey (1981), the present authors intend to consult WHO on the possibilities of expanding this list of symptoms and increasing its sociodiagnostical power on the basis of the experiences with the *International Classification of Health Problems in Primary Care,* second edition (*ICHPPC*-2); with "lay reporting"; and with the proposals of the 1979 Bellagio conference. However, these questions sufficed in their present form to explore the social distribution of health and to locate the social layers, groups, or communities that particularly suffer due to the absence of this value.

The frequency of certain health complaints in different groups is illustrated in Figure 7.13 (the occupational categories are given in accordance with the nomenclature of the Hungarian Central Statistical Office).

As we can see, the frequency of complaints concerning health (or, in other words, the perceived lack of values necessary for health) is distributed very unequally in society. The strata or groups in favorable or unfavorable positions from the aspect of health can be easily located by means of the distribution graphs. This is true not only in the absolute sense, but also in terms of their relative standing in the occupational hierarchy. The structure of inequalities is not identical with the occupational hierarchy (the graphs show strong deviations); the categories of "nonmanuals," "agricultural manuals," and —oddly enough—"managers" are in a relatively bad position compared to their supposed social rank. This relative position is a significant factor, since it can be the source of serious tensions, frustrations, role conflicts, and, indirectly, psychological disorders, if a given stratum is considerably worse off in terms of its values than might be expected from its social position and presumed social prestige.

To conclude, let us turn now to health as a social problem. Figures 7.14–7.17, based on three-dimensional cross-tabulations, show the variation of value levels in the function of two social problems.

Figure 7.12. Complaints of ill health according to age in Hungary, 1977–78.

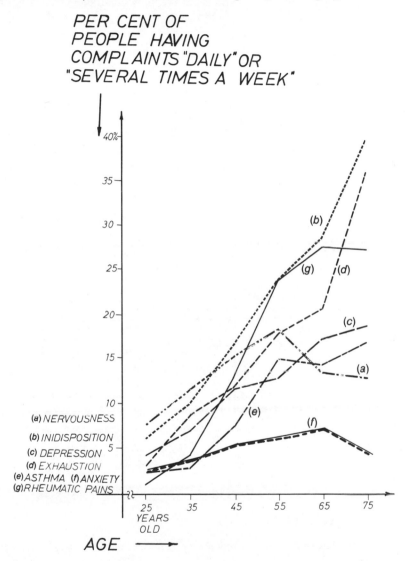

PER CENT OF
PEOPLE HAVING
COMPLAINTS "DAILY" OR
"SEVERAL TIMES A WEEK"

(a) NERVOUSNESS
(b) INIDISPOSITION
(c) DEPRESSION
(d) EXHAUSTION
(e) ASTHMA (f) ANXIETY
(g) RHEUMATIC PAINS

25 YEARS OLD   35   45   55   65   75

AGE ⟶

Source: HQOLS 1977–78, cross-tabulations—see reference 6.

Figure 7.13. Complaints of ill health according to occupation in Hungary, 1977–78.

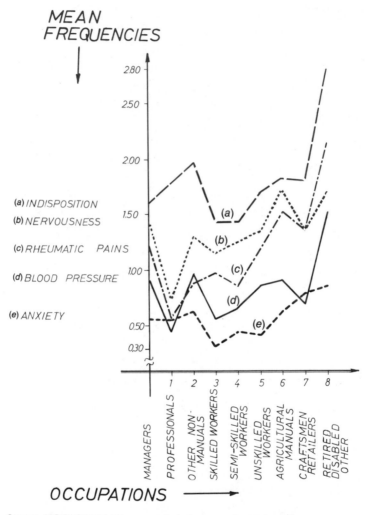

Source: HQOLS 1977–78, cross-tabulations — see reference 6.

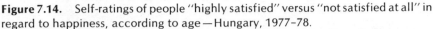

Figure 7.14. Self-ratings of people "highly satisfied" versus "not satisfied at all" in regard to happiness, according to age — Hungary, 1977–78.

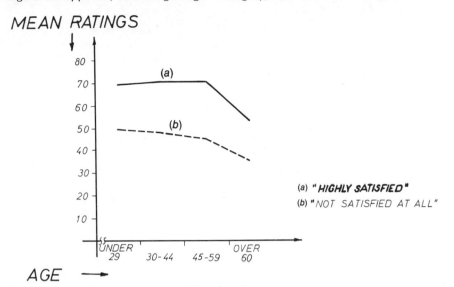

Source: HQOLS 1977–78, cross-tabulations — see reference 6.

Figure 7.15. Self-ratings of people "highly satisfied" versus "not satisfied at all" in regard to success, according to age — Hungary, 1977–78.

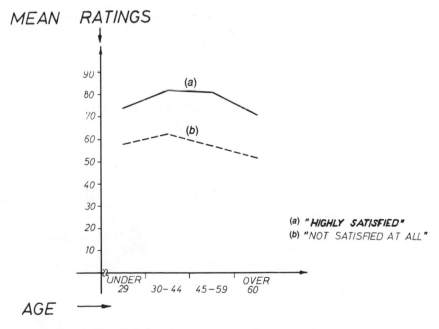

Source: HQOLS 1977–78, cross-tabulations — see reference 6.

Figure 7.16. Self-ratings of people "highly satisfied" versus "not satisfied at all" in regard to perceived power, according to age—Hungary, 1977–78.

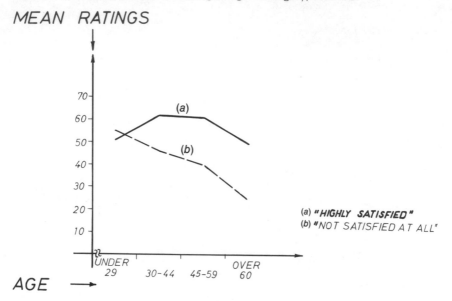

Source: HQOLS 1977–78, cross-tabulations—see reference 6.

Figure 7.17. Self-ratings of people "highly satisfied" versus "not satisfied at all" in regard to perceived importance or indispensability, according to age—Hungary, 1977–78.

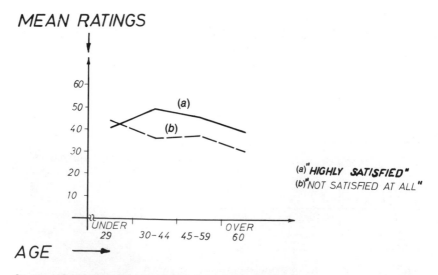

Source: HQOLS 1977–78, cross-tabulations—see reference 6.

As expected, the healthy possess considerably more basic values in each phase of life than do those who are ill. Yet there are values such as the sense of power or usefulness (Figure 7.17), where the value deficiency appears only above the age of 30. This means that here the ill ones are objectively not (or do not perceive that they are) in an unfavorable position. This seems to indicate that the impact of ill health changes with age. As far as perceived power is concerned, the negative impact of ill health increases between the ages of 30 and 60, while its impact on the sense of usefulness is strongest between ages 30 and 45 but is not significant in earlier years and declines after 45.

These and similar questions are analyzed by quality-of-life research, which tries to explore the interrelationships of social and psychological factors affecting health. It would be important to organize an exchange of ideas in this field between sociologists and health care experts.

REFERENCES

1. World Health Organization, "Workshop on Psychosocial Factors Affecting Health: Assessment, Classification, and Utilization" (Geneva: Author, 1979, mimeographed), p. 2.

2. Quoted by WHO, "Workshop on Psychosocial Factors," p. 1.

3. E. Hankiss, "Quality-of-Life Models," in *Indicators of Environmental Quality and Quality of Life,* Reports and Papers in Social Sciences no. 38 (Paris: UNESCO, 1978).

4. Hungarian Academy of Sciences, *QOL Newsletter: The Hungarian Quality-of-Life Research Project,* May 2, 1978, and January 30, 1980. After a series of preparatory and pilot studies since 1972, a national quality-of-life survey was conducted from late 1977 through early 1978. The sample of 1,500 respondents was representative of the Hungarian adult population. The final report is due by the end of 1980. Interim reports and papers analyzing the data (published mainly in Hungarian journals) are listed in the two newsletters cited above. The questionnaires; marginals; cross-tabulations; correlation matrices; and factor, cluster, and regression analysis outputs—issued in 15 copies—are available at the Center for Applied Social Analysis of the Hungarian Academy of Sciences (H-1014 Budapest, Uri utca 49) and in a few major public and specialized libraries in Budapest. These publications are subsequently referred to in this chapter in the following way: HQOLS 1977–78, type of publication (questionnaires, cross-tabulations, etc.).

5. H. Cantril, *The Pattern of Human Concerns* (New Brunswick, N.J.: Rutgers University Press, 1965).

6. Publications of the Hungarian Quality-of-Life Research Project, 1977–78. For further details, see reference 5.

7. N. Rescher, *Welfare: The Social Issues in Philosophical Perspective* (Pittsburgh: University of Pittsburgh Press, 1972).

III

The Classification
of Problems in General
Medical Care

8

Classification of Problems in General Medical Care: Problems and Questions

MACK LIPKIN, JR.

The first part of this volume presents arguments from psychological, epidemiological, and sociological perspectives that multifactorial or multideterminant models of health are required by the masses of data accumulated in this century. This is in contrast to the algebraic or unideterminant models prevalent in the nineteenth century but consistent with the earlier models found in Western history (1), as well as with the dominant models found cross-culturally outside the health systems dominated by Western paradigms (2).

The second part of the volume reviews, through several analytic frameworks, evidence that psychological and social concepts are especially critical in considerations of primary care. Some patients experience their psychological or social problems physically. Others prefer to seek care from nonstigmatizing or nondegrading sources in cultures where medical care is acceptable and mental health care is not or is less so. Most have no choice but to take what they get.

In Part III, Wood first elegantly describes how the varieties of presently available classifications manage psychological and social issues. He points out that the dominant classification scheme, the *International Classification of Diseases* (*ICD*), does not handle adequately 40% of the visits in a primary care office, clinic, or surgery. That a major proportion of primary care is not described, even in the most detailed classification, is significant, even though this is ameliorated somewhat by *ICD*'s Supplementary Classification as he describes.

Regier and his colleagues then add another layer of argument to the debate. They adduce epidemiological data reviewed from the most authoritative sources to suggest that a significant proportion (about 14%) of primary care visits stem from psychological and social reasons for care. They point out that resistance to the psychological and social factors in care is systemic and based in part on the natural need to focus narrowly in order to feel and remain competent in a medical world of explosive increases of knowledge and skill.

Both chapters reflect several main points. The need for a more effective place for classification of psychological and social issues is proven. The existing classifications do make efforts toward this, which are variably successful but have several defects. They are not uniform among themselves. This is not so much because they attempt to measure different phenomena or seek data for different purposes as because they have different histories. The lack of uniformity among classifications diminishes the ability of scholars, statisticians, and planners to compare and compile results.

The emphasis given psychosocial issues may be insufficient, given their relative importance. Their relative present neglect requires correction. For example, they are now in a supplemental portion of *ICD* not integrated directly into its main body.

For all these reasons, the multifactorial and multideterminant nature of health should be fully reflected in its classification through the use of a multifactorial classification scheme. Thus, it is recommended in Part IV of this volume that a three-dimensional or triaxial classification of health problems in primary care be considered for use.

The problems with attempts to devise such a classification are major. First, the usual problems of *reliability* and *validity* are magnified when a classification is used in different cultures and languages. The only way to assess this problem is through the most meticulous and patient field testing in cross-cultural settings—using translation and checking by back translation; using local personnel who can themselves assess validity and appropriateness; and using members of traditional local healing systems who can reveal potential sources of error and confusion (see Chapter 16).

A second concern is that of *medicalization* of social problems. While this concern is beyond the scope of this volume, a brief response to it is offered. In contrast to those like Illich and Szasz, who decry medicine's overexpansion, the present authors' data show that contemporary medicine is too narrow. It omits major factors of central importance for care. The triaxial classification promises to help rather than create a problem concerning the proper scope of care (for a fuller discussion of these issues, see reference 2).

Validity can also be diminished by a "from the top down" approach to generation of the classification. The working groups have therefore clearly indicated that extensive field testing must be done, utilizing methods that would allow full input from local patients and practitioners.

A more realistic concern, perhaps, is that physicians and others underreport these factors for several reasons. First, they are not aware of the mechanisms involved or of the factors themselves. This educational problem is addressed in the final chapter of this volume. Second, they are not in the habit of reporting these factors. While use of a triaxial classification might be hoped to change these habits, the trend could also go the other way. Inertia of nonrecording might doom even the most perfect triaxial classification to incompleteness. Only proven utility of the new classification will lead to its adoption. This would have to be proved on the basis of improved patient care locally. It would have to be accompanied by epidemiological and health services research showing how and why enhanced awareness and recording were beneficial.

One doubt about low effectiveness is the fear, in places where confidentiality is mistrusted, that the potential stigma of recording nonphysical distress will cause underreporting. This problem remains and is major. However, Chapters 17 and 19 show that the use of such data by barefoot psychiatrists in Colombia and the use of complex multifactorial recording in a primary care center in Brazil have led to improve care, greater team satisfaction, and cost-effectiveness.

Finally, the characteristics of a desirable classification must be borne in mind. Its use in primary care suggests that it must be parsimonious—recorded only once and in a form that lends itself to many forms of data collection and aggregation. It must serve all the major purposes of classification. These include self-care, clinical management, direction for investigation, and orientation for treatment. It must be useful for institutional management on the local and central levels. It must be compatible with cultural norms and needs and the local clinical ambience. It must contribute to improved care through two main means: improved relevance and effectiveness of care; and planning better suited to effective, rational, and appropriate resource management.

In practical terms, a usable classification should allow aggregation, tabulation, and interpretation. It should lend itself to experimentation, operational research, and the widening of experience. It cannot be so closed and solipsistic that the medical system cannot learn and expand while using it. It should allow linkage of records. It should allow translation into other important classifications and survey systems. It should permit identification of persons, families, households, and cohorts.

In sum, primary care classifications should be based not on outcomes but experiences—they should be "from the bottom up" systems: the *patients'* experiences should determine *content*. The health care personnel, however, have to be in charge of seeing to the reliability and validity of the use of the system. To that extent, the doctor is in charge of *form*. Finally, pluralism and cultural relativity are just as important as considerations of centralizing utility, since they will determine the validity and truth of the data collected.

The subsequent parts of this book propose a first step toward a classification meeting these criteria, several alternatives, and several applications and problems in their adaptation.

REFERENCES

1. J. M. Janzen, "Medicalization in Comparative Perspective," in *Use and Abuse of Medicine,* ed. M. de Vries, R. L. Berg, and M. Lipkin, Jr. (New York: Praeger, 1982).

2. M. de Vries, R. L. Berg, and M. Lipkin, Jr., eds., *Use and Abuse of Medicine* (New York: Praeger, 1982).

9

The Systematic Assessment
of Psychological and Social Factors
Affecting Health

MAURICE WOOD

A BRIEF HISTORY OF <u>ICD</u> AND <u>ICHPPC</u>

People have always attempted to categorize new ideas and phenomena. Since sentient human beings evolved, categorization has aided and abetted decision making and allowed increasing experience (information) to be used more effectively. It can be seen first in the primitive hunter who classified prey according to whether they were large or small, aggressive or timid, swift or slow. The process described here is like that applied in innumerable other situations. As human information needs evolved, it was inevitable that ultimately there would be a classification of diseases. The earliest physicians, including Hippocrates, ordered and classified the human morbidity they observed, but the first formal classifications of diseases were attempted by Sauvages (*Nosologica Methodica*) and by Linnaeus (*Genera Morborum*) in the mid-eighteenth century.

As data increased in amount, knowledge increased. This required frequent reorganization of the classifications of causes of death to allow increasing specificity. In turn, these changed, as gradually a need developed for classifications of morbidity as well as mortality. Classifications of causes of death became the responsibility of the World Health Organization (WHO) following the creation of the United Nations after World War II, beginning with *International Classification of Diseases,* sixth revision (*ICD*-6). Since then, *ICD* has undergone a series of decennial revisions.

During the early 1950s, Fry and others developed broad classifications evolved from studies of ambulatory care. This was followed in the United Kingdom by attempts to use the then *ICD*-7 to classify this morbidity, but studies from ambulatory care practices showed that 45% of the recorded demand from patients could not be classified by the disease labels, or rubrics, available in *ICD*-7 (1).

This led to the development of a series of compact classifications that allowed the categorization of the mix of signs, symptoms, and disorders identified as occurring in primary care settings. The first attempts at such primary-care-oriented classifications were based on *ICD*. They were produced by the Royal College of General Practitioners (RCGP) of Great Britain in 1959 (2) and the Royal Australian College of General Practitioners (RACGP) in 1965 (3). The Canadian Classification followed in 1969 (4).

By 1971, different general practitioner classifications existed in Great Britain, Newfoundland, Australia, Canada, and the United States. In the United States, a modification of the British Royal College of General Practitioners' classification of 1969 was developed for use with problem-oriented medical records. It added sections on psychological and social problems, on the family history of diseases, and on a selected therapeutic index (5). These five classifications differed from each other in details and in some major elements. This meant that international communication and comparisons of experience was made difficult or impossible.

To remedy the rabble of classifications, the World Organization of National Colleges, Academies, and Academic Associations of General Practitioners/Family Physicians (WONCA) met in Melbourne in October 1972. There, a standing committee on classification was identified and charged with the responsibility to produce an internationally acceptable classification of diseases, disorders, and problems for the discipline of family medicine and general practice and to relate this classification as closely as possible to the *ICD* then extant. Within two years, a trial version of a classification had been agreed upon and put to field tests in 300 sites in nine countries. In November 1974, at the WONCA meeting in Mexico City, the product of this field trial was used to develop a final version of the classification. Later in that month, the council of WONCA accepted the new *International Classification of Health Problems in Primary Care (ICHPPC)*.

Over the next few years, the *ICHPPC* came into widespread use through publication and distribution by the American Hospital Association (AHA), the RCGP, and the RACGP. At the time of development of *ICHPPC,* there had been little interaction between the WONCA Classification Committee and the *ICD* Committee of WHO. The WHO group was involved in developing *ICD*-9, and by 1975, when *ICHPPC* was published, *ICD*-9 was already firmly fixed in form.

In 1978, at the WONCA meeting in Montreux, Switzerland, discussions between the *ICD* unit of WHO and the members of the Classification Committee of WONCA and others, led to an agreement that the Classification Committee of WONCA would modify *ICHPPC*-1 to make it completely compatible with *ICD*-9. This would lead to the *ICD* committee's designating *ICHPPC*-2 as the authorized modification of *ICD*-9 for use in primary care settings. For WHO purposes, *ICHPPC*-2 would be known as *ICD*-9, General

Medicine (*ICD*-9-GM). *ICHPPC*-2 was published by Oxford University Press in 1979 and is now in the process of international distribution.

A RATIONALE FOR CHANGE

The earliest classification of diseases changed in response to the identification of new categories of disease, which provided more detailed causes of death. Little use was made of these classifications to categorize morbidity until after World War II, when the burgeoning growth of specialist and subspecialist care led to a need for greater detail of morbidity classification. The movement toward greater specificity made these classifications less effective for primary care needs. In fact, it was found that a major proportion of the demand in primary care could not be described in terms of the diseases, labels, or rubrics incorporated in even the most detailed classification (6).

As stated well in the eighth revision of the *International Identification of Diseases,* "A statistical classification of diseases or injuries will depend on the use made of the statistics to be compiled" (7). If the "use" is to describe "primary care demands," it is known that many elements of the demands, particularly those expressed as symptoms, signs, and complexes of these, will not be capable of categorization by a standard disease-based classification (8).

In effect, this means that the natural history of morbidity manifest in an unselected patient population of ambulatory patients is different from the natural history of morbidity expressed by a selected group of patients admitted to hospitals. Significantly absent from the morbidity of the hospitalized patient would be problems of behavior and coping response or conditions representing reactions to aberrant social situations.

Few of these "illnesses" are life-threatening, and so such "illnesses" were totally absent from the original classifications of causes of death. It was only when classifications came to be used to describe the content of real-world situations involving ambulatory patients that these psychological and social conditions or "problems of living" became identifiable. In addition, this movement required the acceptance of new concepts of illness or nonwellness, which included conditions precipitated or modified by factors within or external to the individual or the environment. As yet, this concept has not attained universal acceptance by specialist physicians. But few experienced primary care physicians would question it.

An examination of *ICD*-7, *ICD*-8, *ICD*-9, and their authorized modifications shows a steady increase in the use of the classifications to record medical morbidity in the form of diseases, disorders, conditions, injuries, and accidents. Classifications of psychiatric and psychological diseases and disorders have lagged behind the organic diseases in the specificity and detail of their categories. Perhaps this is because the research activity in the psychological domain has been less intense and more recent than it has been with respect to physical diseases. Not until *ICD*-9 do we begin to see "problems of living" or illnesses presumed to be caused by social factors being categorized. Then they appear in a "Supplementary Classification" as an addition. They seem, therefore, to be less important.

Such relegation seems to be inappropriate, considering the present "total health" and primary care orientation of WHO. Also, as documented in this volume, there is widespread recognition that much degenerative morbidity is due to social factors in both developing and developed countries. It would seem that any future edition of *ICD* should recognize and reflect the equivalence of physical, psychological, and social morbidity.

TERMS AND DEFINITIONS

Since many terms and definitions are used in the classification and categorization of diseases and problems, a short glossary is helpful. The following are terms and definitions used in this chapter:

central coding   the classification and coding of medical information by trained personnel located elsewhere than at the point of contact with the patient/ client

classification   the systematic arrangement of items in groups or categories according to preestablished criteria

demography   the statistical study of human populations with regard to size, density, and vital statistics

encounter   a face-to-face contact between a person who assumes a patient or client role and a provider of health services

encounter coding   the classification of these encounters in an orderly manner

rubric   a term under which conditions, descriptions, diseases, or disorders are classified

exclusion term   a term, condition, or description specifically listed as excluded from a rubric

inclusion term   a term, condition, or description specifically listed as included in a rubric

optional hierarchy   the capability to subdivide a rubric to allow the identification and coding of specific problems, disorders, or diseases included in that rubric; for the purposes of intercenter comparison, subsequent reversion to the parent rubric should be possible

peripheral coding   the coding and classification of a symptom, sign, diagnosis, disorder, or condition by the health care practitioner at the point of contact and interaction with the patient/client

recorder   a health care practitioner who is responsible for recording as well as providing health care services

residual   a term used to describe "other" rubrics that contain all the remaining conditions in a section or category classification that have not been specified previously

taxonomer   a scientific classifier; a person who classifies things in an orderly manner according to their presumed relationships

REVIEW OF THE CLASSIFICATIONS

In this chapter, the sections on "Psychiatric Disease," "Symptoms," and "Social Problems" of three existing classifications are reviewed and compared. These classifications are the following:

1. *ICD*-9 (and its agreed U.S. clinical modification, *ICD*-9-CM).
2. *ICD*-9-GM, otherwise known as *ICHPPC*-2.
3. NAMCS-*RVC*. This is the *Reason for Visit Classification* developed by Schneider and colleagues of the American Medical Records Association from data of the National Ambulatory Medical Care Survey (NAMCS) (9).

Each of these classifications is currently in use in clinical practice. These classifications are also compared with Chapter P, "Mental and Life Problems," from the draft classification of the *Reasons for Contact in Primary Care* (*RFC*), prepared in 1978 by a group of consultants for the *ICD* Committee of WHO. This classification is in development, as only two categories have been completed.

In a systematic assessment of the psychological and social factors affecting health, any classification of psychiatric disease and social problems must be seen as part of an overall classification of problems. It cannot exist alone. Primary health care, which includes first-contact care, requires multiple coding of problems in biological, psychological, and social terms. In developed countries, many primary care practitioners record and code the data themselves at the time of assessment or diagnostic decision. This can be called *peripheral coding,* as distinct from *central coding,* which is done by trained coders in the record room of an institution.

In practice, clinical decision making is based on a diagnostic formulation, so any classification, to be acceptable to the average physician will need to have an orientation toward diagnosis or definition of the problem. As a corollary to this, the physician of first contact has a responsibility to identify and confirm with the patient the reason for the patient's contact with the physician (10).

No classification can meet all user needs; this is inevitable, as it is impossible for taxonomers to know in advance all future uses of the data. However, the data should provide accurate information, which aids in decision making. The classic decision-making process is this:

$$\text{Data} \rightarrow \text{Information} \rightarrow \text{``Intelligence''} \rightarrow \text{Decisions}$$

Detailed data, in theory, should give more information, which leads to better decisions. But detailed classifications are difficult, time-consuming, and expensive to use and code. Because primary care deals with large numbers of contacts of short duration, and many visits are repeat visits for the same problem, any classification used in primary care must be as short and simple as possible. It must code the common problems with unique (specific) codes and the uncommon problems in residuals with low frequency. As only a small proportion of primary care patient visits lead to hospital admission or interaction with community-based resources, any classification used must be compatible with those in use in other fields of medicine and social work.

There is evidence that the majority of primary care physician-recorders, using both peripheral and central coding, do not record psychological and social problems as compulsively as they do biological problems. For example, at one primary care training site within the Virginia system of residencies, retrospective review of the problem lists of all cases of asthma showed only 6% with recorded psychological problems. A detailed, retrospective review of the progress notes showed that 40% of the charts contained note of some form of psychological stress (11,12). The recorder's explanation for this included concern about confidentiality and the sensitivity of the information. Another major problem is that many physicians are unwilling to identify such problems because subsequent management and intervention may be ineffective or unrewarding. In addition, the education of medical students is such that the graduate is thoroughly imbued with a biological orientation on leaving medical school. Primary care training and experience can modify this. But in developed countries such change is difficult, because status and reimbursement patterns are such that the largest rewards derive from the use of technology and procedures in hospital.

As a first step toward review and comparison of these four classifications, Tables 9.1–9.3 are presented. Table 9.1 compares the NAMCS-*RVC* "Psychiatric Disease" module, Chapter 5 of *ICD*-9-CM and of *ICHPPC*-2, and the "Diagnosis and Disease" component of Chapter P, "Mental and Life Problems," of the *RFC* classification, WHO. Table 9.2 compares Chapter

16, "Signs/Symptoms and Ill-Defined Conditions," of *ICD*-9-CM, "Symptoms Referable to Psychological and Mental Disorders" of NAMCS-*RVC*, the symptoms included in Chapter 5 of *ICHPPC*-2, and the "Symptom" component of Chapter P, "Mental and Life Problems," of the *RFC*. Table 9.3 compares the Supplementary Classification of *ICD*-9-CM and that of *ICHPPC*-2, the "Diagnosis and Screening," "Treatment," "Injury and Adverse Effects," and "Administration" modules of NAMCS-*RVC*, and the "Diagnosis and Disease" component of Chapter P, "Mental and Life Problems," of the *RFC*. Any element not available in all four classifications is designated with an asterisk (*).

Careful comparison of these lists shows that, despite the different focus of the four classifications, they all contain rubrics in which most of the mental and social problems of people can be classified. The specificity of the rubrics varies among the classifications. As would be expected, *ICD*-9, particularly in its clinical modification form, has the greatest degree of specificity. However, although *ICD*-9 has by far the largest and most detailed classification in the biological areas, this does not apply in the mental and life problem areas. Specific mental diseases are delineated in detail, but the rubrics representing life and social problems are little more specific than those available in *ICHPPC*-2, NAMCS-*RVC*, and *RFC*. In fact, when one compares all classifications available in this area from either medical or social environments, there is remarkably little difference in the "content" of the classifications, but there are considerable differences in the conceptual framework.

An ideal classification for use in primary care should incorporate certain essential elements. It should be specifically designed for use in primary care; be patient- and problem-oriented; and address the total range of physical, social, and psychological problems and "other" reasons for visiting a primary care physician. Further, it should be short enough to be used by peripheral (practice-based) recorders, to be in wide use, and to be capable of being directly linked with other classifications used in other parts of the health care system. Table 9.4 identifies the presence or absence of these essential elements in each of the four classifications being reviewed and highlights their limitations and capabilities.

SIGNIFICANT OR UNIQUE ASPECTS OF THE FOUR CLASSIFICATIONS UNDER REVIEW

ICD -9 and ICD -9-CM

ICD-9 and *ICD*-9-CM are only useful in circumstances where central coding is possible because of the large number of rubrics. Even then, the recorder must know the content of the whole classification, including the supplementary section. This is a difficult task for a recorder of first-contact care. In ad-

Table 9.1. Comparison of NAMCS-RVC "Psychiatric Disease" module, Chapter 5 of ICD-9-CM and ICHPPC-2, and "Diagnosis and Disease" component of Chapter P, "Mental and Life Problems," of RFC

NAMCS-RVC	ICD-9-CM	ICHPPC-2	RFC
Psychoses			
Organic psychoses	Organic psychotic condition	Organic psychoses	Organic psychoses
Organic brain syndrome	Senile and presenile	Schizophrenia	Schizophrenia (all types)
Senile dementia, alcoholic-psychotic	Alcoholic	The affective psychoses	The affective psychoses
	Drug	Other unspecified psychosis	Other unspecified psychosis
	Transient organic psychosis		
Functional psychoses	Other organic psychoses		
Schizophrenia paranoid	Schizophrenia affective psychosis		
Manic-depressive psychosis NOS[a]	Paranoid psychosis child*		
Neuroses	Anxiety state	Anxiety disorder state	Personality and character disorder
Depressive neurosis	Personality disorder	Hysterical and hypochondriac disorder	Mental retardation
Depressive reaction	Sexual deviations	Depressive disorder	Transient situational disturbances
		Neurotic depressive	
			Social
Anxiety reaction	Alcohol dependence syndrome	Other neuroses	Suicide attempt
Obsessive-compulsive neurosis NOS[a]	Drug dependence		Economic problem
			Housing problem

Personality and character disorder

Alcohol and drug dependence

Drug addiction

Other Mental and Psychological disorders

Mental retardation
Other mental diseases
Transient situational disturbances
Adolescent adjustment reaction
Grief reaction
Sexual deviation

Nondependent drug abuse

Physiologic malfunction from mental factors
Special symptoms NEC[b]

Adjustment reaction to stress
Adjustment reaction
Nonpsychotic mental disorder due to organic brain damage*
Depressive disorder NEC[b]
Disturbance of conduct NEC[b]
Disturbance of emotions
  —Child
  —Adolescent
Hyperkinetic syndrome
Specific reading disorder*
Psychological factor with diagnosis in E class*
Mental retardation

Specific learning disturbance and delay in development of skills for schooling
Insomnia
Tension headaches; etc.
Transient situational disturbances
Grief
Behavioral disorders
Psychogenic disturbance of sexual function
Chronic abuse of alcohol
Acute alcohol intoxication (drunk)
Abuse of tobacco
Other drug abuse, habit, or addiction
Personality and character disorders

Problem caring for sick person

Marital problems

Problems with being homosexual
Psychogenic disorder of sexual function
Parent-child problem
Problems with parents or in-laws
Family description
Other problems of family relationships

Specific learning disturbances
Educational problems
Pregnancy out of wedlock
Social maladjustment
Occupational problem
Phase-of-life psychosocial problems
Child-adolescent-change of life
Legal problems
Chronic abuse of alcohol
Acute alcohol intoxication
Abuse of tobacco
Other drug abuse
Other mental and psychological disorders

[a]Not otherwise specified.
[b]Not elsewhere classified.

Table 9.2. Comparison of NAMCS-RVC "Symptoms Referable to Psychologic and Mental Disorders," Chapter 16 of ICD-9-CM, Chapter 5 of ICHPPC-2, and "Symptom" component of Chapter P, "Mental and Life Problems," of RFC

NAMCS-RVC	ICD-9-CM	ICHPPC-2	RFC
Anxiety and nervousness	Signs and symptoms that point definitely to a given diagnosis are assigned to Chapter 5. The following cover ill-defined conditions.	For suicide or attempted suicide code, the nature of the self-inflicted injury or adverse effect as well as any underlying emotions or social problem	Anxiety and nervousness
Fear and phobias			Fears and phobias
Depression			Depression
Anger			Anger
Problems with identity and self-esteem			Restlessness
Restlessness			
	General symptoms	Suicide tendency	Behavioral Disturbances
Behavior Disturbances			
	Coma and stupor	Other neuroses, Chapter 5	Antisocial
Antisocial behavior	Syncope and collapse		Hostile
Hostile behavior	Convulsions		Temper problems
Hysterical behavior	Dizziness and giddiness	In other mental and psychological disorders, Chapter 5	Obsessions and compulsions
Temper problems	Sleep disturbances		Feeling hysterical
Obsessions/compulsions	Pyrexia of unknown origin	Other signs, symptoms, and ill-defined conditions, Chapter 16	
Disturbances of sleep	Malaise and fatigue		
Insomnia			Sleep Disturbances
	Hyperhidrosis		
Sleepiness	Other symptoms general		Insomnia
Nightmares			Sleepiness

128

Sleepwalking
Smoking problems
Alcohol-related problems

Abnormal drug usage
Delusions and hallucinations

Psychosexual Disorders

Frigidity, loss of sex drive
Homosexuality, concerns with
Impotence
Premature ejaculation
Masturbation, excessive concerns about
Orgasm, problem with
Other symptoms and problems relating to psychological and mental disorders NEC[a]
Nail biting

All Other Symptoms Presented by Body System

Nervous and musculoskeletal
Skin
Nutrition metabolic
Head and neck
Cardiovascular system
Respiratory system and chest
Urinary system
Abdominal and pelvis

Other and unspecified Psychoses, Chapter 5
Other mental and psychological disorders, Chapter 5

Nightmares
Sleepwalking

Delusions and Hallucinations

Other Symptoms and Problems Relating to Psychological or Mental Disorders NEC[a]

Neurasthenia
Anxiety causing somatic complaints involving
Musculoskeletal system
Respiratory system
Cardiovascular system
Digestive system
Male genital system
Female genital system
Urinary system
Skin
Other—general

[a]Not elsewhere classified.

Table 9.3. Comparison of Supplementary Classification of ICD-9-CM and ICHPPC-2, the "Diagnosis and Screening," "Treatment," "Injury and Adverse Effects" and "Administration" modules of NAMCS-RVC, and "Diagnosis and Disease," "Diagnostic Screening and Prevention Procedures," "Therapeutic," and "Administrative" components of Chapter P, "Mental and Life Problems," of RFC

NAMCS-RVC	ICD-9-CM	ICHPPC-2	RFC
General psychiatric and psychological examination	Personal diagnosis of mental disorders	Medical examination	Administration of intelligence test
Psychiatric examination required by court or school	Other personal diagnosis	Problems external to the patient (Anxiety in third party)	Administration of psychological test
Psychotherapy	Psychology trauma*	Economic problems—poverty	Other psychological evaluation and testing with general psychiatric or psychological examination
Counseling	Mental and behavioral problems	Housing problems	
		Problem caring for sick	
Social Problem Counseling	Housing, Household, and Economic Circumstances	Marital problems	Interviews and consultations focused on mental disorders and life problems
Economic, educational	Lack of housing	Parent/child problems	
Marital, parent/child	Inadequate housing	Problems with parents or in-laws	Therapeutic Component
Other problems of family relationships	Inadequate material resources	Family disruption	Psychopharmacological
Occupational, legal	Person living alone	Other family problem relationships NEC[b]	Other medication
Social adjustment, other social problems	No one to render care	Educational problems	Individual psychotherapy
Suicide attempt	Holiday relief care*	Illegitimacy	Psychoanalysis
Adverse effect of drug abuse	Person in residential institution*	Social maladjustment	Hypnotherapy
Adverse effect of alcohol abuse	Other housing or economic circumstances	Occupational problems	Behavior therapy
Psychotherapy		Phase-of-life problems NEC[b]	Individual therapy for psychosexual dysfunction
Chemotherapy	Other Family Circumstances	Legal problems	Crisis intervention
Counseling NOS[a]	Family disruption	Other social problems	Play psychotherapy
Uncodable entries	Marital problems	All other problems NEC[b]	
	Parent and child problems		
	Problem with aged parent/in-law		

Health problems in family
Other Psychosocial Circum-
stances
Unemployment
Adverse effect of work
Other occupational circum-
stances
Education circumstances
Social maladjustment
Legal circumstances
Refusal of treatment—religion*;
conscience
Other psychosocial or physical
stress NEC[b]
Unavailability of other medical
facilities*
"Worried well"*
General psychiatric examina-
tion requested by authority
General psychiatric examina-
nation other—unspecified
Observation for suspected
mental condition*
Special screening for mental
disorders and developed
handicaps*

Exploration verbal psycho-
therapy
Supportive verbal psycho-
therapy
Biofeedback
Other psychotherapy and
counseling
Group therapy for psychosocial
dysfunction
Family therapy
Psychodrama
Other group therapy
Drug addiction counseling
Alcoholism counseling
Other counseling
Other therapy

Administration Component

Other reason for contact required by party other than
patient or provider including
psychological exam required
by court
Uncodable entries

[a]Not otherwise specified.
[b]Not elsewhere classified.

Table 9.4. Essential Elements, Limitations, and Capabilities of Four Classifications

NAMCS-RVC—Short	ICD-9-CM—Long	ICHPPC-2—Short	RFC—Short
	ESSENTIAL COMPONENT		
Designed for primary care	Designed for hospital care	Designed for primary care	Designed for primary care
Patient-oriented	Provider-oriented	Provider-oriented	Focused on patient-provider interaction
Problem-oriented	Diagnosis-oriented	Problem-oriented	Problem-oriented
Total range of problems and reasons	Limited range of problems and reasons	Total range of problems	Total range of problems and reasons
Limited comparisons with ICD-9	Good comparison with ICD-9	Limited reasons	Not in use
Limited use	Wide use	Good comparison with ICD-9 and ICD-9-CM	Allows peripheral coding
Allows peripheral coding	Requires central coding	Allows peripheral coding	Allows good comparison with ICD-9 and ICD-9-CM

132

LIMITATIONS

Two recorders needed	Hospital-based only	No reason for visit	No severity
Not linked to hospital data	No reason for visit	No severity	No duration
Poor audit capabilities (cf. Goldberg)[1]	No preventive orientation	No duration	
No severity	No severity	No therapy codes	
No duration	No duration		
	No therapy or screening codes		

CAPABILITIES

Reason for visit	Good audit access	Links ambulatory and hospital data	Links ambulatory and hospital data
Preventive orientation		Preventive orientation	Confirms reasons for contact
Includes therapy and screening and administration code		Good audit access	Preventive screening and treatment orientation
			Good chart audit capability

133

[1]G. A. Goldberg, "Implementing University Hospital Ambulatory Care Evaluation," *Journal of Medical Education* 50(1975):435–42.

dition, *ICD*-9 must be used with some form of encounter coding to describe the patient seen and the types of contact. *ICD*-9 is the base classification for reimbursement purposes in most developed countries.

ICD-9-CM, Chapter 5

This represents a detailed classification of psychiatric morbidity.

Classification of Psychological Services

ICD-9-CM has rubrics for *general psychiatric examination requested by an authority* and *general psychiatric examination [requested by] other—specified*. In addition, it has a very detailed list of mental and behavioral problems in personal, family, housing, household, and economic circumstances.

ICHPPC -2

ICHPPC-2 also has to be used in conjunction with some form of encounter coding that identifies the age and sex of the patients and the type of contact. However, it has only 371 rubrics, and approximately 50% of the total content of primary care is contained in 18 rubrics. Although the other 50% is distributed over the remaining 353 rubrics, it is possible to print the classification on one sheet and have it immediately available to the recorder at the place and time of the patient contact. The common codes are easy to learn, and the time necessary to find the right rubric is minimal. There is evidence that in both teaching and nonteaching environments, physicians are willing to use the classification and record data themselves (rather than have a clerk do so) (13, 14,15,16).

The concept of optional hierarchial expansion (17; see also Glossary, p. 122) is available and can be used on a local basis to expand any aspect of the classification to meet local needs and interests. Comparability with other recorders can still be achieved by collapsing the optional hierarchy to the original *ICHPPC*-2 rubrics before comparing the data. Its direct relationship with *ICD*-9 allows this classification to be used for reimbursement purposes. *ICHPPC*-2 is almost completely compatible with *ICD*-9, as only 7% of its rubrics are split from *ICD*-9 rubrics.

ICHPPC-2's Chapter 5, called "Mental Disorders," is divided into three major sections: namely, (1) "Psychoses," (2) "Neuroses," and (3) "Other Mental and Psychological Disorders." The 21 three- and four-digit categories in this chapter are the same as in *ICHPPC*-1. This represents at least 90 three- or four-digit categories in *ICD*-9.

The *ICHPPC*-2 Supplementary Classification—"Social, Marital, and

Family Problems and Maladjustments"—contains a preamble that defines the mode and use of this section: (1) Use of this section requires that the problem be explicitly discussed with, and accepted by, the patient as being of significance. (2) More than one code may be used. (3) The codes may be used alone or as additional codes to show the interdependence between organic and mental disease and the social milieu. (4) A contact with an emissary for the patient (i.e., problems external to the patient) is coded by an extra rubric in the "Miscellaneous" section of the Supplementary Classification. (This section of the Supplementary Classification is divided into 15 separate four-figure rubrics and one residual. They cover 55 three- and four-figure rubrics in *ICD*-9-CM.)

ICHPPC-2 includes the "psychiatric" medical examination in *general medical examination*, but as mentioned previously, it does allow the recording of problems external to the patient (i.e., anxiety in a third party). Like *ICD*-9, it does not allow the designation of *suicide* as such, but only of *suicide tendency*. It is stated in the "Symptoms" section that for *suicide* or *attempted suicide* it is necessary to code the nature of the self-inflicted injury or adverse effects, as well as any underlying emotional or social problem. In the instructions to recorders, it is pointed out that multiple coding is encouraged.

NAMCS-RVC

"Disease" Module—"Mental Disorders"

This section is coded in seven three-digit categories. All of the seven categories, except two, contain inclusions. The categories are as follows:

Organic psychoses	*Alcoholism and drug dependence*
Functional psychoses	*Mental retardation*
Neuroses	*Other mental disease*
Personality and character disorders	

This module covers much the same field as *ICHPPC*-2, but includes as separate rubrics *adolescent adjustment reaction, grief reaction,* and *sexual deviation,* which *ICHPPC*-2 does not.

"Symptom" Module

This module contains a section on "Symptoms Referable to Psychological and Mental Disorders" and consists of 14 three-digit categories. Some of these categories are broken down into four-digit elements, and all contain inclusions in the original rubrics.

"Diagnosis, Screening, and Treatment" Module, "Injury and Adverse Effects" Module, "Administration" Module

These modules contain the classification for psychosocial services in the NAMCS-*RVC*. The social problems are identified under "Social Problem Counseling" in the "Diagnosis, Screening, and Treatment" module. The *RVC* expands to include *general psychiatric and psychological examination* and *psychological testing*. It also allows a unique code for *psychiatric examination required by a court or a school*. It identifies *psychotherapy* and *counseling* and provides a large list of inclusions in the psychosocial section, which are listed under "Social Problem Counseling." This list allows the definition of *suicide attempt*. The following is a list of social problems.

Educational	*Other social problems*
Economic	*Adverse effect of drug abuse*
Marital	*Adverse effect of alcohol abuse*
Parent and child	*Psychotherapy*
Other problems of family rela-	*Chemotherapy*
tionships	*Counseling, not otherwise specified*
Occupational	*(NOS)*
Legal	*Uncodable entries*
Social adjustment	

RFC, Chapter P, "Mental and Life Problems"

"Diagnosis and Disease" Component

This component is the equivalent of Chapter 5 of *ICD*-9 and *ICHPPC*-2 plus the Supplementary Classifications of *ICHPPC*-2 and *ICD*-9. The incorporation of mental diseases and psychological and social problems together is unique in classification, and one effect may be that it can direct physicians' attention equally to mental and social problems and perhaps give them some degree of equivalency. The device is logical and appropriate, because the rubrics are mutually exclusive and multiple coding is recommended in the instructions.

This component includes 36 separate rubrics, 16 of which relate to *ICD*-9 and *ICHPPC*-2, Chapter 5, and are very similar to the *ICHPPC*-2 breakdown. The other 20 rubrics relate to the Supplementary Classification of *ICHPPC*-2 and are very similar. One or two specific elements, including *suicide attempt,* have been broken out.

"Symptom" Component

This component contains 33 rubrics and is similar to the NAMCS-*RVC* module. A major difference is that *anxiety causing symptomatic complaints* is listed by the body system structure of the chapters of the *RFC*. The detail available in this component allows the patient and the physician a wide range of latitude in determining the "reason for contact."

"Diagnostic, Screening, and Preventive Procedures"
Component, "Therapeutic" and "Administrative" Components

These components contain a considerable amount of detail and reflect to some degree the content of the NAMCS-*RVC* modules of the same name. They allow the capability to record the full range of examinations and tests specific to mental and social problems, and the "Therapeutic" section provides a comprehensive list of therapeutic interventions.

The "Administration" component includes *other reasons for contact required by a party other than a patient or a provider,* which include *a psychiatric or psychological examination required by court or school;* it also includes a rubric for *uncodable entries.*

CONCLUSION

It is hoped that a review such as this will help the reader to recognize more clearly the shortcomings of current classifications of disease in categorizing the total spectrum of biological, psychological, and social problems that beset humanity. Only by developing more appropriate classifications will more accurate descriptions of demand and need for health care services be possible in all societies.

Further, it is hoped that, should new classifications of mental/psychological and social problems be developed as a result of this volume, that they will undergo taxonomic evaluation by criteria similar to those used by Schneider and Appleton in the *Evaluation of the NAMCS Symptom Classification: Final Report* (18).

REFERENCES

1. The Royal College of General Practitioners, "Morbidity: Continuing Observation and Recording of Research Committee," *Journal of the Royal College of General Practitioners* 1(1958):107–28.

2. The Royal College of General Practitioners, Research Committee, "Classification of Disease," *Journal of the Royal College of General Practitioners* 2(1959): 140–59.

3. Royal Australian College of General Practitioners, *Australian Morbidity Study* (1965).

4. R. C. Westbury and M. Tarrant, "The Classification of Disease in General Practice," *Canadian Medical Association Journal* 101(1969):82.

5. Medical College of Virginia/Virginia Commonwealth University, Department of Family Practice, *Coded Classification of Disease* (Richmond: Author, 1972).

6. The Royal College of General Practitioners, Research Committee, "Classification of Disease"; The Royal College of General Practitioners, Research Committee, "Classification of Disease: Amended Version," *Journal of the Royal College of General Practitioners* 6(1963):207-16.

7. U.S. Department of Health, Education and Welfare, *International Identification of Diseases, Adapted for Use in the United States,* 8th revision, vol. 1, Public Health Service Publication no. 1693 (Washington, D.C.: Government Printing Office, 1968), p. xiii.

8. The Royal College of General Practitioners, Records and Statistical Unit, "The Analysis of Routine Medical Records," *Journal of the Royal College of General Practitioners* 11(1966):34-40.

9. D. Schneider, L. Appleton, and T. McLemore, *A Reason for Visit Classification for Ambulatory Care,* Vital and Health Statistics Series 2, no. 78, DHEW Publication no. (PHS) 79-1352 (Hyattsville, Md.: National Center for Health Statistics, 1979).

10. *International Classification of Diseases* Committee of the World Health Organization, *Classification of the Reasons for Contact in Primary Care,* draft (Geneva: Author, 1978).

11. The Virginia Family Practice Data System, Medical College of Virginia/Virginia Commonwealth University, unpublished data.

12. R. O. Haight, D. W. Marsland, and G. S. Mitchell, "Clinical and Educational Implications of a Longitudinal Audit for Asthma," *Journal of Family Practice* (1976): 481-85.

13. M. Wood, F. Mayo, and D. W. Marsland, "A Systems Approach to Patient Care, Curriculum, and Research in Family Practice," *Journal of Medical Education* 50(1975):1106-12.

14. D. W. Marsland, M. Wood, and F. Mayo, "The Content of Family Practice," *Journal of Family Practice* (1976):23.

15. R. O. Haight, C. A. McKee, and J. R. Barkmeier, "Morbidity in the First Year of a Family Practice and Its Comparison to the Virginia Study," *Journal of Family Practice* (1979):295-99.

16. D. W. Lawrence, "Sources of Patients in First Two Years of Solo Urban Family Practice," *Journal of Family Practice* (1977):867-70.

17. J. Anderson and R. Lees, "Optional Hierarchy Expansion of *ICHPPC,*" *Journal of Family Practice* (1978):1271-75.

18. D. Schneider and L. Appleton, *Evaluation of NAMCS Symptom Classification: Final Report* (Chicago: American Medical Records Association, 1976).

10

The Need for a Psychosocial Classification System in Primary Care Practice

DARREL A. REGIER
LARRY G. KESSLER
BARBARA J. BURNS
IRVING D. GOLDBERG

In this era of increasing sophistication in medical science, the national and international attention accorded primary health care is particularly striking. Legislation supporting an increase in the relative proportion of primary care physicians compared with specialists has been passed in the United States (Public Law 94-484, 12 October 1976), and the World Health Organization (WHO) (1976, 1978) has given a major priority to primary health care services.

The reasons for the increasing interest in primary care are multiple, including concerns about overemphasis on narrowly focused specialty treatments, maldistribution of specialty health personnel, and concerns about fragmentation of health care (Pardes and Daniels 1977; Regier 1977). Although the WHO definition of *health* (Andrews, Schonell, and Tennant 1977) as a state of complete physical, mental, and social well-being is often seen as somewhat idealistic, there is general concern that providers of primary care should attend to the many and varied needs of their patients. Health care providers cannot solve all of the physical, mental, and social problems of their patients; but they are clearly being asked to reassess the general medical, mental health, and social support roles they do perform.

One cannot lightly dismiss the barriers that limit the additional attention physicians can give to their mental health and social support roles. The explosion in biomedical knowledge and the need to specialize in order to obtain a high level of competence in any area of medicine will not change. In the effort to cover basic biomedical knowledge adequately in medical education, rela-

Reprinted from *International Journal of Mental Health* 8(1979):16–29, with the permission of the publisher, M. E. Sharpe, Armonk, New York 10504.

tively little curriculum or training time is devoted to mental health and social support roles as they are practiced in primary care settings. Inadequate training produces a lower level of competence and confidence in the provision of effective treatments for mental health and social problems. It is thus natural for primary care physicians to gravitate toward problem definitions and treatments with which they are familiar. Finally, there is a lack of financial incentives to provide such social support and mental health services when the health insurance system preferentially rewards treatment of physical health problems.

This discussion focuses principally on the role of a classification system for medical and psychosocial conditions. It is the present authors' contention that the existing major classification system poses significant barriers to effective primary care practice because it does not provide a means of describing what primary care practitioners do. The direct result is that their mental health and social support roles are not recognized in statistical data. Since primary care practice requires both a health services research base and a psychosocial and biomedical research base to enable practitioners to fulfill their multiple public health roles, accurate description and classification of their activities are essential.

Accurate description and classification are also the first step in taking effective clinical action, since failure to make a good differential diagnosis results in nonspecific and possibly inappropriate care. Hence, a classification is necessary to facilitate both clinical management and health services research activities and to make statistical analyses of morbidity and mortality rates in the populations served.

The major existing classification system is the *International Classification of Diseases,* which is now in its ninth revision (*ICD*-9) (World Health Organization 1977). This system does not have a clinical or health services research focus, and is structured so as to classify diseases primarily according to etiology rather than by phenomenological descriptive manifestations. This is in keeping with the historical concerns of medical statistical classification systems, starting from the time of William Farr (Israel 1978). These systems have been structured to group diseases by anatomical site to facilitate the vital-statistics function of recording causes of death. Hence, the strength of the current *ICD* system is that it promotes an etiologically oriented approach to clinical diagnosis and the pathological description of causes of death and morbidity. However, it fails to provide clinicians with a useful tool for describing physical, mental, or social symptoms and conditions for which a unitary, etiologically based diagnosis is either inappropriate or impossible.

The inadequacies of *ICD* have been recognized, and major modifications have been made to facilitate more clinical and descriptive approaches. Examples of these modifications include the *International Classification of Health Problems for Primary Care* (*ICHPPC*) (American Hospital Association 1976), developed by the Classification Committee of the World Organization of National Colleges, Academies, and Academic Associations of General Practitioners/Family Physicians (WONCA), and the U.S. clinical modification of *ICD*-9, entitled *ICD*-9-CM (U.S. Commission on Hospital and Professional Activities 1978). In addition, the American Psychiatric Association (1978) is making final revisions of the third edition of its *Diagnostic and Statistical Manual of Mental Disorders* (*DSM*-III), which attempts to emphasize a phenomenological, descriptive approach to diagnosis that avoids etiological presumptions about certain diagnostic categories, such as neurosis (e.g., that anxiety states now termed "neurotic" are *necessarily* caused by intrapsychic conflicts). *DSM*-III also takes a multiaxial approach to diagnosis that includes clinical syndromes, personality disorders, physical disorders, psychosocial stressors, and functional status assessments.

CLASSIFICATION REVISIONS FOR PRIMARY CARE PHYSICIANS

As noted above, the major revision of *ICD* for primary care practice has been that made by WONCA. The resulting *ICHPPC* represents a merger of many previous similar classifications developed in Australia, Britain, Canada, the United States, and other countries.

In the psychosocial area, the principal effect of the *ICHPPC* revision of *ICD* has been to decrease the number of major Section 5 three-digit categories from 26 to 15 and to decrease the total number of listed three- and four-digit codes from 184 to 21. The supplementary classification of relevant psychosocial terms has been enlarged to include 16 items in a section of social, marital, and family problems and maladjustments. Hence, the total psychosocial section includes only 37 separate identifiable items, instead of the approximately 200 such items included in *ICD*.

The reduction in categories of mental disorder and the increase in categories covering social, marital, and family problems were thought to be more reflective of the level of specificity required for primary care practice. In this regard, the major criterion of the usefulness of classifications in such settings is whether or not identification makes a difference in the treatment provided.

An even more fundamental change in the framework for classification of general practice is provided by the recently developed U.S. National Ambulatory Medical Care Survey's *Reason for Visit Classification* (*RVC*) (U.S. National Center for Health Statistics 1979). *RVC* is intended to serve a separate function from the *ICD* diagnoses and to exist as a parallel classification system for recording the patient's "diagnosis" as opposed to the physician's diagnosis of the reason for a visit. Major objectives of this classification are to identify why patients use the health care system and to assist in determining the relative roles of self-care, family care, and professional care (both primary and specialty) in meeting patient needs. It is intended to be used as an aid to physicians in classifying reasons why patients are coming to them for care under one of the following seven basic categories: (1) symptoms; (2) clearly defined diseases; (3) diagnostic, screening, and preventive reasons; (4) specific treatments; (5) injuries and adverse effects; (6) obtaining of test results; and (7) administrative reasons.

The emphasis on the patient's reason for visit is consistent with other research in the mental health area by Lazar and coworkers (Eisenthal, Emery, Lazar, and Udin 1979; Lazar, Eisenthal, and Wasserman 1975), which focuses on the processes of negotiation between patient and health professional to define the health problem, of arriving at an acceptable treatment plan, and of enhancing compliance or cooperation in following through with the agreed-upon treatments.

If used properly, *RVC* should enable physicians to characterize the extent to which they are expected to function in a general medical, a mental health, a social support, or an administrative role. Insistence on physicians' recording the patients' reason for contact is an attempt to force them to perform a review of reasons for contact before embarking on a more typical medical review of systems. The physician is still expected to make a diagnosis, however; and it remains to be seen whether physicians will really extend themselves to differentiate between their concept of patients' reasons for visits and their diagnosis of the patients' actual disorders.

Hence, two separate classification systems have now been provided: one, a classification of the patient's reason for visit (which can include a specific diagnosis if the patient says the diagnosis is the reason for contact), and the other, a health-provider diagnostic system, such as *ICHPPC* or *ICD*. Nevertheless, a new classification for the physician's *response* to a reason for visit is not yet available. In the final analysis, an adequate description of primary care practice will require descriptions both of what the physician actually thinks and does during the visit and of what he or she thinks the patient wants him or her to do during such a medical encounter.

In view of all of the concern for classification in primary care settings, it is necessary to ask for evidence of the scope of existing problems within the current system. One way of examining this issue is to compare the relative rates of psychosocial problems identified by three different methods: (1) routine medical records, (2) special surveys of general practitioners, and (3) direct psychosocial interviews of general-practice patients. If there are marked discrepancies in these rates, they can be attributed to problems of recording, problems in interpretation of the available categories, or problems in identification of persons with such psychosocial conditions. The actual classification system may contribute to any of these problems by being irrelevant, overly complex, or insufficiently balanced to give enough visibility to these areas of concern.

That there are major discrepancies in rates obtained for psychosocial conditions is clearly evident from the following data. The National Ambulatory Medical Care Survey (NAMCS) of U.S. office-based physicians has consistently found fewer than 4% of visits to primary care physicians to be associated with a principal diagnosis of mental disorder. Since surveys that concentrate on visits with a routinely recorded diagnosis of mental disorder tend to underrepresent the proportion of patients with such diagnoses in one year by a factor of about two, the maximum annual number of patients with such recorded mental disorder diagnoses would be estimated at less than 8% (Regier, Rosenfeld, Burns, and Goldberg 1979).

The data from the 1975 NAMCS for primary care physicians, including general and family practitioners, internists, and pediatricians, are presented in Table 10.1 (U.S. National Center for Health Statistics, 1978). Relatively low rates (1–4%) of recorded mental disorder diagnoses are observed when only the principal diagnoses are analyzed. For all patients seen in primary care, the proportion of visits with a diagnosis of mental disorder increases from 2.9% to 4.9% when any one of three diagnoses is examined for a recorded mental disorder. (These estimates are somewhat higher when patients under the age of 15 are excluded from the table.)

Table 10.2 shows more recent unpublished National Center for Health Statistics data from the 1977 NAMCS. The total proportion of visits associated with a principal diagnosis of mental disorder declined slightly from the 2.9% 1975 data to 2.6% overall. An additional proportion of the visits is associated with a primary diagnosis in the Section 16, "Symptoms and Ill-Defined Conditions," subcategory of nervous symptomatology, making a total of 3.2%.

Table 10.1.   Percentage of All Visits to Office-Based Physicians with Principal or Any Diagnosis of Mental Disorder, by Primary Care Physician Specialty

	Percentage of All Visits with Diagnoses of Mental Disorder			
	All Patients		Patients Aged 15 and Over	
Primary Care Specialty	Principal Diagnosis	Any Diagnosis	Principal Diagnosis	Any Diagnosis
Total Primary Care	2.9	4.9	3.4	5.9
GP/family practice	3.0	5.0	3.4	5.7
Internal medicine	3.6	6.6	3.7	6.7
Pediatrics	1.0	1.7	4.0	4.8

Source: National Center for Health Statistics, unpublished data from 1975 National Ambulatory Medical Care Survey (NAMCS).

It is interesting to compare NAMCS *ICD* mental disorder rates with *R VC* psychosocial data collected for the first time in 1977 (Table 10.3). The greater number of potential categories for recording psychosocial problems would lead one to expect a higher recorded rate. However, Table 10.3 shows that lower rates of *R VC* psychosocial problems are recorded than are *ICD* Section 5 rates. Of all visits to primary care physicians, 1.8% are classified as resulting primarily from symptoms of a psychological nature ("Symptom" module). Presenting primary diagnoses of mental disorder (in the "Diagnosis" module) and psychotherapeutic and social problem counseling visits (in the "Treatment" module) account for only another 0.2% of all primary care visits. Hence, the total percent of visits associated with any *R VC*-identified psychosocial problem is only about 2%, compared with the 3% for *ICD* mental disorders.

These data may be compared with those generated by National Institute of Mental Health (NIMH) studies of patients (rather than visits) in several other settings. In studies of private physicians' offices, hospital-based general medical clinics, and offices of family physicians, only slightly higher rates of presenting psychosocial problems can be found (Locke, Finucane, and Hassler 1967; Locke and Gardner 1969; Rosen, Locke, Goldberg, and Babigian 1972). Table 10.4 shows that chief or presenting complaints of emotional symptoms and requests for advice or counseling were identified in about 4–7% of patients. Although these estimates may be increased somewhat by adding

Table 10.2. Percentage of All Visits with Principal Diagnoses of Mental Disorder and Related Symptoms, by Primary Care Physician Specialty

	Primary Care Specialty			
ICDA Category	GP/Family Practice	Internal Medicine	Pediatrics	Total
Total*	3.6	4.1	0.7	3.2
All mental disorder diagnoses (290–315)	3.0	3.0	0.7	2.6
Symptoms of nervousness and debility (790)	0.6	1.0	(0.0)	0.6

Source: National Center for Health Statistics, unpublished data from 1977 NAMCS.

Note: Figures shown in parentheses have a relative standard error greater than 30%. Quantity more than 0 but less than 0.05 is indicated by 0.0.

*Total may differ from sum of rows because of rounding.

Table 10.3.   Percentage of Distribution of Principal Reasons for Visit, by *Reason for Visit Classification (RVC)* Module and by Primary Care Physician Specialty

RVC Modules and Reasons for Visit	All Primary Care Specialties	Primary Care Specialty		
		GP/Family Practice	Internal Medicine	Pediatrics
Total, All Reasons*	100	100	100	100
Psychosocial problems*	1.9	2.1	2.4	(0.5)
All other problems*	98.1	97.9	97.6	99.5
"Symptoms"				
Psychological and mental disorders	1.8	1.9	2.1	(0.5)
All other symptoms	56.9	58.7	52.6	54.6
"Disease"				
Mental disorders	(0.1)	(0.1)	(0.1)	—
All other diagnoses	9.2	8.4	14.6	5.8
"Treatments"				
Psychotherapy	(0.0)	(0.0)	—	—
Social problem counseling	(0.1)	(0.1)	(0.1)	(0.0)
All other treatment	5.8	5.5	5.3	7.3
"Injuries and Adverse Effects"				
Suicide attempt	(0.0)	(0.0)	—	—
All other	4.0	5.1	1.4	2.4
All other modules	22.3	20.1	23.6	29.4

Source: National Center for Health Statistics, unpublished data from 1977 NAMCS.

Note: Figures shown in parentheses have a relative standard error greater than 30%. Quantity more than 0 but less than 0.05 is indicated by 0.0. Quantity zero indicated by —.

*Total may differ from sum of rows because of rounding.

the combination categories, patient presentations of such complaints were far less frequent than physician diagnoses of mental disorders (9–22% of patients).

The actual diagnosed frequency rates for mental disorders are consistent with those found by Shepherd, Cooper, Brown, and Kalton (1966) in their study of psychiatric morbidity detected by British general practitioners. In those practices, formal mental illness was diagnosed in about 10% of patients, the categories being psychoses, mental subnormality, dementia, neuroses, and personality disorder. Three groups of associated conditions—psychosomatic conditions, organic illness with a psychiatric overlay, and

Table 10.4.   Percentage of Distribution of Patients by Presenting Complaint and Percentage Diagnosed with Mental Disorder at First Study Visit in Three General Medical Practice Settings

Chief or Presenting Complaint	Private Office Practices of General Physicians and Internists		Hospital-Based General Medical Clinics
	Prince George's County, Md.[1]	Monroe County, New York[2]	Monroe County, New York[3]
Primarily emotional symptoms — advice or counseling	3.5	6.6	6.2
Primarily physical symptoms	61.9	61.9	59.1
Preventive or diagnostic procedures	20.2	26.2	17.0
Accident or injury	8.8	5.1	0.5
Combinations of above, other, and unknown	5.6	0.2	17.2
Total	100.0	100.0	100.0
Percentage diagnosed with mental disorder	9.0	16.9	22.0

[1]White patients age 15 and over (Locke et al., 1967).
[2]White patients age 15 years and over (Locke & Gardner, 1969).
[3]All patients age 15 years and over (unpublished data from Rosen et al., 1972).

psychosocial problems—constituted about 5% of visits. Because of some overlap, the total consulting rate for psychiatric morbidity was 14%.

More detailed examinations of patients in general-practice settings by means of standardized psychiatric interviews or by patient self-report symptom questionnaires reveal that there are a substantially greater number of patients with mental disorders and a considerable amount of hidden mental morbidity that are neither recognized in general-practitioner survey studies nor reported in medical records (Goldberg and Blackwell 1970; Rawnsley 1966). Recent data from a study of primary care physicians in Marshfield, Wisconsin (Hoeper 1979), revealed that some 27% of adult patients in these settings may be identified as having specific mental disorders, and some 30% are identified as having a high level of symptoms on a patient self-report questionnaire—the General Health Questionnaire (GHQ) (Goldberg 1972). The classification used for this survey was the Research Diagnostic Criteria

(RDC) (Spitzer, Endicott, and Robins 1978), which is the basis for part of the *DSM*-III. Although the utility of this classification system has been demonstrated in psychiatric settings, it has not yet been tested in primary care practices.

DISCUSSION

Data from the above studies indicate that recording the patient's reason for visit will not substantially increase our knowledge of the physician's mental health and social support functions. Moreover, the routine recording of *ICD* Section 5 or 16 diagnoses will also tend to underrepresent the prevalence rates of mental disorders or other psychosocial problems. Limiting the number of disorders general practitioners have to consider, as was done in *ICHPPC* and by Shepherd and coworkers (1967), may encourage reporting, although rates approaching 15% have not been published for routine medical reporting studies, as they have in special surveys focusing exclusively on mental disorders.

The solution to the current dilemma may well be an entirely separate diagnostic axis of psychosocial problems that would be recorded for all *ICD* diagnoses. Such a multiaxial approach would clearly demonstrate the psychosocial roles of primary care physicians. It would have the added benefit of providing data on the relationship between psychosocial stress and all physical diagnoses as well (Looney, Lipp, and Spitzer 1978). Medicine has certainly moved beyond unitary etiologic hypotheses for most medical conditions, and such a separate axis could help promote a multifactorial approach.

In the face of wide discrepancies between routinely reported diagnoses and rates obtained from direct surveys of primary care practices, one is forced to reexamine both the reporting practices and the current classification system. Moreover, the issue of hidden morbidity poses particular problems for training (Feldman 1978). Medical records that inaccurately record the presence of a mental disorder or other psychosocial problem have a markedly reduced utility for patient care, for monitoring the quality of care, and for teaching and planning for needed services (American Psychiatric Association 1977).

There is good reason to suspect that the framework provided by the classification of physical, mental, and social problems has a major impact on physicians' expectations of their roles. As a result, there appears to be a conscious effort to shift the relative proportion of biomedical, mental health, and social categories in the routine classification used by primary care physicians in an attempt to reflect more accurately the proportion of time spent in physical medicine, mental health, and social support roles. Nevertheless, a classification change will not in itself effect a change in clinical practice. Physicians tend to screen all patients for illnesses or conditions that have been studied. Today's primary care physicians, most of whom were trained without adequate emphasis on emotional or social conditions, rarely screen for such conditions routinely. This behavior stems not only from a lack of diagnostic and interviewing training, but also from training deficits in the treatment or management of the conditions now listed. Health providers will not persist in screening for conditions they can do nothing about—especially if such conditions have an attached social stigma. Moreover, even when they can recognize mental health problems and provide specific treatments and social support, the reimbursement available for these functions will greatly influence diagnostic and recording practices. An insurance system that forces health providers to report a partial truth or untruth about what they are doing for patients will not serve anyone's interest.

Hence, changes in classification must be considered a necessary but not sufficient action in support of primary care practice. A concomitant increase in training to identify and treat psychosocial problems and shifts in reimbursement policies will be required if primary care is to meet the broad and humane expectations of the society that fostered its rebirth.

REFERENCES

American Hospital Association. 1976. *International Classification of Health Problems in Primary Care.* Chicago: American Hospital Association.

American Psychiatric Association. 1977. *The Problem-Oriented System in Psychiatry.* Task Force Report 12. Washington, D.C.: American Psychiatric Association.

American Psychiatric Association. 1978. *Diagnostic and Statistical Manual of Mental Disorders.* 3rd ed., draft. Washington, D.C.: American Psychiatric Association.

Andrews, G., M. Schonell, and C. Tennant. 1977. "The Relation between Physical, Psychological, and Social Morbidity in a Suburban Community." *American Journal of Epidemiology* 105:324.

Eisenthal, S., R. Emery, A. Lazar, and H. Udin. 1979. "Adherence and the Negotiated Approach to Patienthood." *Archives of General Psychiatry* (Chicago) 36: 393.

Feldman, A. 1978. "The Family Practitioner as Psychiatrist." *American Journal of Psychiatry* 135(6):728.

Goldberg, D. P. 1972. *The Detection of Psychiatric Illness by Questionnaire.* Maudsley Monographs No. 21. London: Oxford University Press.

Goldberg, D. P., and B. Blackwell. 1970. "Psychiatric Illness in General Practice: A Detailed Study Using a New Method of Case Identification." *British Medical Journal* 2:439.

Health Professions Educational Assistance Act of 1976. Public Law 94-484, 20 October 1976.

Hoeper, E. 1979. "Observations on the Impact of Psychiatric Disorder Upon Primary

Medical Care," in *Mental Health Services in General Medical Care.* Washington, D.C.: National Academy of Sciences.

Israel, R. A. 1978. "The *International Classification of Diseases:* Two hundred years of development." *Public Health Reports* 93:2.

Lazar, A., S. Eisenthal, and L. Wasserman. 1975. "The Customer Approach to Patienthood: Attending to Patient Requests in a Walk-In Clinic." *Archives of General Psychiatry* (Chicago) 32:553.

Locke, B. Z., and E. A. Gardner. 1969. "Psychiatric Disorders among the Patients of General Practitioners and Internists." *Public Health Reports* 84:167.

Locke, B. Z., D. L. Finucane, and F. Hassler. 1967. *Emotionally Disturbed Patients under Care of Private Nonpsychiatric Physicians.* Psychiatric Research Report no. 22, pp. 235–48. Washington, D.C.: American Psychiatric Association.

Looney, J. G., M. R. Lipp, and R. L. Spitzer. 1978. "New Method of Classification for Psychophysiologic Disorders." *American Journal of Psychiatry* 135(6): 304.

Pardes, H., and R. S. Daniels. 1977. "The Primary Care Dilemma." *Journal of Psychiatric Education* 1:123.

Rawnsley, K. 1966. "Congruence of Independent Measures of Psychiatric Morbidity." *Journal of Psychosomatic Research* 10:84.

Regier, D. A. 1977. "Psychiatry's Dilemma with Primary Care." *Journal of Psychiatric Education* 1:137.

Regier, D. A., A. H. Rosenfeld, B. J. Burns, and I. D. Goldberg. 1979. "The Nature and Scope of Mental Health Problems in Primary Care." Paper presented at the Institute of Medicine Conference on "The Provision of Mental Health Services in Primary Care Settings," National Academy of Sciences, Washington, D.C., April 1979.

Rosen, B. M., B. Z. Locke, I. D. Goldberg, and H. M. Babigian. 1972. "Identification of Emotional Disturbance in Patients Seen in General Medical Clinics." *Hospital Community Psychiatry* 23:364.

Shepherd, M., B. Cooper, A. C. Brown, and G. W. Kalton. 1966. *Psychiatric Illness in General Practice.* London: Oxford University Press.

Spitzer, R. L., J. Endicott, and E. Robins. 1978. "Research Diagnostic Criteria." *Archives of General Psychiatry* (Chicago) 35:773.

U.S. Commission on Hospital and Professional Activities. 1978. *International Classification of Diseases, Ninth Revision—Clinical Modification.* Ann Arbor, Mich.: Commission on Hospital and Professional Activities.

U.S. National Center for Health Statistics. 1978. *The National Ambulatory Medical Care Survey: 1975 Summary, U.S., January–December 1975.* Vital and Health Statistics, Series 13, no. 33, DHEW Publication PHS 78-1784. Washington, D.C.: Government Printing Office.

U.S. National Center for Health Statistics. 1979. *A Reason for Visit Classification for Ambulatory Care.* Vital and Health Statistics, Series 2, no. 78, DHEW Publication PHS 79-1352. Washington, D.C.: Government Printing Office.

World Health Organization. 1976. "Psychosocial Factors and Health—Report of the Director-General to the 57th Session of the Executive Board." *Official Records of the World Health Organization,* nos. 231 and 232.

World Health Organization. 1977. *Manual of the International Classification of Diseases, Injuries, and Causes of Death*. 1975 revision, 2 vols. Geneva: World Health Organization.
World Health Organization. 1978. *Primary Health Care*. Geneva: World Health Organization.

IV

Proposed Classifications
of Psychological Symptoms
and Social Problems
in Primary Care

11

A Proposed Classification of Social Problems and Psychological Symptoms for Inclusion in a Classification of Health Problems

DARREL A. REGIER
JACK D. BURKE, JR.
BARBARA J. BURNS
ANTHONY W. CLARE

WALTER GULBINAT
MACK LIPKIN, JR.
ROBERT L. SPITZER
JANET B. W. WILLIAMS

MAURICE WOOD

The World Health Organization (WHO) in 1946 defined *health* as "complete physical, mental, and social well-being" (1). This definition is significant in its emphasis on health as a positive state, and not merely as the absence of disease. This represents an important change in concept from previous notions that a state of health is one in which the individual is merely free of disease and symptoms. The WHO definition describes health as well-being in not only the physical, but also the psychological and social, areas of functioning. In other words, to be healthy is to have adequate functioning in these three important areas of living.

The goal of physicians and other health care personnel is to promote health. If one accepts the WHO definition of health, then, one can extrapolate that health care personnel must deal with the psychological and social as well as the physical areas of living. Problems develop in all three of these components of life, and all must be dealt with to achieve a state of health.

There is little dispute nowadays over the fact that psychological and social problems can be important influences affecting physical well-being, and often coexist with physical disease. It may be that psychosocial problems cause physical disease; that physical disease causes psychosocial problems; and/or that the same people are vulnerable to physical, psychological, and social problems. But whatever the mix, the evidence is clear that patients with

Prepared for the working group by Janet B. W. Williams.

psychosocial problems have a higher rate of incidence of physical problems (2). It follows, then, that psychosocial problems should not be ignored in a comprehensive approach to health care.

The front-line health provider is the first to make contact with patients seeking health care. Many patients, especially the middle-aged (in particular, women) and the elderly, present with a mixture of complaints—with symptoms of physical distress and psychological or social stress. It is essential that the physician of first contact make some assessment of the patient's problems, including a judgment about the relative interdependence of the physical, psychological, and social complaints, so that appropriate intervention can be planned.

It is also known that most patients with "emotional problems" present themselves to the health care system complaining of a variety of physical symptoms and do not identify themselves as in need of psychiatric treatment (3). Often this occurs because patients with emotional problems find it difficult to express their problems in psychological terms, so they are said to "somaticize" their psychological and social problems. It is the physician of first contact who must make the judgment of whether physical complaints are an indication of organic illness, and what is the most appropriate target of treatment.

Even when patients acknowledge that their chief complaint is a psychological or social problem, they may be unwilling to go to a mental health specialist because of the stigma involved. They may feel it is much less stigmatizing and therefore more acceptable to be treated by a general practitioner. The general practitioner must be sensitive to this view, and must not risk losing these patients from any kind of treatment by making an immediate referral to a mental health specialist. In other words, in such cases, the general practitioner must be prepared to manage the psychosocial problems as best he or she can, if that is the only vehicle for treatment that the patient is willing to accept.

Finally, as some patients present with purely physical complaints, some also present with problems only in the areas of psychological and social functioning, without accompanying physical distress. The primary care health practitioner cannot ignore these other problem areas.

The WHO definition of health is an affirmation of the responsibility of primary care personnel for the multiple needs of their patients. Indeed, they are distinguished from their specialist colleagues by the greater need to consider the psychological and social problems of their patients, as well as the physical—that is, to have a basically holistic orientation. Patients treated by specialists in medicine, psychiatry, and social work often reach those specialists by referral from primary care practitioners. In this way, primary care personnel fulfill screening and triage functions for the rest of the health care delivery system. To serve this function, primary care providers must be very aware of the multiple needs of patients seeking care, and must have an under-standing of problems in all three areas of functioning. While for a variety of reasons they cannot actively intervene in all problems in all areas of a patient's life, primary care personnel must be responsive to multiple needs.

In addition to serving as the point of entry into the health care system, pri-mary caretakers often perform an important supportive function with regard to psychosocial problems. The support they provide by listening, counseling, and in some cases referring for specialized treatment is an important and val-uable aspect of their primary care role. And, whatever the treatment, they should assume the role of "case manager"; that is, they should provide and facilitate continuity of care and coordination of the various health care serv-ices to which the patient is exposed. Primary care personnel should have the "overall picture" in mind; they should be aware of the degree to which the entire "physical, mental, and social well-being" (to quote the WHO defini-tion again) of the patient is impaired, and can thus judge best what priority to give the treatment of each of the patient's problems.

Communication between the general practitioner and health specialists should be strong, and liaisons with public health and social agencies should be solidified. An important advantage to the health care system of primary care practitioners' serving this function is that there is less likelihood that a patient will drift from specialist to specialist seeking care, if that patient's overall treatment is overseen by one person or by a primary health care team.

Despite the need for primay health care personnel to be attuned to and un-derstanding of all the problems of their patients, and especially aware of psy-chological and social problems, evidence suggests that many general practi-tioners tend to overlook psychological and social problems. The reasons for this lack of attendance to psychosocial problem areas are many. Studies sug-gest that, when practitioners are reminded to be cognizant of such difficul-ties, the reporting of problems in these areas increases markedly.

The medical training of general practitioners does not include much, if any, training in the recognition and diagnosis of psychosocial problems. Ev-idence suggests that the sensitivity of general practitioners to detecting psy-chiatric problems is very low (4,5). Furthermore, because there is some vari-ation in sensitivity, interclinician agreement on what constitutes an emotional problem is very low, as each practitioner uses his or her own biases and thresh-olds in detecting mental illness (6). Obviously, given the points made in the discussion above, it is essential that there be some standardization in the skills and criteria used for detecting psychiatric problems. Accurate diagnosis of psychological and social problems is the first step toward effective treatment, and the ability to do this with some consistency should be an important com-ponent of primary care practice.

Once the detection of psychological or social problems has been made, pri-mary care practitioners have basically three options. Patients can either be referred to a specialist; be treated by the primary caretakers themselves; or be managed as part of a multidisciplinary health team, in which case a general practitioner's role is a combination of liaison and direct care provider.

Referral to a specialist is only a viable choice if appropriate specialists are available and if a patient is willing to seek care from a specialist. In general, there is a shortage of psychiatrists and other mental health professionals, especially in rural environments and in developing countries. Because of this shortage, there may not be an available specialist, and the majority of patients in primary care who have a recognized mental disorder are not referred.

If the most appropriate action in some cases is for primary care personnel to treat the patients themselves, another level of skill beyond that required to detect the problems in the first place is necessary. Unfortunately, the training of most primary care personnel in the past has not fully equipped them to treat the psychological and social problems of their patients. Although all training programs include training in the skills necessary to develop a sound "doctor-patient" relationship, medical education has been focused mainly on the treatment of physical problems. Most primary care personnel have no specialized knowledge of the use of psychotropic medications, psychotherapeutic techniques, or appropriate social intervention techniques. To be sure, many primary care providers perform an important supportive function with regard to the psychosocial problems of their patients. The support they provide by listening, reassuring, and in some cases counseling, is an important aspect of their primary care role. The lack of more sophisticated skills undoubtedly contributes to the lack of attention paid to psychological and social problems by primary care personnel; they tend to ignore or overlook what they cannot do much about.

Finally, there is the possibility in some sophisticated settings of making use of a therapeutic team or liaison approach. In the team approach, generally, a mental health professional or multidisciplinary team (including a social worker, psychiatrist, and a psychologist) and a primary care physician work together to manage the patient's physical, mental, and social problems. A liaison approach requires the availability of specialists in the treatment of psychological and social problems to serve as consultants to the primary care provider as he or she manages the patient directly. The availability of these resources contributes to the increased attention by the primary care provider to the psychological and social components of health.

The fundamental reasons for the tendency of most primary care clinicians to overlook the existence and importance of the psychosocial problems of their patients, then, are the lack of detailed knowledge about these factors and the lack of availability of effective interventions. Obviously, these are separate problems, and this chapter deals only with the first. It should be recognized, however, that the only purpose in facilitating more accurate differential diagnosis and understanding of psychological and social problems is the fact that this represents the essential first step in determining effective strategies for management and treatment.

The first step in promoting accurate diagnosis of psychosocial problems is to have a classification of these problems that can be used by those charged with the identification of these problems. The need for a classification of psychosocial problems for use by primary health care personnel has been acknowledged in Chapter 10 of this volume. To address this need, an advisory group of individuals with special expertise and interest in the area of psychosocial factors related to health gathered in October 1979 at the National Institute of Mental Health. What follows is a summary of this group's approach to the problem and a draft proposal.

The specific domain of problems to be classified is determined by the purposes such a classification is designed to serve.

THE PURPOSES OF A CLASSIFICATION OF PSYCHOSOCIAL PROBLEMS

Clinical Management

An essential purpose of such a classification is that it be clinically useful. That is, categorization according to this classification should suggest the most appropriate intervention. For example, the classification of a patient's troubles under the rubric of *marital dissatisfaction* should suggest the possibility of a need for marital therapy. This intervention may or may not be available. When a particular problem is frequently categorized and no appropriate intervention is available for it, this suggests the need for a new intervention, specific for that problem. For example, classification of a problem as *financial*—that is, the patient cannot pay bills and is deeply in debt—suggests that a social intervention, such as referral to the public assistance system, may be indicated. In an area with no such system available, the assessment of financial problems may suggest that such services are needed.

Resource Planning

Resource planners as well must know what problems are being presented by patients for the attention of the health care system. Only by understanding the relative frequencies of such problems, and ultimately what treatments each requires, can planners properly develop and allocate health care resources. In the community, planners must know the extent to which various psychosocial factors become psychosocial problems and constitute the presenting complaints of patients entering the health care system. If, for example, family-related problems are a major reason for seeking health care intervention in a particular community, this may suggest that family counseling services should be instituted or expanded.

Research

As particular types of problems begin to be more accurately recorded—a condition that presupposes an adequate classification system—we can begin to learn more about them. Rates of prevalence for different problems in different settings, reported by different types of patients, can be studied; this information can increase our understanding of the etiology of these problems and can be important for study of the effectiveness of resource allocation and management techniques. Researchers can begin to learn the role of psychosocial problems in health status in general, and, more specifically, can determine whether certain of these problems contribute more than others to ill health. Findings of this type would parallel the finding of epidemiologists, for example, that crowded living conditions predispose people to the development of epidemics of disease. One would expect particular psychosocial problems to be more related to certain kinds of physical illness than others, and in some cases this is known. For instance, it has been found that loss of a parent in early life apparently makes an individual more likely to develop depressive illness later in life. Likewise, certain substandard living conditions make individuals more susceptible to developing tuberculosis. Once these connections are made, it is easier to discover the most effective ways of dealing with these problems. It must first be clear what the problems *are* before anyone is able to determine what best to do for them, and a suitable classification is a prerequisite for research of this type.

Education

Finally, the use of such a classification in practice should serve an educational purpose. Such a classification should help primary care clinicians become more aware of the multifactorial nature of health problems, as well as the importance of psychological and social problems in the health of their patients. The documentation that primary care personnel spend a significant proportion of their time dealing with the psychosocial problems of their patients will dictate the need for increased training in management techniques for these problems, such as (1) psychotherapeutic techniques; (2) the appropriate use of psychotropic medications; (3) effective social intervention techniques; and (4) effective methods of referring patients to specialists. Eventually, education at the undergraduate level will be influenced so that primary care clinicians are trained to be more sensitive to psychosocial problems at the outset and to have a better idea of how to deal with them.

WHAT TO CLASSIFY

In beginning construction of a classification of anything, one must have a clear notion of the domain of items to be classified. In other words, it is necessary to know the boundaries of the set of items under consideration so that it is clear what will be included and what will be excluded. In the case of psychosocial factors, there are two decisions to be made: whether to classify psychosocial factors or psychosocial problems, and exactly what these comprise.

Psychosocial Factors versus Psychosocial Problems

Psychosocial *factors* exist in everyone's lives. To name just a few, there are environmental, interpersonal, and familial factors that influence all of us, some in positive ways and some in negative ways. It is only when a psychosocial factor causes us difficulty and affects our physical, psychological, or social well-being that it becomes identified as a psychosocial *problem*. Psychosocial problems are psychosocial factors that cause distress or disability of some kind—that is, factors that have a negative influence on our "well-being." Psychosocial factors are of value for clinicians to consider in general or specialized practice; however, they are only germane to a classification of health problems when they become psychosocial problems. No patient will seek health care contact for a psychosocial factor in his or her life. It is only psychosocial *problems* that may constitute reasons for visits. The psychosocial problems that a patient reports are an indication of how he or she is coping with the psychosocial factors in his or her environment. It is psychosocial *problems* that are clinically significant for attention by health care personnel.

Psychosocial Problems: One Classification or Two?

In discussing the boundaries of the realm of "psychosocial problems," it becomes clear that, although psychological problems often have a social component, and social problems frequently have accompanying psychological distress, they are really two domains of information that are best considered separately. (This proposal focuses on psychological *symptoms* rather than on mental *disorders,* because symptoms are most often the complaints presented to primary care personnel.) Clinicians are accustomed to thinking of psychological symptoms occurring together in patterns called *syndromes*. These syndromes are sometimes diagnosed as mental disorders. By tradition, mental disorders are conceptualized separately from physical disorders and social problems. The *International Classification of Diseases (ICD)* has always contained a separate chapter for mental disorders, and although the boundaries of this concept are not always clear, it does seem useful to conceptualize the categories in that chapter as distinct from physical and social problems.

Whereas psychological problems are generally conceptualized as occurring within an individual, the locus of social problems tends to be thought of as in the interaction of an individual with other people or with the environment. Social problems are not generally thought of as associated with social "symptoms" in the same way as mental disorders are associated with psychological symptoms. Granted, in some cases the distinction between a social problem and a psychological problem is somewhat arbitrary; however, both tradition and clinical usefulness support this distinction.

For these reasons, this proposal contains drafts of two classifications: one for social problems and one for psychological symptoms.

THE CLASSIFICATION OF SOCIAL PROBLEMS

Before determining the categories in a classification of social problems, it is wise to consider classifications already in use.

International Classification of Health Problems in Primary Care

Realizing that *ICD* was inadequate for use by primary care providers, the World Organization of Colleges, Academies, and Academic Associations of General Practitioners/Family Physicians (WONCA) organized a major revision in *ICD* specifically for use in primary care practice; the result was the *International Classification of Health Problems in Primary Care,* or *ICHPPC* (7). Basically, *ICHPPC* groups the detailed *ICD* rubrics into a shorter list of conditions significant in primary care practice. The first version of *ICHPPC* was revised on the basis of field testing and the influence of *ICD*-9 to become the currently used *ICHPPC*-2. This classification was field-tested internationally and found useful in the wide variety of settings served by primary care personnel: in rural or urban settings, and with ambulatory or in-hospital patients. Although *ICHPPC* contained major revisions in the listing of physical problems, it simplified Chapter 5 ("Mental Disorders") of *ICD* in the area of psychological problems, decreasing the number of major *ICD* categories from 26 to 15, and decreasing the total number of listed codes from 184 to 21 (see Appendix A). In addition, a separate section for "Social, Marital and Family Problems and Maladjustments" was added to the Supplementary Classification of relevant psychosocial terms. The entire psychosocial section was simplified to include only 37 separate items instead of the 200 items in *ICD* (Appendix B).

Reason for Visit Classification

The patient's perception of why he or she is seeking treatment is often discrepant with the health care personnel's assessment of the individual's problem. As discussed above, this occurs often when the patient's primary complaint is of a psychological or social problem. For this reason, clinicians should become more aware of what the patient perceives as the problem. If a patient is being treated for a physical illness, for example, and sees his or her concomitant feelings of depression as the main problem, the clinician should attend to that complaint, especially as it undoubtedly affects the patient's physical health.

In an effort to classify reasons for seeking primary health care from the patients' point of view, the *Reason for Visit Classification (RVC)* was developed by the National Center for Health Statistics (8). The purpose of this classification was to serve as a system parallel to *ICD* as the physician's classification of the reasons for a visit. The instrument was designed primarily for use in research and not as an aid to the clinician in diagnosis and patient management. Patients' reasons for seeking medical care can be classified in one or more modules as follows: symptoms; clearly defined diseases; diagnosis screening and prevention; treatment; injuries and adverse effects (of drugs, alcohol, or the environment); obtaining of test results; or administrative reasons. These different modules were developed to facilitate the gathering of data on the frequencies of various reasons for treatment. The "Symptom" module includes "Symptoms Referable to Psychological and Mental Disorders," and the "Disease" module contains a section for "Mental Disorders" (Appendix C). A section in the "Treatment" module for "Social Problem Counseling" is actually a classification of social problems (Appendix D) and includes nine specific categories and one residual category. Each specific category is described by a brief list of specific problems that would be included in that category. For instance, the category *occupational problems* includes *unemployment, out of work, job dissatisfaction,* and *problem with boss or coworkers.*

Although *RVC*'s main purpose is to classify reasons for visits as stated by the patients, it will facilitate the specification of what problems primary caretakers are expected to deal with, and what treatments are administered for them.

General Practice Research Unit Classification

In order to develop a vehicle for the systematic collection of data recorded in social service case records, an instrument was developed that included a classification of social problems for which clients are referred to social workers (9). The list of problems was constructed from the results of a national survey of case-recording systems in use in the United Kingdom. The resulting problem classification (Appendix E) was developed primarily for use by researchers, and with the following principles in mind: that there be clear definitions of terms and clear boundaries of the categories; that the categories themselves be mutually exclusive; that multiple categories could be recorded for any individual; that the directions to the rater be clearly stated as to from whose point of view the recording was made, at what point in time, and whose problem was being recorded (e.g., the client's, or a family problem that directly affects the client). In addition to nine categories of "Social Factors," there are sections for "Personal and Social Relations," consisting of *relationship problems* and the problem of *lack of relationships,* and one for "Problems Related to Health," such as minor and major *physical ill health* and *problems associated with reproduction.*

Social Maladjustment Schedule

In an effort to develop an instrument that would be adequate for assessing social adjustment for use by a wide range of personnel, including family physicians, Clare and Cairns constructed the Social Maladjustment Schedule (10). This instrument lists six areas of an individual's social life that are of particular importance in affecting social functioning. These areas are as follows: housing, occupation/role, economic situation, leisure/social activities, family and domestic relationships, and marital. An individual's functioning in each of these areas is to be rated with respect to "material conditions," that is, in light of the individual's objective social circumstances; "social management," that is, the subject's management of his or her social affairs, activities, and relationships in each area of functioning; and "satisfaction," or the individual's subjective assessment of his or her satisfaction in each area of functioning. Within each subject area, items are specified for rating on a 4-point scale, ranging from "satisfactory, no difficulties, satisfied" to "severe difficulties, severe dissatisfaction." This entire schema is presented in Appendix F. Subjects are rated on only those items that are applicable, and alternative sections of the schedule have been constructed to be used with individuals in alternative social roles, such as the chronically unemployed, and for alternative domestic situations. A high degree of interrater reliability on individual items was obtained in a reliability study of 48 subjects. Although this instrument requires a reasonably high level of training, it is basically simple and easy to score.

International Statistical Classification of Diseases, Injuries, and Causes of Death (ICD-9)

The ninth revision of the *International Classification of Diseases* (*ICD*-9), which went into effect in 1978, contains a separate chapter (Chapter 5) for mental disorders (11). For the first time, a glossary of definitions of the various disorders is included within this chapter. (The *ICD*-8 also had a glossary, but it was published separately.) The *ICD*-9 classification of mental disorders is far longer and more detailed than necessary for use in primary care practice.

In addition, there is a separate section, the V Codes, which is a "Supplementary Classification of Factors Influencing Health Status and Contact With Health Services." This section contains a number of categories of social problems (Appendix G). These are grouped into three large categories: housing, household, and economic circumstances; other family circumstances; and other psychosocial circumstances. Within each of these large categories there are a number of more specific problem areas, most with examples of problems that would be included in each rubric. The *ICD*-9 classification of social problems is quite long and unduly complicated, with many categories, such as *holiday relief care* and *person living in residential institution,* that describe situations rather than social problems. For this reason, this classification has not been deemed suitable for use by primary care personnel, although some of its categories have been included in the classification proposed in this chapter.

Diagnostic and Statistical Manual of Mental Disorders

The third edition of the American Psychiatric Association's *Diagnostic and Statistical Manual of Mental Disorders* (*DSM*-III) provides a multiaxial system for the evaluation of individuals with mental disorders (12).

The first of two of five axes contain all the mental disorders, with two classes of disorders ("Personality Disorders" and "Specific Developmental Disorders") placed separately on Axis II because they are often overlooked when attention is directed toward the usually more florid Axis I diagnosis. Axis III is for recording physical disorders and conditions that are relevant to the understanding or management of the individual being evaluated. Disorders recorded here are taken from the *ICD*-9-CM classification, outside Chapter 5. Axis IV provides for a recording of the severity of psychosocial stressors that have contributed to the development or exacerbation of the mental disorders recorded on Axis I and Axis II. Although no specific classification of "Psychosocial Stressors" is provided, a list of ten categories of stressors is suggested for use as areas of inquiry in evaluating whether the severity of a significant stressor should be recorded (Appendix H). Finally, Axis V provides a rating scale for noting the highest level of adaptive functioning that the individual was able to sustain for at least a few months during the year prior to the evaluation. This information is assumed to be of prognostic significance and may be relevant to treatment planning.

PROPOSED CLASSIFICATION OF SOCIAL PROBLEMS

As can be seen by comparing the appendices, each of the classifications of social problems contains basically similar categories, differing only in the boundaries between categories.

Experience tells us that for a classification system to be used by busy clinicians, it must be clearly and simply constructed. The number of categories classified must be limited to a minimum number necessary for the specificity required. For this reason, the proposed classification contains a limited number of major categories, with several examples within each (Table 11.1).

Table 11.1.   Proposed Classification of Social Problems

---

1. Housing problems
    Includes: overcrowding
                lack of housing
                inadequate housing
2. Change in residence
    Includes: immigration
                moving out of parental home
3. Financial problems
    Includes: cannot pay bills or debts
                cannot afford food of sufficient quality or quantity
4. Problems within a family
    a. Conjugal (marital or nonmarital problems)
        Includes: marital discord
                    spouse abuse
                    sexual problems (not due to physical or mental disorder)
    b. Parent-child problems
        Includes: child abuse or neglect
                    excessive parental control
                    deficient parental control
                    child deprived of parental attention
                    conflict over rules
    c. Family disruption
        Includes: divorce
                    separation
                    death
                    family member leaves home
    d. Other problems of family relationships
        Includes: problems with relatives other than parent or children
                    problems with siblings
    e. Problems of caring for sick person (includes family members and friends)
        Includes: aged parent
5. Other nonfamily interpersonal problems
    Includes: problems with peers, neighbors
                social isolation
                death of a friend

Table 11.1. (*continued*)

6. Educational or learning problems
    a. Educational problems
       Includes: school failure
                  school refusal
                  lack of schooling
                  absenteeism (truancy)
                  inadequate educational opportunities
                  cheating
                  quarrels with teachers
    b. Learning problems
       Includes: reading problems
                 arithmetic problems
7. Occupational problems (includes problems as housewife)
    Includes: problems with coworkers
               role dissatisfaction
               unemployment
               difficulties at work or in adjusting to work situation
8. Legal problems
    Includes: imprisonment
               prosecution
               litigation
               legal investigation
9. Personal and environmental circumstances that impede access to health care
    or are hazardous to physical health
    Includes: lack of transportation
               ignorance of significance of symptoms
               rigid appointment schedules of health facility
               advertising of a proprietary medicine for treating the patient's
                  symptoms
               religious beliefs or cultural attitudes
               air pollution
               water pollution
10. Conflict with the practices or belief systems of a social or cultural institution
     Includes: nonconformity with religious ritual
                crisis of religious or political persecution
                conscientious objection
11. Other social problems
     Includes: unwanted pregnancy
                persecution or discrimination (on the basis of politics, religion, sex,
                   or race)
                excommunication
                hexing

For problems not easily categorized in a specific area, there is a residual category. Hopefully, the classification is such that the frequency of problems assigned to this category will be very low; that is, that most of the social problems presented for categorization can be classified in the specific categories. Ideally, the frequency of problems assigned to the residual category should not exceed a maximum of 5% of all problems classified. Recognizing that many patients complain of several social problems occurring together, multiple coding in this classification is encouraged. No one problem should be assigned to more than one category, but several categories may be indicated, if there are several different social problems.

The order of items is arranged hierarchically, to approximate the relative importance of the problem categories. For example, the most basic needs of housing, financial adequacy, and family relations are listed first, before the categories of occupational and legal problems. The first-listed categories refer to needs essential to even a minimal level of functioning, while those listed later are only relevant if a minimum level of functioning is already established.

In order to arrive at the particular categories to be classified, the *ICHPPC* was used as a baseline, and all the other systems were reviewed for what they could add to this list. The group picked the best of each classification scheme for use in this proposed list.

Problems to be recorded are only those related to physical health status or otherwise constituting the reason for visit. The relation to health status may be defined as causal—that is, the social problem may be the cause of the physical problem (as when business pressures cause an ulcer) or may be due to the physical problem (as in a diabetes-induced depression). When the social problem constitutes the reason for visit, there may or may not be a related health problem (as complaints of occupational role dissatisfaction, without accompanying physical distress).

This classification is limited to the identification of *categories* of social problems; it does not include mechanisms for coding dimensional characteristics, such as severity and duration. The inclusion of these additional parameters would have resulted in a more complex system that would probably have tried the patience and spirit of cooperation of its users.

PROPOSED CLASSIFICATION OF PSYCHOLOGICAL SYMPTOMS

When an individual with psychological symptoms is evaluated by a clinician, an attempt is made to assess whether or not there is a mental disorder that accounts for the psychological symptoms. However, many individuals who consult primary care physicians are bothered by psychological symptoms that do not correspond to any particular pattern or syndrome that can be identified as a specific mental disorder. For example, complaints of anxiety or depressed mood are common even when an anxiety or an affective disorder cannot be diagnosed. Therefore, there is a need for a classification of psychological symptoms that would supplement a classification of mental disorders.

In most of the classifications reviewed above, there is a section that includes psychological symptoms. All of these were reviewed, and *RVC* was used as the basis for developing the following classification (Table 11.2). The list does not include such symptoms as phobias and obsessions, included in some classifications, since it was determined that if a patient actually complained of such symptoms, the diagnosis of the corresponding mental disorder (e.g., phobic neurosis or obsessive-compulsive neurosis) would be made. Symptoms appropriate for children have been included. It is expected that frequently multiple symptom categories will be recorded.

Table 11.2. Proposed Classification of Psychological Problems

1. Feeling anxious or nervous
   Includes: apprehension
             bad nerves
             panicky feeling
             tension
             upset
             worried
             fears
2. Feeling depressed
   Includes: crying excessively
             dejected
             feeling low
             hopelessness
             sadness
             unhappy
             low self-esteem
             guilt
             shame
3. Disturbances of sleep
   Includes: trouble sleeping
             sleeping too much
             nightmares
4. Sexual problems
   Includes: excessive concerns about masturbation
             concern with sexual performance (e.g., potency)
             concern with size and shape of sexual organs

(*continued*)

Table 11.2. (*continued*)

5. Eating problems
   Includes: loss of appetite
            excessive appetite
            concern with weight

6. Ideas of suicide
   Includes: attempts

7. Feeling angry or irritable
   Includes: bitterness
            temper tantrums
            violence or homicidal

8. Psychomotor restlessness
   Includes: hyperactivity
            overactivity

9. Trouble with concentration or memory
   Includes: forgetfulness
            confusion
            distractibility

10. Problems with identity
    Includes: no confidence
             loss of identity
             identity crisis

11. Social withdrawal
    Includes: avoiding people
             excessive shyness

12. Personality trait
    Includes: dependence
             oppositional or antisocial behavior
                dominant behavior (e.g., provocative, negativistic)
                cruelty to people or animals
                destructiveness
                fire setting
                stealing
                other behavior

13. Substance-related problems
    Includes: alcohol problems
             tobacco problems
             other drug problems

14. Delusions, hallucinations, or incoherence
    Includes: seeing things
             hearing things
             overly suspicious

15. Phase-of-life problems

Table 11.2. (*continued*)

Includes: problems adjusting to developmental stage such as adolescence
or retirement
16. Age-specific developmental problems (excludes learning problems)
  Includes: bedwetting
  ancopresis
  thumb sucking
  delay in early development (e.g., acquisition of motor skills or
  language)
17. "Psychophysiological" problems (including any physical symptoms
exacerbated by psychological factors)
  Includes: skin problems
  respiratory problems
  gastrointestinal (GI) problems
18. Other psychological problems
  Includes: "can't cope"
  "going crazy"
  "losing my mind"
  rituals
  stuttering

CONCLUSION

A comprehensive evaluation of health status requires consideration of the
physical, psychological, and social components of health. This chapter presents a classification of psychological symptoms and a classification of social
problems for use in evaluation by a primary care provider. One way that these
classifications could be used is by incorporating them into a triaxial evaluation system with each component on a separate axis. Axis I would consist of a
classification of physical disorders and a supplemental list of physical symptoms. In a parallel fashion, Axis II would consist of a classification of mental
disorders and a supplemental list of psychological symptoms, as proposed
here. Finally, Axis III would consist of the classification of social problems
presented here.

The use of such a system would encourage the clinician to consider areas of
health that are frequently overlooked; would be a guide to him or her in planning appropriate interventions; would be a guide to rational planning for resource allocation; and finally, would provide the research investigator with
data about the interrelationship of social, psychological, and physical components of health.

APPENDIX A:
ICHPPC -2 CLASSIFICATION OF "MENTAL DISORDERS"

Psychoses (except alcohol and drug induced)

294 Organic psychosis
incl. nonalcoholic acute or chronic delirium, senile and presenile dementia

295 Schizophrenia, all types
incl. paranoid states and reactions

296 The affective psychoses
incl. psychotic depression, involutional melancholia, mania, hypomania, manic-depressive, reactive depressive psychosis

298 Other and unspecified psychoses
excl. alcoholic

Neuroses

3000 Anxiety disorder, anxiety state
excl. anxiety causing a somatic complaint

3001 Hysterical and hypochondriacal disorders
incl. factitious disorders, compensation neurosis, conversion hysteria, hysterical state, anxiety causing a somatic complaint, hyperventilation syndrome, cardiac neurosis
excl. psychogenic disorders of sexual functions, tension headache, insomnia

3004 Depressive disorder (neurotic depression)
incl. depression, NOS
excl. brief depressive stress reactions

3009 Other neuroses
incl. neurasthenia, phobic state, obsessive-compulsive disorders, occupational neurosis, neurosis, NOS

Other mental and psychological disorders

315 Specific learning disturbance and delay in development of certain skills needed for schooling
excl. mental retardation

3074 Insomnia and other sleep disorders

3078 Tension headache, psychogenic backache and other pain of mental origin (psychalgia)
excl. headache, NOS, migraine, lumbalgia

308 Transient situational disturbance, acute stress reaction, adjustment reaction

incl. grief reaction, bereavement, brief depressive reaction; may have additional code for cause

312 Behavior disorder (any age), disturbance of emotions specific to childhood and adolescence
incl. hyperkinetic child, delinquency, kleptomania (any age)
excl. character disorder

3027 Psychogenic disorder of sexual function
incl. frigidity, impotence and loss of libido, psychogenic dyspareunia
excl. marital problems, vaginismus NOS and dyspareunia NOS in female

Other psychosomatic disorders of genitourinary system

3031 Chronic abuse of alcohol
incl. alcoholism, alcoholic psychosis
excl. nondependent alcohol abuse

3050 Acute alcohol intoxication, drunk, excessive alcohol intake, NOS

3051 Abuse of tobacco

3048 Other drug abuse, habituation, or addiction
(*incl.* drug-induced psychosis)
incl. diazepam, cannabis, LSD, barbiturates, laxatives, glue sniffing, etc.

301 Personality and character disorders

317 Mental retardation

316 Other mental and psychological disorders
incl. sexual deviation, tic, habit spasm, stammering and stuttering, anorexia nervosa, psychological causes of diseases classified elsewhere, psychological effects of head injuries
excl. enuresis *not* clearly of psychological origin

APPENDIX B:
ICHPPC -2 CLASSIFICATION OF "SOCIAL, MARITAL, AND FAMILY PROBLEMS AND MALADJUSTMENTS"

Note: This section is for social problems and maladjustments (inside the family or outside) that have been explicitly discussed and that are accepted by the patient as a significant problem. More than one of these codes may be used alone to describe the substance of an encounter, or may be used as additional codes to show the interdependence between organic or mental disease and the social milieu of the patient *excl.* contact with person acting as emissary for another person who is experiencing problems.

V602 Economic problem, poverty

V600 Housing problem

V614 Problem of caring for sick person (e.g., alcoholic family member)
excl. patient lacking person able to render care (V624)

V611 Marital problem
incl. problems of the relationship between a man and a woman, whether married or not
excl. problems limited to sexual activity (3027)

V612 Parent-child problem
incl. concern about behavior of child, problems related to adopted or foster child, child abuse, battered child, child neglect

V613 Problem with aged parents or in-laws

V610 Family disruption, with or without divorce, affecting the couple or others
excl. bereavement (308)

V619 Other problem of the family relationship NEC

V623 Educational problem

V616 Pregnancy out of wedlock (illegitimate pregnancy), illegitimacy

V624 Social maladjustment
incl. social isolation, persecution, cultural deprivation, political, religious, or sex discrimination

V620 Occupational problem
incl. unemployment, difficulties at work or in adjusting to work situation, career choice problem or frustration

V627 Phase-of-life social problem NEC

V625 Legal problem
incl. imprisonment, prosecution, litigation, legal investigations

V629 Other social problems
incl. refusal of treatment for reasons of religion or conscience

APPENDIX C:
RVC CLASSIFICATION OF "SYMPTOMS REFERABLE TO PSYCHOLOGICAL AND MENTAL DISORDERS" (S100–S199)

S100.0 Anxiety and nervousness
Includes: apprehension
bad nerves
panicky feeling
tension
upset
worried

S105.0 Fears and phobias

S110.0 Depression

Includes: crying excessively
dejected
feeling low
hopelessness
sadness
unhappiness

S115.0 Anger
Includes: bitterness
hostile feelings
Excludes: temper problems (S130.4)

S120.0 Problems with identity
Includes: no confidence
loss of identity
identity crisis
don't like myself
guilt

S125.0 Restlessness
Includes: hyperactivity
overactivity

S130.0 Behavioral disturbances

S130.1 Antisocial behavior
Includes: avoiding people
excessive shyness
social isolation
withdrawal

S130.2 Hostile behavior
Includes: aggressiveness
criminality
cruelty
destructiveness
negativism
quarrelsome

S130.3 Hysterical behavior

S130.4 Temper problems
Includes: blowing up
losing temper
temper tantrum

S130.5 Obsessions and compulsions

S135.0 Disturbances of sleep
S135.1 Insomnia
Includes: sleeplessness
can't sleep
trouble falling asleep

S135.2 Sleepiness (hypersomnia)
       Includes: drowsiness
                can't stay awake

S135.3 Nightmares

S135.4 Sleepwalking

S140.0 Smoking problems
       Includes: smoking too much
                can't quit smoking
       Excludes: smoker's cough (S440.0)
                physical symptoms of smoking
                (*see* particular symptom)

S145.0 Alcohol-related problems
       Includes: drinking problem
       Excludes: adverse effects of alcohol (J915.0)
                alcoholism (D320.0)

S150.0 Abnormal drug usage
       Includes: drug abuse
                frequent or excessive use of stimulants, hallucinogens,
                depressants, etc.
       Excludes: drug addiction (D320.0)
                overdose, unintentional (J910.0)
                intoxication with drugs (J910.0)

S155.0 Delusions or hallucinations
       Includes: seeing things
                hearing voices
                medicine is poisoned

S160.0 Psychosexual disorders

       S160.1 Frigidity, loss of sex drive, lack of response

       S160.2 Homosexuality, concerns with

       S160.3 Impotence

       S160.4 Premature ejaculation

       S160.5 Masturbation excessive, concerns about

       S160.6 Orgasm, problem with

S165.0 Other symptoms or problems relating to psychological and mental disorders, NEC
       Includes: can't cope
                going crazy
                losing my mind
       Excludes: character disorder (D315.0)
                personality disorder (D315.0)

       S165.1 Nailbiting

       S165.2 Thumbsucking

APPENDIX D:
RVC CLASSIFICATION OF "SOCIAL PROBLEM COUNSELING" (T700-T799)

T700.0 Economic problem
    Includes: too little income
               can't pay bills

T705.0 Marital problems
    Includes: problem with husband, wife
               alcoholic spouse
               marriage counseling, NOS
               premarital counseling
               divorce, desertion, separation

T710.0 Parent-child problems
    Includes: working mother
               concern about childhood behavior
               discipline
               maturation problems
               child neglect and abuse
               adopted or foster child

T715.0 Other problems of family relationship
    Includes: aged parents or in-laws
               problems with relatives
               family fights and disruptions

T720.0 Educational problems
    Includes: absenteeism, truancy
               problems with teachers
               hates school
               school behavior problems

T725.0 Occupational problems
    Includes: unemployment
               out of work
               job dissatisfaction
               problem with boss or coworkers

T730.0 Social adjustment problems
    Includes: loneliness
               social isolation
               neighborhood and community relations problems
               discrimination problems
               don't have any friends

T735.0 Legal problems
    Includes: imprisonment, prosecution
               lawsuits, litigation

T740.0 Other social problems

Includes: pregnancy out-of-wedlock
               disasters
               housing and clothing problems

APPENDIX E:
GENERAL PRACTICE RESEARCH UNIT
CLASSIFICATION OF "SOCIAL PROBLEMS"

I. Social Factors

1. Housing:
   a. homelessness
   b. tenancy problems
   c. physically unsuitable for needs
   d. overcrowding
   e. poor conditions
   f. other (specify)

2. Finance:
   a. low income
   b. poor management
   c. indebtedness
   d. other (specify)

3. Occupation:
   a. unemployment
      i. extrinsic
      ii. intrinsic
   b. occupational difficulties (e.g., job dissatisfaction, need for sheltered work)
   c. other (specify)

4. Problems with formal institutions:
   (e.g., D.H.S.S., legal system, police, race relations board)
   specify:

5. Problems of cultural adaptation:
   a. religion
   b. language
   c. social behavior
   d. other (specify)

6. Education:
   a. problems at school/college
   b. school refusal
   c. inadequate or inappropriate educational provision
   d. other (specify)

7. Problems with home management:
   a. personal care of self

      b. domestic care of family
      c. other (specify)
- 8. Environmental factors:
      a. neighborhood environmental factors (e.g., noise, smell, traffic)
      b. other (specify)
- 9. Problems associated with delinquency/crime:
      a. juvenile
      b. adult

II. Personal and Social Relations

- 1. Relationship problems:
      a. marital
      b. parent/child
      c. intrafamilial
      d. problems with extended family
      e . problems with close personal relationships outside the family (e.g., boyfriends)
      f. problems with neighbors
      g. problems with workmates
      h. other (specify)
- 2. Lack of relationships:
      a. social isolation
      b. bereavement
      c. absence from home of parent/spouse
      d. other (specify)

III. Health

- 1. Physical health:
      a. minor physical ill health
      b. major physical ill health
- 2. Mental health:
      a. minor psychiatric/emotional disturbance
      b. major psychiatric/emotional disturbance
- 3. Problems associated with reproduction:
      a. contraception
      b. pregnancy
      c. infertility
      d. infant behavior problems (infants under 12 months)
      e. other (specify)

APPENDIX F:
SOCIAL MALADJUSTMENT SCHEDULE

	Rating Category
Subject Area	Material Conditions
Housing	Housing conditions Residential stability
Occupation/social role	Occupational stability Opportunities for interaction with workmates*
Economic situation	Family income
Leisure/social activities	Opportunities for leisure and social activities* Opportunities for interaction with neighbors*
Family and domestic relationships	Opportunities for interaction with relatives* Opportunities for domestic interaction (i.e., with unrelated others or adult offspring in household) Situational handicaps to child management*
Marital	

*This group of items rates objective restrictions that might be expected to impair functioning in the appropriate area. "Situational handicaps to child management" assesses difficulties likely to exacerbate normal problems of child rearing (e.g., inadequate living space, an absent parent). Objective restrictions on leisure activities include extreme age, physical disabilities, heavy domestic or work commitments, isolated situation of the home, and the like.

APPENDIX F: (continued)

Rating Category

Social Management	Satisfaction
Household care Management of housekeeping	Satisfaction with housing
Quality of personal interaction with workmates	Satisfaction with occupation/social role (includes housewives, unemployed, disabled, retired) Satisfaction with personal interaction with workmates
Management of income	Satisfaction with income
Extent of leisure and social activities Quality of interaction with neighbors	Satisfaction with leisure and social activities Satisfaction with interaction with neighbors Satisfaction with heterosexual role
Quality of interaction with relatives Quality of solitary living Quality of domestic interaction (i.e., with unrelated others or adult off-spring in household) Child management	Satisfaction with interaction with relatives Satisfaction with solitary living Satisfaction with domestic interaction Satisfaction with parental role
Fertility and family planning Sharing of responsibilities and decision making Sharing of interests and activities	Satisfaction with marital harmony Satisfaction with sexual compatibility

APPENDIX G:
ICD -9 CLASSIFICATION OF "SOCIAL PROBLEMS"

V60 Housing, household and economic circumstances

   V60.0 Lack of housing
          Hobos
          Social migrants
          Tramps
          Transients
          Vagabonds

   V60.1 Inadequate housing
          Lack of heating
          Restriction of space
          Technical defects in home preventing adequate care

   V60.2 Inadequate material resources
          Economic problem
          Poverty, NOS

   V60.3 Person living alone

   V60.4 No other household member able to render care
          Person requiring care (has) (is):
              family member too handicapped, ill, or otherwise unsuited
                 to render care
              partner temporarily away from home
              temporarily away from usual place of abode
          Excludes: holiday relief care (V60.5)

   V60.5 Holiday relief care
          Provision of health care facilities to a person normally cared
             for at home to enable relatives to take a vacation

   V60.6 Person living in residential institution
          Boarding school resident

   V60.8 Other

   V60.9 Unspecified

V61 Other family circumstances
     Includes: when these circumstances or fear of them, which affect
               the person directly involved or others, are mentioned
               as the reason, justified or not, for seeking or receiving
               medical advice or care

   V61.0 Family disruption
          Divorce
          Estrangement

   V61.1 Marital problems
          Marital conflict

Excludes: problems related to psychosexual disorders (302.-),
             sexual function (V41.7)

V61.2 Parent-child problems
Child: abuse, battering, neglect
Concern about behavior of child
Parent-child conflict
Problem concerning adopted or foster child
Excludes: effect of maltreatment on the child (995.5)

V61.3 Problems with aged parents or in-laws

V61.4 Health problems within family
Alcoholism in family
Care of sick or handicapped person in family or household
Presence of sick or handicapped person in family or house-
    hold

V61.5 Multiparity

V61.6 Illegitimacy or illegitimate pregnancy

V61.7 Other unwanted pregnancy

V61.8 Other

V61.9 Unspecified

V62 Other psychosocial circumstances
Includes: when these circumstances or fear of them, which affect
             the person directly involved or others, are mentioned as
             the reason, justified or not, for seeking or receiving medi-
             cal advice or care
Excludes: previous psychological trauma (V15.4)

V62.0 Unemployment
Excludes: when main problem is inadequate material re-
             sources (V60.2)

V62.1 Adverse effects of work environment

V62.2 Other occupational circumstances or maladjustment
Career choice problem
Dissatisfaction with employment

V62.3 Educational circumstances
Dissatisfaction with school environment
Educational handicap

V62.4 Social maladjustment
Cultural deprivation
Political, religious, or sex discrimination
Social: isolation, persecution

V62.5 Legal circumstances
Imprisonment

        Litigation
        Prosecution

V62.6 Refusal of treatment for reasons of religion or conscience

V62.8 Other psychological or physical strain, not elsewhere classified

V62.9 Unspecified

APPENDIX H:
DSM-III CLASSIFICATION OF "PSYCHOSOCIAL STRESSORS" (AXIS IV)

I. Conjugal (marital and nonmarital):
Engagement
Marriage
Discord
Separation
Death of spouse

II. Parenting:
Becoming a parent
Friction with child
Illness of child

III. Other Interpersonal (all problems with one's friends, neighbors, associates or nonconjugal family members):
Illness of best friend
Discordant relationship with boss

IV. Occupational (includes work, school, homemaker):
Being unemployed
Retirement
Problems at school

V. Living Circumstances:
Change in residence
Threat to personal safety
Immigration

VI. Financial:
Inadequate finances
Change in financial status

VII. Legal:
Being arrested
Being in jail
Involved in a lawsuit or trial

VIII. Developmental (the meaning given to phases of the life cycle):
Puberty

Menopause
"Becoming 50"

IX. Physical Illness or Injury:
Illness
Accident
Surgery
Abortion

Note: A physical disorder is listed on Axis III whenever it is related to the development or management of an Axis I or II disorder. A physical disorder also can be a psychosocial stressor if its impact is by virtue of its meaning to the individual, in which case it would be listed both on Axis III and on Axis IV.

X. Other Psychosocial Stressors:
Natural or manmade disaster
Persecution
Unmarried pregnancy
Out-of-wedlock birth
Rape

XI. Family Factors—children and adolescents—(in addition to the above, for children and adolescents, the following stressors may be considered):
Cold or distant relationship between parents
Overtly hostile relationship between parents
Physical or mental disturbance in family members
Cold or distant parental behavior toward child
Overtly hostile parental behavior toward child
Parental intrusiveness
Inconsistent parental control
Insufficient parental control
Anomalous family situation: single parent, foster family
Institutional rearing
Loss of nuclear family members

REFERENCES

1. World Health Organization, *Basic Document,* 26th ed. (Geneva: Author, 1946).

2. M. R. Eastwood and M. H. Trevelyan, "Relationship between Physical and Psychiatric Disorder," *Psychological Medicine* 2(1972):363–72.

3. World Health Organization, *Psychiatry and Primary Medical Care: Report on a Working Group Convened by the Regional Office for Europe of the World Health Organization* (Oslo: Regional Office for Europe, World Health Organization, 1973).

4. D. P. Goldberg and B. Blackwell, "Psychiatric Illness in General Practice: A

Detailed Study Using a New Method of Case Identification," *British Medical Journal* 2(1970):439–43.

5. L. Zabarenko, R. A. Pittenger, and R. Zabarenko, *Primary Medical Practice: A Psychiatric Evaluation* (St. Louis: Warren Press, 1968).

6. M. Shepherd, B. Cooper, A. C. Brown, and G. W. Kalton, *Psychiatric Illness in General Practice* (London: Oxford University Press, 1966).

7. World Organization of National Colleges, Academies, and Academic Associations of General Practitioners/Family Physicians, *International Classification of Health Problems in Primary Care,* 2nd ed. (Chicago: American Hospital Association, 1979).

8. D. Schneider, L. Appleton, and T. McLemore, *A Reason for Visit Classification for Ambulatory Care,* Vital and Health Statistics, Series 2, no. 78, DHEW Publication no. (PHS) 79-1352 (Hyattsville, Md.: U.S. National Center for Health Statistics, 1979).

9. R. Fitzgerald, "The Classification and Recording of 'Social Problems,'" *Social Science and Medicine* 12(1978):255–63.

10. A. W. Clare and V. E. Cairns, "Design, Development, and Use of a Standardized Interview to Assess Social Maladjustment and Dysfunction in Community Studies," *Psychological Medicine* 8(1978):589–604.

11. World Health Organization, *Manual of the International Statistical Classification of Diseases, Injuries, and Causes of Death,* 9th revision, vol. 1 (Geneva: Author, 1977).

12. American Psychiatric Association, *Diagnostic and Statistical Manual of Mental Disorders,* 3rd ed. (Washington, D.C.: Author, 1980).

12

A Child-Oriented
Psychosocial Classification
for Primary Health Care

BARBARA J. BURNS
JACK D. BURKE, JR.
DARREL A. REGIER

The special characteristics of children that need to be considered in the development of a psychosocial classification system for use in primary care serve as the major focus of this chapter. The classification system is defined to include mental disorders, psychological symptoms, and social problems. Special characteristics of children are discussed in relation to (1) the need for such classification, (2) issues and problems reflected in current systems, and (3) recommendations for change.

BACKGROUND

The 1978 World Health Organization (WHO) Alma Ata Conference on Primary Health Care made a series of extensive recommendations related to the availability and quality of primary health care services; two are particularly pertinent here. They are, first, that the content of primary health care should include the "promotion of mental health," and second, that "high priority be given to the special needs of women, [and] children" (1). Following these recommendations, the WHO Medium-Term Programme for Mental Health identified "the promotion of mental health, exemplified by work concerning the psychosocial development of the child" (2) as one of three main concerns; it also proposed increasing the effectiveness of general health services through appropriate utilization of mental health skills and knowledge.

Recent U.S. efforts have been made in the same direction. These efforts include strengthening the primary health care sector (Public Law 94-484, Health Professions Educational Assistance Act); identifying children as a priority group for mental health services; and emphasizing the importance of coordination between the general health and mental health sectors (3). Further, both professional organizations for both pediatric and family practice have moved toward formalizing a mental health role. The Council on Pediatric Practice of the American Academy of Pediatrics identified the provision of parental support and guidance and developmental screening as part of well-child care (4), and a recent Task Force on Pediatric Education concluded that behavioral and social problems should receive more attention in the education of primary care practitioners (5). Childhood psychosocial problems described by pediatricians as the "new morbidity" represent a shift in pediatric practice away from a strictly biological orientation, according to Haggerty, Roghmann, and Pless (6). Family-practice residencies include a training requirement in the behavioral sciences.

The tendency for children to be underserved by mental health services has been reflected both in major reviews of the status of the mental health of U.S. children (7) and in legislation targeted at meeting special needs (e.g., The Education for All Handicapped Children Act of 1975, Public Law 94-142). Nevertheless, in 1975 less than 1% of children in the United States received services from an organized mental health facility (8).

NEED FOR PSYCHOSOCIAL CLASSIFICATION IN PRIMARY CARE

The major purpose of reexamining psychosocial classification systems used by primary care practitioners (PCPs) is to improve the delivery of mental health services for children through increased recording of existing psychosocial problems by PCPs. The underlying assumption is that documentation of a problem will lead to clinical intervention, ranging from prevention and early intervention to management and referral. The child psychiatry epidemiological literature reviewed by Robbins (9) and Rutter, Tizard, and Whitmore (10) estimates that the prevalence of mental disorder in children ranges from 5% to 15%. However, routine diagnostic recording by pediatricians, family practitioners, and nurse practitioners (based on several studies) rarely exceed 1%, whether the percentage of children or of visits is counted (11,12). Several studies, which queried physicians specifically about the presence of psychological problems, reported higher rates—one reported a rate of 3.5% in children under 18 with pure psychological problems and 25.7% with a psychological component in visits to general practitioners (13); in a second study of this type, pediatricians reported a 5% rate of children with emotional or behavioral problems (14). The preceding studies suggest that physician recognition of such problems is greater than routine recording indicates. A future question to investigate is whether systematic attention is given to problems that are not normally recorded. Reasons for the disparity between true prevalence rates and practitioner recording are discussed subsequently.

Although specific information on the link between recording practices and clinical intervention is not available, there is some evidence to the effect that the classification system itself is a factor in the extent of health provider recording. Starfield and colleagues (15), in a study of five health care facilities using the *International Classification of Health Problems in Primary Care* (*ICHPPC*), reported that psychosocial diagnoses made in one year by pediatric and family-practice services varied from 5% to 15% across settings. This range is similar and closer to the estimates of general prevalence noted above (9,10) than it is to the *International Classification of Diseases* (*ICD*) diagnostic recording of health practitioners cited (11,12). This contrast between *ICHPPC* and *ICD* findings may point toward greater compatibility of the *ICHPPC* categories with practice (e.g., type of problems recognized and perceived as within the domain of health providers) than the recording of mental disorders as spelled out in Section 5 of the *ICD*.*

There is a range of possible explanations for limited primary care recording of psychosocial problems. Some are associated with inadequacies in existing classification systems, while others are related more to characteristics of practice. Problems with current systems may include the following: (1) a lack of consistent, clear, and comprehensible psychiatric terminology; (2) the absence of major categories seen frequently in practice; (3) the cumbersome nature of systems with highly specific diagnoses, designed primarily for use by mental health specialists; (4) an emphasis on mental illness instead of a focus on psychological symptoms and social problems, which would be more consistent with the health promotion orientation of PCPs; (5) practitioner awareness of the limited agreement among mental health specialists regarding an adequate child psychiatric classification system.

Other factors associated with low recording of psychosocial problems are relatively independent of the classification systems. One may be related to the role perceptions of the pediatric or family PCP who maintains a biological orientation in contrast to a biopsychosocial one. Such perceptions may derive from training that has not prepared the practitioner to elicit, assess, and manage the psychological, emotional, and developmental problems of children. Both role perceptions and the mental knowledge and skills of PCPs may be in the process of changing given the recent impetus for increased training in the behavioral sciences and mental health (5,17,18). Personality characteristics (e.g., "interest and concern") and conservatism are also known to influence the mental health role and skills of practitioners (16). Another factor that affects provider recording relates to potential negative social consequences associated with labeling children (17–24), unless such labels have clear implications for provision of services by one of the helping professions.

ICHPPC is a simplified version of *ICD,* with fewer diagnostic categories that are compatible with practice, and it also emphasizes social problems.

The lack of adequate reimbursement for mental health services may also contribute to underrecording (15).

Resolution of the classification-related issues for PCPs could contribute to changes in the preceding practioner-related issues. The development of an appropriate and acceptable classification system could provide an impetus for pursuing directions associated with improving the clinical management of psychosocial disorders in primary care. A first step involves obtaining further understanding of the magnitude of psychosocial disorders in primary care with respect to the overall level of disorders and the distribution of specific types of problems. Primary care prevalence data could be contrasted and composed with service delivery data on the detection, diagnosis, management, and referral of children with such problems by PCPs. The bases for gaps between the presence of psychosocial problems in children and clinical intervention by PCPs, as well as the outcome of such mental health services, could be assessed. Findings from such research could have long-range implications for training PCPs and for differentiating the mental health role of PCPs from the role of mental health specialists. Information on the level and type of mental health services provided by health and mental health practitioners could be used for estimating personnel needs for each type of practitioner and for identifying organizational relationships for the provision of coordinated health and mental health services.

GENERAL ISSUES RELATED TO CLASSIFYING CHILDREN

Initial steps toward revising existing psychosocial classifications for children or proposing alternate approaches include delineation of the scope of clinical problems that will be considered and identification of child-specific needs in such a system. With respect to the first task, addressing the scope of problems that will be viewed as psychosocial problems, there are several levels that might be considered. Factors that influence the development, adjustment, and general health of a child range from the problems of a society to those inherent in individuals. Although interaction occurs between children, their immediate social world, and their community, for the purpose of clinical application it might be possible to delineate three levels: (1) those stemming from the environment at large as "risk factors" (e.g., consequences of war, poverty, pollution, overpopulation); (2) problems emanating from children's interaction with the immediate environment as "social problems" (e.g., family disruption, child abuse); and (3) problems manifested in the behavior, cognition, and feelings of children as "mental disorders and psychological symptoms." Classification for the purpose of clinical management is likely to emphasize the second and third levels, which are the focus of the remainder of this chapter. While the first level provides important data for assessing the overall health of a child from a public health perspective, the presence of "risk factors" does not describe individual functioning per se.

Child-specific considerations—those that differentiate children from adults—include the critical roles of development and the dependent status of children. Since behavior or a cluster of behaviors may be seen as abnormal at one developmental stage and normal at another, the relationship between development and disorder must be explored before designating and defining problems. As key writers have emphasized, the effects of rapid growth where symptoms or syndromes are subject to change must be considered (22–25). Limited stability has been reported for most childhood disorders, with the exceptions of antisocial behavior (26), mental retardation, and childhood schizophrenia. Limited knowledge about the prognosis and course of childhood disorders requires a more tentative approach to classification than is appropriate for adult disorders; this caution is necessary to avoid labeling children as having expected long-term conditions that may in fact be developmental in nature.

The dependent status of children requires that they be viewed in the context of relationships with the key adults providing their care. At a minimum, information about home and school are necessary to understand the nature of the input which a child receives from his or her environment. A classification system for children's problems must also take into account the need for including parents or other important adults in the assessment process and recognition that such information is derived from sources other than the children. For older children, understanding of peer group influences and sociocultural milieu are necessary to assess levels of psychosocial functioning. The goal of a classification system for a child's social problems is to describe the child's interaction with these elements in his or her environment, not the environmental factors themselves.

In summary, children must be seen as being molded by the environment while developing internally both psychologically and biologically. These factors contribute to the complexity of assessing and classifying children and therefore must influence the formulation of a classification system. Additional problems of limited empirical evidence on the prevalence, etiology, prognosis, and effectiveness of treatment of psychological and social problems in children, as well as health provider needs for a concise and practical system that will be applicable to a busy practice situation, place further constraints on the current efforts to design a classification system.

ASSESSMENT OF EXISTING PSYCHOSOCIAL CLASSIFICATIONS FOR CHILDREN

In constructing a general classification for psychosocial problems, three types of problem categories should be considered. These include a classification of mental disorders, a classification of psychological symptoms, and a classification of social problems that are related to health status and functioning. How these three components can best be structured in a psychosocial classification system has not yet been determined, but it is important for all three portions of the final system to make adequate provision for the special features for children. Since all three of these problem types interrelate, they are discussed here to demonstrate how they can be developed appropriately for children. Also, the lack of agreement among child mental health specialists on a single classification for childhood mental disorders means that this problem must be considered explicitly, since classifying mental disorders of children is a more complicated matter than it is with adults. For the classification of mental disorders, a review is made of the existing systems for children in terms of their suitability for primary care, and a new proposal by Williams and Spitzer (see Chapter 13 of this volume) is presented. For the classification of psychological symptoms and social problems, the system presented by Regier and colleagues (given in Chapter 11 of the present volume and based on an NIMH planning meeting for the WHO conference in Bellagio, Italy, in November 1979,) will be reviewed, along with slight modifications that have been made to increase applicability to children.

Mental Disorders

The five major current classification systems for childhood mental disorders have been developed by different groups for different reasons, and none has achieved uniform acceptability. Two of these have been proposed as state-of-the-art systems for use by child mental health specialists particularly; two others have been adopted by a sanctioning organization as an official disease-reporting system for both specialty and nonspecialty clinicians; and one was designed specifically for use in primary care settings. Each of these can be examined in terms of its approach to four basic problems of classifying childhood mental disorders:

1. Logical structure of the classification, such as the degree of precision in differentiating disorders and the relative tendency to be primarily descriptive (based on reporting observable clinical phenomena without much abstraction or conceptualization of a disorder) or primarily conceptual (based on an abstract formulation of an illness, incorporating beliefs about etiology, course, treatment, etc.) (27,28).
2. The degree to which it depends on general classification systems developed for adult disorders, including use of similar terminology and the degree of integration or segregation of terms specifically applicable to children.
3. The extent to which it allows consideration of special problems of

childhood, such as developmental changes and healthy reactions to a difficult situation.

4. The primary intended users of the system, such as child mental health specialists or general PCPs.

The five major systems are reviewed with respect to the preceding characteristics, and an outline of the points discussed is presented in Table 12.1.

Group for the Advancement of Psychiatry (GAP) (29)

The GAP system (1966) provides a comprehensive outline of childhood disorders:

1. The categories are precise, specific, and primarily conceptual rather than descriptive, as they are based on a psychodynamic model of etiology and mechanism.

2. The system stands independent of any more general classification schemes for adults. It uses terminology typically applied to adults, such as *neurosis* and *personality disorder*, but individual disorders in these categories are defined in accordance with their presentation in children.

3. Throughout the system, reference is made to the role of development and change in childhood, and both specific developmental disturbances and healthy responses/adjustment reactions can be reported.

4. The system is intended primarily for child mental health specialists.

Multiaxial Classification (MAC) (30,31)

A WHO seminar proposed (1969, 1975) a triaxial, now multiaxial, system for children:

1. The clinical syndromes reported on Axis I are primarily descriptive, but in important instances are not subdivided beyond broad topic headings (for example, *neurosis*).

2. The system was published without specific linkage to any more general classification system, but it does include terms like *neurosis* and *personality disorder* without much elaboration of their suitability or applicability to children.

3. Some consideration is given to the changing nature of childhood disorders, but the general role of development is not directly addressed. Provision is made for specific developmental disorders and for normal variation-adaptation reactions.

4. The system is intended, after further development, to be used by child mental health specialists.

Table 12.1. Comparison of Classification Systems for Childhood Problems

	GAP	HAC	ICD-9	DSM-III	ICHPPC-2
Logical structure	Conceptual; specific	Descriptive; variable specificity	Descriptive; specific	Descriptive; very specific	Descriptive; very broad
Etiology related to syndromes	Yes (psychodynamic)	No	No	No	No
Relation to general (adult) system	Separate (parallel); similar terms	Separate (parallel); similar terms	Separate but linked; different terms	Separate; different terms	Fully integrated; similar terms
Developmental phases considered in system	Yes	Moderately important	Not important	Moderately important	No
Provision for normal variants	Yes	Yes	Limited	Limited	No
Social problems considered	No	Yes (Axis IV)	Yes (supplementary codes)	Yes (Axis IV and V codes)	Yes (supplemental codes)
Multiple diagnoses allowed	Yes	No	Yes	Yes	Yes
Information reported	1. Clinical disorders 2. Specific symptoms 3. Duration Severity Developmental period	I. Clinical syndrome II. Intellectual level III. Biological influences IV. Psychosocial influences	Clinical disorder (and supplementary codes for social problems)	I. Syndromes II. Developmental disturbance III. Physical disorders IV. Psychosocial stressors V. Level of functioning	1. Clinical syndrome 2. Supplementary codes for social problems

International Classification of Diseases,
Ninth Revision (ICD-9) *(32)*

The *ICD*-9 system (1979) has the following elements:

1. It provides very specific, primarily descriptive categories for childhood disorders.
2. These categories are integrated throughout Chapter 5, with other categories applicable to all age groups; a partial attempt has been made to provide separate categories for children to allow coding of problems that do not fit in a category traditionally appropriate to adults (e.g., *disturbance of emotions specific to childhood and adolescence* vs. *neurosis*).
3. No general statement about the role of development appears, but specific developmental disturbances and acute stress reactions/adaptation reactions can be coded.
4. The *ICD*-9 is intended for all health personnel.

Diagnostic and Statistical Manual of Mental Disorders,
Third Edition (DSM-*III*) *(33,34)*

The American Psychiatric Association's *DSM*-III is a multiaxial system:

1. Its categories on Axis I are compatible with *ICD*-9, but are even more specific than *ICD*-9. Diagnoses are primarily descriptive, although each one is accompanied by a list of diagnostic criteria and by current beliefs and knowledge about associated features, prevalence, etiology, and so forth.
2. Specific categories for children are listed together in a separate grouping, and terms used commonly for adults are generally avoided (for example, personality disorders on Axis II for adults are not applicable to children).
3. The issue of developmental change is not addressed separately, but developmental disturbances can be coded either in selected Axis I categories or on Axis II. Acute reactions to stress can be coded only in terms of a specific syndrome.
4. Mental health specialists in the United States began using this system after January 1980.

International Classification of Health Problems
in Primary Care, *Second Edition* (ICHPPC-2) *(35)*

A compact version of *ICD*-9, *ICHPPC*-2 (1979) has been developed for primary care settings:

1.   Categories in *ICD*-9 have been condensed into global categories for *ICHPPC*-2 or placed into a single large residual, so little specificity is possible in classifying childhood disorder.

2. With this simplification has come much greater overlap with categories for adult disorders than occurs in *ICD*-9.

3. Developmental change receives little consideration, and only developmental disturbances relating to learning and school functioning can be coded in a separate category, apart from the global residual.

4. The intended users are primary care clinicians.

The difficulty in using *ICHPPC*-2 to record children's disorders can be seen from Table 12.2, which presents the *ICHPPC*-2 equivalents of diagnoses made by pediatricians who used the MAC Axis I system, and by family practitioners who used the Royal College of General Practitioners system, in two different studies (14,36). The usefulness of categories for anxiety and depression can be seen from the family practitioners' study, but in both cases translating reported diagnoses from the study data into *ICHPPC*-2 categories resulted in creating very large final residual categories (29.4% and 55.5%).

A Proposed Classification

With the same intent as evidenced in *ICHPPC*-2, Williams and Spitzer have demonstrated that it is possible to construct a collapsible hierarchical classification system of mental disorders that is compatible with *ICD*-9 and *DSM*-III and suitable for use in primary care practices. The system presented in Table 12.3 represents an elaboration of the "Childhood" component of the general classification system proposed by Williams and Spitzer (see Chapter 13). It satisfies the needs for a classification system identified with the four principles that have been used as a basis for examining the existing classification systems:

1. The proposed classification is based on descriptive categories, using terminology developed for *ICD*-9.

2. The system can be integrated into a general adult classification scheme, as shown by Williams and Spitzer, or it can be used separately—for example, by pediatricians or family practitioners. It avoids use of terms such as *neurosis* and *personality disorders* for children; other adult categories that can reasonably be applied to children or adolescents are noted specifically.

3. A separate statement emphasizes the importance of considering the child's developmental status in making a diagnosis; the proposal contains categories for specific developmental delays; and it contains categories for normal or transiently pathological reactions to environmental stress.

4. Global categories can be coded (for example, *disorders of emotion specific to childhood and adolescence*), or greater specificity can be obtained when needed by clinicians (for example, *disorder of emotion with shyness*). This system is not dependent on precise distinctions or unusual terminology,

Table 12.2. Translation of Data for Equivalent Diagnoses into *ICHPPC*-2

ICHPPC-2 Diagnostic Category	Rochester (Pediatricians)[a] (Patients)	Virginia (Family Practitioners)[b] (Problems)
298 Other and unspecified psychoses	2 (1.1%)	57 (4.6%)
3000 Anxiety disorder or state		152 (12.3%)
3001 Hysterical and hypochondriacal disorders		0
3004 Depressive disorder		52 (4.20%)
3009 Other neuroses	7 (3.7%)	39 (3.2%)
315 Specific learning disorder and delay in development for school	32 (17.1%)	0
3074 Insomnia and other sleep disorders		23 (1.9%)
3078 Tension headache; psychogenic backache; other pain of psychic origin		54 (4.4%)
308 Transient situational reaction; acute stress reaction; adjustment reaction	44 (23.5%)	27 (2.2%)
312 Behavior disorder; disturbance of emotions; hyperkinetic disorder	37 (19.8%)	30 (2.4%)
3027 Psychogenic disturbance of sexual functions		1 (0.1%)
3031 Chronic abuse of alcohol		0
3050 Acute alcohol use; drunk; excessive alcohol use not otherwise specified (NOS)		11 (0.9%)
3051 Tobacco abuse		0
3048 Other drug abuse		2 (0.2%)
301 Personality and character disorder		23 (1.9%)
317 Mental retardation	10 (5.3%)	80 (6.5%)
316 Other disorders	55[c](29.4%)	687[d](55.5%)
Total	187	1238

Note. The Rochester pediatrician study used the MAC, and the Virginia family practitioner study was based on the Royal College of General Practitioners (RCGP) system.

[a]From reference 14 (Table V, p. 895).

[b]From reference 36 (pp. 51–53).

[c]Includes 23 (12.3%) unknown and 9 (4.8%) other.

[d]Includes 282 (22.8%) from RCGP Residuals and 36 (2.9%) as *other chronic adult situational reaction.*

Table 12.3.   Proposed Classification of Mental Disorders of Childhood and Adolescence

---

Disorders of childhood and adolescence should be diagnosed with consideration of the developmental status of the patient. For example, enuresis and encopresis will normally not be diagnosed in children under four years of age.

Reactions to environmental stress (309.9)
   Healthy response—no disorder (V71.0)
   Adjustment reaction—no pre-existing disorder (308,309)

Mental retardation (319)
   Mild—2+ SD below mean (317)
   Moderate—3+ SD below mean (318.0)
   Severe—4+ SD below mean (318.1)
   Profound—5+ SD below mean (318.2)

Disorders of emotion specific to childhood and adolescence (313.9)
   With anxiety (313.0)
   With sadness (313.1)
   With shyness or withdrawal (313.2)

Disorders of conduct (312.9)
   Unsocialized or aggressive disorder of conduct (312.0)
   Socialized, group-based disorder of conduct (312.1)

Hyperkinetic syndrome (314.9)

Disorders with predominantly physical manifestations (307.9)
   Anorexia nervosa (307.1)
   Other eating disorders (307.5)
   Stuttering (307.0)
   Tics (307.2)
   Sleep disorders (307.4)
   Enuresis (307.6)
   Encopresis (307.7)
   Psychiatric conditions associated with physical disorders (306,316)

Specific developmental delays (315.9)
   Reading delay (315.0)
   Arithmetic delay (315.1)
   Other learning disorder (315.2)
   Speech or language delay (315.3)
   Motor coordination delay (315.4)

Childhood psychosis (299.9)
   Infantile autism (299.0)
   Disintegrative psychosis (299.1)

Diagnoses of adulthood occasionally applicable to children or adolescents
   Schizophrenic psychoses (295)
   Affective psychoses (296)
   Drug abuse and dependence (304,305)

Table 12.3.   (*continued*)

Alcohol use and abuse (303,305.0)
Sexual deviations (302)

Notes. If the system is to be used separately—for example, by pediatricians—from a general classification system for all adult disorders, then the categories specified as occasionally applicable to children and adolescents should be included as above. If the system is to be used as one component of a general system, then some categories included (e.g., reactions to environmental stress) may also be designated as suitable for adults. Numbers in parentheses are the corresponding codes in *ICD*-9.

and it is relatively compact. For these reasons, it is expected that it could be used by either family practitioners or by pediatricians.

Psychological Symptoms

Integrating special considerations for children into a general classification of psychological symptoms is less complex than in the case of mental disorders. Since symptoms are essentially descriptive and issues of duration, stability, severity, or causality do not necessarily arise, many symptom categories (for example, *feeling depressed*) can be applied to both adults and children with little confusion.

The proposed classification of psychological symptoms presented by Regier et al. (see Chapter 11) is based on an adaptation of the *Reason for Visit Classification* (*RVC*) of psychological symptoms (37). In Table 12.4, an elaboration of this proposed classification demonstrates the minor additions that have been made to produce a general symptom list applicable to children. The following four points refer to the list presented in Table 11.4 and illustrate how special characteristics of childhood can be integrated into a general symptom list with little difficulty.

First, the role of developmental change and regression still produces a need for categorizing both developmental delays and specific disturbances that are inappropriate to a given age or developmental period. A specific category for this problem area has been included in this list.

Second, common symptom classes might or might not be considered necessary for adults, but seem essential for children. For example, adding a category for disturbances in bodily functions, or for psychophysiological symptoms, would provide coverage of common functional bodily complaints of children. A category such as the one for *psychophysiological problems* could also be compatible with corresponding adult complaints.

Third, some symptomatic behaviors are especially relevant to children but

Table 12.4. Proposed Classification of Psychological Symptoms

---

   I. Anxiety or nervousness
      Includes: apprehension
               bad nerves
               panicky feeling
               tension
               upset
               worried
               fears
  II. Feeling depressed
      Includes: crying excessively
               dejected
               feeling low
               hopelessness
               sadness
               unhappy
               low self-esteem
               guilt
 III. Feelings of anger or irritability
      Includes: bitterness
               temper tantrums
 IV. Restlessness
      Includes: hyperactivity
               overactivity
  V. Trouble with concentration or memory
      Includes: forgetfulness
               confusion
               distractibility
 VI. Problems with identity
      Includes: no confidence
               loss of identity
               identity crisis
 VII. Social isolation or withdrawal
      Includes: avoiding people
               excessive shyness
VIII. Hostile or antisocial behavior
      Includes: violence
               criminality
               cruelty to animals
               fire setting
               stealing
 IX. Disturbances of sleep
      Includes: trouble sleeping
               sleeping too much
               nightmares

Table 12.4.   *(continued)*

   X. Substance-related problems
     Includes: alcohol problems
           tobacco problems
           other drug problems

  XI. Delusions, hallucinations, or incoherence
     Includes: seeing things
           hearing things
           overly suspicious

  XII. Sexual problems
     Includes: excessive concerns about masturbation
           concern with sexual performance (e.g., potency)
           concern with size and shape of sexual organs

 XIII. Eating problems
     Includes: loss of appetite
           excessive appetite
           concern with weight

 XIV. Age-specific developmental problems
     Includes: bed-wetting
           encopresis
           thumb-sucking
           delay in development (e.g., acquisition of language)
           learning failure

  XV. Psychophysiological problems
     Includes: skin problems
           respiratory problems
           GI problems

 XVI. Other behavior problems
     Includes: A. Dominant behavior—bullying, fighting
           B. Dependent behavior—clinging, whining, and demanding
           C. Oppositional behavior—provocative, negativistic

 XVII. Learning problems
     Includes: reading problem
           arithmetic problem

XVIII. Other symptoms or problems relating to mental disorders
     Includes: "can't cope"
           "going crazy"
           "losing my mind"
           rituals
           stuttering

---

do not apply to adults. Besides categories for *social isolation* and *hostile or antisocial behavior,* an additional list to cover other recognizable patterns of behavior in children has also been included. Whether these are listed as separate categories will depend on the overall structure of the symptom classification system, but the categories under *other behavior problems* in Table 12.4 represent a collapsible category, adapted from the GAP symptom list (29).

Another example of a category primarily relevant to children is *learning problems.* If a clinician is not certain that a formal mental disorder can be diagnosed (for example, without full access to school records or psychometric testing), he or she can report the condition as a symptom. This example demonstrates the interrelationship between mental disorder diagnoses and psychological symptoms within the classification system. It is especially important to allow reporting of these problems as symptoms if they do not satisfy the diagnostic criteria or if there is insufficient information (e.g., absence of psychosometric testing) to make a formal diagnosis of a learning disorder.

Fourth, the general categories and lists of examples can be expanded to include additional examples that are suitable to children. For example, under *hostile or antisocial behavior,* such specific acts as *fire setting* and *stealing* have been added.

This discussion assumes that clinicians will code categories (*feeling depressed*) rather than specific items (*crying excessively*). In some practice settings, or possibly after the results of the field testing have been assessed, it might be desirable to allow coding of specific symptoms instead of the global categories. In that case, more precise lists of childhood symptoms would need to be used. Two sources provide comprehensive lists of individual signs and symptoms that can guide construction of a more complete list of specific symptoms. First, the GAP classification system (29) includes a list of psychological symptoms to supplement the GAP classification of mental disorders. Second, symptom checklists that provide thorough lists of observable problem behaviors have been devised by several investigators for use by parents and teachers. These lists have recently been reviewed by Achenbach and Edelbrock (25), who have found that the lists are easily used by non-mental health raters and that the results are similar for similar populations of children studied by different investigators using slightly different instruments.

Social Problems

The classification of social problems associated with three of the systems reviewed under "Mental Disorders" above—the GAP, MAC, and *DSM*-III systems—are important on their own but, because of their different aims, are not relevant to the task to be considered here. The Supplementary Classifications in *ICD*-9 and *ICHPPC*-2 are mutually compatible and are more relevant to this task.

Two considerations seem important in constructing a social problem classification for children. First, at the basic level, categories appropriate to a child's functioning and health status need to be included. Second, the problem statement should be presented in a way to bring attention to the child's position. This point is especially important because the parent, school official, or other adult is often the informant, and problems between parent and child or teacher and child are often defined only in terms of the adult's perception. For example, a parent might complain to a clinician about a child's "unruly behavior." With some investigation of the complaint, the clinician might uncover evidence of the parent's harsh, inflexible, and controlling behavior toward the child, with only mild transgressions of the parent's unreasonable expectations by the child being seen by the parent as a serious disciplinary problem. In such a case, the clinician would likely redefine the problem as one of "excessive parental control" rather than simply recording the initial complaint of "unruly behavior." To some extent, a classification system might encourage a balanced, thorough clinical assessment by providing in its coding scheme appropriate examples of both perspectives on a problematic situation. In this instance, both "unruly behavior" and "excessive parental control" would be listed as examples under the global heading of *parent-child problem*. The clinician's own judgment, based on the clinical assessment, would determine the proper intervention. Although the problem coded would be expressed in general terms, such as *parent-child problem,* the list of illustrative examples with appropriate alternatives included would support a balanced assessment of the presenting problem. This consideration also serves as a reminder that the ultimate aim of such a classification system is to produce improvements in clinical practice through the proper documentation of clinical problems.

Giving so much attention to the child's interaction with the environment is even more important than it is with adults, for two reasons. First, the child's major developmental tasks include development of increasing skill in coping with the environment. Second, in view of a child's relatively immature and limited capacity for coping with the environment, some greater level of environmental intervention by a clinician might be indicated, in the role of a child advocate, than would be appropriate with adults.

In general, the classification system of social problems presented in Chapter 11 seems appropriate for children. It has been presented in Table 12.5 with slight modifications under two categories, *parent-child problem* and *educational problems,* to show how the specific illustrative examples cited can cover a broad range of alternatives in a given problem area. Further examples of specific problems can be developed either from the classification of psy-

Table 12.5.   Proposed Classification of Social Problems

   I. Housing problems
      Includes: overcrowding
              lack of housing
              inadequate housing

  II. Change in residence
      Includes: immigration
              moving out of parental home

 III. Financial problems
      Includes: cannot pay bills or debts

 IV. Conjugal (marital or nonmarital) problems
      Includes: marital discord
              spouse abuse
              sexual problems

  V. Parent-child problems
      Includes: child abuse
              unruly behavior
              excessive parental control
              deficient parental control
              child deprived of parental attention
              running away

 VI. Family disruption
      Includes: divorce
              separation
              death
              family member leaves home

 VII. Other problems of family relationships
      Includes: problems with relatives other than parents or children
              problems with siblings

VIII. Problems of caring for sick person (includes family members and friends)
      Includes: aged parent

 IX. Other nonfamily interpersonal problems
      Includes: problems with peers, neighbors
              social isolation
              death of friend

  X. Phase-of-life problems
      Includes: problems adjusting to developmental stage, such as adolescence
              or retirement

 XI. Educational problems
      Includes: school failure
              school refusal
              absenteeism (truancy)
              inadequate educational opportunities

Table 12.5. (*continued*)

                    cheating
                    quarrels with teachers
XII. Occupational problems (includes problems as housewife)
     Includes: problems with coworkers
                    role dissatisfaction
                    unemployment
                    difficulties at work or in adjusting to work situation
XIII. Legal problems
     Includes: imprisonment
                    prosecution
                    litigation
                    legal investigations
XIV. Other social problems
     Includes: unwanted pregnancy
                    persecution or discrimination (on the basis of politics, religion,
                    sex, or race)
                    excommunication
                    hexing

chosocial functioning in children created by Prugh (22) or from Axis IV of the MAC system (31).

CONCLUDING COMMENTS

The major emphasis of this chapter has been on the special attention that must be given to childhood disorders in the formulation of a classification system to be used in primary care settings. Two characteristics of childhood —rapid development and growth, and children's dependent and reactive relationship with their environment—indicate that children cannot simply be classified using diagnostic terms developed for adults. However, constructing an appropriate system for children is not a simple matter. The disagreement among child mental health specialists about the best approach to classifying mental disorders for their own use illustrates the difficulty in applying general principles about children to a classification system; this disagreement reflects the relative lack of research into childhood problems and the resulting lack of an adequate conceptual framework for understanding and treating them.

Although no single classification system currently meets the needs of primary care clinicians for reporting mental disorders, psychological symptoms, and social problems of children, modifications of existing proposals might be field-tested as a first stage in the development of an acceptable system. Specific recommendations to be field-tested are briefly reviewed here.

Mental Disorders

In the classification of mental disorders of childhood, it seems clear that the categories should be primarily descriptive with a focus on observable affects, behaviors, and clinical conditions, with minimal abstraction from basic clinical phenomena (for example, depression). To provide useful information and to meet the needs of the users, the classification system of mental disorders should provide specific categories for the major problems that are most commonly seen so that no large residuals are produced; for this reason, it seems clear that the "Mental Disorder" component of *ICHPPC*-2 is inadequate for children (see Table 12.2).

The need to maintain compatibility with the system of classifying mental disorders of adults seems clear. However, the review in this chapter indicates that special considerations for children cannot be adequately handled simply by using existing classification systems designed primarily for adults. As a result, it appears useful to follow the practice of *DSM*-III and to publish diagnoses intended specifically for children together in their own category, and not to integrate them into the single list for all disorders as has been done in *ICD*-9. This separate listing for children could include a general statement about the need to consider the appropriateness of a problem in terms of a child's developmental period (e.g., to diagnose enuresis as a problem only when it is age-inappropriate) and could indicate the need to consider special developmental disturbances (such as delayed speech). This separate listing of disorders for children could also include a specially defined category for normal or mildly pathological reactions to difficult external situations.

Such a classification system of mental disorders in childhood will probably be consistent with the practice of the clinicians who will use it. Primary care clinicians increasingly use problem-based medical records. In some studies in the United Kingdom, it has been shown that only half of the problems seen in primary care practice reach a level of understanding that permits them to be changed into a formal diagnosis of a disease (38,39). The common occurrence of problems that cannot be understood at a level sufficient to justify a diagnosis, and the typical practice of seeing patients in a series of multiple brief visits instead of in a single comprehensive evaluation, encourage the use of a descriptive, problem-based classification system. Such a system would emphasize convenience in use, clear terminology, and provision for the most frequent problems, so that residual categories with miscellaneous labels are not often used. It is anticipated that the childhood component of the classification proposed by Williams and Spitzer (see Chapter 13), as modified in

Table 12.3, will meet the needs of the first round of field testing of an overall primary care classification system.

Psychological Symptoms

The list of psychological symptoms to accompany the list of diagnoses of mental disorders should also be carefully formulated to provide accurate reporting of children's signs and symptoms of an emotional or behavioral nature. This list of psychological symptoms would be compatible with the classification system for mental disorders described above. Practitioners could report the occurrence of psychological problems whenever they were not able, on the basis of clinical judgment, to determine the presence of a diagnosable mental disorder. Although many symptom categories can apply equally to children and adults, some special features have been included to make the list applicable to children, as presented in Table 12.4.

Social Problems

Since many of the child's most important developmental tasks depend on attaining skills in relating to parents, other family members, other adults, and peers, as well as to the larger society, the need for an effective classification of social problems is also clear. The dependent status of children and their reactive relationship to the environment make their interactions with the environment an important consideration in reporting areas of psychological distress and dysfunctioning. One hazard that should be avoided in focusing on social problems, however, is the temptation to view all of a child's problems exclusively from the perspective of the family or the environment. Although a family focus during the assessment and management of the problem is crucial, it is important not to have such a broad focus as to lose sight of the individual child. The clinician needs to make a balanced assessment by considering problems of the child as well as those of the broader family or environmental context in which the child functions. This rule is especially important, since information the clinician gathers will often be provided by adults, not by the child. If the classification system of social problems can increase the capacity of the primary care clinician to identify concerns from the child's viewpoint, it will improve the chances that the clinician can act as an effective child advocate. To further this goal, the social problem list should include major areas of the child's functioning, such as dealing with school, parents, peers, heterosexual relationships, and so on. Important categories of social problems, such as *parent-child problems,* should also refer to problems from the child's standpoint and not simply reflect complaints that the parent has about the child. The list of social problems, modified slightly to show these concerns, is presented in Table 12.5.

Field Testing

Although it is difficult to generalize from the existing data on the use of classification systems for children, it seems likely that a well-constructed and convenient classification system for psychological and social problems of children will increase the capacity and willingness of primary care clinicians to report these problems. During the field testing of the classification system, special consideration should be given to the effects of having a segregated category for children within the mental disorder system; to the effect of different practice modes of different providers (such as pediatricians vs. family and general practitioners); to cultural differences in the nature of the sociocultural functioning expected of children; and to the mechanics of reporting problems (such as the questions of routine reporting vs. special survey or queries to the provider, and a listing of a primary diagnosis vs. multiple diagnoses and problems). Field testing would also offer an opportunity to explore relationships among mental disorders, psychological symptoms, and social problems in different settings. Another important aspect of the field testing in general—one that is especially important, considering the relatively less developed state of classification for children's psychological and social problems—is the opportunity to revise and improve the classification system after field testing has been completed. Once an effective classification system for psychological and social problems has been developed, further research into the nature and extent of existing problems and the role of primary care clinicians in dealing with them can begin.

In summary, such a classification system for psychological and social problems of childhood would appear to meet the needs of primary care users. It would be primarily descriptive, and would be expressed using definable terms to report easily observable behavior or conditions. By specifying the categories applicable to children, the system would also be easy to use in primary care settings. It would maintain the important goal of emphasizing problems from the child's point of view instead of making them appear secondary to adult concerns of problems, and it would help define the clinician's role as an effective child advocate.

REFERENCES

1. World Health Organization, "The Alma Ata Conference on Primary Health Care," *WHO Chronicle* 32(1978):407–58.

2. World Health Organization, "Medium-Term Programme for Mental Health 1975–1982," in *Report of the General Director* (Geneva: World Health Organization, 1978), p. 2.

3. *The President's Commission on Mental Health* (Washington, D.C.: Government Printing Office, 1978).

4. Council on Pediatric Practice, *Standards of Child Health Care* (Evanston, Ill.: American Academy of Pediatrics, 1972).

5. Task Force on Pediatric Education, *The Future of Pediatric Education* (Evanston, Ill.: American Academy of Pediatrics, 1978).

6. R. J. Haggerty, K. J. Roghmann, and I. B. Pless, *Child Health and the Community* (New York: Wiley, 1975).

7. The Joint Commission on Mental Health of Children, *The Mental Health of Children: Services, Research, and Manpower* (New York: Harper & Row, 1973).

8. B. M. Rosen, "An Overview of the Mental Health Delivery System in the United States and Services to Children," in *Basic Handbook of Child Psychiatry,* vol. 4, ed. J. D. Noshpitz (New York: Basic Books, 1979).

9. L. N. Robbins, "Mental Disorders in Children," in *The President's Commission on Mental Health* (Washington, D.C.: Government Printing Office, 1978).

10. M. Rutter, J. Tizard, and K. Whitmore, *Education, Health, and Behavior* (London: Longmans, 1970).

11. T. M. Ezzati, *Ambulatory Care Utilization Patterns of Children and Young Adults,* Vital and Health Statistics, Series 13, Data from the National Health Survey no. 39, DHEW Publication no. (PHS) 78-1790 (Hyattsville, Md.: U.S. Department of Health, Education and Welfare, 1978).

12. I. D. Goldberg, D. A. Regier, and B. J. Burns, eds., *Use of Health and Mental Health Outpatient Services in Four Organized Health Care Settings,* National Institute of Mental Health, Series DN no. 1, DHHS Publication No. (ADM) 80-859 (Washington, D.C.: Government Printing Office, 1980).

13. V. Bailey, P. Graham, and D. Boniface, "How Much Child Psychiatry Does a General Practitioner Do?" *Journal of the Royal College of General Practitioners* 28(1978):621–26.

14. I. D. Goldberg et al., "The Role of the Pediatrician in the Delivery of Mental Health Services to Children," *Pediatrics* 63(1979):898–909.

15. B. Starfield et al., "Psychosocial and Psychosomatic Diagnoses in Primary Care of Children," *Pediatrics* 66(2)(1980):159–67.

16. J. N. Marks, D. P. Goldberg, and V. F. Hillier, "Determinants of the Ability of General Practitioners to Detect Psychiatric Illness," *Psychological Medicine* 9(1979):337–53.

17. D. Goldberg, "Detection and Assessment of Emotional Disorders in a Primary Care Setting," *International Journal of Mental Health* 8(1979):30–48.

18. B. J. Burns and W. Cromer, "The Evolving Role of the Psychologist in Primary Health Care Practitioner Training for Mental Health Services," *Journal of Clinical Psychology* 7(1978):8–12.

19. L. Phillips, F. G. Draguns and D. P. Bartlett, "Classification of Behavior Disorders," in *Issues in the Classification of Children,* ed. N. Hobbs (San Francisco: Jossey-Bass, 1975).

20. T. S. Szasz, "Psychiatric Classification as a Strategy of Social Constraint," in *Ideology and Insanity,* ed. T. S. Szasz (Garden City, N.Y.: Doubleday, 1969).

21. R. Rosenthal and L. Jacobson, *Pygmalion in the Classroom: Teachers' Expectations and Pupils' Intellectual Development* (New York: Holt, Rinehart & Winston, 1968).

22. D. G. Prugh, "Psychosocial Disorders in Childhood and Adolescence: Theoretical Considerations and an Attempt at Classification," Appendix A in *The Mental Health of Children: Services, Research, and Manpower,* by the Joint Commission on

Mental Health of Children (New York: Harper & Row, 1973).

23. M. Rutter, "Classification and Categorization in Child Psychiatry," *Journal of Child Psychology and Psychiatry* 6(1965):71–83.

24. R. L. Cromwell, R. K. Blashfield, and J. S. Strauss, "Criteria for Classification Systems," in *Issues in the Classification of Children,* ed. N. Hobbs (San Francisco: Jossey-Bass, 1975).

25. T. M. Achenbach and C. S. Edelbrock, "The Classification of Child Psychopathology: A Review and Analysis of Empirical Efforts," *Psychological Bulletin* 85(1978):1275–1301.

26. L. N. Robbins, "Follow-Up Studies of Behavior Disorders in Children," in *Psychopathological Disorders of Childhood,* ed. H. C. Quay and J. S. Werry (New York: Wiley, 1972).

27. R. K. Blashfield and J. G. Draguns, "Toward a Taxonomy of Psychopathology: The Purpose of Psychiatric Classification," *British Journal of Psychiatry* 129 (1976):574–83.

28. P. Williams, "Deciding How to Treat: The Relevance of Psychiatric Diagnosis," *Psychological Medicine* 9(1979):179–86.

29. Group for the Advancement of Psychiatry, *Psychopathological Disorders in Childhood: Theoretical Considerations and a Proposed Classification* (New York, Jason Aronson, 1966).

30. M. Rutter et al., "A Tri-Axial Classification of Mental Disorders in Childhood: An International Study," *Journal of Child Psychology and Psychiatry* 10(1969): 41–61.

31. M. Rutter, D. Shaffer and M. Shepherd, *A Multi-Axial Classification of Child Psychiatric Disorders* (Geneva: World Health Organization, 1975).

32. World Health Organization, *Manual of the International Statistical Classification of Diseases, Injuries, and Causes of Death,* 9th revision, vol. 1 (Geneva: World Health Organization, 1977).

33. American Psychiatric Association, *Diagnostic and Statistical Manual of Mental Disorders,* 3rd ed., draft (Washington, D.C.: American Psychiatric Association, 1978).

34. American Psychiatric Association, *Diagnostic and Statistical Manual of Mental Disorders,* 3rd ed., Micro-D, draft (Washington D.C.: American Psychiatric Association, 1979).

35. World Organization of National Colleges, Academies, and Academic Associations of General Practitioners/Family Physicians, *International Classification of Health Problems in Primary Care,* 2nd ed. (London: Oxford University Press, 1979).

36. D. W. Marsland, M. Wood and F. Mayo, "A Data Bank for Patient Care, Curriculum, and Research in Family Practice: 526,196 Patient Problems," *Journal of Family Practice* 3(1976):25–68.

37. D. Schneider, L. Appleton, and T. McLemore, *A Reason for Visit Classification for Ambulatory Care,* Vital and Health Statistics, Series 2, Data Evaluation and Methods Research no. 78, DHEW Publication no. (PHS) 79-1352 (Hyattsville, Md.: U.S. National Center for Health Statistics, 1979).

38. Editorial, "Behavioral Problems in General Practice," *Journal of the Royal College of General Practitioners* 29(1979):323–27.

39. D. C. Taylor, "The Components of Sickness: Diseases, Illnesses, and Predicaments," *Lancet* 2(1979):1008–10.

13

A Proposed Classification of Mental Disorders for Inclusion in a Multiaxial Classification of Health Problems

JANET B. W. WILLIAMS
ROBERT L. SPITZER

The essential feature of all multiaxial classification systems is the placement of different classes of information onto different axes such that the clinician is expected to assess each patient on each axis. The many multiaxial systems proposed differ in the number of axes and the kinds of information included.

In recent years there has been much interest in developing multiaxial classification systems for use in mental health assessment, largely for two major reasons. First, there is recognition that certain kinds of diagnostic information are frequently overlooked or are inconsistently noted. For example, in developing a multiaxial system for the evaluation of children, it was noted that learning disturbances were often overlooked when associated with more florid behavioral disturbances, such as conduct disorder. The milder symptomatology of the learning disability was overshadowed by the more disruptive behavior of the conduct disorder. For this reason, an axis for "Developmental Delays" was included separately (1).

Second, and perhaps more significantly, there is recognition of the importance of including certain classes of nondiagnostic information in a comprehensive assessment. For example, information about social functioning and social problems is crucial to the most effective planning of treatment or other interventions, such as referral to an appropriate social agency.

This chapter describes the *DSM*-III multiaxial system (2,3,4) and reports on experience with its use in a large field test. In addition, it describes how a simplified classification of mental disorders, adapted from both the *DSM*-III and the *International Classification of Diseases,* ninth edition (*ICD*-9) (5), could be incorporated into a triaxial classification system for a comprehensive assessment of health suitable for use in primary care.

THE DSM-III MULTIAXIAL SYSTEM

The *DSM*-III multiaxial system provides five axes:

- Axis I: "Clinical Syndromes" (e.g., *schizophrenia, major depression*)
  "Conditions Not Attributable to a Mental Disorder that are a
  Focus of Attention or Treatment" (e.g., *marital problem*)
- Axis II: "Specific Developmental Disorders" (e.g., *developmental reading disorder*)
  "Personality Disorders" (e.g., *schizoid personality disorder*)
- Axis III: "Physical Disorders and Conditions"
- Axis IV: "Severity of Psychosocial Stressors"
- Axis V: "Highest Level of Adaptive Functioning Past Year"

Axes I and II comprise all the mental disorders. Axis II is reserved for those disorders in children and adults that are most frequently overlooked when attention is directed toward the usually more florid Axis I disorder. For example, in an individual with alcoholism, the presence of a coexisting dependent personality disorder is likely to be overlooked. Axis I includes all the mental disorders, except for specific developmental disorders and personality disorders.

Axis III is for physical conditions that are potentially relevant to the management or treatment of the individual being assessed. The physical condition may be etiologically related to the Axis I disorder, as when a neurological disease causes a dementia. Or the physical condition may be an important consideration for the management of the individual—for example, diabetes in a child with conduct disorder.

Axes IV and V provide nondiagnostic information that may be valuable for treatment planning. Axis IV is for recording, on a 7-point scale, the severity of psychosocial stressors that are judged to have contributed to the initiation or exacerbation of the Axis I and II disorders (Table 13.1). This axis was chosen for inclusion in *DSM*-III to encourage the clinician to consider potentially modifiable stresses in the patient's environment to which attention should be directed. Originally, in the development of this axis, a rather complicated classification of 40 categories of psychosocial stressors was included in addition to the scale of severity, and clinicians were expected to categorize the relevant stressors for each individual being assessed. However, this complexity proved too unwieldy for clinical use; only the rating scale is included in the final version, with a simplified categorization of ten areas of potential stress being recommended for evaluation.

In making the rating, the clinician is instructed to take into account the total number of stressors, the extent to which each stressor is a desirable one, the extent to which each stressor is under the individual's control, and the

Table 13.1. *DSM*-III Axis IV: "Severity of Psychosocial Stressors"

Code	Term	Adult Examples	Child or Adolescent Examples
1	None	No apparent psychosocial stressor	No apparent psychosocial stressor
2	Minimal	Minor violation of the law; small bank loan	Vacation with family
3	Mild	Argument with neighbor; change in work hours	Change in schoolteacher; new school year
4	Moderate	New career; death of close friend; pregnancy	Chronic parental fighting; change to new school; illness of close relative; birth of sibling
5	Severe	Serious illness in self or family; major financial loss; marital separation; birth of child	Death of peer; divorce of parents; arrest; hospitalization; persistent and harsh parental discipline
6	Extreme	Death of close relative; divorce	Death of parent or sibling; repeated physical or sexual abuse
7	Catastrophic	Concentration camp experience; devastating natural disaster	Multiple family deaths
0	Unspecified	No information, or not applicable	No information, or not applicable

Source: Reference 2.

amount of change each stressor effects in the individual's life. The clinician should then rate the severity based on the amount of stress that an "average" individual in similar circumstances and with similar sociocultural values would experience, given the same stressor(s). In most cases, the stressors will have occurred within the past year; in some cases, the stressor will be the anticipation of a future event (e.g., retirement). Information on this axis is assumed to have prognostic significance, in that a full recovery is more likely from an episode of illness that has occurred in reaction to a severe stressor than from an episode occurring after only a mild stressor.

Axis V provides a 7-point scale for rating the highest level of adaptive functioning that an individual has been able to sustain for at least a few months during the year prior to the evaluation (Table 13.2). In making this judgment, the clinician should take into account the individual's level of social function-

Table 13.2. *DSM*-III Axis V: "Highest Level of Adaptive Functioning During Past Year"

Levels	Adult Examples	Child or Adolescent Examples
1 Superior		
Unusually effective functioning in social relationships, occupational functioning, and use of leisure time	Single parent living in deteriorating neighborhood, takes excellent care of children and home, has warm relationships with friends, and finds time for pursuit of hobby	A 12-year-old girl gets superior grades in school, is extremely popular among her peers, and excels in many sports; she does all of this with apparent ease and comfort
2 Very Good		
Better-than-average functioning in social relationships, occupational functioning, and use of leisure time	A 65-year-old retired widower does some volunteer work, often sees old friends, and pursues hobbies	An adolescent boy gets excellent grades, works part-time, has several close friends, and plays banjo in a jazz band; he admits to some distress in "keeping up with everything"
3 Good		
No more than slight impairment in either social or occupational functioning	A woman with many friends functions extremely well at a difficult job, but says "the strain is too much"	An 8-year-old boy does well in school, has several friends, but bullies younger children
4 Fair		
Moderate impairment in either social relationships or occupational functioning, *or* some impairment in both	A lawyer has trouble carrying through assignments; has several acquaintances, but hardly any close friends	A 10-year-old girl does poorly in school, but has adequate peer and family relationships
5 Poor		
Marked impairment in either social relationships	A man with one or two friends has trouble keep-	A 14-year-old boy almost fails in school and has

Table 13.2. *(continued)*

Levels	Adult Examples	Child or Adolescent Examples
or occupational function-ing, *or* moderate impair-ment in both	ing a job for more than a few weeks	trouble getting along with his peers
6 Very Poor		
Marked impairment in both social relationships and occupational func-tioning	A woman is unable to do any of her housework and has violent outbursts toward family and neigh-bors	A 6-year-old girl needs special help in all subjects and has virtually no peer relationships
7 Grossly Impaired		
Gross impairment in vir-tually all areas of func-tioning	An elderly man needs supervision to maintain minimal personal hygiene and is usually incoherent	A 4-year-old boy needs constant restraint to avoid hurting himself and is al-most totally lacking in skills
0 Unspecified		
	No information	No information

Source: Reference 2.

ing, occupational functioning, and (when there is no impairment in social or occupational functioning) use of leisure time. Social functioning, because of its greater prognostic significance, should be given greatest weight. Again, the information recorded on this axis has important prognostic significance and is thus an important consideration for treatment planning, in that an individual usually returns after an episode of illness to his or her level of premorbid func-tioning.

Experience with the <u>DSM</u>-III Multiaxial System

More than 500 clinicians throughout the United States took part in field test-ing *DSM*-III and its multiaxial system (6). Each clinician was asked to use the *DSM*-III in evaluating 40 of his or her patients (adults and children) over a two-year period. Despite the added task of making a multiaxial evaluation, 68% of the clinicians who responded to an anonymous questionnaire agreed that it was useful to divide the mental disorders into Axis I and Axis II conditions. A total of 81% agreed with the statement: "The *DSM*-III multiaxial system will be a useful addition to traditional psychiatric diagnosis." Although many of the clinicians questioned the approach taken for Axis IV, in which only those stressors judged causally related to the onset or exacerbation of the mental disorder are considered, 52% favored leaving Axis IV in that form. Some 38% indicated that they found it "clinically useful in deciding a treatment approach and in evaluating prognosis."

Axis V was more acceptable; fully 63% judged it useful, and only 10% did not.

A large reliability study (6,7) involving pairs of clinicians making independent assessments indicated fair reliability for Axis IV (intraclass R = .64) and good reliability for Axis V (intraclass R = .76).

Problems with Existing Classifications of Mental Disorders for Use in Primary Care

At the present time, or in the near future, the most widely used classifications of mental disorders are the "Mental Disorder" section of *ICD*-9, the "Mental Disorder" section of the second edition of the *International Classification of Health Problems in Primary Care* (*ICHPPC*-2) (8), and the *DSM*-III classification.

Both the *ICD*-9 and the *DSM*-III classifications of mental disorders are far too detailed for use by primary care personnel, since the distinctions are too fine for the range of therapeutic techniques available to primary care personnel. Undoubtedly, this is the reason that the *ICHPPC*-2 classification of mental disorders is far simpler, consisting of only 21 categories. However, the *ICHPPC*-2 suffers from failure to make distinctions of importance to primary care personnel. For example, both acute delirium associated with infection and senile or presenile dementia would be coded merely as *organic psychosis*. Another example is the inclusion of both hyperkinetic syndrome and delinquency in the same category of *behavior disorder*. Furthermore, the categories are not defined other than by the listing of several inclusion and exclusion terms.

A PROPOSED CLASSIFICATION OF MENTAL DISORDERS FOR USE IN PRIMARY CARE

By examining the major classes of the *ICD*-9 and *DSM*-III classifications of mental disorders, and the *ICHPPC*-2 classification, the present authors have constructed a classification of mental disorders that includes 12 major classes with a total of 27 separate categories (Table 13.3). It may be argued that this system has several advantages over the *ICHPPC*-2 system and over a classification using only the major classes from either *DSM*-III or *ICD*-9.

ICHPPC-2 divides the entire classification into *psychoses, neuroses,* and *other mental and psychological disorders.* It is now generally recognized that the psychotic-neurotic distinction includes unproven etiological assumptions that are not very useful and do not accurately reflect current thinking. For this reason, the proposed system instead contains major categories distinguished from each other largely on the basis of descriptive features rather than etiological hypotheses.

Whereas the *ICHPPC*-2 classification has only three categories specifically appropriate for children, the proposed classification includes nine specific categories. This expansion seems appropriate in view of the importance of recognizing and treating disorders in children.

The proposed system divides affective disorders into two categories: *major affective disorders* (which includes *affective psychoses*) and *minor affective disorders* (which includes *mild depressive reactions to stress*). The *ICHPPC*-2 system has a single category of *affective psychoses,* a term that is confusing since individuals with such a disorder are not necessarily psychotic at any or every point in the course of their illness, but only suffer from a disorder that in *some* individuals is of psychotic proportions. The distinction between a major and a minor affective disorder is of more treatment relevance than the distinction between psychotic and nonpsychotic.

If the proposed system is considered for adoption, it would be very helpful to develop a brief glossary so that each category would be defined. This would undoubtedly result in more uniform use by clinicians of varying experience and orientation. An example of such a definition follows:

8.0 Personality disorders

Inflexible and maladaptive patterns of perceiving, relating to, and thinking about the environment and oneself, that are exhibited in a wide range of important social and personal contexts, and cause either significant impairment in social or occupational functioning, or subjective distress.
Includes: antisocial personality disorder, paranoid personality disorder

THE USE OF THE PROPOSED CLASSIFICATION OF MENTAL DISORDERS IN A TRIAXIAL CLASSIFICATION SYSTEM

As noted elsewhere (see Chapter 11 of this volume), it is useful to conceptualize a comprehensive assessment of health as involving inquiry about three areas of functioning: physical, psychological, and social. A useful multiaxial

Table 13.3.   Proposed Classification of Mental Disorders for Use in Primary Care

1.0 Disorders Usually Arising in Childhood
    1.1 Mental retardation
    1.2 Hyperkinetic syndrome of childhood
    1.3 Conduct disorder of childhood
    1.4 Eating disorders
        Includes: anorexia nervosa, bulimia
    1.5 Tics
    1.6 Childhood disorders with predominantly physical manifestations
        Includes: enuresis, stammering, pavor nocturnus
    1.7 Childhood psychosis
    1.8 Specific developmental delays
    1.9 Other childhood disorders
        Includes: disturbance of emotions specific to childhood and adolescence
2.0 Organic Mental Disorders (other than due to alcohol or drugs)
    2.1 Senile and presenile dementias
        Includes: arteriosclerotic dementia
    2.2 Transient organic psychoses
        Includes: delirium associated with endocrine, metabolic, and cerebrovascular disorders
    2.3 Chronic organic psychoses NEC
        Includes: dementia associated with metabolic or neurological disorder
    2.4 Other organic mental disorder
3.0 Alcohol Use Disorders
    Includes: alcohol abuse or intoxication, alcohol dependence
    3.1 Alcoholic psychoses
        Includes: delirium tremens, alcoholic dementia
4.0 Drug Use Disorders
    Includes: abuse of drugs other than alcohol, dependence on drugs other than alcohol
    4.1 Drug-induced psychoses
        Includes: drug withdrawal syndromes, drug intoxication states
5.0 Affective Disorders
    Includes: affective psychoses
    5.1 Major affective disorders
    5.2 Minor affective disorders
        Includes: mild depressive reaction
6.0 Other Nonorganic Psychoses
    Includes: schizophrenia, paranoid states, brief psychotic reaction
7.0 Neurotic Disorders

Table 13.3. *(continued)*

Includes: anxiety states, hypochondriasis, hysteria, psychogenic pain
Excludes: minor affective disorders

8.0 Personality Disorders
Includes: paranoid personality disorder, antisocial personality disorder

9.0 Sexual Dysfunctions
Includes: frigidity, impotence, dyspareunia

10.0 Adjustment Reaction
Excludes: minor affective disorders

11.0 Psychological Factors Associated with Physical Disorders
(classified elsewhere)

12.0 Other Mental Disorders
Includes: gender identity disorders (e.g., transsexualism), sexual deviations
(e.g., pedophilia)

classification for primary care providers that would involve a separate axis for each of these may be proposed. Axis I would consist of a classification of physical disorders and a supplemental list of physical symptoms. An apparently satisfactory classification for this purpose exists in *ICHPPC*-2. Axis II would consist of a classification of mental disorders, such as proposed here, along with a supplemental list of psychological symptoms, as proposed in Chapter 11. Finally, Axis III would consist of a classification of social problems, also proposed in Chapter 11.

The present authors believe that the use of such a multiaxial system by primary care personnel would facilitate a comprehensive assessment of health of value to clinicians, patients, planners of resource allocation, and research investigators.

REFERENCES

1. M. Rutter, D. Shaffer, and M. Shepherd, *A Multi-Axial Classification of Child Psychiatric Disorders* (Geneva: World Health Organization, 1975).

2. American Psychiatric Association, *Diagnostic and Statistical Manual of Mental Disorders,* 3rd ed. (Washington, D.C.: American Psychiatric Association, 1980).

3. Janet B. W. Williams, "*DSM*-III: A Comprehensive Approach to Diagnoses," *Social Work* 26(1978):101–6.

4. Janet B. W. Williams, and Robert Spitzer, "NIMH Sponsored Field Trial: Interrater Reliability," in *Diagnostic and Statistical Manual of Mental Disorders,* 3rd ed. (Washington, D.C.: American Psychiatric Association, 1980).

5. World Health Organization, *Manual of the International Statistical Classifica-*

tion of Diseases, Injuries, and Causes of Death, 9th revision vol. 1 (Geneva: World Health Organization, 1977).

6. Robert L. Spitzer and Janet B. W. Forman, "*DSM*-III Field Trials: II. Initial Experience with the Multiaxial System," *American Journal of Psychiatry* 136(1979):6.

7. Robert L. Spitzer, Janet B. W. Forman, and John Nee, "*DSM*-III Field Trials: I. Initial Interrater Diagnostic Reliability," *American Journal of Psychiatry* 136(1979): 815–17.

8. World Organization of National Colleges, Academies, and Academic Associations of General Practitioners/Family Physicians, *International Classification of Health Problems in Primary Care,* 2nd ed. (Chicago: American Hospital Association, 1979).

14

Classification of Social Problems Affecting Health: A New Conceptual Framework

DENISE DELIEGE

INTRODUCTION: THE USEFULNESS OF A TAXONOMY OF SOCIAL FACTORS

Health has been defined as a state of physical, mental, and social well-being. This has caused more attention to be paid recently to the third item, "social well-being," and the influence of social factors on physical and mental health. Knowledge of and action in this field are much less developed than in the other two. This is due to the fact that social science is both younger and more complex than the so-called "exact" sciences. Positive experimentation on "society" is hardly possible, as social groups are composed of numerous individuals, each one living independently and reacting in various ways to environmental factors according to his or her own past experience and sensitivity. Progress in this field can only be achieved by multiplying careful observations of events among numerous individuals whose living conditions remain unchanged.

In the field of health, such an objective requires that every social factor that can be associated with the state of health be recorded.

To be fruitful, such observations should be recorded on the basis of a good taxonomy. The latter will be useful in many respects; it should help to improve not only general knowledge, but also medical education and efficiency of social action.

Usefulness for Research

The validity and significance of research in the field of "social well-being" will strongly depend on the quality of the classification being used. Each aspect of knowledge will be better supported: description, analysis, relation of findings to other types of phenomena (for instance, diseases or psychological

219

symptoms), and conception of a good explanatory model and an overall theory.

Usefulness for Teaching

A still larger number of experts advocate better training of physicians in the field of social problems. Such training requires a good conceptual framework. A rational classification can serve indeed as a basic tool to build up adequate training in this field; doctors-to-be must have a clear understanding of problems, as much for didactic purposes (easier understanding and memorizing) as for using such a classification in their daily professional practice.

Usefulness for Action: Individual Practice and Planning of Resources

In order to help practitioners and decision makers to solve the problems encountered, these should be identified not only as to the field of social life from which they stem, but also as to the type of question they raise. The question being clear, one can usually better identify the action needed to solve the problem.

However, the relation between the type of problem and the type of solution is not perfect. Compared to a system recording only the "field of the problem," one identifying the "type of problem" enhances overall insight into the actions to be taken. But straight conclusions about such actions are certainly not valid at an individual level, nor are they 100% valid for groups of populations. In fact, a decision about action should take into account two other dimensions of social reality: the actual origin or "cause" of the problem encountered, and the probability of the various possible solutions' being accepted. Obviously, such detailed thought can only take place at the case level, after careful investigation of every aspect of each problem. This remains outside the scope of a general classification.

DEFECTS OF PREVIOUS CLASSIFICATIONS*

Previous classifications seem to have grown out of medical practice, with both the advantages and the defects of such roots: They seem simple and easy to use, but do not appear efficient for the purposes of teaching, research, problem solving, and planning of resources. Some categories are too broad,

---

*These include the following: the "Social Problems" section of the *International Classification of Diseases,* ninth revision (*ICD*-9); the "Social, Marital, and Family Problems and Maladjustments" section of the *International Classification of Health Problems in Primary Care,* second edition (*ICHPPC*-2); the "Social Problem Counseling" section of the *Reason for Visit Classification* (*RVC*); and the General Practice Research Unit classification of "Social Problems."

as they sometimes mix different areas of social life; a few items are classified in the wrong area; no attention is paid to identifying the real *type* of problem encountered; quite a few social problems are not mentioned. In short, the classifications seem out of date for present problems encountered in the industrialized world and are not always well adapted for problems prevalent in the developing countries. An improved conceptual framework seems needed.

Some Categories are Too Broad

Very often, problems pertaining to different areas are included in one category; for instance, *housing, household, and economic problems* are considered as one sole category, whereas they actually form different aspects of social life. As an example of this, one can be inadequately housed, even without any financial problem. Conversely, one may have a suitable home and still be hit by economic problems. Similarly, bad household management is quite different in nature from experiencing housing problems.

A Few Items are Classified in Wrong Areas

A few problems are inadequately classified into certain fields, because of careless thought about their real nature. The following are two examples of such misclassification:

Hobos, Tramps, Vagabonds

To classify hobos, tramps, and vagabonds as having *housing problems* is to oversimplify the reality of their condition by confusing it with its most obvious consequence. In fact, providing such people with a decent home would not help a great deal, because they probably would not use it. Their problem is more basically a lack of integration into society at large.

Multiparity

Multiparity is sometimes considered as a problem and in such a case inappropriately classified as a *family problem.* Of course such a situation usually occurs in the context of a family, but the problem thus raised is not a family one, but rather an economic one or, more often, one of difficulty in managing a household.

Various Problems Can Be Mixed within a Certain Field

When a broad field such as *educational problems* is not split into smaller categories, various problems, quite different in nature, are mixed under one excessively large heading (e.g., lack of education or opportunities, inadequate facilities, interruption in schooling, truancy, trouble with cotrainees and/or teachers, etc.).

Obviously, the significance of each of these items, their probable impact in terms of risks, and the actions they call for are quite different. Therefore, the *type* of problem met, along with the *area* to which it pertains, should be recorded.

The same reasoning can be applied to any field that could be used as a single category for classification, such as *employment* or *housing*.

A Few Problems Are Not Mentioned

Quite a few important problems are not mentioned in previous classifications; either they were already existing but not perceived as social problems, or they have grown within the last decades as consequences of modern social life.

Predicaments Only Recently Perceived as Social Problems

Problems Pertaining to Women's Status.   The problem of women's status has been only recently recognized as a specific concern. Hardly any attention is paid in previous classifications to women's specific difficulties: Problems pertaining to managing a household are not mentioned, nor is the situation of battered women (even when *battered child* is noted), whereas the recent opening of refugee homes for abused women has revealed the magnitude of the latter problem. Perhaps most striking is the fact that abortion is never mentioned, although innumerable women have resorted to it since time immemorial.

Difficulties during Childhood.   More evidence is put forward every year to point out how important the first years of childhood are for the individual's development and integration into social groups. Could difficulties during childhood be considered as *psychological trauma* (i.e., item V 15.4 of the *ICD*-9)? It hardly seems possible, because most of such predicaments do not involve one precise dramatic event, but rather a long-lasting, insidious situation.

Problems of Political or Social Disruption.   Since the beginning of human life, struggles for power have regularly brought trouble to communities, be they clans, tribes, or larger units such as states, nations, or blocs. The state of insecurity and violence thus involved is of course dangerous. The impact on social well-being can vary according to individuals' attitudes toward the new regime; some will be threatened by it, while others will prosper. It is highly questionable, however, whether such circumstances, affecting a major part of the population, can be efficiently acknowledged as a pathogenic factor by people living in the area undergoing the crisis.

New Types of Problems Evolving from Recent
Societal Developments

Present and Future Evolution of Men's and Women's Roles.   New types of problems have evolved within urban developed societies: social isolation of housewives, due to the absence of personal relationships and social life within urban dwellings; plurality of occupations; more and more people assuming responsibilities within the home as well as professional jobs outside. It might seem strange at first to consider the latter circumstances as pathogenic, since they are considered signs of major progress by women's liberation movements. While any value judgment about the opportunity to promote or discourage such plurality of roles should be avoided, it should be noted that, for classification purposes, this evolution requires that separate items should be provided for *employment* and for other occupational circumstances, such as *household conditions.*

It should also be noted that this plurality of roles, considered nowadays as a typical women's problem, will soon become common to both sexes.

Evolution of the Family.   The community of life has evolved very rapidly within half a century; from the extended group, it has been reduced to the nuclear family in the industrialized countries. Further changes are already noticeable. Conjufal life, for example, is no longer the privilege of officially married people; new types of common living are experienced, either within groups (sects, mixed families, etc.) or with homosexual partner. Clinicians should be able to classify predicaments evolving from all such circumstances: They should all be considered *family problems,* according to an extended definition of this basic community of life.

Evolution of Employment Problems.   Plurality of occupations has already been mentioned for men and women, sharing responsibilities of a job and a household. It can also apply to students carrying out a job during their studies. This is another reason for separating the various forms of occupations in a classification.

Another new predicament is the long distance between job and home, requiring exhausting commuting twice a day.

Evolution of Housing Problems.   Beside bad conditions of the home itself, quite a few predicaments have evolved from the neighborhood environment in the crowded industrial cities, such as noise and traffic, smell and emanations, unsafe areas, and so on.

Evolution of Marginalization Problems.   Maladjustment to one's own social group can lead to all types of flight from the group or rejection of it, including behavior opposed to social norms. Among the traditional ones, one can note alcoholism and delinquency; among the ones presently increasing in frequency, one should include drug addiction, deviant behavior, processes of marginalization and anomia, and illegal political action and terrorism. Of course alcoholism and drug addition are already included in *ICD*-9 as actual diseases; still, all these factors should be included in a classification of social predicaments, independently of the *ICD,* to allow for the use of such a classification by social workers.

Change and Threat of Change.   Change has always existed and can be considered as a major means of progress for humanity. In the past, however, change took place slowly over generations, so that a single person could hardly perceive the contrasts within his or her own life. A major characteristic of the present era is the growing importance of change in a person's life; an increasing number and frequency of changes affect each individual in the course of his or her life (1).

As a consequence, people live in a world so different from the one they knew 20 or 30 years earlier that they sometimes hardly recognize it. They have to accept physical as well as mental mobility—frequent removals, new jobs, new ways of living, new social relationships, new ideas, new beliefs, new values, and so on. As their capacity to adapt is limited, these changes are not always well accepted or easily borne, inducing anxiety and stress. Up to now, change in itself has hardly been perceived as a real pathogenic factor. On the basis of various epidemiological surveys, however, it may be assumed that it is becoming a major one (2).

Therefore, important changes endured by anyone should be recorded as risk factors. This is obvious for family disruption (which has already been recognized as a social predicament), but also applies to removals, crisis in belief, or change of employment, to name a few examples. It also holds true for happy events such as marriage, birth, or promotion, because they all require social adjustment and new responsibilities (3).

Of course, the impact of a change on someone's health might differ according to its proximity in time. A recent event is particularly disturbing; more detailed classification should thus take into account the fact that such an event took place within the last 12 months. But even if they have occurred a long time ago, important events might have left profound wounds and should be recorded.

Furthermore, a threat of change also puts burdens on the individual, as it induces anxiety for the future. Such a threat, too, should be given due recognition as a health problem.

PROPOSALS FOR A NEW CLASSIFICATION

General Principles

In spite of the disadvantages described above, previous systems of classification form good points of departure. The present author has begun with *ICD*-9 (V Codes 60–68) and has attempted to bring it up to date and to palliate the defects listed above.

In the proposed classification, presented as Table 14.1, there are nine broad areas of problems: food, housing, economics, family or clan, home management, employment, education, conditions of life, and social and political structures.

Within each of these fields, items should be classified in such a way that the *type* of problem can be identified. Two main types of problems can occur: either present predicaments or predicaments associated with an individual's "life story." (In order to simplify the recording system, this dichotomy does not appear as such in the proposed classification.) Four types of present predicaments can be identified in each area: *lacks, defects, personal maladjustment,* and *interpersonal relationships.* Predicaments associated with "life story" are referred to as *changes*—either perturbing past events or recent changes, or simply the threat of a change. As complementary categories, *other* and *unspecified* items are always provided for.

The items taken into account are these: (1) social predicaments, thought to be associated with health and illness, in the present state or to be potential threats to health in the future; (2) indications of social maladjustment, except for signs and symptoms of psychological or mental disorder (these are listed on a separate axis of classification).

Advantages and Limits

Updating and Clarification

The proposed classification updates and improves the previous systems, which seem to reflect the problems of males living in industrialized countries during the 1950s or 1960s. Normally, it allows for better description of the social factors associated with health and avoids the earlier confusions among various fields and types of problems encountered within each field.

It is also much more useful for action, either at the individual level or at the level of resource planning. Actions to be taken are highly dependent upon the types of problems they mean to tackle. We can assume that the problems classified under *lack of opportunities* or *inadequate facilities* require that appropriate opportunities or facilities be created through public funds. Defects can be of different natures: A few call for technical improvements, while others

Table 14.1.   Proposed Classification of Social Problems (Risk Factors)

10 FOOD

11 *Lack*
    111 Not enough food available
    112 No drinkable water available in the neighborhood
    113 No source of energy available to warm food

12 *Defects*
    121 Lack of hygiene to prepare food
    122 Unbalanced type of food
    123 Inadequate food habits
    124 Need for special dietary counseling

13 *Personal maladjustment*
    131 Cannot bear usual food
    132 Anorexia

20 HOUSING PROBLEMS

21 *Lack*
    211 Unsettled migrants or refugees
    212 Victims of disasters or expulsions
        Excludes: hobos, tramps, vagabonds (see 934)

22 *Defects*
    221 Inadequate housing conditions
        221.1   Overcrowding
        221.2   Lack of water supply
        221.3   Lack of sewage system
        221.4   Lack of source of energy
        221.5   Lack of heating/cooling
        221.6   Lack of ventilation or light
        221.7   Lack of sanitary facilities
        221.8   Unsafe or damaged construction
        221.9   Slums
        221.10 Physically unsuitable for needs (e.g., staircases for handicapped; technical defects preventing adequate care)
        221.11 Long distance from workplace
    222 Neighborhood environmental factors
        222.1   Pollution (e.g., noise, smell, traffic, toxic emanations)
        222.2   Impersonal dwellings
        222.3   Unsafe area
        222.4   Long distance to important services

23 *Personal maladjustment*
    231 Frustration issued from housing conditions

Table 14.1. (*continued*)

24 *Interpersonal relationships*
    241 Troubles with neighbors
    242 Ostracism
25 *Important change over time*
    251 Simple moving
        Excludes: moving out of parental home (see 452)
    252 Important change of environment (e.g., rural to urban)
        Excludes: migration (see 952)
    253 Expulsion
    254 Residential unstability
        Includes: transient, tenancy problems
26 *Other*
    261 Person living in residential institution
        Excludes: jail (see 932)
                transient homes (see 254)
27 *Unspecified*

30 ECONOMIC CIRCUMSTANCES
31 *Lack*
    311 Lack of financial resources (e.g., money, land, cattle)
    312 Poverty
32 *Defects*
    321 Indebtedness
    322 Insufficient resources (i.e., financial resources or prevalent resources in the area)
33 *Personal maladjustment*
    331 Poor management of resources
35 *Important change over time:* Drastic drop of economic level
    351 Bankruptcy
    352 Sudden debt
    353 Loss of property (natural disasters, fire, social disruption)
36 *Other*
37 *Unspecified*

40 FAMILY, CLAN, OR COMMUNITY OF LIFE
41 *Lack*
    411 Has no relatives
42 *Problems or defects*
    421 Inadequate rearing (deprived of parents or affection during childhood)

(*continued*)

Table 14.1. (*continued*)

---

422 Problems associated with procreation
     422.1 Infertility
     422.2 Unwanted pregnancy
     422.3 Abortion
     422.4 Out-of-wedlock birth

423 Incomplete family
     423.1 Single parent
     423.2 Long absence from partner

424 Incest and other sexual taboos

43 *Personal maladjustment*

  431 Frustration

  432 Discord about values

44 *Interpersonal relationships*

  441 Problem with partner
     Includes: conjugal (marital or nonmarital) problem, homosexual partner
     441.1 Discord
     441.2 Battered partner
     441.3 Abuse

  422 Problem with younger children (parent-child or extended family versus child)
     442.1 Discord about behavior
     442.2 Child abuse or neglect, battered child

  443 Other problems of family relationships
     443.1 Problems with relatives other than partner or younger children (siblings, in-laws, extended family)
     443.2 Other members of the community of life

45 *Changes over time*

  451 Family disruption
     451.1 Death
     451.2 Divorce
     451.3 Separation

  452 Left parents' home or community

  453 Recent marriage or birth

46 *Other*

  461 Foster family

  462 Institutional rearing

47 *Unspecified*

50 HOME MANAGEMENT PROBLEMS

51 *Lack*

Table 14.1.   (*continued*)

---

511 No one cares for household or personal care

52 *Problems or defects*

521 Bad hygiene of housekeeping

522 Presence of a disabled person
Includes: handicapped child, aged parent, sick or injured relative, alcoholism or drug addiction in home

523 Temporary overload

523.1   Need for holiday relief care
523.2   Need for temporary help (e.g., because of illness or absence of partner or multiparity)

53 *Personal maladjustment*

531 Cannot cope with demands (e.g., too many children)

532 Role dissatisfaction of housekeeper

54 *Interpersonal relationships:* See family (44)

55 *Important change over time*

551 Loss of person caring for household

56 *Other*

57 *Unspecified*

60 EMPLOYMENT
Excludes: Occupational problems other than related to employment (see 50, 70)

61 *Lack*

611 Unemployment

612 Looking for a job (even if not recorded as "unemployed")

62 *Defects:* Adverse effects or work environment

621 Working hours

622 Toxic matters

623 Other dangers

624 Rhythm

625 Monotony

626 Noise

627 Light

628 Smell

629 Bad sanitary conditions

63 *Personal maladjustment*

631 Difficulties in adjusting to work situation

631.1   Demands exceed possibilities
631.2   Need for sheltered work

632 Overload

(*continued*)

Table 14.1. (*continued*)

    632.1 At work
    632.2 Due to various circumstances (e.g., employment + household or employment + long distance)

64 *Interpersonal relationships*
  641 Problems with workmates or peers
  642 Frustration

65 *Change over time*
  651 Loss of employment
  652 Retirement
  653 New job
  654 Occupational instability (threat of firing or closing the company)
  655 Career choice

66 *Other*

67 *Unspecified*

70 EDUCATION

71 *Lack*
  711 Lack of opportunities for training, or lack of objective possibilities
  712 Lack of education, inducing other types of problems

72 *Defects*
  721 Inadequate educational opportunities
  722 School refusal

73 *Personal maladjustment*
  731 Truancy
  732 Hates school

74 *Interpersonal relationships*
  741 Trouble with cotrainees
  742 Trouble with teachers

75 *Change over time*
  751 Had to interrupt training
  752 School failure
  753 Threat of interruption or failure
  754 Threat of change

76 *Other*

77 *Unspecified*

80 CONDITIONS OF LIFE

82 *Defects*
  821 No leisure time

Table 14.1. (*continued*)

83 *Personal maladjustment*

    831 No interest in life, no activity

    832 Bad hygiene

    833 Not enough physical exercise

    834 Not enough sleep

    835 Works too much

    836 Smoking habit

    837 Drinking, alcoholism

    838 Drug addiction

90 SOCIAL AND POLITICAL STRUCTURES

91 *Lack*

    911 Anarchy, revolution, war

92 *Defects*

    921 Social isolation: no contacts outside home

    922 Social abuse: rape, torture, concentration camps

    923 Cultural deprivation

    924 Political, religious, racial, ethnical, caste, or sex discrimination

    925 Persecution, legal terror

93 *Personal maladjustment*

    931 Legal problems

        931.1 Ligitation, lawsuits

        932.2 Prosecution, legal investigation

    932 Imprisonment

    933 Attempted suicide

    934 Anomia, tramps, hobos, vagabonds

    935 Delinquency

    936 Illegal political activities: terrorism

94 *Interpersonal relationships*

    941 Bad influence of reference groups

95 *Change over time*

    951 Phases of life: puberty, menopause

    952 Migration

    953 Crisis in belief or value

    954 Excommunication, exile

    955 Important past sufferings: previous rape, torture, concentration camps

96 *Other*

97 *Unspecified*

can be solved by provisional help (extended by volunteers or nonprofit services). Problems of relationships can best be tackled by psychosocial action (therapy, counseling, training groups), whereas problems of recent change or threat of change call mainly for nonprofessional support to be provided by the community itself.

Better Adaptability to Problems of Developing Countries

Items listed in previous classifications seem better adapted to industrialized societies than to developing countries. For example, such a major predicament as lack of food is not mentioned.

The proposal made in this chapter allows for adaptation to each country without major change. As "types of problems" are identified, each nation or group can list under each heading items that are specific to its own situation. First steps in this direction might include the following:

- As economic problems, one might add under the heading *lack, lack of food, lack of land,* or *lack of cattle.*
- As housing problems, one could add *lack of light or ventilation* under the heading *defect of housing conditions.*
- As family problems, those pertaining to extended families could be included.
- As defects of social structure, one might have to add *caste discrimination.*

Descriptive versus Explanatory Theory

The proposed classification should not be considered as an explanatory theory; the items as such form a step of the analysis. Additional thought is needed at a later stage for interpreting the results. The present author does not claim to have identified anything like the social "causes" of illness—only to have pointed out "factors of risk." The social etiology remains to be studied through further research.

Usefulness for Interpretation versus Ease of Coding

This new classification is probably more difficult to handle; it is somewhat longer and more intricate than previous ones. It demands that users find out the real meaning of problems encountered, rather than classifying them as they are perceived at first sight. This apparent loss of simplicity is compensated for by the classification's discriminating power and its validity as a tool for research, training, and action.

In any event, the proposed system allows for more or less detail according to the purpose of the study; one can choose to use two, three, or four significant digits.

Frustration versus (Dis)satisfaction or Psychological Disorders

A few ambiguities remain in this classification: It does not aim at measuring anything like "satisfaction" in regard to the items considered; nor does it take symptoms of psychological disorder into account, these being classified on a different axis, for which various types of classification can be found (e.g., *ICD-9*, items 300–816).

However, such distinctions might be subtle. For instance, various forms of personal maladjustments, such as *frustration, role dissatisfaction,* or *expectations not met,* obviously lie at the borderline between social predicament and psychological reaction to it. The use of the term *dissatisfaction* also seems to contradict the previous statement of not taking "satisfaction" into account. Actually, previous research has shown that satisfaction and dissatisfaction are not just two extremes on one single scale: dissatisfaction occurs when current expectations are not met, as these pertain to needs already supposed to be fulfilled. If such needs are perfectly met, they will thus not produce any type of positive satisfaction. The latter only arises when extra events occur, able to meet the individuals' aspirations, located higher on the hierarchy of needs.

In any case, the purpose is not to find out about the individual's own feeling of satisfaction or dissatisfaction, but to allow a professional to record under the heading *maladjustment* his or her own appraisal of the patient's frustration.

Signs of Maladjustment versus Disease

Some signs of deviant behavior reflecting maladjustment are also considered as actual diseases (e.g., alcoholism, drug addiction, or suicide attempts). It is appropriate to keep them in this classification, as it may be used by nonmedical professionals working in fields related to health, such as social work.

Meaning of Social Well-Being: Anomie versus Normality

Meaning of Social Well-Being.   To record social factors associated with health does not mean that one has succeeded in measuring anything like "social well-being." An attempt to set up indications of physical, mental, and social well-being has been made lately (4), but it is a difficult task, because *social well-being* can have two meanings:

- The personal adaptation of the individual to his or her environment, regardless of the "objective" quality or defects of this environment.
- The state of social conditions compared to a point of reference.

The second aspect seems more objective than the first one, but it still rests on ambiguities and value judgments. A similar dichotomy exists for more traditional aspects of "health." "Needs for care" are based either on the subjective appraisal of the individual looking for help or on the doctor's "professional appraisal," based on clearly identified symptoms. The first is a "need" in the socioeconomic conceptual framework (the wish for specific consumption); the second is a "need" in the medical tradition, according to the grid of judgment developed in medical training and depending on the technical possibilities of medical knowledge.

To return to social well-being, the ambiguity of both approaches prevents us from constructing a scale of measurement for either of them.

Each Individual's Adaptation.   The way an individual adapts to a specific social context depends on personal factors and on group factors.

1. Similar contexts can induce different reactions, and similar reactions can stem from different contexts. Individual behavior indeed stems not only from the context itself, but from the conformity (or lack of it) between this context and expectations. For instance, a job can either be positively appreciated or lead to frustration, according to previous experiences in life. A migrant with no opportunities in his or her home country will accept a difficult job more readily than a highly skilled worker from an industrialized society will. Similarly, very inadequate housing can be accepted without major difficulty by people who have always lived in such dwellings, whereas a minor defect can deeply affect families belonging to well-off classes.

2. The type of reaction to various social predicaments can be twofold: (a) social deviation from the usual behavior, or (b) personal maladjustment, together with conformity to expected behavior.

The first phenomenon accounts for all types of social anomie, such as drug addiction, delinquency, or other forms of marginalization (the existence of hobos and tramps, etc.). These reactions should be included in any classification of social factors affecting health, such as the one proposed in this chapter.

The second phenomenon accounts for various types of psychological reaction, ranging from simple dissatisfaction (not taken into account in a classification of factors of health, except when it leads to more severe disturbances) to symptoms of genuine psychological disorder, such as insomnia, depression, and so on.

Abnormal Social Conditions and Deviant Behavior. Social conditions may be classified as showing a lack, an inadequacy, or a change; in such cases, they may be thought of as predicaments and thus labeled as potential or actual threats to health.

One should be aware, though, that the identification of specific conditions as predicaments is strongly dependent on one's personal frame of reference and personal implicit judgment about the risk such conditions induce, taking into account the specific characteristics of the individual one is dealing with.

For instance, a home with stairs can be assessed as perfect for a young family and also as unfit for an elderly or handicapped person. A home without heating could be considered as a predicament in well-off groups, whereas it might appear a dream to workers dealing with slum dwellers.

Variations in assessment are still larger from one country to another. Poor housing conditions, unemployment, and lack of education might be categorized as "abnormal" according to the criteria of industrialized countries, whereas they might be part of the normal and usual life in rural areas of developing countries.

Differences of assessment occur in sociopolitical fields as well, and will thus affect the way in which people are labeled as deviant or normal. A Marxist, for instance might be categorized as a "deviant" in a few right-wing dictatorships; similarly, the fighter for human rights might be considered a dangerous "hooligan" in some contexts. The member of a traditional clan trying to build up his or her career and well-being apart from the clan's solidarity will be considered "deviant" and will suffer from various forms of pressure, whereas the Western adult who wishes to escape from the consumption pattern and joins a sect that aims at more solidarity will be considered "deviant" in his or her home country.

These "deviations" are puzzling only if one does not realize the aims and limits of the proposed classification. It endeavors to point out risk factors in a specific context and according to reference norms prevailing in the individual's group. It does not aim at measuring objective living conditions. Thus, it does not allow for comparison at that level. For instance, defects of the home will be assessed quite differently in different countries and in different social classes within one country. The Marxist and the human rights activist will be considered as "deviants" or not, depending on the values prevailing in their societies. Even if their opinions diverge strongly, their positions might be similar as they fight the social order of their home countries. Both might be threatened by social and economic pressure and thus might suffer from exactly the same type of predicament.

CONCLUSION

The choice of a good classification system is important for training, research, professional practice, and planning of resources. The proposed classification updates the previous ones, allows better adaptation to various cultural contexts, and is constructed along a coherent conceptual framework. It has been presented in full detail, but can of course be used in a much shorter way, using only two significant digits. It is an important tool in working toward better recognition of social factors affecting health. It should not, however, be used as an explanatory model of social aspects of health, nor should it be considered as a scale of "social health" or as a means to compare social predicaments among various cultural contexts.

REFERENCES

1. A. Toffler, *Future Shock* (New York: Random House, 1970).
2. J. Cassell, "The Contribution of the Social Environment to Host Resistance," *American Journal of Epidemiology* 104(1976):107–23.
3. B. Dohrenwend and B. Dohrenwend, *Stressful Life Events: Their Nature and Effects* (New York: Wiley, 1974).
4. D. Deliege, *Les indicateurs de bien-etre physique, mental, et social* (Geneva: World Health Organization, 1980).

15

Proposed Classifications of Psychological and Social Problems in Primary Care: Comments and Questions

MACK LIPKIN, JR.

This part of *Psychosocial Factors Affecting Health* has presented four possible solutions to the problems of classifying psychological and social problems in primary care. Regier and colleagues set the stage in Chapter 11, and the three subsequent chapters play variations on the theme. Regier's group clearly states its purposes in Chapter 11: clinical care, resource allocation, research, education. They outline a series of desiderata for a primary care classification. It should be empirically derived, reliable, valid, simple to use, hierarchical in construction so that more or less complexity can be included, and multiaxial because health problems are multidimensional. Perhaps most importantly, it should be fully field-tested in a variety of primary care settings in the developed and developing nations in order to assess its utility and to refine it.

The primary focus of the new classification is the primary care setting. It is possible that it might be useful for epidemiological or hospital settings, but that is for later.

In the primary care setting, the most important issue is the care of patients. The new classification should be an aid rather than another bureaucratic nuisance. How might it help? First, it may sensitize practitioners to diagnostic possibilities they had not previously considered. The actual effort of classifying and familiarizing themselves with the glossaries may increase the focus of primary care workers on psychosocial problems. It may point to management considerations that they had not previously entertained, such as pursuit of more information, referral to an appropriate specialist, referral to an appropriate nonmedical care provider, or mobilization of community resources in the interest of the patient's recovery.

A second benefit of the triaxial classification is less direct. The use of three

Table 15.1　Desiderata of a Primary
　　　　　　　Care Classification

- Empirically derived
- Reliable
- Valid
- Simple to use
- Multipurpose
- Hierarchically expandable
- Multidimensional (axial)
- Field tested

---

axes may demonstrate correlations among items that lead to expanded knowledge of disease causation, disease precipitation, healing, failure to heal, and the like. That is, by counting and comparing these categories, new relationships may reveal themselves, or the data may suggest focuses for deeper investigation with more refined epidemiological methods. Presently there is much work in this area, but it suffers frequently from the use of noncomparable rating methods and problem categories, from very small numbers, and from sampling that is not population-based. Widespread adoption of a classification such as this could help correct these problems. It would generate sufficiently large numbers that subtle correlations might emerge, which studies with small numbers are not sensitive enough to detect. Presently, we know relatively little about the phenomenology of psychosocial aspects of primary care, as suggested in the introduction to this volume. Use and continuing refinement of a triaxial classification can be part of coming to know more.

A third way in which a new triaxial classification can be useful is through the generation of more realistic and complete data about how patients and health personnel spend their time together. As reviewed in Chapter 10, a significant portion of primary care effort is related to psychological and social problems. Sometimes these problems are primary and the direct cause of a visit to a primary care provider. At other times, they precipitate physical or mental disorder. They complicate treatment adherence and the gathering of reliable data in the interview. They affect when and how patients relate to clinics. Yet commonly these factors are not included in planning, in part because they do not enter into the relevant statistics. Clearly, a better-rounded statistical picture of primary care can lead to improved planning.

These benefits all coalesce in education, since the content of present educational efforts would be improved by clinical care, learning from the outset to think multidimensionally, and having more complete data-based paradigms of care.

These hoped-for benefits, however, may be questioned. One concern is that the addition of extra dimensions for consideration may tax the energy, intellect, or good will of already overburdened primary care workers. Their willingness to adopt a new classification can be questioned. Is it an accident that these matters are presently omitted? Is it coincidence that even programs and institutions that have charismatic, effective role models of integrated approaches to care still predominantly reflect the traditional biotechnical paradigms? Assuming that the new classification turns out to be of proven benefit and becomes adopted widely, what will be given up to make room for it? This is clearly the beginning of a long effort in which competing choices and forces within medicine will struggle.

A larger unknown concerns the feasibility of achieving reliability (i.e., reproducibility) and validity (i.e., measurement of what the instrument says it will do) with such a simple instrument across vastly different cultures. Even if it works in selected settings, chosen for their interest, will it work in average settings? If, as some argue, primary care workers lack the appropriate clinical tools to detect these problems, will their records be sufficiently accurate to warrant collecting? Detailed responses to these worrisome questions are found in Part V. But in brief, some centers have been successful in shifting the attention of their primary care workers toward a more integrated approach and seem to be satisfied with the results. A small, growing literature supports this. Yet how generalizable such approaches will prove remains to be seen and studied.

Finally, there are specific questions about each of the proposed classifications. The consensus of the working group in Bellagio in November 1979 was that there were convincing reasons to favor the classification set forth in Chapter 11 by Regier and his colleagues. First, it is based on existing and tested symptoms from primary care settings. It was based primarily on the *Reason for Visit Classification* but modified in the light of the proposals of Burns's group and Williams and Spitzer (see Chapters 12 and 13) to include items that handle the special needs of children and the situation of identified mental disorders. Under this system, mental disorders would be removed from the first axis (e.g., the ninth revision of the *International Classification of Diseases* or the second edition of the *International Classification of Health Problems in Primary Care*) and coded on the second axis. This then would replace an entry from the psychological symptoms classification. It was agreed that each of these categories might have to be expanded hierarchically in settings where important and frequent occurrences or distinctions occurred. This would become apparent only after field testing of the classification in a given locale.

Finally, some considerable progress has been made in the plans for field testing. Seven sites have been chosen, representing a cross-section of primary care settings around the world. Each site will generate a series of case vignettes typical of their practice. These will then be translated for use by each of the other sites. From these, a set of case vignettes will be classified by primary care workers from each site. On the basis of this experience, a modification of the classifications will be made. The principal changes anticipated are that some items will prove so infrequent as to not warrant separate status. Others will emerge as subitems that are of sufficient frequency to warrant status as separate rubric. This experience will also show which items suffer from ambiguity, imprecision, or cultural narrowness. More broadly, the initial studies will give some indication as to the acceptability and utility of the use of the triaxial classification. These studies were planned at two meetings, the first at the Rockefeller Foundation in March 1980 and the second at Bellagio, Italy, in February 1981. The Division of Mental Health of the World Health Organization, under the direction of Norman Sartorius, is responsible for executing these field trials.

V

Applications of Classifications of Primary Health Care

Part V of this volume turns from the general and theoretical to consider some of the practical problems encountered in the use of multidimensional approaches to classifying health problems. Four issues are paramount.

First, psychological and social aspects of care are deeply embedded in local culture and conditions. The meaning and weight of individual issues vary enormously across cultures and within them. Because of this, the validity of a general classification may be questioned. In Chapter 16, Serpell discusses in detail the problems of obtaining valid data across cultures, using Zambian experiences as examples. He notes that the meaning of data may only become clear over time and several visits. Thus, he questions the value of any given classification used at only one point in time. Serpell notes that so-called "cosmopolitan" views of medicine and illness are frequently paralleled by traditional views more firmly embedded in the local culture. The extent to which parallel belief systems are included in the initial testing of a classification may determine its final validity. Serpell therefore calls for extensive grassroots participation in the testing of the new triaxial classification. These notions are reinforced in Chapter 17 by Burton-Bradley, who draws on examples from Papua New Guinea.

A second set of practical issues centers around the identity of those using the new classification. Specialists trained in highly developed tertiary centers might well use the same instrument differently than lay persons trained as health aides or physician's assistants. In Chapter 18, Climent details the ex-

241

perience in Cali, Colombia, in order to compare the functioning of specially trained auxiliary nurses and health promoters to that of psychiatrists. After careful epidemiological analysis, he asserts that the principles underlying success are not a function of the degree level of the health worker. Rather, an emphasis on health, methodological simplicity, and effectiveness in communicating determine whether or not a health worker will satisfactorily identify psychosocial issues. Climent also analyzes the aspects of patients that may affect illness phenomena and notes that any classification should include items that reflect the patients' beliefs, attitudes, and socioeconomic conditions. For example, attitudes such as tolerance, submission, family orientation, and distrust may affect the care the patients seek, what they reveal, and how they react to prescriptions and diagnoses. In Cali, the use of indigenous auxiliary nurses has led to improved case finding, more complete diagnosis, more complete treatment, and lowered costs of care.

Even when using appropriately sensitive and knowledgeable workers, the mechanics of recording may influence the success of the new classification. In Chapter 19, Busnello demonstrates one recording system that concretely expresses a multidimensional approach to patient care. He documents the model used, the system used, and some of its effects. An unusual feature is that of giving the patients part of their own records. Busnello anecdotally details the benefits of using a multiaxial records system.

Finally, even the best classification, expressed in an ideal record system, still depends on the individual health worker for proper application. In Chapter 20, Lipkin discusses the problems of educating, as well as training, primary care health workers in the psychosocial aspects of primary care. He discusses the central importance of psychosocial issues in the individual encounter. Then he establishes goals for education. He provides an outline for content, for processes to be taught, and for skills to be learned. He then goes into the practical issues of establishing appropriate curriculum, techniques, and principles of teaching, and of overcoming resistance. The central principle throughout is that success in educating primary care workers about psychosocial aspects of care requires more than a mechanical approach and more than didactic completeness. Integration of the knowledge, skills, and attitudes must be accomplished, so that the worker can feel good about the new learnings, can apply them with success, and can see that the benefits outweigh the discomforts and sacrifices involved.

16

Social and Psychological Constructs in Health Records: The Need for Adaptation to Different Sociocultural Environments

ROBERT SERPELL

THE RELEVANCE OF PSYCHOLOGICAL AND SOCIAL DATA FOR HEALTH PLANNING

Human illness is reflected in behavior. Contemporary biomedical science, however, often construes such behavior as a superficial manifestation or by-product of a more fundamental, underlying physical process of disease. As a result, practitioners trained in the new worldwide, cosmopolitan tradition of modern medicine are sometimes accused of failing to treat their patients as human beings in a state of conscious suffering.

Whereas the major advances of medical science during the nineteenth and early twentieth centuries took the form of demonstrating that complex and reversible physical processes in the human body are responsible for the conscious experience of illness, recent decades have seen the growth of a complementary body of knowledge in the field of social medicine, which emphasizes the role of psychological and social processes in both the manifestation and the etiology of physical disease. The conceptualization of just how psychological and social factors enter into the causation and definition of illness has not yet reached the level of rigorous consensus that informs the biomedical tradition. Nevertheless, the importance of these factors is sufficiently widely

The author is grateful to Professor Alan Haworth, of the University of Zambia School of Medicine, for assistance in locating some of the relevant literature and for access to his unpublished observations. The Ministry of Health of the Government of the Republic of Zambia has kindly given permission for the reproduction of the record form in Figure 16.1. Last, but not least, thanks are due to the various health workers who have given time to share their experiences in this difficult and important domain.

recognized that they form an essential part of the data base on which international, national, and local health planning must draw.

One group of psychological and social factors affecting health operates by increasing the physical vulnerability of the individual. It is clear, for instance, that both public and domestic sanitation in human settlements exercise a direct influence on the spread of infectious diseases. Both individual and social behavior play an essential part in the effectiveness of all forms of toilet systems, especially such low-cost forms as can realistically be projected for most low-income populations in countries of the Third World. Again, malnutrition is known to be responsible for a high proportion of illness in the poor countries of the world. In addition to the political and economic causes of poverty, many social and psychological variables enter into the cycle of behavior that maintains the inadequate intake of essential nutrients; these variables include migration and employment, inefficient land use, food storage and preparation, dietary preferences, and so on. Other examples of major health hazards with obvious psychological and social antecedents are road traffic and industrial accidents and the abuse of alcohol, tobacco, and other drugs.

A second group of factors, which partially overlaps the first, enters into the definition of certain forms of illness. Mental disorders of all kinds evidently manifest themselves in psychological symptoms, while many are known to have specific social origins. Mental stress has also been implicated in numerous "physical" afflictions, such as asthma, bronchitis, high blood pressure, and heart disease.

A third group of factors can be roughly characterized as reactions to disease and impairment. Individual and group differences exist in the threshold of intensity to which physical symptoms must rise before a sick role is adopted, as well as in the emotional and behavioral correlates of that role (1). The type of treatment that a patient will seek is, of course, also greatly influenced by cultural and social factors. Each form of treatment, in its turn, is socially structured and carries implications for the future social behavior of the treated individual. Notorious examples of unintended social consequences arising from treatment are the stigmatization and social incompetence often associated with patients discharged after long stays in medical institutions.

Finally, the correlation between certain broad demographic variables and the incidence of various diseases is probably a reflection of one or more of the three types of influence outlined above. For instance, the higher incidence of certain mental disorders among groups of lower socioeconomic status may reflect patterns of social organization that make them more vulnerable to certain precipitating factors such as marital discord; or it may reflect different cultural styles of expressing symptoms of mental stress; or, again, it may reflect different situational factors influencing a patient's mode of response to the illness experienced (e.g., some groups may have a greater need to escape completely from the responsibilities of normal social roles once the illness has reached a certain threshold).

SOURCES OF PSYCHOLOGICAL AND SOCIAL DATA RELEVANT TO HEALTH

Psychological and social factors of the kind listed above are clearly relevant to the interpretation of illness and to the design of health services. But rather little information about these factors is normally generated by systems for national health recording and reporting. A patient treated for gastroenteritis at a health center may be enjoined to wash his or her hands after using the toilet, but no record is likely to be obtained of the sanitary facilities to which he or she has access at home. Even patients treated for malnutrition are seldom requested to declare their income in countries where poverty is widespread. Moreover, some of the psychological and social factors that influence health-seeking behavior may be quite inaccessible to practitioners trained in the cosmopolitan tradition of modern medicine because of their particular social status and image. Home cures and visits to indigenous traditional healers may not be reported to the "cosmopolitan" health worker, either because the patient recovers without consulting him or her, or because they are deliberately concealed by the patient for fear of reprimand or ridicule.

It may be questioned, however, whether the social data needed for planning health services must necessarily be collected at the level of the individual patient. If a correlation has been well established between a certain environmental variable and the incidence of a disease, it may be sufficient to collect survey data on the environmental variable in isolation. For instance, in Zambia, public health assistants based in rural areas could be required to monitor the number and the quality of maintenance of pit latrines constructed in the catchment area for a rural health center by an annual survey, instead of requiring the medical assistants to ask patients who attend the center with gastric infections to give details of their domestic sanitation facilities.

Other categories of data may be more accessible to the agents of different social services than to health workers. Agricultural assistants and demonstrators might, for instance, find it easier to estimate the food supply available to individual families in rural areas of Zambia than public health assistants might. Teachers at the local primary schools, on the other hand, would be in a better position to monitor the daily food intake of malnourished children attending school. And community development assistants may be the best placed to record details of local dietary preferences and supplies of drinking water. Traditional healers in Zambia, as in many other countries in the Third World, treat a considerable range of illnesses and could, with appropriate efforts, be enlisted to record certain types of data concerning the social dynamics of the communities they serve.

Moreover, there is much to be gained, both in the promotion of public health and more generally in the reduction of wasteful duplication of efforts, by a greater integration of social services at the grassroots level. It has been observed in Zambia (2) that front-line agents of the various social services operate within an administrative framework that provides few incentives for intersectoral cooperation. Relevant institutions such as the district development committees and local councils exist in name, but generally lack the political and economic resources necessary to coordinate effectively the work of the various agencies. Instead, each front-line worker depends for guidance on a long, vertical chain of command within the particular national ministry against whose establishment he or she is appointed.

Decentralization is recognized by the Zambian government as a key requirement of successful rural development (3). A mechanism for pooling information resources at the local level would be a valuable contribution toward the implementation of such a policy. Access to information is, of course, only one of the necessary conditions for its accurate and regular recording and reporting. In addition, the officer to whom this task is entrusted needs to be appropriately trained and motivated. The tradition of professional specialization within cosmopolitan medical services may lead some medical experts to question the competence of primary school teachers to make a clinical assessment of a child's nutritional intake, or of community development assistants to judge the hygienic adequacy of a village's water supply. The best solution to this kind of problem seems to be for health educators to participate in the design of curricula and in the actual training of the relevant, allied professional and paraprofesional staff.

To enlist the participation of nonprofessional members of rural communities in the recording and reporting of health-related information is a difficult proposition, especially in Third World countries, given the low level of formal education of the general population. Nevertheless, the World Health Organization (WHO) has made a firm commitment (endorsed by some 134 national governments) to the concept of primary health care that "requires and promotes maximum community . . . participation in the planning, organization, operation, and control of primary health care, making fullest use of local . . . resources—and to this end develops through appropriate education the ability of communities to participate" (4). The peculiar contribution that traditional health practitioners may be hoped to make to the understanding of psychological and social factors affecting health is discussed in more detail below. Suffice it to note at this juncture that their unique access to certain categories of information would certainly justify a considerable investment of effort in training them to record and report such data (5).

The proposal that agents outside the Ministry of Health should be involved in the collection and reporting of data relevant to health would require for its implementation a variety of systematic orientation and training programs. Conflicting demands may be anticipated in this context between the economies of scale that could be achieved with centralized training and the greater situational relevance that can be ensured by training *in situ*. An ideal strategy would be to incorporate the general principles of collecting health-related information within the basic training of relevant categories of social service agents as well as in the curriculum of basic primary education, and to mount periodic local-level seminars aimed at bringing various agents together and at teaching highly specific routines in the context of actual local constraints, which otherwise undermine the feasibility of sophisticated recording systems devised from the perspective of a central planner (see below for examples).

RECORDING AND REPORTING BY HEALTH WORKERS

The Working Group on Primary Health Records convened by WHO at Rijeka (6) distinguished three main types of purpose for maintaining health records: (1) as a clinical *aide-mémoire* for the health worker who makes the record; (2) for communication about a patient to other health workers or agents of other social services; and (3) for the generation of statistical data. The last of these purposes is of greatest concern to health planners and administrators, who use such statistics for the computation of workloads, of the costs and coverage of health services, and so on. Such statistical aggregates are, however, seldom made available to the front-line health worker who makes the initial records. For him or her, the main purpose of keeping records is as a reminder of what transpired when the patient last came to the clinic, so that the progress of the prescribed treatment can be monitored.

Inspection of the practice in a rural health center in Zambia suggests that the requirements of these two contrasting purposes (the first and third) have little in common. For their own *aide-mémoire,* the medical assistants keep a card for each patient on which they record the date of consultation, the presenting symptoms of the ailment, and the treatment prescribed. The card is numbered and filed in consecutive numerical order, and the patient is given a small card with the same number on it, which he or she presents when returning for further treatment. If the patient returns more than two months after the last consultation, he or she is treated as a new case. For statistical purposes, medical assistants also keep on their desk two checklists for outpatients. One, for new cases, provides 32 options for classifying the diagnosis, and an assistant crosses off the next number in the appropriate box as well as entering in a register the patient's card number, name, sex, age, home village, ailment, and treatment. The other checklist is for returning patients and simply provides a consecutive list of numbers, one of which is canceled for each case.

The effect of this parallel recording procedure is that the medical assistant seldom has any need to consult the patients' record cards when compiling the monthly returns required by the Ministry of Health headquarters (Figure 16.1). Most of the data required is already contained on the checklist for new cases, and the remainder (breakdown by sex and age) can be retrieved from the register. The only exceptions are the small number of inpatients, as well as tuberculosis (TB) and leprosy outpatients, about whom a greater amount of detail is required in the reports.

When the reporting system is examined for its coverage of psychological and social factors, it becomes apparent that these are generally filtered out, not only by the limited set of categories provided on the monthly return forms but also by the overall recording procedure. Since (with the exception of inpatients, TB, and leprosy patients) details of a patient's ailment are only included in the data base for onward reporting on the occasion of the first consultation, any subtle or latent etiological factor is most unlikely to find its way into the records. The 32 categories supplied by the checklist are all based on the physical symptoms that are likely within the cosmopolitan biomedical tradition to command initial attention during a first consultation. The alleviation of these symptoms is the principal apparent motive of the first consultation, and by comparison their etiology tends to receive only subsidiary attention.

An evaluation of how appropriate this approach may be to the treatment of outpatients at a small health center must depend on a number of considerations, including the proportion of cases in which organic disease is the principal cause of the reported symptoms, and the effectiveness of purely "physical" treatment for the majority of cases. A study of patients attending a specialist medical clinic in the capital city of Dar es Salaam, Tanzania, concluded that "90% of patients complaining of chest pain and 75% of those with abdominal pain . . . were thought not to have organic disease as a basis for their symptoms" (7). In a study of outpatients at a small town's health center in Ethiopia, 19% of the cases were judged to display "conspicuous psychiatric morbidity," of which nearly half reported physical symptoms without any identifiable organic cause, and a further quarter showed abnormal psychological reactions to an indisputable physical illness (8). A very similar incidence of "conspicuous psychiatric morbidity" (22%) was found in a study of outpatients at a health center that serves a low-income suburb of Lusaka, Zambia (9). Both of the latter studies identified a significant proportion of the cases displaying psychiatric morbidity as patients who presented themselves as suffering from diseases of the respiratory or gastrointestinal system, the two largest causes of illness recorded by health institutions in Zambia (2).

These and other scattered indications suggest that psychological factors play a considerable role in the causation and manifestation of illnesses that are referred to general health centers in several Third World countries. General health workers, however, seem to detect only a small proportion of such cases. The baseline studies in Colombia, India, Senegal, and Sudan for WHO's study on strategies for extending mental health care have so far indicated that less than 40% of the definite cases of mental disorder confirmed by psychiatric interview were detected by the staff of general health centers during the initial consultation (10). As we have seen, no provision exists in Zambian rural health centers for the staff to record such a condition specifically, even when it is detected. The case must simply be recorded as a specific physical ailment or as one of "all other diseases" (see Figure 16.1).

For treatment and management, the health staff members have a number of options. They can attempt to treat the physical symptoms as if they have an organic cause; they can prescribe a placebo; they can refer the case to a specialized psychiatric unit; or they can attempt to mobilize other community resources, such as the patient's escorts and other members of the family, a social worker (in the rare cases where one is accessible), or a law enforcement agency. Finally, in the rare cases where a psychiatric condition has been clearly identified, the health staff can, if suitably supplied, dispense appropriate psychopharmacological drugs.

Only if a patient is referrred to a specialized psychiatric unit will his or her illness be recorded and reported to the Zambian Ministry of Health as a specific category of mental disorder. In addition to the large mental hospital in the capital (which has an inpatient capacity of more than 500 beds), eight general hospitals and ten rural mental health units in Zambia have facilities for mental inpatients. There are also facilities at 20 localities in Zambia for outpatient treatment of mental disorders. The inpatient caseload for the nation as a whole (with a total population of about 5 million) in 1978 was about 6,000, and the outpatient caseload about 16,000 (11). The scope of this specialized mental health service is unusually wide for Africa. The constraints faced by its recording and reporting system can therefore be taken as an underestimate of those faced by other national health services on the continent in keeping track of mental health morbidity.

A recent visit to the mental health unit of a general hospital located in a small provincial capital town revealed record-keeping problems of a different nature from those faced by the rural health center. Here the caseload is confined to inpatients (between 1,000 and 2,000 per year), and each patient has a file. A register of patients is also kept; it starts each month with a list of those carried forward from the previous month and then records each new admission with a file number, date of admission, date of discharge, "absconding" or death, name, age, residence, and reason for admission. The principal medical assistant in charge of the unit has estimated that at least three-quarters of his admissions are brought in by the police with a detention order, while the remainder are voluntary patients or transferred from other, smaller units in the same province.

The monthly returns to the Ministry of Health are derived from the admis-

Figure 16.1. Checklist for returning patients, for use by medical assistants in Zambia.

MINISTRY OF HEALTH

Monthly Returns

Medical Form No. 4

D443 27/8 2A

FOR HEALTH CENTRES AND SUB-CENTRES

Full Name of Unit _____ Officer No. _____

Full Address and Box No. _____ Actual Skeds _____ Cat. _____

District _____ Province _____ Month _____ Year _____

PART A — New Cases this Month

	MAIN DIAGNOSIS FOR NEW IN-PATIENT ADMISSIONS						MAIN DIAGNOSIS FOR OUT-PATIENT ATTENDANCES					
	MALES		FEMALES				MALES		FEMALES			
	Adults	Children	Adults	Children			Adults	Children	Adults	Children		
Abdomen: Diarrhoea												
Jaundice												
Other abdominal cases												
Fevers: Malaria												
Sleeping Sickness												
Other fevers												
Infectious diseases: Chickenpox												
Measles												
Smallpox												
Whooping cough												
Other infectious diseases												
Chest: Upper respiratory tract infections												
Pneumonia												

Other pulmonary cases

Skin:	Scabies								
	Ulcers								
	Other skin cases								
Worms:	Bilharzia								
	Hookworm								
	Other worm infections								
Disease of:	Ear								
	Eyes								
	Teeth								
Genito urinary disease									
Anaemia									
Leprosy									
Tuberculosis—Non-pulmonary, suspected									
Veneral ciseases									
Malnutrition and other deficiency									
Injuries									
All other diseases									
Maternity Admissions									
TOTAL NUMBER OF NEW CASES (New this Month)									

NOTES: (i) Only NEW ILLNESSES THIS MONTH should be recorded here. A patient who was already attending for the SAME illness last month is a Re-Attender.

(ii) CHILDREN—UP to 15 years: ADULTS—15 years and over. The age group 5#14 includes all children up to the age of 15 but not 15.

Source: Ministry of Health, Zambia

sions register and make almost exclusive use of three categories: A69 (*psychoses*), A70 (*alcoholic*), and A74 (*epileptics*).* Earlier records of the unit had also occasionally used A71 (*neurotics*), but such cases are not part of the current workload as perceived by the principal medical assistant. This pattern of diagnoses and referrals stands in marked contrast to epidemiological studies from industrialized countries and to the preliminary results of the WHO (10) study in rural areas of Colombia, India, Senegal, and Sudan, where the majority of those identified as mentally ill fall into the neurotic group. The phenomenon may be understood either as a threshold effect, with only the more serious cases reaching the hospital, or as a product of a communication failure, with society preselecting the cases that it brings to the hospital on the basis of a limiting stereotype of the scope of "cosmopolitan" psychiatry. The latter possibility receives more detailed consideration below.

Another facet of the recording system that gives grave cause for concern is its handling of readmissions. The principal medical assistant has estimated that about three-quarters of his caseload are readmissions, with some patients being readmitted as often as ten times in one year. Yet, not only is the service inadequately equipped to follow up such cases in the patient's home community, but the record system itself is poorly designed for maintaining continuity of care in hospital over several consecutive admissions. Files of current and recently discharged patients are stacked neatly in piles according to alphabetical order of the patients' surnames. But every year this classified stack is cleared by tying all inactive files into a bundle, which is stored on a high shelf in a cupboard. The principal medical assistant has recognized this as a serious problem and has itemized administrative constraints that have delayed the construction of suitable shelving for the orderly storage of past years' files. But, of course, even with such improvements, a caseload of 1,000 per year would rapidly overload such a system.

As is the case in the rural health center, the clinical functions of record keeping in this mental health unit seem to be totally divorced from the systematic classification and ordering of data that is carried out for statistical purposes. In this instance, it is clear that a locally usable card index would greatly facilitate the delivery of continuous care to chronic psychiatric patients, as well as provide a more reliable basis for generating statistics on readmission. The absence of an effective system for tracing a patient's record is probably a source of distortion in Zambia's medical statistics, even in the case of outpatient treatment over a period of a few days or weeks. For instance, Haworth (9) reports that records kept by researchers over a sample of six days

---

*The glosses cited here are those provided by the health worker in charge of the unit. A69 was the most frequently used and seems to combine categories 210, 211, 212, and 213 of the Basic Tabulation List in the ninth revision of the *International Classification of Diseases* (*ICD*-9) (12). A70 and A74 correspond quite closely with *ICD*-9's 215 and 225, while A71 resembles 214.

at an urban clinic yielded an estimate of 5,000 attendances by new patients per month, whereas the statistics of this monthly index reported to the Ministry of Health over the preceding five months ranged from 15,000 to 21,000. No doubt, part of the error may arise from reattending patients failing to produce an identification number. But the penalty for such a failure at an urban Zambian clinic is a very considerable delay in receiving treatment. The most important cause of the inflated record of new attendances seems likely to be the unwieldy filing system, which prevents health staff from tracing many of their reattending patients' earlier records. Indeed, Haworth reports that "after the survey had been completed the only experienced records clerk was removed from the clinic (to work at the headquarters of the Ministry of Health), and it then became impossible to trace increasing numbers of medical record cards attending the clinic and, finally, many thousands were destroyed when the situation had become completely chaotic" (9).

Before ending this discussion of the practical difficulties of generating useful and reliable records of psychological and social factors in Third World health institutions, mention must be made of the problem of multiple causation. The practice of ticking items off a checklist while examining new cases militates against the clinical principle of resolving a problem only up to the level of specificity that is warranted by the available information. In order to choose among the necessarily limited set of categories on the checklist, the health worker must at an early stage of treatment make unwarranted and arbitrary decisions (e.g., whether to record a case as *diarrhea,* as *anemia,* or as *malnutrition*—cf. Figure 16.1). For clinical purposes at this stage, the conscientious health worker needs to record a variety of symptoms and to keep open a number of alternative diagnoses. If psychological and social factors are to be introduced into the record form, the need for multiple coding will be further highlighted. Rutter, Shaffer, and Shepherd (13), for instance, showed that mental retardation was significantly less often coded by experienced psychiatrists using *ICD*-8 than when using a multiaxial system, which required them to specify an intellectual level for each patient.

The V Codes included in *ICD*-9 specify a number of psychological and social "factors influencing health status and contact with health services," but their use is explicitly "supplementary" and optional and thus fails to command priority attention from busy health workers. The use of a more elaborate classification scheme will clearly afford an opportunity for improving the scope and reliability of health records. But it would only be realistic to attempt to introduce such a system in busy clinics if the demands of the clinical and statistical functions of records can be successfully integrated. Under the circumstances described above, the health worker, especially within the psychiatric service, may enter psychological or social factors in the etiology of a case into the clinical record, but this record is seldom consulted when reporting for statistical purposes to a higher level.

THE NEED FOR SOCIOCULTURAL ADAPTATION
OF INFORMATION SYSTEMS

It has already been noted above that different users of medical records have different objectives in consulting them, and that an ideal record for the clinical purposes of the front-line health worker may not be ideal for generating statistical returns to central planners, or vice versa. This is a particular instance of a more general problem of communication to various audiences. The problem has long been of concern to social scientists and semantic theorists, and has acquired a special importance in cross-cultural research.

Pike (14) drew an influential analogy between the problem faced by the social scientist seeking to represent the social world of a culture to which he or she is new, and the task of constructing an appropriate description of the sound system of a newly encountered community's language. In both cases, the theorist's success depends on identifying the contrasts that are important to members of a given culture. Within the realm of phonology, such contrasts are termed *phonemic* and can be shown empirically to be a relatively small subset of the range of *phonetic* distinctions of which the human vocal and auditory organs are capable. Not only does the foreign adult experience difficulty in pronouncing the sounds of a new language, but he or she also fails to notice the difference between certain pairs of sounds in that language when spoken by a native speaker. The learning process that enables one to become a fluent speaker of a given first language tends to disable one from hearing or pronouncing the signficant sounds of a structurally different language. The result is known by some students of linguistics as *first-language interference,* a phenomenon all too familiar to the participants in international conferences. (A limitation of interference theory is described below.)

Borrowing from this analysis of contrastive phonology and its behavioral consequences, Pike proposed that in any field of social behavior a set of concepts that are significant to a particular cultural group may be identified, and that these should be termed *emic* concepts for that group. The full range of possible concepts in the domain in question is conversely termed *etic* by analogy with the International Phonetic Alphabet. Some cross-cultural psychologists have been inspired by this analysis to set themselves the task of deriving from multicultural studies a set of universally applicable, etic constructs that can describe behavior effectively, irrespective of its cultural setting (15,16).

Judging from the case of phonology, however, the usefulness of such etic constructs would be confined to a small group of specialists who seek to take an "Olympian view" of the full range of human behavior (17). Indeed, it is arguable that the goal of such a detached impartiality is partly responsible for the fact that so much psychological research in the Third World has "been addressed to an international audience of scholars, with little or no concern for whether the interpretations it offers have any meaning for the people who were studied" (18). In the field of health, as in other domains, the layman in every society "expects that the understanding which the psychologist offers will bear some relation to the understanding he himself already has. If the psychologist offers explanations which bear no relation to this, or suggests or implies that his everyday understanding is of no significance, the layman is inevitably puzzled or dissatisfied" (19).

Such dissatisfaction is all too easily dismissed as reactionary conservatism by those who see in the dramatic advances of contemporary science a panacea for all human ills. The categories of the physical sciences, these critics claim, have an objective truth value that sets them above the emic criteria of any given culture. Many philosophers of science would reject such a view. Kuhn, for instance, interprets most "normal" scientific "research as a strenuous and devoted attempt to force nature into the conceptual boxes supplied by professional education" (20). Nevertheless, the demonstrable effectiveness of modern, "cosmopolitan" medicine might seem to impart in many parts of the world a pragmatic validity to its model of disease. Against this cogent argument must be set the evidence that many populations, especially in the Third World, seem to adopt an eclectic attitude toward "cosmopolitan" medicine, and to find no incompatibility between, on the one hand, drawing on the services of "cosmopolitan" health workers while, on the other hand, concurrently consulting indigenous traditional healers whose theories of illness are entirely different. In Zambia's capital city of Lusaka, for instance, Leeson and Frankenberg (21) found that 90% of their sample of over 1,000 patients of ng'anga (traditional doctors) had first consulted a "cosmopolitan" medical agency, while Khan, Kaunda, and Maguire (22) assert that 95% of their sample of children admitted to hospital had first seen a traditional healer or been treated by their grandmothers. When it is recognized that contemporary "cosmopolitan" medicine admits that it is unable to successfully treat a wide range of the complaints and conditions that it encounters, there remains little room for doubt that alternative, widely used medical systems deserve serious consideration.

Another important counterargument against the charge of conservatism is that the demand for intelligibility is not incompatible with creative innovation. An *emic* construct may be defined "as a representation which conforms with the conventions of a system known to members of a given culture" (18). Such conventions are instances of what Searle (23) has called *constitutive rules.* In chess, the rules that specify the possible moves for each piece constitute the essence of the game. Their logical status is thus quite different from that of *regulative rules,* such as the conventions that a player may not change a move after letting go of the piece moved or that a move must be made within a certain specified period of time. The grammar of a language may be said to be constituted by a set of rules in the same way that a game is constituted by its rules. Now in both these types of systems, it is possible to create new and original applications of the rules. In the domain of language, for instance, entirely new words can be coined that adhere to the phonological rules, and new sentences can be composed that conform to the syntactic rules. Indeed, through the use of metaphor, poets and scientists can "talk what is nonsense on the face of it, but in such a way that the recipient may have the meaning suggested to him" (24). The secret of acceptable innovation, as Gombrich (25) has succinctly put it for the domain of art, is to devise "comparisons that work." The call for social scientists to phrase their interpretations of behavior in emic terms is not a demand that they repeat what their audience already knows or believes, but that they strive to make their message comprehensible to that audience.

The domains of psychological and social factors pose special communication problems for the "cosmopolitan" health planner, since these are precisely the spheres in which the explanatory constructs of local traditional medicine generally carry the greatest weight with the local population. In Zambia, "the service offered by traditional practitioners differs from the national health service in two major respects: it is more firmly embedded in the social environment of the patient, and it is more personalised" (16). Moreover, a subtle shift occurs in the logical relation between a representation and that which is represented as we move from the domain of physical phenomena to that of mental and social life. For, as Taylor has argued, "the vocabulary of a given social dimension is grounded in the shape of social practice in this dimension: that is, the vocabulary wouldn't make sense, couldn't be applied sensibly where this range of practices didn't prevail" (26). For example, Taylor considers the case of a traditional society founded on

> a powerful form of consensus, which put a high premium on unanimous decision. Such a consensus would be considered shattered if two clearly articulated parties were to separate out, pursuing opposed aims and attempting to vote down the opposition or push it into a settlement on the most favorable conditions for themselves. . . . Now the difference between our [American] society and one of the kind just described could not be well expressed if we said we have a vocabulary to describe negotiation which they lack. We might say, for instance, that we have a vocabulary to describe the heavens which they lack, viz., that of Newtonian mechanics; for here we assume that they live under the same heavens as we do, only understand it differently. But it is not true that they have the same kind of bargaining as we do. (p. 23)

Likewise, it may be quite proper to assume that bacteria and parasites invade and infect human organisms in a standard way irrespective of those humans' belief systems, but it is much more difficult to justify the assumption that psychiatric syndromes or social pressures operate independently of the sociocultural setting.

On the contrary, we may propose that psychological and social health constructs will only be of use if they are carefully designed to be intelligible to members of the cultural group whose health is at stake. This proposition can be defended with two lines of reasoning. First, there is danger that, if an internationally standardized construct is introduced into two different cultures, it will carry different connotations within each culture, thus undermining the theoretical foundations on which its explanatory validity has been premised. We may term this the *danger of cultural distortion or interference*. Second, there is the *danger of perceived irrelevance*. Since human cognitive and conative processes are necessarily involved in the course of psychological and social forms of illness, the health practitioner in this domain, like Joynson's hermeneutical psychologist, "can be of practical value only in so far as he succeeds in increasing the laymen's self-understanding, and only to the extent that he contrives to enlist the layman's self-control" (19).

The theoretical problems discussed above have both political and practical implications. The political implications have been well stated by the Director General of WHO as follows:

Most behavioral science has been developed in the industrialized countries of Europe and America. The concepts, methods, and findings of the studies done in these areas may not be applicable in other sociocultural settings, and new strategies and research techniques may be necessary to supplement the approaches to psychosocial problems in the developing countries. Moreover, particularly in a psychosocial program, radical steps must be taken to avoid the donor/recipient relationship in which the developing countries are/were consumers of methods and projects prepared elsewhere. The fact that in many instances researchers in developing countries serve at best as data collectors for outside experts is contrary to the very nature of a psychosocial program in which the methods, concepts, and approaches must be developed in the setting in which work takes place, by people who understand it and are part of it, and with a full understanding of the temporal and sociocultural dimensions of the problems under study. (27)

The political dilemma that arises in the international arena from the unequal distribution of scientific institutions and resources between more and less industrialized countries is reenacted on the domestic scene between the town and country and between the educated elite and the illiterate mass of the population. Theories and technologies conceived in isolation by central planners based in Third World nations' ministerial headquarters run the same risk of failing to respond to the essential health needs of peripheral rural communities as do those transferred blindly from industrialized countries. It is therefore necessary to envisage grassroots community participation at an early stage in both the setting of priorities and the generation of strategies. If members of the community, front-line health workers, and other social service agents are to be responsible for the collection and utilization of psychological and social data, they must understand the need for those data from the perspective of their own situations.

There are also more concrete, practical reasons for adapting information systems to the sociocultural characteristics of the communities to which they refer. The environment of many peripheral communities in Third World countries is characterized by a scarcity of basic economic infrastructure, educated personnel, technological artifacts, documentary resources, and reliable supply lines for externally produced commodities. Many information systems that seem intrinsically well designed are liable to encounter operational problems in such an environment. A computerized system may break down completely, for instance, because of inadequate technical support facilities (28). Even a card-filing system needs to be assured of regular supplies of preprinted, standard-format record cards—which is far from assured in rural health centers in Zambia. Two of the health units that the present author visited recently—one in a remote rural setting, the other in the hospital of a small provincial town—were using entirely inappropriate printed forms as record cards, for lack of any alternative.

The resourcefulness of front-line workers in the face of such constraints commands respect, but the particular coping strategies that they adopt are liable to sacrifice essential features of an information system unless they are thoroughly familiar with its total rationale. For instance, a clinical *aide-mémoire* scarcely needs to record the sex of the patient, but this variable is precoded on statistical returns for significant epidemiological reasons.

One way of safeguarding a reporting system against the omission of essential information under the pressure of local expediency would be to train front-line workers to calculate their own local statistical data for their own interest and use. Plotting a graph to reveal the monthly incidence of certain major conditions, for instance, is well within the capabilities of Zambian medical assistants. Such a practice would provide an incentive for keeping complete and accurate records. It could also help the national or provincial health system to respond more efficiently to fluctuating local needs. A sudden rise in the incidence of a given infectious disease would be readily documented at the level of a single clinic, and this could form the basis of a quantitative estimate of the clinic's needs for an emergency supply of drugs.

PROBLEMS OF ADAPTATION AND STANDARDIZATION IN A THIRD WORLD COUNTRY

The indigenous or emic system of representing psychological and social information in a Third World community often departs from basic premises of professional training in Western industrial societies. There are two domains in which this can give rise to misunderstanding by cosmopolitan health workers: first, the classification of basic social information, and, second, communication about illness. The latter is a slippery business at the best of times, especially when one party is a health worker who claims some expert knowledge that may be used to redefine and reify the patient's problem. The difficulty is, however, further aggravated in Third World societies, where so many of the conceptual tools of "cosmopolitan" medicine are foreign to the predominant local cultural norms.

Two anecdotes from clinical case conferences at the mental hospital in Lusaka serve to illustrate the communication problems that this situation can generate. On one occasion, a medical officer (himself born and bred in another Third World country, but trained in a Western institution) was interviewing an elderly woman patient through an interpreter. When she proved unable to tell him the calendar date on which she was being interviewed, he interpreted this as evidence of "disorientation in time." Now anyone who has lived for a few days in a Zambian village is well aware that the passage of time is not indexed by calendar date among most of the adult women.

Indeed, attempts by researchers to establish the date of birth of a young child in a Zambian village encounter the following constraints. The mother can pinpoint the year of birth if the child is less than five years of age, and is often able to specify the season with reference to the presence or absence of rain and the growth cycle of crops. But it is to the inside of the father's Bible or to a school-going elder sibling that one must turn for a calendar date. The child will often be uncertain on the matter of his or her own age even in the upper grades of primary school, although a "school age" can be readily given. In the lower grades, this statistic adds little to the knowledge of the grade in which the child is enrolled, since almost all children register in first grade as being either seven or eight years old in order to conform with the regulations of the Ministry of Education, irrespective of their real age.

The concept of chronological age is scarcely of any importance within Zambian village cultures. What matters is seniority. Early in life this is represented in relation to one's siblings and neighbors in the same general stage of physical maturity. Later in life it is marked by the milestones of puberty, marriage, and parenthood; still later by multiple parenthood and the age and number of one's children and grandchildren; and finally by the physical signs of aging and debility. Under these circumstances, the psychological and social information related to age may be more reliably elicited in a form that requires the informant to interpret the situation of the target individual rather than by requesting an absolute number. Many rural Zambian informants, whose estimates of the chronological age of lifelong acquantances would be unreliable within a range of five years, could more reliably indicate for instance whether they have reached puberty, how many children they have, or whether they have any grandchildren of school-going age. In the case of children, emic milestones are more difficult to specify, but many parents may be able to state quite reliably whether a child was seriously delayed in walking or talking within the first two years of life.

A second anecdote from the hospital concerns a young male patient who was recounting through an interpreter the events that had led to his being arrested by the police. A fight was described in which the patient claimed that he was knocked over and the identity of his assailant was in question. After some probing, the nurse who was interpreting announced that the assailant was the patient's mother-in-law. The audience burst into laughter at the idea of the traditional tension between son-in-law and mother-in-law giving rise to such unladylike violence. The clinician presenting the case interpreted the report as evidence of blatant projection and/or confusion. But after the mirth had subsided, the nurse was prevailed upon to check on the sex of the alleged assailant and the patient was quite definite that it was a man who had struck him.

The confusion in this instance was created by a mistranslation. None of the Zambian languages encode the gender of personal pronouns, and the word for *mother-in-law* also means *father-in-law*. Because of the low idiomatic availability of the English sex-free term *parent-in-law,* which is the nearest equivalent to *mpongozi,* the interpreter has to decide each time whether to translate it as *mother-in-law* or *father-in-law*. Had the clinician interviewed this patient in his own language, the ambiguity of his utterance would have been apparent and would have been resolved through the usual contextual information. As it was, the excitement generated by the confusion over sex identity diverted the attention of the case conference from the more significant fact of violence being alleged between a man and one of his parents-in-law, which in all the indigenous Zambian cultures constitutes a very serious breach of traditional taboo.

The whole domain of family relationships is a rich source of misunderstanding across cultures. If such data are to be recorded routinely by health staff members, great care will need to be exercised in the design of record forms so as to avoid forcing the actual data into inappropriate categories. For instance, there are several different forms of marriage prevalent in Zambia. The main categories are common-law marriage, customary marriage, and statutory marriage. Different laws pertain to each of these forms of marriage (29), but there is widespread ignorance of the relevant law as well as numerous legal anomalies; reform in this area, especially with regard to inheritance, is regarded as a priority by the National Law Development Commission (30). Ordinary language usage fails to distinguish among the different types of marriage, unless a series of probing questions is asked. Research is needed to establish whether different forms of marriage in Zambia are correlated with different patterns of health, and a preliminary contribution will be made in this field by the WHO-sponsored study of community response to alcohol-related problems (31). In the absence of such research, decisions on how to code marital status in health records in Zambia and many other multicultural countries must remain highly problematic.

A related family variable, which has received considerable attention in Western research on mental health in childhood, is the integrity of the home. "Broken homes" have been postulated as injurious to children's mental health for a number of theoretical reasons (32,33). It has, however, been widely recognized that the structure of families and patterns of parenting vary greatly from one culture to another. In Zambia, the identity of a central parental figure may sometimes be hard to specify. For instance, in the tradition of the extended family, a child normally has several "mothers" and several "fathers." Close questioning will reveal which of the persons so designated are a child's biological parents, but this may or may not be an important distinction in respect of the child's relationship to those adults.

Within a small, stable village community, child care responsibilities may be systematically shared among several relatives at different ages. Grandparents, for instance, traditionally play an important role in caring for children between the ages of two and seven in Chewa society (34) and in many other Zambian communities. Elder siblings also carry much more explicit responsibility for child care in most Zambian families than is the case in Western industrialized societies. In low-income urban settlements, far from undergoing change in the direction of Western cultural norms, the role played in child care by elder siblings is very prominent, perhaps because of the lesser accessibility of grandparents (35). Given the complexity and variability of family environments across different sociocultural groups, the selection of appropriate key variables to index family stability and integrity will require extensive research. Whereas the marital status of a target child's biological parents may account for a substantial proportion of the variance in mental health within a Western city culture, the same variable may carry very little weight in certain rural cultures of the Third World.

Socioeconomic status is another demographic variable widely held to correlate with health in industrialized countries. The construction of an index for this variable need not pose a serious problem in a Third World country. But the rapid social and economic change that a society is undergoing may require that the criteria for demarcating categories be frequently revised. Moreover, in the dual economies of many Third World nations, two separate scales might prove most appropriate, one for the rural sector and one for the urban sector.

Communication about illness itself is, by its nature, especially prone to problems of definition. A patient's dominant preoccupation is most often with subjective experience, while that of a physician is with observable disorders of function. The success of a practitioner depends to a considerable extent on his or her ability to reach consensus with the client on a particular conceptualization of the health problem. From this conceptualization are derived both the criteria of recovery and a rationale for the type of intervention that is to be prescribed. An observer, be it patient or practitioner, conceptualizes a particular case by drawing on one or more general theories of illness. Such a theory, or *nosology,* encompasses a variety of explanatory constructs. Some are simple, empirical generalizations, such as that linking swelling and pain with a twisted ankle. Others involve complex inferences and hypothetical intervening processes, such as infection, bewitchment, or repression. Not all of these theoretical constructs are explicitly invoked in any given discussion of a patient's problem, but they constitute a framework of implicit assumptions that give meaning to the overt diagnosis and treatment. One of the purposes of health education is to implant in the minds of the general public the rudiments of "cosmopolitan" medicine's currently dominant nosological constructs, such as the germ theory of disease. In many societies such education is in competition with one or more, less formally transmitted, alternative nosologies that inform much of the public's thinking about illness.

For simplicity of exposition, let us first consider the situation portrayed in Figure 16.2, which postulates just two nosological systems to which members of a particular society have access. One of these, termed "cosmopolitan medicine," represents the body of knowledge incorporated in such documents as *ICD* (12). The other system, termed "indigenous traditional medicine," represents a body of oral tradition of which certain local specialists have an extensive knowledge. Members of the general population from which the patients attending health centers are drawn typically have a patchy and incomplete knowledge of each of these two systems. The small circles in the diagram represent nosological constructs of various kinds, such as TB, affective psychosis, gastroenteritis, and so on. These examples would all belong within the larger right-hand circle representing the system of cosmopolitan medicine. If the community in question were a group of Chewa villages in eastern Zambia or in Malawi, constructs featuring in the system of indigenous traditional medicine (represented by the larger left-hand circle) would include *mizimu* and *mdulo* (36,37).

The first problem that may confront cosmopolitan health workers in such a situation is the different logical status of the traditional medical constructs invoked by some of their patients to explain their illnesses, on the one hand, and on the other hand the cosmopolitan medical constructs that their training has prepared them to use. A well-known anecdote illustrating this problem is that of the Western-trained scientist who sought to persuade a believer in African witchcraft that the fever he was experiencing was caused by malaria. The traditionalist, after listening carefully, replied, "Yes, I accept that what you say is true: An anopheles mosquito bit me, and I therefore caught malaria. But your account does not explain why the mosquito bit *me* at this point in time rather than anyone else." In such cases a patient is likely to seek two different kinds of diagnosis and treatment concurrently: one, derived from cos-

Figure 16.2. Access to the repertoire of nosological constructs in a bicultural community.

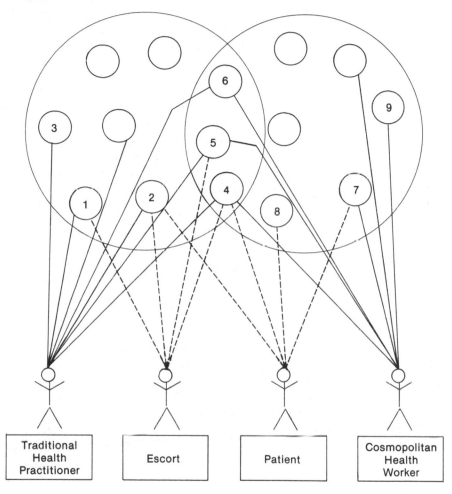

Source: Compiled by the author.

mopolitan medicine, to alleviate the physical symptoms of disease; the other, derived from traditional medicine, to explain its origin and to prevent its recurrence. Often such parallel treatments can proceed without mutual interference, but occasionally they come into direct conflict. An example cited by a medical assistant in charge of a rural health center in Zambia's Eastern Province was the aftercare of children diagnosed by cosmopolitan medicine as suffering from measles. The traditional medical treatment for this condition indigenous to the area prohibits the mother from washing the child. This sometimes results in the skin sores left by the disease becoming infected. In such a case, cosmopolitan medicine prescribes a line of action incompatible with the indigenous traditional prescription.

The resolution of such a conflict will depend on a variety of factors. If the illness under consideration is explained by a patient and by the person escorting them to the clinic in terms of a traditional construct (e.g., number 2 in Figure 16.2) that is unknown to the health worker, while he or she in turn explains the same illness in terms of a cosmopolitan construct (e.g., number 9 in Figure 15.4) that is unknown to both patient and escort, a full-scale battle of wills must ensue. In favor of the health worker's diagnosis will be his or her status as a recognized healer, especially if the initiative for the consultation has come from the patient and/or the escort. But, unless the patient is admitted for continuous supervision, the responsibility for adhering to the health worker's prescription rests with the patient and his or her immediate family. Often, in that context, the traditional system will carry the greater weight.

Communication about the patient's illness, however, will normally bring into play a number of different types of explanation, many of them being attempts to define symptoms rather than to name a specific disease entity. Some of these lower-order constructs are held in common between the two medical systems (e.g., numbers 4, 5, and 6 in Figure 16.2). Although they use quite different pharmacopoeias, the two systems may agree on the principle of prescribing palliatives for external sores, etc. By focusing attention on such bridging constructs, especially if they are known to patient, escort and health worker (e.g., number 4), a degree of consensus may be more readily attained. It is, however, highly desirable that the health worker should understand the emic significance of such constructs within the local community's culture, since without such background knowledge he or she may suggest unintended connotations by invoking a particular construct to explain or describe the patient's condition.

The two systems of medicine in Figure 16.2 can be likened to two linguistic codes. Just as most people in a multilingual society have a knowledge of more than one language, members of a multicultural society have a repertoire of cognitive systems on which they draw for different situations (38). Hence the patient in Figure 16.2 is represented as having a knowledge (albeit partial) of both medical systems. Indeed, in many Third World urban communities, an individual typically has some contact with three or more alternative nosological systems that overlap in a variety of different ways, as illustrated speculatively by Figure 16.3. Many of the African independent churches, for instance, hold rituals of healing that are informed by a distinctive combination of ideas derived from Christianity and other African traditions (39). One way of understanding how an individual chooses which of the available systems to apply to the interpretation of his or her illness is the model of situational code switching (40). The situational variables that can be shown to affect a bilin-

Figure 16.3. Patterns of overlap among the multiple systems of medicine coexisting in a multicultural society.

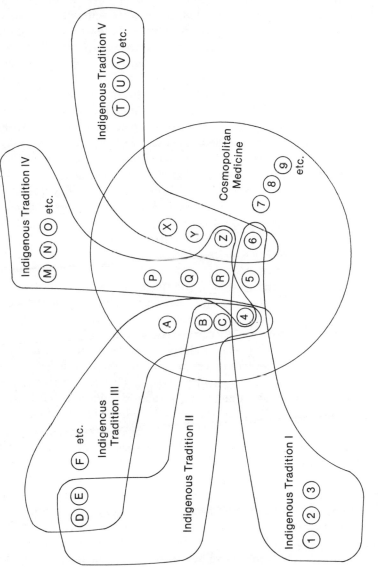

Source: Compiled by the author.

gual speaker's choice of code include the social setting (e.g., home or school); the social situation or constellation of personnel (e.g., a classroom lesson or a game of football); and the topic of conversation (e.g., presenting a lesson or requesting a student to clean the board). In the same vein, we may expect the multicultural patient to come to a cosmopolitan clinic with a predisposition to interpret his or her illness—at least in overt speech—in terms of cosmopolitan medical constructs, while bringing a complementary appropriate disposition to a consultation with a traditional herbalist or to a faith-healing ritual.

What precipitates the decision to refer one particular case of illness to a given agency is still in need of clarification through research. Certainly, the range of conditions commonly referred to the specialized psychiatric service in Zambia falls far short of the theoretical scope of such a service. Very few children are referred to the service, especially in rural areas; mental subnormality in itself is scarcely ever a reason for referral; and neurotic conditions are relatively seldom seen outside the urban hospital. A priority reason for referral to the service appears to be violence, but much more needs to be established concerning the criteria by which a very small proportion of all violent incidents leads to a referral to the psychiatric service.

Leeson and Frankenberg (21) found significant differences in the distribution of complaints among the patients of a sample of 23 ng'anga, traditional healers based in a suburb of Lusaka, and the patients of a cosmopolitan private practitioner serving the same catchment area. The ng'anga were consulted by relatively fewer children, fewer educated adults, and more women than the cosmopolitan doctor. A higher proportion of the ng'anga's patients had been ill for more than a year. Particularly salient among their clientele relative to the cosmopolitan practice were cases complaining of infertility (20%) and mental problems, including epilepsy (8%). The latter phenomenon reflects a widespread belief among the Zambian population that certain illnesses are "African" and can only be successfully treated by African traditional doctors.

The interplay between symptoms and diagnostic categories can be well illustrated by the case of fits. Haworth (9) interviewed a number of Zambian traditional ng'anga and found that, although they used a wide variety of terms, they all clearly distinguished between the conditions of grand mal epilepsy and spirit possession. The general public, however, including some paramedical staff of the cosmopolitan health service, tends to confuse the two syndromes because of a loose definition of the symptom of fits (9). A dramatic case of code switching in health-seeking behavior, precipitated by this symptom, was described to me by the medical assistant in charge of a Zambian rural health center. A woman had brought her young child to the center for treatment of a high temperature and was waiting in the queue outside. The child went into a series of intense convulsions, whereupon the mother attempted to leave the line, declaring that this condition could only be treated by a traditional *ng'anga*. She was eventually persuaded to allow the medical assistant to attempt treatment. Diagnosing high fever brought on by malaria, the medical assistant dispensed a combination of phenobarbitone, chloroquin, and paracetamol, which, according to his report, proved highly effective. Needless to say, he was not informed about any other, traditional treatment which may have been administered later in the day by a traditional *ng'anga*. If such treatment was sought, the mother may well have attributed the cure to it rather than to the cosmopolitan clinic's medicine.

In general, nonprofessional people seeking treatment for their illness seem to be eclectic with regard to theory. The fact that institutional forms tend to prohibit the simultaneous application of cosmopolitan and traditional medicine should not blind us to the clear implication of the high prevalence of parallel consultation (21,22). The multicultural individual sees no incompatibility between the two systems. Once again, the analogy with speech behavior may be illuminating. Various forms of accommodation have been described in multilingual communities between the various languages and/or dialects in their repertoire.

> Words and sentences of language A are frequently spoken with a compromise phonology that reflects the transfer of patterns from language B to language A. Lexical forms are freely borrowed from one language into the other, and sometimes even the syntax of one language is transferred. According to one research tradition, these patterns of interaction are construed as cases of "first-language interference," a significant source of difficulty in the mastery of a second language. If, however, the two linguistic systems are treated as components of a single community's shared, multiple repertoire, their convergence into hybrid forms may be interpreted as a natural process of integration. The problem is not how well each ethnic group can master the other's language, but rather how effective a consensus all elements in the community can achieve on forms of communication. (41)

In the domain of health-seeking behavior, such a consensus would involve at least ensuring that the various types of health practitioner acquire a familiarity with alternative medical systems. In the terms of Figure 16.2, this would mean more lines of access for the cosmopolitan health worker to the traditional system and more lines of access for the traditional health practitioner to the cosmopolitan system. This is illustrated in Figure 16.4. In addition to understanding alternative systems, the various practitioners would need to establish forms of coordination so as to minimize cases of direct conflict, such as the treatment of measles described above. Lambo's renowned innovation of providing for traditional healers to se up consultation centers within the premises of Aro Mental Hospital at Abeokuta, Nigeria, constitutes one institutional mechanism for facilitating such coordination (42). On the other hand, one of the greatest apparent strengths of the indigenous healing sys-

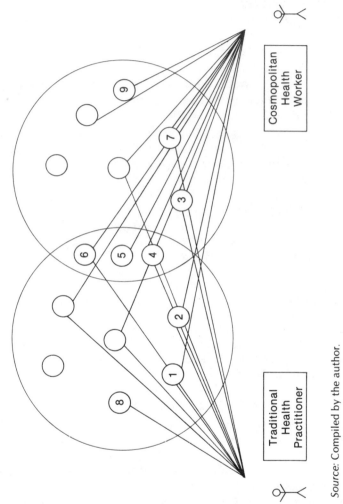

Figure 16.4. Increased lines of access to each other's medical repertoire by different kinds of health practitioners.

Source: Compiled by the author.

tems in Zambia is their social embeddedness in the communities they serve. Rather than bringing traditional healers into the urban hospital, a more productive strategy may be to provide support for their existing practices in the form of training and supplies, so as to amplify their contribution to primary health care. A small beginning has been made in this direction in Zambia with the training program for traditional birth attendants (2).

In the longer term, consensus may be further enhanced by increasing fusion of alternative medical systems. In the idiom of Figure 16.2, this would be represented by increasing the area of overlap between the two large circles, as illustrated by Figure 16.5. The better publicized attempts to formalize this process have tended to be unidirectional, with cosmopolitan medicine offering its own interpretation of the mechanism by which alternative medical systems achieve their results—for example, Melzack's theoretical account (43) of analgesia induced by Chinese traditional acupuncture. The elaborate scientific armory and institutional development of cosmopolitan medicine is bound to give it an advantage over local traditional systems in this regard. However, the socially embedded status of traditional medical practices places them at a complementary advantage in respect of influencing public attitudes. And, as noted above, the establishment of points of contact with the lay person's self-understanding is an essential preliminary to enlisting his or her self-control—a high priority within a "psychosocial" program of primary health care.

STRATEGIC CONSIDERATIONS IN THE ADAPTATION OF PSYCHOLOGICAL AND SOCIAL HEALTH CONSTRUCTS TO PARTICULAR SOCIOCULTURAL ENVIRONMENTS

It has been argued in the preceding sections that psychological and social factors play a significant part in the causation of human illness, in its definition, and in responses to it; that such factors therefore need to be monitored by health planners to a greater extent than is presently done; that information systems should be adapted to the unique characteristics of the sociocultural environment of the population they are designed to serve; and, finally, that numerous problems can be anticipated in adapting an information system for monitoring psychological and social factors relevant to health so that they are appropriate for the sociocultural environments that obtain in certain Third World countries. In this concluding section, some preliminary suggestions are offered for a strategy designed to overcome the kind of problems described in this chapter. Most of these are already implicit in the earlier discussion.

The first and most general principle to be advocated here is that local-level personnel be given an opportunity to make use of the health data that they re-

Figure 16.5.   Increased fusion of two alternative medical systems.

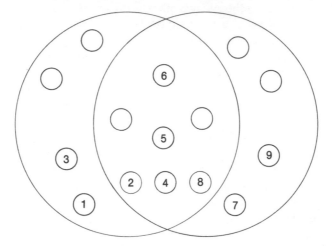

Source: Compiled by the author.

cord, and that they be required to critically review the health-reporting system in which they participate. The practices currently prevailing in health centers in Zambia are both wasteful of effort and defective in efficiency with respect to the local user's clinical objectives. Front-line workers are aware of these defects and could easily be motivated to undertake a review designed to overcome them. In addition, there is a real danger that when faced with an excessively demanding report form designed for statistical purposes, the front-line worker will resort to coping strategies that distort the data in significant ways. Instead of merely transmitting their monthly returns to various regional and central officers, local-level health workers should be required to analyze and interpret the statistical data they generate. In this process, they may more readily detect anomalies arising from erroneous recording procedures than is possible for central planners looking at aggregated data that they have played no part in generating. In addition, regional and central offices should undertake as a major responsibility the periodic feedback to front-line workers of comparative and aggregated data analyses.

   The assumption of greater responsibility for the utilization and review of the health reporting system by front-line workers may be expected thus to contribute toward two objectives: the greater clinical usefulness of health records and the greater reliability and validity of reported health data. In addition, if the information system is to be revised to include psychological and social data, a likely consequence of involving front-line workers in the selection of appropriate categories will be to enhance their sensitivity to such factors in the course of their clinical work. The "from the bottom up" generation of ideas and techniques in this field, in addition to increasing the likelihood of their local relevance and comprehensibility, may thus also pave the way for changes in the orientation of service delivery by arousing in front-line agents a sense of the need for a change in policy.

Secondly, clients and their escorts may contribute more useful information if they are asked to interpret psychological or social facts than if they are required to supply estimates of objective variables. Thus in designing health records, rather than precoding objective values on such dimensions as age, marital status, and parentage, it may prove to be both more valid and more reliable to code values on higher-order dimensions with greater psychological or social relevance, such as a culturally defined stage in the life sequence or the degree of continuity and consistency of a child's care. Another dimension on which the escorts of patients could usefully be required to provide coded information refers to the reasons for referral. It should be possible in most instances of psychiatric referrals by police to specify a more detailed reason than "detention order," and a rough classification of the forms of behavior that lead to such referral would provide valuable clues to community attitudes. Such information is relevant not only to the treatment of the individual patient, but also to the planning of the service and to coordination with other formal and informal social service agencies.

Continuity of individual patients' records is a third concern to emerge from this review of current practices in Zambia. The inclusion of a patient's previous medical history was classified as an "optimal" characteristic of the unit record by the Rijeka meeting of the Working Group on Primary Health Records (6). From the perspective of a "psychosocial" health program, however, this would seem to be an essential minimum requirement. Many psychological and social factors exercise a long-term influence on the individual's health that can most easily be detected by monitoring the recurrence of illness over a period of several months or years. Such a long-term record is, moreover, a valuable resource for collaboration with other social service agents such as community development, educational, agricultural, or police officers.

Turning to the realm of mental disorders, recording symptoms or presenting behaviors in addition to diagnoses seems to be a strategy that deserves some exploration. The discussion in the previous section suggested that symptoms of illness are more likely than higher-level diagnostic categories to command a consensus between cosmopolitan and traditional medical systems (i.e., to fall into the region of overlap between the systems portrayed in Figures 16.2–16.5). It is interesting to note that in the realm of phonology, etic (phonetic) categories are more narrowly defined than emic (phonemic) categories. Each phoneme in a language typically includes within its range a number of phoentically distinguishable variants. In a similar way, it may prove fruitful in exploring the potential for coordination and fusion between alternative medical systems to concentrate on lower-level, closely defined, directly observable symptoms.

Another advantage of such a recording principle is that it reduces the need for training and thus facilitates the recruitment into the health care system of nonspecialized members of the community. It is already common practice in cosmopolitan medical circles to delegate the recording of symptoms to para-professional staff, while reserving the diagnosis for the doctor or medical assistant. It may, at first glance, seem to place an excessive burden on those front-line health workers who lack ancillary support to require them to record both symptoms and diagnoses separately. On the other hand, a separate record of symptoms has considerable cliinical advantages for detecting an initial mistake in diagnosis, and it is apparent that the prevailing Zambian practice described earlier of assigning a single code to each new case of illness presents the clinician with a need to make arbitrary and unwarranted decisions.

Given that the inclusion of psychological and social factors in general health records almost certainly demands a multiaxial system, it may not be unreasonable to propose that one criterion for the development of such a system should be the separation of symptoms from diagnoses. Furthermore, given the apparent importance of traditional medicine in the treatment of psychogenic and mental health problems, it may be considered desirable to encourage front-line health workers to elicit and record the patient's own interpretation of the cause of his or her illness. Such information will prove clinically useful in cases with a strong psychological component of etiology, and statistical data generated from such records could throw valuable light on community attitudes toward various kinds of illness.

REFERENCES

1. H. Fabrega, "Group Differences in the Structure of Illness," *Cult Med Psychiatr* 1(1977):379–94.

2. United Nations International Children's Fund, *Children and Women in Zambia* (Lusaka, Zambia: Author, 1979).

3. Government of the Republic of Zambia, *Decentralised Government: Proposals for Integrated Local Government Administration* (Lusaka: Zambia Information Services, 1978).

4. World Health Organization, *Primary Health Care: Report of the International Conference on Primary Health Care, Alma Ata, USSR, 6–12 September, 1978* (Geneva: Author, 1978).

5. R. Serpell, W. Anokhbonggo, A. Haworth, and A. Veno, *A Strategy of Increased Cooperation between Traditional and Government Health Services in Zambia* (Lusaka: University of Zambia, 1979).

6. World Health Organization, *Primary Health Records: Report of a Working Group, Rijeka, October 1977,* Publication no. WHO/HS/NAT.COM/78.357 (Geneva: Author, 1978).

7. J. A. Holmes and A. N. Speight, "The Problem of Nonorganic Illness in Tan-

zanian Urban Medical Practice, *East African Medical Journal* 52(1975):225–36.

8. R. Giel and J. N. van Luijk, "Psychiatric Morbidity in a Small Ethiopian Town," *British Journal of Psychiatry* 115(1969):149–62.

9. A. Haworth, "Psychiatric Morbidity in Patients Attending a Lusaka Suburb Health Centre" (unpublished manuscript, University of Zambia, 1979).

10. World Health Organization, *Strategies for Extending Mental Health Care: Report of the Second Meeting of Investigators held in Khartoum, October 1977,* Publication no. MNH/78.7 (Geneva: Author, 1978).

11. Ministry of Health, Republic of Zambia, *Priorities in Mental Health in Zambia* (Lusaka: Author, 1979).

12. World Health Organization, *Manual of the International Statistical Classification of Diseases, Injuries, and Causes of Death,* 9th revision, vol. 1 (Geneva: Author, 1977).

13. M. Rutter, D. Shaffer, and M. Shepherd, *A Multiaxial Classification of Child Psychiatric Disorders* (Geneva: World Health Organization, 1975).

14. K. L. Pike, *Language in Relation to a Unified Theory of the Structure of Human Behaviour,* 2nd ed. (The Hague: Mouton, 1967).

15. J. W. Berry, "On Cross-Cultural Comparability," *International Journal of Psychology* 4(1969):119–28.

16. R. W. Brislin, "Comparative Research Methodology: Cross-Cultural Studies," *International Journal of Psychology* 11(1976):215–29.

17. F. K. Berrien, "Methodological and Related Problems in Cross-Cultural Research," *International Journal of Psychology* 2(1967):33–44.

18. R. Serpell, "Cultural Validation in Psychological Research," in *Cross-Cultural Contributions to Psychology,* ed. L. Eckensberger, Y. Poortinga, and W. J. Lonner (Amsterdam: Swets & Zeitlinger, 1979), p. 288.

19. R. B. Joynson, *Psychology and Common Sense* (London: Routledge & Kegan Paul, 1974), p. 14.

20. T. S. Kuhn, *The Structure of Scientific Revolutions* (Chicago: University of Chicago Press, 1962), p. 5.

21. J. Leeson and B. Frankenberg, "The Patients of Traditional Doctors in Lusaka," *African Social Research* 23(1977):217–34.

22. A. A. Khan, W. Kaunda and J. M. Maguire, *Traditional Healing Practices in Diseases of Childhood: Observations by Clinicians* (Lusaka: Republic of Zambia, Ministry of Health, 1977).

23. J. Searle, "What Is a Speech Act?" in *Philosophy in America,* ed. M. Black (New York: Allen & Unwin, 1965).

24. O. Barfield, "Poetic Diction and Legal Fiction," in *The Importance of Language,* ed. M. Black, 2nd. ed. (Englewood Cliffs, N.J.: Prentice-Hall, 1962), p. 67.

25. E. H. Gombrich, *Art and Illusion* (London: Phaidon, 1960).

26. C. Taylor, "Interpretations and the Sciences of Man," *Review of Metaphysics* 25 (1971):3–51.

27. World Health Organization, *Psychosocial Factors and Health: Report of the Director General,* Publication no. EB57/22 (Geneva: Author, 1975).

28. World Health Organization, *Reporting, Processing, and Using Data Generated from Nonhospital Health and Medical Records,* Publication no. WHO/HS/NAT.Com./79.364 (Geneva: Author, 1979).

29. M. Ndulo, "Liability of a Paramour in Damages for Adultery in Customary Law," *African Social Research,* in press.

30. M. P. Mvunga, "A Call for Reform in the Law of Succession in Zambia," *ZANGO: Zambian Journal of Contemporary Issues* 4/5 (1978):18–23.

31. A. Haworth and M. Mwanalushi, *Report on the Pilot Survey Carried Out in George Compound, Lusaka* (Lusaka: University of Zambia, School of Medicine, 1978).

32. J. M. Bowlby, *Child Care and the Growth of Love* (Harmondsworth, England: Penguin, 1953).

33. M. Rutter, *Maternal Deprivation Reassessed* (Harmondsworth, England: Penguin, 1972).

34. J. Bruwer, "The Composition of a Chewa Village (Mudzi)," *African Studies* 8 (1949):191–98.

35. S. Goldberg, *Infant Care in Zambia: Measuring Maternal Behavior,* HDRU Reports 13 (Lusaka: University of Zambia, 1970).

36. A. M. Drake, "Illness, ritual, and social relations among the Chewa of Central Africa" (Ph.D. dissertation, Duke University, 1976).

37. A. B. Chilivumbo, "The Social Basis of Illness," *Central Africa Journal of Medicine* 20 (1974):181–85.

38. R. Serpell, "Learning to Say it Better: A Challenge for Zambian Education," in *Language and Education,* ed. L. N. Omondi and Y. T. Simukoko, Communication 14 (Lusaka, Zambia: Institute for African Studies, 1978).

39. B. Jules-Rosette, *The New Religions of Africa* (N.J.: Ablex, 1979).

40. J. J. Gumperz and J. P. Blom, "Social Meaning in Linguistic Structures: Code Switching in Norway," in *Language in Social Groups,* ed. J. J. Gumperz, selected and introduced by A. S. Dil (Berkeley: University of California Press, 1971).

41. R. Serpell, "Context and Connotation: The Negotiation of Meaning in a Multiple-speech Repertoire," *Quarterly Newsletter of the Institute for Comparative Human Cognition* 1 (1977):10–15.

42. T. A. Lambo, "A Form of Social Psychiatry in Africa," *World Mental Health* 13 (1961):190–203.

43. R. Melzack, *The Puzzle of Pain* (Harmondsworth, England: Penguin, 1973).

17

Diagnosis of Social Problems in Non-Western Countries

The term *diagnosis* is derived from the Greeks, who saw the procedure as a device to elucidate the nature of any diseased condition as they understood it. In modern times it is perhaps more strictly applied to the precise organic pathology and/or introduced noxae of the sick person to be clearly separated from all other such entities. The term *social problem* is inherited from the sociologist and applies to a situation considered intolerable and a threat to the values of the society to which it refers, and is thought to be correctable by group action. Social problems include such things as mental illness, crime, drug addiction, prostitution, poverty, unemployment, and delinquency. But it is also used synonymously with the term *social pathology,* which deals with people who are socialized in such a way as to develop disapproved deviations. We are now getting closer to the individual. The primary health care worker will certainly be concerned with the individual as such at the first level of contact, not only by virtue of the subjects' psychopathology derived, in part, from endogenous sources, but also by virtue of his or her linkage with family, language group, and culture.

In the proposed procedure for the triaxial recording and classification of health problems that present in primary health care settings in Chapter 11, too little mention is made of the *cultural* component subsumed under the term *social.* Because I consider it of critical importance in the achievement of adequate primary care classification, this chapter emphasizes the cultural component of social problems.

I apply the word *culture* to the totality of customs of a given group of people who speak the same language. This is not surprising, as custom stems from language and cuts across national and political boundaries.

Culture in diagnosis is, of course, a particular example of all transcultural observation and communication, and applies to subcultures in a multicultural society and even to age and sex in a simple society, not to mention class and occupation. This chapter is, in part, a plea for protection and preservation of

275

the nonliterate nosologies of traditional peoples, each one of which is in danger of extinction. I believe that the traditional label, like the eponymic label, contains *additional* information and alerts the primary health care worker to a broader and more appropriate disease or problem model. The traditional nosology can exist side by side with other classifications, and in some cases can be incorporated within them.

I first became interested in the cultural factor while Colombo Plan Psychiatrist in what was then the British Crown Colony of Singapore during the 1950s. At that time there was no such thing as transcultural psychiatry and, according to the textbooks of the day, cultural factors were of no significance. But it was virtually impossible to carry on any reasonable form of diagnosis and therapy without noting language, customary behavior, sorcery and spirit beliefs, marriage rules, kinship obligations, socialization patterns, the vastly different value systems of the Chinese, Malay, Tamil, Sikh, Arab, and Eurasian peoples, and many other themes that derive from *culture-specific* contexts. While it was true there were certain similarities with Anglo-American psychiatry in basic psychopathology and the mental mechanisms involved, it was clear that the mental mechanisms operated in different ways. This became even clearer in Papua.

Papua New Guinea consists of a mainland and hundreds of smaller islands. It is the largest and most densely populated part of Melanesia, although it is economically poorer than Fiji or New Caledonia. There are about 3 million people, and a full range of morphological types occurs. There are wide variations in such vivid and immediately perceived characteristics as facial appearance, hair texture, and skin color. But more important than all these is that, of the world's 2,800 languages, Papua New Guinea alone contributes about 750! These are discrete languages, not dialects. This is a unique situation. Each of these miniature systems of speech communication has its own culture, its own social character, its own pattern of psychiatry, and its own set of social problems.

The majority of these cultural microunits has, until very recent times, remained comparatively isolated from the rest of the world. Particularly this has been the case with those from remote, rural areas. I have had to take these facts into account in the course of my clinical and field work with all the different peoples. Over the past two years I have studied 40 of these cultural-linguistic groups in great detail by direct contact. First I present an account of the methodology employed in which one immerses onself in the culture; then a brief survey of some of the findings is given.

METHOD

Ethnography is the scientific method first employed by the late Bronislaw Malinowski in Papua New Guinea during World War I. Prior to this, accounts of nonliterate peoples were usually anecdotal and based on reports of such doubtful observers as traders, missionaries, and raconteurs. Malinowski lived with the Trobriand Islands peoples of the Milne Bay Province from 1917 to 1919 and absorbed their way of life by direct observation during this period. While he was clearly a major figure in *scientific* anthropology as it applies to social and cultural factors, his understanding of psychological matters was of a lesser order.

It has been my practice to examine all the people in a village who are involved in some form of social problem, and sit down with the villagers and record their past experiences in dealing with issues of this kind. It is also my practice to tell them about social problems, including psychiatric illness in my own country, to see if similar entities exist among them. Whenever and wherever possible I confer with the traditional practitioner in each case, although he is, at times reluctant to be interviewed. He saw me as a competitor who might put him out of business. But he could be encouraged with a few goods or a little monetary remuneration. The method provides the maximum degree of information possible under the circumstances. Both verbal and nonverbal communication play its part, with the duration of contact the crucial factor.

RESULTS

Perhaps the most interesting result from such observations is that the traditional practitioner *has* produced a culturally based mental health system in each case. This is done without the adjuncts of modern physical therapies, guided only by his own awareness of his linguistic group, and leaning heavily on oral traditions of his own people. In its simplest form, the mental health system consists of three people: the *disturbed person,* the *concerned observer* of the disturbance, and the *diagnoser,* who is called in because of his experience with previous disturbances. Such a triad is the nucleus upon which a culturally elaborated system develops and within which the so-called culture-bound syndromes come to be recognized.

Highly pertinent to this work are the categorizations of the people themselves and the cultural embellishments of the individual illness entities. (In passing it should be mentioned that such a nucleus may well be the basis upon which most mental health systems have developed throughout history.) The next most important thing to notice is that the people have developed their own elementary systems of classification and nosology without any help from outside sources. In the groups I have examined it is clear that they separate nonconformist behavior into both its forensic and its medical dispositions. They distinguish the obligatory nonconformist, or disturbed person, from the facultative or nonobligatory nonconformist, or criminal, and treat such a person accordingly. What is important is that, in each case, they have a *name* in their own language for each of these categories. Among the obligatory nonconformists, they recognize the following:

1. An apathetic withdrawn person who speaks rarely and has a dream life of his own.
2. A hyperactive person who runs around for no immediately discernible reason, and continues to do so until exhausted or overpowered by others.
3. The sufferer from epilepsy who has recurrent episodes of grand mal seizures with intervening periods that include nonnormative aggressive behavior.
4. The person with mental disorder due primarily to physical causes (e.g., head injury). Two subvarieties are recognized:
   a. Those instances thought to be due to accident alone.
   b. Those that are the result of accident, but assigned to the machinations of a sorcerer.
5. The mentally retarded person whose illness has existed from birth or early life onward.
6. The so-called culture-bound syndromes (CBSs). This concept grew from the work of Yap Pow Meng and the dissatisfaction of Asian psychiatrists with Western psychiatry. It is doubtful that it was his intention to infer that similar entities do not occur in other geographical areas. But he clearly recognized that a formal noncultural diagnosis, based on remote European constructs, failed to convey what he felt were the essential elements in such conditions.

There are those who believe that Western nosologies as such will, in due course, come into their own with the aid of carefully translated lexical categories. There are at least three reasons why this is unlikely to occur with any reasonable degree of accuracy. First, there is the nature and mechanism of translation. Here we have an attempt to transpose and reshape a perceptual experience from one mode of cultural expression to another, to interpret in a different medium, and to carry over from one device to another. We seek a quasi-geometrical fit in the transfer. But no two languages are sufficiently similar to guarantee this fit or to delineate the exact social reality with all its consequences for our interpretation of behavior. In addition, the vocabulary of a language is the encoding of *its* culture's cognitive categories and such vocabulary is incorporated into the perceptual experience of both the examiner and the person examined. It structures the perceptual field with all the consequent behavioral sequelae.

Second, the lexical categories theory is part of a confused attempt to achieve allegedly scientific precision. But the underlying ethnic and cultural bias of a CBS (irrespective of whether it is consciously intended or not) is most readily detected by those to whom it is directed, if not by others. Communication is the construction of channels to carry signals from source to destination. So we may be dealing with a defective instrument, particularly when it happens to be, as it so often is in traditional societies, through the medium of Christian missionary dictionaries designed for other purposes. There is distortion and error. There is a concatenation of minds and speakers and loss of the qualitative and culturally unique aspects of person-to-person interactions. In short, the need to be scientifically respectable is quite different from being scientific in fact. A science that excludes the cultural dimension in dealing with people's minds and lives is no science at all.

Third, Western psychiatric nosologies are based upon and derive from only a fraction of humanity. Rendering generalizations from such a sample is a tenuous and very risky procedure. English-language and continental-European nosologies have tended to dominate modern psychiatry. The terms and concepts of these linguistic confines have their derivation in a patient population of a few limited geographical areas in Vienna, Munich, and Zurich. Great merit is due to these sources in setting us on our way. But the aberrant forms of culturally mediated behavior of the rest of the human species, which constitutes the vast majority, still remain with us. Although in modern times both Occidental and indigenous psychiatrists have worked conscientiously in so-called developing and other non-Western countries, very few indeed among them have moved out of the larger towns for any great length of time in the course of their work. In other words, when one considers the populations of Africa, China, the Indo-Pakistani subcontinent, the Soviet Union, Southeast Asia, and South America, it is apparent that most members of the human species have never been examined by a potential nosologist.

The goals of diagnosis are different for different people, for clinician, administrator, or researcher, although these roles are, at times, contained within the one person. The diagnostician may seek a marker in order to develop statistics, an elusive and hazardous process when dealing with the emotional states that stem partly from social problems. The mathematization of social relationships, so highly prized in modern times, is fraught with difficulty. Human behavior and social change in myriad cultures and subcultures display a type of complexity not readily reducible to the deductive mathematical pattern. One does not always know what one is counting. Even if one did, the end product of alleged truths mathematically arrived at still has to be communicated to the power brokers for whom it is designed and who may or may not act upon it.

The diagnosticians may wish to support existing classifications for a multitude of reasons, not least of which are the prospects of preferment and emolument within the profession. He or she may seek pattern recognition or causation or, as in the case of psychoanalytical diagnosis, he or she looks for help in understanding the meaning of the patient's behavior. The diagnostician may seek any, some, or all of these things. But, in most cases, he or she will undoubtedly seek to help the patient, which is what we are primarily concerned with.

In Papua New Guinea one encounters cargo-cult syndromes, spirit possession syndromes, sorcery syndromes, *amok* runners, Mekeo Madness, *ston het, longlongs, kavakavas, dabanapaias,* bongbongs, and many others. These entities are well known to the people themselves, who use their own names for them in their own languages. Their identification helps to unravel the difficulties in communication and alerts the physician to group networks peculiar to the patient under examination. They are a shorthand gestalt readily understood by almost everyone. They broaden the doctor's horizon. To ignore their cultural content by the application of a European label is to throw out the baby with the bathwater. It is within the restricted linguistic-geographical area as outlined above that cargo-cult syndromes arise among the cult leaders. Not all cult leaders suffer in this way, but many do, and when they do, their mental disorder is characterized by grandiose delusions, hallucinations, and associated physical inferiorities, all occurring in a specifically cargo-cult context. Like some other paranoics these patients have a specific motivation to establish a following. They are compulsive characters with a high narcissistic need and tend to settle conflicts by an appeal to exogenous sources in the persons of their followers rather than by self-imposed endogenous penalties. Should such a Melanesian sufferer travel abroad, as happens in modern times, he or she runs the risk of receiving a Western diagnostic label and a corresponding Western pattern of treatment, which may well be unsuccessful.

In short, a case has been stated for the preservation of the traditional nosology, which is, at the present time, an endangered species. The foregoing account in a small way highlights the significance of the cultural factor in social problems of non-Western countries as an important component in the alleviation of human suffering. In the proposal to develop triaxial recording and classification of health problems, there exists the danger that traditional nosologies may be ignored or inadvertently suppressed through overgeneralization. This would result in considerable loss in the comprehensive understanding and treatment of sick and disturbed people. Any proposed classification should include machinery to construct devices that make clear the crucial significance of the cultural factor so that it remains foremost in the mind of the primary health care worker.

18

Challenges in the Utilization of a Triaxial Classification of Disease in a Primary Health Care Setting

CARLOS E. CLIMENT

INTRODUCTION

The contribution of primary care in the delivery of health services has been clearly established as an international priority for the next two decades (1). The potential participation of those services to improve the health of populations is great, but it has been limited to some actions in a few fields. It is in this area where most changes are expected to occur in the future.

The success of such actions would be more complete if serious considerations were given to the utilization os psychosocial variables as a basis for developing new health strategies. The major potential contribution of primary health workers (PHWs)* lies precisely in their ability to recognize social and psychological variables associated to disease, thanks to their close contact to the patients in their own habitat. The capability of PHWs in the identification and utilization of variables that are frequently beyond the reach of more sophisticated (but for the most part busier) health workers is perhaps the most important resource still to be used in health care programs.

This chapter deals with several observations made in the course of conducting a series of projects for extension of mental health services to marginal urban communities in Cali, Colombia (2,3). The main goal of these projects is to extend services through the use of local health teams† working in peripheral health centers in which PHWs are in charge of handling clinical cases as

Carlos Leon helped in the integration of experiences and ideas into concepts. Maria Victoria de Arango contributed many examples of field work.

*For the purposes of this work, PHWs are auxiliary nurses (ANs) and health promoters (HPs).

†A health team consists of an MD and an RN (and/or an AN and/or a PH).

part of their daily tasks. The psychiatrist acts only as a supervisor of the health team.

An important element in the work of the team is the identification and management of psychosocial variables of disease in these populations. Observations of the performance of PHWs with low levels of training (ANs and HPs) confirmed their ability to carry out certain actions in mental health as an integral part of their work. This is possible through specific training, adequate supervision, and permanent quality control mechanisms. In contrast to what is expected traditionally, PHWs as members of health teams are able to carry out therapeutic actions that include identifying psychiatric cases through the use of questionnaires; obtaining clinical data and elaborating a narrative history; identifying major psychopathology through simple mental status descriptions reported in a narrative form; presenting data to a supervisor; following up treatment plans as recommended by a supervisor, which includes supervising psychopharmacological treatments, including side effects; and submitting recommendations regarding modifications of dosages or discontinuation of psychopharmacological agents in certain cases. Other tasks include listening to patients; providing support; giving guidance about specific problems when social information is required; talking to relatives or neighbors; carrying out home visits and making some assessment of the home situation; and referring cases to higher levels.

Many of the clinical activities described above are beyond the routine work of professionals with a more sophisticated level of training, mostly due to lack of time, but also because PHWs are able to maintain better communication with patients.

The success of PHWs in carrying out such therapeutic actions is in most cases an explicit instance of something they have already been doing. Most of them are in fact the natural counselors of their communities. Because of this, they have a good understanding of the psychological, economic, and social factors affecting the lives of the people involved.

The previous experiences in Cali have led us to conclude that trained and supervised PHWs can do the following:

1. Identify adequately the psychosocial variables affecting the health of patients in deprived populations.
2. Provide treatment and follow-up to patients suffering from disorders in which emotional components play an important role.
3. Constitute the more adequate resource to carry out these health actions, especially in low-income populations.

The challenge resides in the adequate detection, registration, and utilization of psychosocial variables of disease through the existent medical resources. Specialists, generalists, nurses, and PHWs are potentially well qualified to gather such data. Nevertheless, they need training, supervision and specific consideration of certain aspects, both at the level of the provider and the receiver of health.

ASPECTS RELATED TO THE PROVIDER OF HEALTH

Limited Emphasis on Health

Limited emphasis on health and disproportionate interest in disease does not help the recognition and utilization of psychosocial variables of disease. In any environment, but more so among deprived populations of less developed countries, disease is frequently a consequence of social, economic, and psychological concomitants. The complete picture is usually presented by the patient in detail from the beginning, but the health personnel often hear without listening; attention is paid to the signs and symptoms of disease but the psychosocial factors of disease are frequently overlooked.

This problem has been documented by Puffer and Serrano (4), who showed that there is a wealth of psychosocial information waiting to be used and incorporated as contributing causes of death within present classifications of diseases. These authors compared information gathered from death certificates with information gathered through a series of complementary data. (Such information was available for inclusion in death certificates to begin with, but was never used.) This study demonstrated that over 50% of all deaths due to malnutrition as a basic cause of death were classified as diarrhea, pneumonia, or influenza. The basic causes reported by death certificates were in agreement with the research findings in only 52.4% of the cases. This indicates severe deficiencies in the utilization of statistics that affect the use of data for health-planning purposes. Based on these certificates, a cause of death as common as measles would be known only in 55.4% of the cases, and no information would be available to uncover the real cause, which is malnutrition in about 80% of the cases. Automobile accidents and alcoholism constitute additional examples in which death certificates reflect the final outcome and say nothing about the really important psychosocial correlates. These and other factors deserve to be taken into account, because they contribute to ambiguous and erroneous information about psychosocial correlates of morbidity and death.

Many factors could be used to explain this situation. One could be that there has been little training available in this field; therefore, medical personnel have not been adequately sensitized regarding the importance of psychosocial variables. As a general rule, the emphasis in the medical curricula is on pathology, and interest in psychosocial matters as contributing causes of diseases is mostly theoretical.

One example might be a patient with intestinal parasitism, for whom the appropriate drug is prescribed. A description of the environmental circumstances is requested as part of the routine examination, but its real importance is minimized. Consequently, appropriate episodic treatment is given, but real long-term help to the patient is minimal—reinfestation usually occurs.

The successful model doctor does not need to demonstrate interest in the important role of economic, social, or psychological variables; his or her success is associated with the ability to take care of signs and symptoms of disease. It is assumed that very little, if anything, could be done to modify these related variables.

The emphasis on disease is linked to the orientation of training programs at the health sciences schools. There is a need for stimulating the interest of students in the preventive aspects of medicine or in community programs that eventually will modify these attitudes.

Simple Methods

Sophisticated methods are not necessarily better than simple methods in the registration, diagnosis, and treatment of health problems. Interest in sophisticated methods and excessive dependence on specialists and specialized institutions reduce the possibility of progress in this field. One reason for this is that it increases the distance between the patient and the health personnel.

The medical profession should see simplicity as something desirable, since the patient is interested in the relief of suffering through useful, effective, and humane methods. Patients are not specifically interested in obtaining help from the most sophisticated health worker. They are looking for kindness in the understanding of their problems and effective therapeutic actions, and if this is offered by PHWs they will be satisfied.

The design and use of standardized questionnaires and procedure manuals, supervision, quality control, and training programs are some of the important elements to be incorporated if simple procedures are to be adapted.

Communication

Adequate communication between health provider and patient may contribute effectively toward the relief and comfort of patients. Assessment of psychosocial factors affecting health is not easy through the existing communication mechanisms. When health professionals try to communicate with patients from a deprived sociocultural level, many barriers exist on both sides because of the circumstances and the realities of such exchanges. For one thing, doctors usually do not fully understand the psychosocial environment; in the vast majority of cases they have not even seen it, and the language they use is frequently difficult for patients to understand. The patients feel the distance and barely provide the information that they feel will please the people in charge.

Such interviews are generally short, and doctors are forced to make a diagnosis without knowing much about the patients' psychosocial correlates. Even if they had a list of them they would be in trouble, however, because their knowledge about the patients' social atmosphere, living conditions, feelings, and sufferings is limited. In consequence, "good" patients are the ones who give a clear idea of their signs and symptoms—who do not "mix" psychosocial correlates with "clean" reports of their physical disorders.

Lack of communication also occurs when doctors assume that the patients understand the indications given, or assume that prescriptions are obtained by patients and followed with precision. It is well known that only a small proportion of patients buy the medications prescribed and even fewer take them; yet few providers of health seem concerned about this.

From the semantic viewpoint, however, there are barriers regarding even the apparently simplest items. For example, an *attack,* usually assumed to be an epileptic fit, means to many patients a hysterical episode, tinnitus, dizziness, faintness, anger, asthma, laughter, and so on. The term *headache* is used frequently to mean dizziness, tension (anxiety), anger, or worry. *Depression* is often confused with *anxiety.*

The problem is worsened when patients are unable to express this in a precise form and the health personnel is not aware of the difficulty. Consequently, no effective effort is made to clarify the doubt.

Interest in the Human Aspects of Medical Care

A successful program to make the health profession more aware of the human aspects of medical care is an important priority, since it is the best motivation to make people think about the psychosocial variables of disease. The health services—their administrative infrastructure and health care programs—emphasize the scientific aspects of medical care, but minimize the human needs of patients; this contributes to an inadequate delivery of services. It is rather common in a hospital ward to see a patient with medical or surgical problems and with obvious psychological difficulties who is handled as two separate individuals. In the best of circumstances, a consultation is requested for "the psychiatric problem," but in the majority of the cases this component is ignored, with subsequent deterioration of the patient's condition. The crude presentation of diagnosis to patients; the lack of interest in the possible impact on them of such information; the poor awareness regarding the emotions of the severely ill, the dying, and the impact of all these events on relatives—these are only a few examples of the dehumanization of medical care as a consequence of failures in medical education. A pilot experience (5) has demonstrated the great impact that fuller awareness of these aspects has on the health personnel of an institution. A group of interns, after dealing with these concepts, was able to assimilate them with enthusiasm and defend this new knowledge with vigor. There was evidence of change in the behavior and attitudes of the persons involved when compared with the group that did not participate in the experience. Otherwise, the psychosocial variables of disease were systematically ignored, actively resisted, or bluntly denied.

A classification of diseases that incorporates psychological and social aspects should help in the modification of this situation by making health workers aware of new variables that permit a more comprehensive and gratifying practice.

ASPECTS RELATED TO THE PATIENT

As a minimal requirement for acknowledging the point of view of the patients, the design of a triaxial classification of diseases should consider at least their beliefs, attitudes, and socioeconomic conditions.

Beliefs

The beliefs of populations could be important assets for the adequate use of health services. By the same token, if no attention is paid to these aspects, the consequence is a reduction in the efficacy of efforts in the delivery of health care. The majority of people have secret but firm beliefs regarding medical services; they make use of established systems only when all other efforts have failed, and the possibilities of success through the established medical systems are minimal. In fact, many people consult healers before going to doctors. In a study of a rather deprived population in the outskirts of Cali (6), 41% of the interviewed sample did not use the health services when faced with an illness; 70% of the people firmly believe in the "evil eye" as a cause of diarrhea in children (7).

The reasons for not using the health services are not simply cultural or religious, but also include the patients' fear of being reprimanded by authoritarian health providers for having used alternative services as a first choice.

Another factor to be taken into consideration in this regard is that knowledge of sociocultural organizations of the different regions could help explain the emphasis given by different people to social, organic, or other factors as associations to disease. It has been demonstrated, for example, that the causes people attribute to mental problems are not random, but rather appear to vary between and within cultural units (8). Research into these and similar factors operating in a region should shed light on relevant psychosocial correlates.

Attitudes

Submission

Psychosocial correlates of disease are difficult to assess, identify, and utilize, because people from deprived groups passively accept the realities of their lives; in the face of suffering and disease, they act with submission. The vast majority ignore the alternatives available to them; they are used to living under intolerable psychosocial conditions, and they do not foresee any better future. The consequence of this attitude is the incapacity of health workers to identify the psychosocial variables affecting the organic problems that prompted the consultation. If this factor is taken into careful consideration at all times, our actions as health providers and the detection of psychosocial variables would be more effective.

Tolerance

The enormous tolerance of these populations to many problems—for example, to mental illness—is demonstrated not only at the familial or social level, but also when the individual makes use of the health services, as this example indicates:

> An 18-year-old female accompanied by her mother consulted the health center due to vaginal bleeding and abdominal pain. The diagnosis was an ovarian dysfunction; symptomatic treatment was prescribed and the patient was sent home. Personnel from the mental health program at the health center became accidentally interested in the patient and decided to refer her to this program. Upon questioning, it became clear that the patient had been suffering obvious psychiatric symptoms for months but no one at home felt that a consultation was necessary and spontaneous information was not given. She was finally diagnosed as a catatonic schizophrenic. (9)

Many other examples could be given: Alcoholism is rarely considered a disease; depressive or anxiety-related neuroses are considered "forms of life," and therefore their modification is rarely judged necessary. Paranoid attitudes and even psychosis are often tolerated for years without questions even being raised about the need for medical intervention.

A different sort of tolerance occurs regarding somatic complaints that constitute a frequent chief complaint at health centers. Gastrointestinal, respiratory, genitourinary, and sexual disorders are presented daily as isolated signs and symptoms of disease. They are supposedly independent of the emotional, marital, familial, or economic circumstances, although these factors are intimately related to the origin, severity, inadequate handling, and perpetuation of the disease. In consequence, the somatic complaints are chronically and frequently repeated.

Distrust

In deprived populations of less developed countries, people live in isolation in their homes and distrust neighbors and visitors. A permanent migration contributes to the isolation. Social insecurity increases the fear of communicating with other people; the fear of being attacked, robbed, or raped enormously affects the peace of these people's lives, contributing to the limited utilization of medical services. The result is silence regarding many psychosocial aspects of disease that seriously affect these patients. Consequently, in order to obtain reliable data from them, several visits from PHWs are usually necessary. Adequate knowledge of these aspects should enhance the efficiency of health personnel faced with these patients.

Family Tradition

The vast majority of health actions are related to family tradition; this factor determines the type of services people choose. For example, a young mother will follow birth control methods or will attend an institution for pregnancy control or delivery only if her mother and grandmother have done so. If this has not been the case, whatever method the family tradition has established will carry more weight than any health education programs.

Socioeconomic Factors

Economic variables that affect health in these populations cannot be ignored. Unfortunately, the health services appear to be designed for the well educated, those with economic resources, and/or those with adequate public services. The consequence of this is that doctors prescribe treatment without knowing whether the patient can obtain it. It is crucial, therefore, to know the patient's conditions in a precise form. But this is not an easy task, since people will not confess that they lack the money to buy medication. They receive the prescription submissively, and they may even come back to the following interview without having taken it; they are ashamed to reveal such a fact to the doctor unless very direct questions are asked.

The availability of public services is an extraordinarily important variable. The existence of many services (e.g., potable water, electricity, sewage, garbage collection, paved roads, and adequate transportation systems) is erroneously assumed. All these services are basic elements that affect health, and those with a responsibility in the delivery of health care should know these variables well, since the absence of such basic conditions makes it very difficult to follow even the simplest health recommendations.

Household conditions are another important variable, since crowding exists in a high proportion of homes in many of these populations and is associated with a series of negative aspects, of which infectious diseases, incest, and severe situational reactions are just some of the more commonplace.

CONCLUSIONS

The adequate utilization and assessment of psychosocial factors affecting health in a primary health care setting require careful consideration of variables, from the point of view of both the provider and the receiver of health. PHWs can play an important role in the identification, recording, and utilization of psychosocial data, but they need very specific training. A new technology will have to be developed in this field, and training should stimulate students in all areas to become advocates of health rather than experts in morbidity.

Training should consider the communication barriers and the human elements inherent to the receiver-provider relationship. Simple methods of training are not necessarily low-quality methods; in fact, they require sophisticated techniques to make them simple but efficient at the same time. Therefore, the best-qualified people should be called upon to cooperate in the design of texts and manuals. The use of simple standardized questionnaires is mandatory, but it should be kept in mind that even the apparently simple could be difficult for most of the populations.

Each region should produce its own list of psychosocial correlates of disease; this process should be carried out through community consultation with advice given by experts. The list should be agreed upon in sufficiently flexible, general categories, so as to be applicable in the different social and cultural settings. It should be based on the studies carried out in each region regarding people's attitudes and beliefs about health, disease, medical services, and psychosocial correlates of health.

Active governmental involvement must be emphasized. It has been found in Cali that official decisions regarding acceptance of certain changes in the delivery of health services are not sufficient. In spite of having received support from the directors of institutions and governmental health officials, new ideas regarding mental health programs have met a number of obstacles before their final implementation. The main reason has usually been passive and active resistance at all levels, due to the fact that something new was about to be added to an already loaded schedule.

Simplicity has been tried out through the design of standardized scales to be used by PHWs. The results of these trials indicate that it is possible to use very simple questionnaires to gather almost any psychosocial information that is needed from patients or relatives. The instruments designed for use by PHWs in a World Health Organization (WHO) collaborative study on strategies to extend mental health services (9) demonstrates that it is possible to provide these services through PHWs with various resources in different countries. It has also shown that the detection and management of psychological correlates of disease can be carried out by PHWs under certain conditions of supervision.

PHWs have a good working knowledge of the psychosocial factors relating to health. They live closer to patients' environments and can establish better communication with them. They are able to obtain psychiatric histories and psychosocial information to the point that specialists, to confirm diagnoses, do not have to see the patients directly. They listen to and read the information collected by the PHWs and then make their diagnoses and therapeutic decisions. This is not to say that professional personnel do not play a crucial role in the process of detection, recording, and utilization of psychosocial variables affecting health, but they are often prevented from doing so because of their busy schedules and the obstacles to communication.

The challenges, as well as the possibilities of success, are many. If appropriate actions are taken, it is possible to make PHWs readily available to participate in the utilization of psychosocial data. PHWs should be more active participants in this process; it has been demonstrated that they are well qualified to carry out the identification, recording, and reporting of this information, but this potential has not been adequately used as yet.

The ultimate challenge resides in our ability to design training methods and recording mechanisms to increase the communication between PHWs, who are closer to patients' psychosocial realities, and other health workers. The knowledge and effective utilization of such data would help health workers at all levels to feel more satisfied with their work, and the final outcome would be better and more humane medical care for the populations they serve.

REFERENCES

1. World Health Organization, *Primary Health Care: Report of the International Conference on Primary Health Care, Alma Ata, USSR, 6–12 September 1978* (Geneva: Author, 1978).

2. C. E. Climent, M. V. de Arango, R. Plutchik, and C. A. León, "Development of an Alternative, Efficient, Low-Cost Mental Health Delivery System in Cali, Colombia. Part I: The Auxiliary Nurse," *Social Psychiatry* 13(1978):29–35.

3. C. E. Climent and M. V. de Arango, "Development of an Alternative, Efficient, Low-Cost Mental Health Delivery System in Cali, Colombia. Part II: The Health Center," in press, 1980.

4. R. R. Puffer and C. V. Serrano, *Caracteristicas de la Mortalidad en la Niñez* (Washington, D.C.: Pan American Health Organization, 1973).

5. C. E. Climent and R. Guerrero, *Humanization of Medical Care: An Experimental Program at the University Hospital in Cali, Colombia* (in preparation, 1979).

6. Barreto, Ramirez, y Delvasto. *Estudio de Comunidad del Barrio "El Diamante"* (Cali, Colombia: PRIMOPS, 1977).

7. C. A. León and C. E. Climent, "Anotaciones Sobre el Ojo en Cali," *Acta Psiquiátrica Psicológica y de América Latina* 14(1968):23–24.

8. M. Micklin and C. A. León, "Cultural Bases of Images of Causation in Psychological Disorder: A Colombian Survey," *Social Psychiatry* 24/2(1978):79–94.

9. T. W. Harding, M. V. de Arango, J. Baltazar, C. E. Climent, H. A. Ibrahim, L. Ladrido-Ignacio, R. Srinivasa-Murthy, and N. N. Wig, "Mental Disorders in Primary Health Care: A Study of their Frequency in Four Developing Countries," *Psychological Medicine* 10(1980):231–41.

19

A Mechanism for Recording and Reporting Physical and Psychosocial Components of Health in a Community Health System in Porto Alegre, Brazil

E. D'ARRIGO BUSNELLO

INTRODUCTION

This chapter deals with the adaptation of a problem-solving-oriented medical record to be used by families in a community health system that delivers primary health care, as well as in the supporting echelons (1,2,5).

THE PRESENT PROBLEMS OF HEALTH SERVICES

The close relationship between physical, psychological, and social problems of individuals and groups is the object and foundation of an entire scientific and humanistic view of the practice of health sciences. At the present time this has crystallized into a positive definition of *health* as physical, psychological, and social well-being, as well as the absence of illness.

Viewed from this standpoint, the traditional delivery of health services to the population has shown itself to be more and more ineffective. Care is offered to the population in a random form, presenting a clear dissociation among promotion, prevention, treatment and cure, and rehabilitation. To this fragmentation of the process of morbidity is added the dissociation pres-

The author is indebted to his colleagues, the late Dr. Issac Lewin, who introduced the problem-solving-oriented medical record in the state of Rio Grande do Sul; Dr. Sergio Ruschel, who worked with the author and Dr. Lewin in the organization of the model and of its graphic design; and to Dr. T. W. Harding and Mr. W. Gulbinat of the Mental Health Division of the World Health Organization, who encouraged the author to report on this work.

ently existing among concepts of physical, psychological, and social health. Dissociation also exists among the many services of a health institution and among different health institutions, dehumanizing health care by splitting the person into many physical parts and psychosocial aspects.

The community is not consulted when health services are structured. Yet the users would undoubtedly like to have health care delivery services integrated, and to be treated in an integral, continuous, personalized, and participative way.

Perhaps for this reason the population does not see these services in proportion to what is offered. This explains their loss of relevance for the communities they serve: the small and inadequate utilization and scarce coverage; a small part of the population occupying the services with trivial and unsolved problems; the passive care offered; the absence of activity planning and home-delivered services; the minimum coordination between services; the slight emphasis given to primary prevention activities.

The immediate consequence is that both the population and the higher echelons of the health care system no longer exercise pressure over the services, which have a tendency to close in on themselves. These services begin to respond to necessities internally defined. Priorities are established in terms of the ideas and interests of the professionals who work there, and not according to the importance of the problems for the community.

The personal interests of the professionals and the tendency toward individualism create independent groups within the health services that seldom communicate with one another. The rigidity of the roles of the professionals is paralleled only by their resistance to changes. Oriented to the treatment of the episode of the illness within a hospital or an office (their natural habitat), they restrict themselves to the practice of specialties as a defensive measure.

In the area of psychiatric assistance, these faults are compounded by the biased attitude that continues to surround mental illnesses. This is the main reason for the separation between psychiatric and general health services and for the increasing withdrawal of psychiatry from the conjunction of the traditional medical specialties.

As to the care of social problems, more and more valued in the etiological complex of health disorders, the situation is even more critical. Interventions on the social level lack a methodology and must wait for changes of attitude that will allow them to be implemented.

Perhaps the major defect of present health systems, and the greatest harm they cause to medicine and health in general, is that they maintain the dissociation between physical and psychological medicine. To this may be added the dissociation existing between these two and social medicine. Alienated from each other and from the society as well, they are enclosed in themselves and no longer receive the mutual impacts and influences needed to fertilize their thinking. This has led to their stratification and to the discredit into which they have fallen in the eyes of the users.

THE MEDICAL RECORDS

The circulation of information within a health service is vital for its good performance. Information, in general, is collected from what is transcribed in medical records or other special documents related to them. Medical records usually register the actions of physicians and nurses assigned to the care of a patient, and serve as well to establish communication among the various professionals involved in the assistance.

Due to the injunctions of the type of services that use them, medical records are instruments that reflect the episode and not the process of morbidity. They only document the health actions aimed at secondary prevention (early diagnosis, prompt treatment, and disability limitation). The register of biological, psychological, and social antecedents is not considered; the need for primary preventive measures (education and specific protection against illnesses) and tertiary ones (rehabilitation) is considered even less. The records are also not used as guidelines for continuous treatment of the patients' problems, even, at times, within one single institution.

The mechanisms for recording and reporting the biological and psychosocial components of health at the primary health care level and supporting echelons are inadequate, and this has grave consequences for the quality of these services. The medical records generally are the property of the health institution (health post, health center, or hospital). Users may hardly have access to them. For this reason, they often do not use them in their transit through the various services of a single system, and almost never when they seek institutions belonging to other systems that offer physical, psychological, or social care.

Thus, tasks already done are wasted, as well as the time of the professionals, making it still more difficult to meet the needs of the patients. At the same time, the technicians and the users are involved in a series of repetitive efforts that diminish the creative gain of both and raise conflicts of comprehension very difficult to surmount.

Closely connected to the services of health delivery in health systems in almost every case, the medical record is aimed at the episode and not at the whole process—at the care of a specific problem and not of the person in all his or her biopsychosocial complexity. It also does not foresee integral care and continuity of patient treatment. For this reason it is limiting and, so to speak, dies at the end of the episode that justified the care.

As a result of this routine, the impoverishment of the relation between physician and patient is further aggravated; the efficiency of the service rendered is diminished; and the orientation given to the patient becomes disorganized.

Structuring a medical record creates a contradiction between the free employment of creativity, on the one hand, and scientific reasoning and the constraints of the method adopted, on the other hand. To avoid the consequences of a precarious equation of this contradiction, some innovative forms of registers have arisen. Outstanding among these is the problem-solving-oriented medical record (9), which opens the possibility of registering all the biological, psychological, and social problems of the person, and which also allows for the continuity of accomplishing the tasks aimed at elevating health conditions. It also fosters a personal and participative contact with the patient.

A PROBLEM-SOLVING-ORIENTED FAMILY MEDICAL RECORD

The medical record is a document that registers all medical and paramedical acts related to a patient, establishing a communication link between health professionals. A system that is aimed not only at integral health care but also at the close relationship between the professionals and the users of a service, considering the latter in their proper dimension as patients and agents of health actions, should certainly question the objectives of the registration of data as they are formulated in the present health services. An adequate medical record should also indicate the measures taken to preserve health and to maintain the progress reached, as well as serve to communicate with the users.

When the communitarian form of health care is adopted, the need arises for the employment of a kind of medical register that is both practical and functional, expressing clearly the health activities affected.

Adopting a clinical record for the primary health care level and supporting echelons brings to issue the objectives of the system and the dilemmas faced by contemporary medical care. In the conception of such a record, it is necessary to take the following into account: the objective of the care provided—the person who is the patient, and not only his or her illness; a wider communication among health professionals and between these professionals and the users; the integrity and continuity of the care offered; the participation of persons and families in their own treatment. Attention should equally be given to the failures of the usual systems of care, such as the impoverishment of the physician-patient relationship; the low quality of the services rendered, due to the orientation of medical work toward overspecialization; the lack of integrated federal, state, and private social security systems; and the constant change, either of the population assisted, or of the professionals responsible for care delivery.

Another problem is in overcoming the conflict between structuralization and creativity, so as to favor the development of scientific reasoning. In the course of research work, scientists agree to follow norms and receive appraisal without feeling that their creativity and originality is being threatened. On the contrary, critical analysis is welcomed with the intention of improving the results. In the medical area, however, there exists a great resistance toward the proper registration of data, under several pretexts. These range from the possible loss of time to the loss of independence and restriction of creative imagination. Yet with the kind of register that should be employed, the deepest analysis of medical activity would be greatly facilitated (4). The documents generated by this activity would supply data on the relation between the tasks accomplished and the costs of these, between the necessities of the population and the services rendered, making evaluation of these services possible.

The medical record thus may become an incentive to the evaluation of a health task. A problem-solving-oriented medical record forces the team to become more effective in the diagnosis of the patients and more concerned with formulating plans of treatment (8).

In community health systems, a clear association among services rendered, training, and research should exist. Their central focus should be care, around which training and research revolve. The medical record used could also become one more instrument to facilitate the realization of activities related to health, as well as teaching and learning.

The clinical record here presented was tested in the community health care system of the Murialdo Sanitary Unit of the Rio Grande do Sul State Department of Health, Brazil. Its purpose was to include the registration of family groups in an integral way, with a profile of their healthy and morbid aspects, as well as all the problems of physical, psychological, and social health, together with all the preventive, curative and rehabilitation health measures taken with respect to the individuals and the family group. It was thus meant to serve as an instrument and method to improve the care rendered, allowing for the participation of individuals and families in their assistance.

In order to fulfill such objectives, the technique of data registration and the traditional policy in the use of records had to be changed. In view of this, a functional record was contemplated, so as to afford the development of scientific reasoning; to give a view of the interrelationship and continuity of the services rendered; and to overcome the supposed restrictions on creativity raised by the registers. It had to be a record that could be used by professionals as well as by patients and families. It also had to allow for the analysis of the quality of the services rendered and their relation to cost and efficiency. Being a practical and efficient tool for the registration of health actions, it also had to be useful for teaching-learning tasks (4).

In searching for a medical record that would correspond to the purposes of the system, the method proposed by Weed (9), in which every registration is oriented to solving a problem, seemed to better fulfill practical conditions. To reach the desired results, a local adaptation of the Weed method was attempted by applying it to the family group, so as to permit the family as a whole to be the object of the register. Physical, psychological, and social problems of individuals and family groups had to be clearly identifiable to anyone handling the record, with a view to avoiding—for the family as well as for the patients—dispensable reexaminations; to preserving health tasks already accomplished; and to resuming treatments that by chance had been discontinued.

Usually family medical records are a collection of individual sheets grouped in a single folder (3).* The family medical record that supplies general information on the family and requires that the entire family group be followed systematically, registering the evolution of the whole family and of its members, is an innovation that probably will arouse the curiosity of health service administration technicians throughout the world (3). In the preparation of the family medical record adopted by the community health care system of the Murialdo Sanitary Unit, the experience of Lewin (4), who had worked the most for the implantation of the problem-solving-oriented clinical record, was essential in solving the technical difficulties.

The clinical record of the community health care system was intended to be an element for centralizing the activities in the achievement of the aforesaid objectives. With it, it has been possible to achieve the following:

- Communication between the members of the health team who interact with the patients, their families, and the community was facilitated.
- The members of the primary health team, the volunteers, and the personnel in training were more easily turned into health agents.
- The treatment was centered on the social group and not only on the individual.
- The treatment of the patient and of the family group was integral, in terms of prevention, cure, and rehabilitation, as well as in the physical, psychological, and social aspects.
- The continuity of the treatment was maintained, detaching it from the episode and returning it to the process.
- The analysis of care rendered to patients, their families, and the community was facilitated.
- Research into better forms of treatment was fostered.

The family medical record in question is composed basically of three sheets. These sheets are divided into four parts. The first of them, called the front page, contains the *Identification* of the entire family group. In it appear the names and letters that distinguish the members of the family. These letters will be used whenever there is reference to a problem of that individual. Other data include sex, social status, occupation, membership in social security program, educational level, and individual income. The sum of the individual incomes will give the total income; that, divided by the number of adults, added to the number of children up to nine years old, and divided by two,

*Copies of the forms described here and below are available on request from the author.

gives a sum utilizable in classifying the family group above or below the poverty criterion fixed by the system.

The front page also has the *Problems List,* considered the fourth part of the record, where the problems of the family as a whole and of the individuals that constitute it are registered. Each problem receives a number and the letter corresponding to the person affected by it; in the case that such a problem affects the family group, the registration is made under the column entitled *Family.* So, for instance, alcoholism may be the problem of the head of the family, who would be the patient lettered A. Problem 1 of A (which is placed in the first column after the one entitled *Family*) would be *alcoholism.* This same problem could be affecting the whole family group, and then it appears in the column *Family* as Problem 1, in the form of Mental Health Problem A.

Each problem has a square with three lines for filling in. This arrangement facilitates the registration of integral and continuous care.

In one case, a line might read *psychomotor agitation.* If this is later identified as a psychosis, the first phrase is deleted, and is replaced in the line below by *psychosis.* This one in turn is cancelled out when the definitive diagnosis is reached, such as, for instance, *manic-depressive psychosis,* which will be set down on the third line.

The date of identification of the problem is registered under the column headed by the letter R, and under the column headed by the letter S is placed the date of this solution. Thus, if in the column that corresponds to one of the children, there appears in one of the squares the problem *Incomplete Immunizations,* the register will be canceled out as soon as they are completed, by noting the date of such event under the column S.

The date beside the register allows anyone handling the record to look, on the third sheet (*Evolution*), for the data on problems noted in physical, psychological, or social examinations that led to the diagnosis of the case or identification of the problem affecting the patient and the family, as well as the orientation suggested and the treatment routine proposed. In this way, at any moment, any health professional, inside or outside the system, can get acquainted with the case of the family and of the individuals that constitute it, as well as take it into his or her charge.

The second sheet (*Psychosocioeconomic Profile*) presents the characteristics of the family group. It must be filled in immediately after the first contact with the patient and complemented upon the first home visitation. The profile makes explicit the portrait of the family sketched on the front page, showing nuances not contained in the data of the *Identification* and the *Problems List.* On its back, the *List of Environmental Conditions* appears, describing the kind of habitation, its water and light supply, and the general conditions of the environment. On this sheet there is an addendum, entitled *Observations,* where there is reference to some problems that, although inactive (e.g., treated tuberculosis in a member of the family, surgeries undergone, allergies, etc.), can become potentially capable of reactivation and endanger health.

The third sheet, the *Evolution,* follows and serves for all the members of the family and for the family as a whole. The register is sequential, arranged by date of attendance. In the first column is placed the date, name, and/or letter of the patient seen, as well as the number of the problem that induced the appointment, with the respective letter of the family member who was assisted. This is followed by the annotations of the technician, which might refer to either a physical or psychological examination, the identification of a social problem, subsidiary laboratory tests, schedule of the treatment routine, or the measures taken.

The sheets of the record are put in a printed envelope, which bears the name of the Sanitary Unit, of the community health care system, the reference number of the record, the name of the family, and its address, and is kept in a plastic folder.

This record is entrusted to the family, which, with very few exceptions, keeps it with great care, taking it along whenever attending the Sanitary Unit or any other health service (1).

Besides the family record, the primary care team also fills out a priority card when some member of the family presents one of the problems that the Sanitary Unit regards as a priority. At first there were four priority problems used to determine families at risk: immunization, malnutrition, tuberculosis, and alcoholism. Now the following problems are in the process of being put into operation: poor school achievement, pregnancy and family planning, mental disorders, difficulties with adolescents, water supply, major socioeconomic problems, community organization, and dental problems.

Priority cards serve for the planning of interviews and home visits, supervision of programs, and keeping of records on the care given to priority problems by each team. When there is one or more priority problem in a family, this will be considered an *Under Care Family,* for which home visits and regular outpatient attendance are planned.

A nominal card and a residential card are also maintained by the team for controlling the number of residences in each area and the number of persons dwelling in them.

The care given is always registered in the family record, in the priority cards, and in the statistical forms used by the Sanitary Unit.

RECORDING AND REPORTING THE PSYCHOSOCIAL COMPONENT OF HEALTH AT THE PRIMARY HEALTH CARE LEVEL AND SUPPORTING ECHELONS

This family medical record illustrates a means for recording and reporting psychosocial factors affecting health in primary health care settings and supporting echelons. Its use for recording psychosocial factors affecting health, as well as for understanding the interaction between them and the physical problems presented by individuals and their families, is evident.

In a community health system, where this mechanism is used, many psychosocial problems are already being recorded and reported by the health personnel working in it. They have been already listed as capable of characterizing *At-Risk Families.*

From the study of this document, one may assess immediately which are the psychosocial factors affecting health as they are introduced and considered as problems in primary health care settings. Thus, when we refer to *Child At Risk,* there are many psychosocial factors included: death of more than four siblings; difficulties in breast feeding; mental disorder in the family; deprivation of father and mother (abandonment, change, and hospital isolation); families of a different culture in process of adaptation. When *Pregnant Woman At Risk* is characterized, there is clear reference to age, multiparity, unwanted pregnancy, mental disorder affecting the mother, poverty, broken home, unwed mother. Among *Socioeconomic Problems* are listed large families, poverty, unemployment, expulsion from the welfare system, illiteracy, disability, abandonment of family members, and family disorganization. Bad sanitation conditions, overcrowded homes, promiscuity, and contact with contaminated animals are recorded among *Sanitation and Housing* problems.

All these psychosocial factors are recorded when they affect one individual or the family as a group in the *Problems List* (the fourth part of the family medical record) or in the *Psychosocioeconomic Profile* and *List of Environmental Conditions* (the second part of the family medical record).

This form of recording and reporting psychosocial problems is encompassed by the ideology that supports the organization of the community health system in which it is used: the integration of all physical, psychological, and social health services, in preventive, curative, or rehabilitative primary health care settings. It is unjustifiable to have a separate assessment, classification, and recording of mental and social problems in such settings.

COMMENTS

The entrusting of the records to the patients was inspired by the report made by David Morley, after visiting the Murialdo Sanitary Unit in 1974, describing the success he had had in providing the records of his "Under-Five Clinics" to the mothers (6). This success encouraged the present writer to deliver the records to the families; this was begun in one of the areas assisted by the Murialdo Sanitary Unit and, after a long process of study, research, and consultation, was extended to the other areas.

The delivery of medical records to the users has already been depicted in the medical literature (7) as a form of increasing the quality of care, improving the relation between physicians and patients, ensuring continuity, and avoiding excessive bureaucracy. The basis of this policy is that the person who buys the service has the right to keep the product purchased for evaluation. The positive results of this procedure would include better participation of patients in their treatment; the reduction of the number of patients who do not obey recommendations (since, if they have the record in their hands, they do not have to memorize instructions); and the patients' motivation for health education as they try to understand the meaning of his sickness.

In the Murialdo Sanitary Unit, this fact has been proven. Patients have begun admitting, routinely and without prejudice, that they are sick and need treatment for problems such as tuberculosis, psychosis, or alcoholism. Entrusting the records to the patients improves the continuity of the delivery of services, previously impaired by the predominance of medical practices more and more oriented to specialization. In this manner, in sending the patient to specialists or to hospitals, the possibility of exposing them to a whole new set of clinical or subsidiary exams is attenuated. Positive experiences have occurred in this sense when patients of the system have been assisted by other health systems. For example, pregnant women in the system who seek out maternity hospitals, bringing their records with the whole prenatal care duly registered (including characteristics of the pregnancy, if it is normal or of risk) facilitate the work of the obstetrician. In addition, mental health problems that may complicate the clinical or surgical management needed by the patient are at once under the control of the assisting professional in the supporting echelons.

Another benefit is the possibility of establishing a better physician-patient relationship, removing the paranoiac fears caused by the usual dependent attitude of patients toward their physicians. Since in communitarian medicine the free choice of a professional is impaired, providing records to the patients offsets the disadvantages of forcing professionals upon them by fostering dialogue between both groups.

For the physicians there are also advantages, such as the incentive in the evaluation of their work and in the attempts to raise its quality, as offered by the dialogue and by the studies resulting from the records. The satisfaction of the professionals will also be increased to the extent that the distance between academic professionals (who work at university health institutions and who use sophisticated records) and professionals working directly with the patients (who register precariously, or do not register at all, the health actions they take) is diminished. The entrusting of the records also contributes to the work of health service planners or administrators, facilitating audits, which begin to be done more by the professionals themselves rather than by fiscal experts.

Naturally many objections have been addressed to this form of registering health data. Among them are their reliability (for they can be adulterated); the possibility of their being precariously or tendentiously reviewed by the colleagues of the health services or other services; the possibility that the patients would sue the professional because of medical error; and the greater loss of time due to writing and explaining more to the patient.

The objection of loss of time is refuted at once by the elevation of the quality of the first attendances, which will make the link between the professional and the patient so strong that the "lost" initial time will soon be recovered by the facility with which further evaluations of the patient and the family will be made. The other objections, although relevant, can be similarly overcome. Problems of communicating the occurrence of terminal sicknesses and mental disorders may in a way constitute an obstacle to the policy of entrusting the records to the family groups. The Murialdo Sanitary Unit experience has shown, however, that delicate mental problems and marriage conflicts can be registered and kept in secret by the family and the health services they attend. The registration of some problems, however, mainly those related to sicknesses stigmatized by prejudice, or to terminal ones, must be given special individual treatment. The analysis of such problems with patients and their families, who do or do not wish to become aware of them, or who do not want them to be marked down, can answer this question better than years of academic discussions.

The Murialdo Sanitary Unit had one case of an alcoholic who went to his primary care team to ask that his problem not be annotated. In the home visit, relatives and neighbors convinced him, in a meeting of memorable common sense (although absolutely absurd by the standards of what is conventionally called a formal meeting between relatives and health professionals), to accept the diagnosis.

As to professional secrecy, no violations occur, for if the record is entrusted to the family it becomes its private object, accessible only to its owners and to the health services they attend. The secret, in the opinion of the Murialdo professionals, belongs to the family, which sometimes lends it to the health professionals and health services to keep for them. To give them back their medical records is merely to recognize this fact and to use it as a tool for the better management of the family.

REFERENCES

1. E. Busnello, "A Integração de Saúde Mental num Sistema de Saúde Comunitária" (thesis for qualification for Associate Professorship in Psychiatry at the Department of Psychiatry and Legal Medicine of the School of Medicine of the Federal University of Rio Grande do Sul, Porto Alegre, 1977), pp. 10–11.

2. E. Busnello, I. Lewin, and S. Ruschel, "Estudo de um Caso Registrado num

Prontuário de Família Orientado para a Solução de Problemas," accepted for publication, *Revista da Associação Médica do Rio Grande do Sul* (Brazil).

3. H. Cohn and W. Schmidt, "The Practice of Family Health Care: A Descriptive Study," *American Journal of Psychiatry* 131(1975):781–82.

4. I. Lewin, "A Ficha Clínica e o Trabalho Médico: Papel na Assistência, Educação, Comunicação, e Avaliação," *R. Med. ATM* (Porto Alegre, Brazil) 10(1075): 1–28.

5. I. Lewin, E. Busnello, and S. Ruschel, "O Prontuário de Família Orientado para a Solução de Problemas," *Revista da Associação Médica Brasileira* 25(1979):5–8.

6. D. Morley, "The Under-Five Clinics," in *Medical Care in Developing Countries*, ed. M. King (Nairobi: Oxford University Press, 1966).

7. B. Shenkin and D. Warner, "Giving the Patient His Medical Record: A Proposal to Improve the System," *New England Journal of Medicine* (1973):688–92.

8. M. Q. Thorne, Jr., "PSRO: Future Impact on Community Mental Health Centers," *Community Mental Health Journal* 11(4):389.

9. L. Weed, *Medical Records, Medical Education, and Patient Care* (Cleveland: The Press of Case Western Reserve University, 1969).

20

On the Teaching and Learning of Psychosocial Aspects of Primary Care in Developed Countries

MACK LIPKIN, JR.

THE CENTRAL IMPORTANCE OF PSYCHOSOCIAL ISSUES IN PRIMARY CARE

The education and training of primary care workers in psychosocial aspects of primary care touches on all phases of the primary care worker's training and career. This is because psychological and social issues touch each portion of the work of primary care and because primary care workers keep on learning about these issues throughout their careers. For example, sociocultural issues determine whether or not someone chooses to become a patient (1). Social considerations of the availability of care, transport, and wealth determine where a person seeks care. How a problem is conceptualized by a patient is a complex of factors, including the illness models of the patient, the personality of the patient, the patient's language and culture, and the nature of the physical aspects of the problem. How a problem is presented by a person to a health care provider is both personal and cultural. For example, some traditional cultures point to places on totem dolls. Others speak in terms of spirits. Even in less modest cultures, the identical lesion may be presented in enormously varied ways. Some of these variations are due to contextual considerations; others are due to the psychological makeup and experience of the patient (2). Parallel considerations apply to the practitioner as well.

Each illness episode also has psychological and social implications for the patient. The change from self-perception as a well person to a self-perception as an ill person leads to multiple changes but always includes loss of self-esteem, acute grief reaction, heightened dependency, and a wish for help. The social implications may be enormous, including financial deprivation, loss of work, changes in the support system, and so forth.

Similarly, each healing act has psychological and social implications.

Healing often must be presented in such a way as to elicit the cooperation and agreement of the patient. For this to be, the language must be appropriate, the healing processes must be acceptable to and believed in by the patient, and the patient must understand what is required of him or her.

Thus, regardless of the phase of primary care, psychological and social considerations are of major importance. For this reason, teaching about these considerations, to be effective, must touch and pervade all aspects of training. That this is not presently the situation in most training programs may in part account for the uproar of dissatisfaction concerning such programs and their product, modern cosmopolitan medicine (3).

Such issues, sketched in greater detail in other chapters of this volume, lead to a question that is answered in this chapter on educating primary care workers in psychosocial aspects of care. The question, simply, is: Education for what? The purpose of this discussion is to consider basic long-range educational goals, methods, and evaluation, and to survey some present solutions in the developed world.

GOALS OF EDUCATION IN PSYCHOSOCIAL ASPECTS OF PRIMARY CARE: KNOWLEDGE, SKILLS, ATTITUDES

All education in medicine has as an ultimate objective to produce demonstrable effects on defined, desirable, and priority outcomes of care. These include improved morbidity and mortality statistics, increased patient and health personnel satisfaction, and decreased unit and systems costs. However, educational design in medicine is not sufficiently advanced to move rationally and directly from outcome-oriented goals to educational processes. So most authors and programs plan rather in terms of content and knowledge, process and skills, and attitudes and beliefs. (*Knowledge* refers in this context to cognitive aspects of knowledge rather than to knowledge of processes.)

Content

The appropriate content of education concerning psychological and social aspects of primary care is controversial. There is neither agreement nor uniformity in programs. Each program tends to invent its own subset of content from the universe of possibilities, based on the strengths and interests of its faculty or on the local needs of its populations. Further complicating these choices is the diversity of theoretical bases underpinning work in this area. The principal schools of thought diverge along traditional lines of psychological theorizing; they include depth approaches such as psychoanalytic and dynamically oriented views, systems approaches, subpsychiatric approaches (in which the world of primary care is thought of as a lesser version of the world of psychiatry), and humanistic approaches (in which the democratic psychologies are translated into the medical context). That such diversity can persist is evidence, in part, of a lack of a telling empirical analysis that would settle the issue of content. This is, in fact, a major argument for the effort to create a classification of psychosocial aspects of primary care. Until it is possible to identify what the problems actually are, which are the most important and common, and how their presentation in primary care differs from that of the better-studied secondary and tertiary centers, it will not be possible to develop broadly accepted general principles upon which to base the content of service and educational programs in psychological and social aspects of primary care.

In the absence of certain consensus, knowledge and content decisions should be oriented toward the prevalent problems and the most practical available solutions in the defined context of the learner. One list, deriving from an informal consensus process, is that of the recent report of the Society for Research and Education in Primary Care's workshop on interviewing (4). The content areas stressed in the subgroup on curriculum included the following:

1. Basic psychodynamics (e.g., transference, conversion, etc.).
2. The effect of life events on illness.
3. Coping styles of providers and patients.
4. Affective disorders.
5. Growth of the physician as a provider.
6. Psychotropic drugs.
7. Substance abuse.
8. The angry patient.
9. The pain-prone patient.
10. Personality styles in medical practice.
11. Death and dying.
12. Hypochondriasis.
13. Depression.
14. Psychophysiology as it relates to psychoneuroendocrinology and psychoimmunology.
15. Sexual dysfunction and sleep disorders.
16. Basic therapeutics (psychotherapy, behavior modification, hypnosis, etc.).

Similar lists can be generated from the contents of leading texts and numerous reports in journals such as *The Journal of Medical Education*. A selection of such lists is given in Appendixes A–F, including this author's own set of contents and a selection of representative others.

Processes and Skills for Psychosocial Effectiveness in Primary Care

The principal processes essential in primary care are easy to name but difficult to teach. The principal objective is to elicit all data relevant to a defined task in an efficient manner that promotes a positive relationship; initiates therapy effectively; and includes promotion of patient self-help, compliance, and preventive care. Particular emphases with respect to data collection are usually laid on completeness, on use of both direct and indirect data, on the development of active listening, and on use of the self by the primary care worker. Indirect data are sometimes neglected. These include implied or implicit verbal data and nonverbal data such as body language, countertransferential data (data gleaned from the skilled interviewer's reaction to the patient), and symbolically hidden information. Efficiency rests on the use of multiple channels of information simultaneously, including the use of countertransference. This is brought to its extreme in the "flash" technique of the Balints, who assert that the significant psychological and social issues can be recognized most often within the context of the six-minute general practice visit in England (5). Efficiency also depends on cogent use of clinical decision-making processes, astute clinical observation, and the use of data collection outside the clinical encounter itself through the use of screening instruments, questionnaires, and knowledge of the clinical and patient context.

Promotion of a positive relationship is the subject of an enormous literature and covers details from the physical plant through depth-psychological notions concerning identification, *encountering* the patient (a Jungian concept), and the like. Although the literature is inconclusive and no certain principles can be indisputably maintained, it seems that there may be commonalities underlying successful relationships between professionals and patients that span schools of thoughts. These include communication of positive regard in culturally appropriate forms, communication of understanding, optimism about the possibility of help (defined in the patient's terms), lack of ambivalence and ambiguity, effective use of healing suggestions, and a history of prior effectiveness with the patient or patient's circle. Clearly, these qualities assume others, such as physical accessibility, comprehensibility, and (at some level) cultural and linguistic compatibility of practitioner and patient.

Promotion of an effective *therapeutic alliance* or of compliance is again a subject of enormous complexity. Again, the plethora of approaches testifies to the immaturity of the field, as well as to its difficulty. There seems to be little consensus about accepted approaches. It is generally agreed upon that proposed practices must be acceptable to the person, society, and culture of the patient. They must be clear and understandable and must be understood by the patient. They work best if incorporated into the patient's own consciousness. The latter aspects (of promotion of compliance) may be enhanced by active participation by the patient in the formulation of the plan and in repetition of its content. Green has suggested that brevity, organization, primacy, readability, repetition, specificity, and combinations of these may enhance compliance (6).

Recent efforts in this area include use of controlled clinical trials to ascertain the effect of specific educational methods on outcomes of care (7,8), as well as on intermediate parameters such as learning and psychological effect. A second sort of effort is in a natural historical stage. Various efforts are made to characterize the process involved in such aspects of the primary care encounter as the interview. The present author, has, for example, studied the patterns and problems of both psychologically trained and general internal medicine interviewers in primary care settings and has described ten processes that must be completed. These are based on the notions that the interview is not a linear process in which one follows one prescribed step after another, but is a matrix, like a Persian carpet. The warp of the interview consists of ten elements. The first is establishing interest in and commitment to working with the patient. The second is establishing communication with the patient through facilitating communication and by calibrating and overcoming barriers to communication. Next is training the patient to provide the interviewer with the quality and quantity of data that are necessary to accomplish the interview tasks. Surveying the patient's problems permits understanding the full context and setting of priorities. Selection of a priority problem is the next structural element. Reaching agreement about a priority problem and about what the focus of work will be requires negotiation of tasks. Having negotiated a task and focused on a priority problem, development of a narrative thread permits the interview to flow and data to emerge in an organized fashion. Developing hypotheses about the nature of the phenomena is the next step. Typically, this occurs shortly into the interview. Testing of those hypotheses is a major function of the encounter. The final structural element involves using one's self and one's helping skills to develop a helping relationship.

While this particular set of processes is included simply as an example, is arbitrarily selected, and is suited to the needs of one group of practitioners and patients primarily (those in large, urban, middle-class U.S. settings), such analyses must proceed work to identify the critical elements in patient-physician interactions and to begin to show their role and function experimentally. Recent work in this area is contained in Lipkin and Putnam (4) and in Lipkin, Boufford, Froom, and White (9).

Development of Skills in Psychosocial Aspects of Primary Care

As in the area described above, the teaching of specific skills is controversial both with respect to which skills to teach and how to teach them. Clearly, the basics include those skills necessary to do the job desired. Typically, they include assessment of common problems, initiation of the relationship, and continuing care of the patient. Central in this is interviewing skill. Teaching of interviewing has been reviewed by Carroll and Munroe (10). The essential finding is that active participation rather than use of didactic methods is essential. Conjunction to an actual interview experience by the trainee is optimal. Use of standardized stimuli in the form of teaching tapes (audiotapes or videotapes), case vignettes, simulated patients (actors or volunteers), or volunteer patients are all helpful ways to control the student's interview practicum experience to permit focus on specified objectives and to avoid trauma and failure resulting from excess of material that the novice is ill-equipped to manage initially.

It has been the experience of many that certain other qualities enhance the teaching of such skills. The use of organized material that introduces one step at a time, allows progressive, positive experiences, and achieves a sense of growing mastery is helpful. The use of faculty role models who have clinical credibility is of great value. Because of the power of role models, it is probably reasonable to assert that the use of outside experts and of behavioral scientists (if they do not have clinical credibility) places such teachers at a severe handicap. Even when expert clinical faculty participate in learning experiences, modeling both of desirable interviewing traits and also of self-correction or self-criticism by the faculty member through interaction with the student group or through self-criticism facilitates the student's ability to be self-critical and constructive. Choice of examples and materials that have local relevance is of great value in making learning interesting, useful, and perceived as relevant. Finally, setting standards of behavior concerning interviewing and relating to patients that include the material that is taught creates certainty that these skills will be mastered. Such standards can be created through course objectives and through exit requirements, such as examinations for licenses. Ongoing requirements can also be used, such as review of ongoing work, relicensure examinations, and continuing monitoring of care in some sort of real-time review process. These can also promote appropriate behavior. So can the use of economic tools.

CURRICULUM: LEARNER-ORIENTED, FEASIBLE, AND ACTIVE

The principal means of meeting educational goals is through the enunciation of a curriculum, selection of teaching techniques appropriate to the curricular goals and content, and creation of evaluation procedures appropriate to these tasks. Curricular choices concerning psychosocial aspects of primary care seem to be arbitrary at times because of the overlap of the subjects. But there are essentials that are not arbitrary, regardless of how they are expressed. Local choice of curriculum should be based on an analysis of the needs of the learners once they are finished. This analysis should be empirical, not theoretical. Curricular choices should be appropriate neither to idealized notions of the academic field of the senior instructor, nor to the accumulated accretions of a committee created in Noah's Ark fashion to represent one of each type of specialty.

Curricular design should reflect the learning task of the learners and not the teaching preference of the teachers. For example, passive lectures about interviewing, while easy to deliver, are much less useful than interviewing experiences that are active, allow the student to practice skills, and contain useful and noncritical feedback. If teachers prefer to lecture, they must find other teachers to provide active learning for their students.

The curriculum must also be feasible. It must be compatible with available resources. In the few training programs in the United States that explicitly attempt to teach psychosocial aspects of primary care to medical residents (e.g., University of Rochester, University of North Carolina, University of Virginia, University of Washington), a major problem is that the curriculum is ambitious but the time available for it is not. Similarly, teachers often attempt to tag this complex area onto already busy schedules of research, other teaching, service, and administration. This is a first-class ticket to failure, for this sort of work and teaching is intellectually demanding because of the high complexity of the data and phenomena involved; it is also psychologically demanding because of the intensity of the affective issues it raises, because of the extreme neediness of the subset of patients, and because it requires suspension of normal reactions and a high tolerance for ambiguity.

Similarly, this teaching can tax educational resources because not all groups are equipped with one-way mirrors or with videotape and audiotape equipment and skill, and because it is teacher-intensive. It has been found, however, that when the goals of teaching these issues are clear, ingenuity can overcome most resource deficits. For example, if the intention of the teachers is to give students feedback about an interview but they have no videotape or audiotape available, they can use a simulated patient. People are always available for this role, since anyone who has ever been sick can do it. If the teacher is reluctant to use a simulated patient for one reason or another, he or she can have the students critique one another using preformulated and pre-discussed criteria or by having them derive and then use their own criteria. Once goals are clear, many creative solutions to teaching problems usually are available.

Given, then, that the teaching will be active, appropriate, and consistent with local learning needs and local teaching realities, what should be taught? In general, some version of the following areas must be included. Clearly, these could be expressed in a variety of ways, but this list is probably representative.

1. The doctor-patient relationship.
2. Psychological and social problems in primary care.
3. Coping styles of providers and patients.
4. The effect of life events on illness and disease.
5. Death and dying.
6. Basic psychodynamics.
7. Basic psychotherapeutics (suggestion, hypnosis, behavioral modification, biofeedback, psychopharmacotherapy).
8. Transference.
9. Interviewing.
10. Personal growth of the patient.
11. Personal growth of the provider.
12. The life cycle.
13. Sexual and sleep disorders.
14. Substance abuse.
15. Problem patients (angry, pain-prone, hypochondriacal, dependent, psychotic).
16. Local cultural issues (varied patients' health belief models).
17. Local political issues (stigma of mental illness, reimbursement requirements).
18. Local issues of illness classification (e.g., the "hot and cold" system of Puerto Rican patients in New York).
19. Clinical observation, clinical decision making, clinical judgment.
20. Quantitative assessment of one's activities.
21. Legal and professional record-keeping requirements (problem orientation).

Clearly, each of these contains many, many subtopics. As well, there is much overlap, because these aspects of the problems of individuals intersect in multifactorial and multivariate relations.

Complementary to these specific subject areas are *attitude* areas, which include (1) humility in the sense of willingness to do whatever is necessary to help a patient; (2) empathy; (3) nonjudgmental acceptance of the values, strengths, and frailties of one's patients and colleagues; (4) belief based on experience and world view that dealing with the appropriate range of a patient's problems in an integrated fashion is professionally valid, satisfying, and necessary.

Complementary *skills* to these sets of knowledge and attitudes include the following:

1. Mastery of the cognitive base.
2. Skill in acquring data.
3. Skill in analyzing data.

4. Skill in synthesizing relevant data.

5. Initiation and completion of a satisfying and successful healing relationship.

6. Effectiveness in education of patients and colleagues.

7. Effectiveness in counseling.

8. Effectiveness as a referral agent.

9. Effectiveness as an ombudsman for the patient.

10. Effectiveness in recording and evaluating these activities and processes in valid and reliable fashion.

Many other sets of curricular material exist. However, most of the elements are probably contained in the above framework. Several samples, again, are shown in Appendixes A–F.

TECHNIQUES: INTEGRATION ON FOUR LEVELS

Techniques for teaching about psychological and social aspects of primary care are not unique (except in content) in the domain of teaching efforts that attempt to change how a learner acts, thinks, and processes complex phenomena in life. But the area presents some features that render it challenging and that, when ignored, lead to ineffective teaching and to failure to change the learners sufficiently to achieve reasonable goals.

Many teaching programs attempt to teach these issues on a single level. For example, the level may be cognitive; it may be affective, through the use of support groups; it may be at the level of understanding, through teaching about such things as medical anthropology or medical sociology; and so forth. Teachers who teach in this fashion frequently express discouragement because the learning of their students is transient. They observe that their students soon regress to behaviors that reflect the dominant paradigms and modes of behavior in their locale. Because of this, characteristically, teachers of these issues do not last very long. They burn out, drop out, specialize, go into research, and so forth.

This author has presented elsewhere the argument that it is necessary, in teaching about psychological aspects of care, to teach in a fashion that permits learners to integrate their learning into their entire professional and personal lives. As in learning a language, unless learning about these issues includes practice and mastery on the spoken, read, and idiomatic levels and on the level of world view in Whorf's and Wittgenstein's sense, the learner soon drops out of functional competence (11).

To be more specific, learners must first learn to incorporate the new knowledge on the *intrapsychic* level. That is, what they learn must be accepted psychologically and must become part of the psychological and perceptual apparatus of the students. They must also learn on the *interpersonal* level, in the sense that they must be able to use their learning interactionally with other individuals, be they patients or fellow workers. Furthermore, they must learn to use the learning in the *social system* in which they will be functioning and in the social subsystems in which they will be functioning. For medical people, these typically include the clinic, the hospital, and the social service apparatus in their locale. They must be able to translate and integrate their new knowledge into the prevailing language of these systems; they must fit the rules; they must adapt their learning to the modes, mores, and fashions of their practice setting. Finally, they must integrate what they learn into their own *cultural* setting. They must use culturally acceptable and meaningful language and concepts, or they must have ways to translate their new ideas into acceptable aspects of the dominant culture.

The alternative to learning on these four levels—intrapsychic, interpersonal, social system, and cultural—is for the learner to be and to feel alien. When this happens, and it is the most common experience of learners about these issues, they are forced into a choice between remaining a part of their cultural setting or of rejecting the new concepts. In such contests, the new concepts are likely to lose.

It is because of this need for integrated learning on these four levels that the present author has developed *block teaching* in a controlled context to ensure effective initial efforts by students (11). Elements of such teaching, regardless of whether or not it is done in an intensive block format, usually include supervision of encounters with real patients, use of an observer in the room, audiotaping or videotaping, use of one-way screens, and use of simulated patients or automated patient experiences.

Some sort of support group is often coupled to such teaching. In this author's model, an ongoing group (regardless of level) sees patients who come from the learners' practices. A patient is seen in the group, live, most of the time but not all of the time. This permits all the learners to share common data, to model good and bad technique and self-correction, and to share in a supportive setting the realities and difficulties of dealing with real people. The group may elect other topics or activities as well. The group overcomes resistance together, develops a common language, and develops a support system. Such groups provide a bridge that allows the learners to integrate their new learnings into their old settings.

Such teaching is only successful—whether in an intensive block, in a support group, or in a feedback exercise—when it includes role modeling of effective patient care; when it is free of jargon; when it is relevant to the perceived needs of learners; and when the learners have a sense of progress and progressive mastery of material. Use of taped or stock interviews is useful to control content. But this must not be the only experience of the learners, since such passive exercises tend to be unidimensional, unrealistic, and perceived as both.

Once basic skills are acquired, a learning setting that permits progressive increase in conceptual and technical mastery should be provided. Reinforcement of the basic paradigms must occur in this continuity setting. Support for the learners and their new methods, and in their use of them in the demanding situations and challenges of the real clinical world, is essential especially with respect to long-term help and continuity. If this is provided, learners can be helped to a lifelong habit of progressive mastery and growth in psychosocial aspects of primary care. This is highly desirable. The form of such experience may vary as a function of time and talent; again, however, they usually center around a continuing case conference as described above, or around a preceptorial relationship in which a master teacher-clinician supervises others with less experience.

LOCAL NEGOTIATIONS

Because of the demands of learning such new materials—which substantially modify and to some extent disorient the settled life of the primary care worker—and because such teaching requires considerable effort by the trainee if it is to be assimilated, the trainee must be motivated to undertake the rigors of the new materials.

Such motivation fundamentally derives from the validity of the work and its effectiveness in meeting the goals of the learner. However, this needs to be demonstrated, and that may take some creativity. The available techniques include "carrots" of demonstration of usefulness, relevance, enhanced clinical effectiveness, and greater personal satisfaction. Some students and learners can find reward in the intellectual fascination of the area. Others require more practical demonstration that they must master this material if they are to be effective. As well, the "sticks" of examination; monitoring of care; and definition of acceptable standards of interview, therapy, and psychosocial aspects of care, as well as of standards concerning recording of these sorts of issues, are all useful.

Negotiating these "carrots" and "sticks" is essentially a local issue. It must be addressed and formulated according to the priorities of the locale in which the teachers and students work and with respect to the psychological, social, and cultural variables at work in that location. But this is a critical step. These changes cannot be imposed; they must be embraced by the potential recipients.

MEETING RESISTANCE: RESPECT, MODELING, BECOMING A HELPER

Resistance to dealing with psychological and social issues is prevalent in most parts of present-day medicine. The reasons for this are complex. They are symbolized by the present dominance of the biomedical model, with its nineteenth-century biochemical and infectious disease models of care, and the underlying algebraic thinking involved, which is essentially univariate. This is reflected in the greater economic rewards of doing procedures and prescribing medications than of dealing with people. It is reflected in the dominant academic interests—in the biological and the esoteric.

Thus, at present, there is little prestige and glamor in dealing with the mundane ills of the people. In addition, dealing with the complexities of patients' problems is sometimes intellectually and always emotionally taxing. It is subject to ambiguity, which is intolerable to many of those presently selected to become health care personnel. Whether this results from the selection process or the educational process is not, perhaps, clear. But it is clear that health care personnel, like most other people, tend to shun ambiguity and to prefer simple solutions and simple models.

Those attempting to teach about these areas, then, must be prepared to respect the resistance of the learners, to demonstrate that their teachings are worth the pain, and to deal with resistance not by meeting it head on but by turning it to their use. The most simple and direct way of doing this is to show both clinical and intellectual interest and excitement. The surest way to do this is to actually involve one's self and one's students in the care and study of patients. In concrete and real cases, students quickly see the reasons for learning this material. This puts the teacher in the position of helper instead of the position of preacher or dictator of ideas.

Resistance, then, is most readily overcome by effective role modelers in clinically potent roles. Students in this context readily accept the task of helping patients with their problems, in addition to the tasks of doing diagnosis and monitoring physiological changes. The teacher quickly becomes seen as a necessary helper. Lack of the role of necessary helper is a disadvantage that behaviorists and psychological specialists have. They can overcome this disadvantage, but, to do so, they must be willing to *join* the learners at the level at which learners are functioning. If they are unwilling or unable to assimilate, a more suitable role for behaviorists is to help clinical personnel in enhancing their own effectiveness. This is done principally by defining meaningful curricula, by finding effective teaching approaches, and by supporting the clinical teachers in their sometimes discouraging tasks.

Support groups of learners wrestling with psychological and social issues of their patients can also effectively reframe resistance by creating a peer group that is commonly struggling with the new methods.

Essential to this process is the incorporation of a new and coherent paradigm across the four levels cited above—intrapsychic, interpersonal, social system, and cultural. This protects the learner who encounters the dominant care system, which does not use much psychological or social data or reasoning in its care processes. Without this protection, the learner will soon regress and the half-life of the learning will be short.

RESOURCE SHARING

There are some critical, only partially met, needs in the area of teaching about psychological and social aspects of primary care.

First is the accumulation and organization of much more data about the role of these factors at the primary care level. The new classification set forth in this volume is one step in making this process possible. Development of clinical laboratories in which sufficient numbers of cases are seen in a manner that permits reliable data accumulation is essential.

Second is the testing of methods of dealing with problems encountered and catalogued. Until more, and more meaningful, work is done in this area; until it sheds its specialty aura and its need for new languages; and until it becomes available to the level of worker who is actually doing the work—the primary care worker, not the psychiatrist—there will be little but authority to serve as the basis for choice among the babble of voices claiming to have sound approaches.

A third need is the description and testing of ways to teach about what is known to be of clear benefit and use.

A fourth need is the establishment of communications networks about such findings. Recently, a clearing house of information about this has been established by the author and others.

A fifth need is the development of resource sharing, consultative networks, the pooling of expertise, and the use of consortium and matrix approaches to teaching so that each teaching group does not have to develop its own resources from scratch.

THE TRAINING OF WORKERS FOR THE USE OF THE NEW CLASSIFICATION OF PSYCHOLOGICAL AND SOCIAL FACTORS OF PRIMARY HEALTH CARE

Clearly, the training of workers to test this new classification will depend on who they are, where they are, what their needs are, and what their prior levels of education are. This chapter has suggested that education concerning such factors is a *process* that should begin in the beginning of a health worker's education and continue throughout his or her professional life.

APPENDIX A*

Knowledge

A. *Human Developmental and Contextual Assessment*

    I. Personal Assessment

        a. Personality style
        b. Inner resources; coping style
        c. Life stage and situation

    II. Family and Contextual Assessment

        a. Life cycle tasks of family members
        b. Health of family
        c. Cultural factors
        d. Recent events
        e. Environmental factors

    III. Community

        a. Resources, extrafamilial supports

B. *Psychophysiology*

C. *Psychosocial Aspects of Illness*

    I. Psychogenic Illness

        a. Conversion
        b. Hypochondriasis

    II. Psychosomatic Concepts and Illness

        a. General concepts
        b. Asthma
        c. Hypertension
        d. Peptic ulcer
        e. Rheumatoid arthritis
        f. Thyrotoxicosis
        g. Ulcerative colitis and Crohn's disease
        h. Neurodermatitis

    III. Psychosocial Factors in Other Illnesses

        a. Accidents
        b. Alcoholism
        c. Anorexia nervosa
        d. Cardiovascular illness
        e. Diabetes
        f. Drug abuse
        g. Leukemia, cancer
        h. Multiple sclerosis

Source: Mack Lipkin, Jr., and Penny Williamson, *Select Bibliography of Psychosocial Aspects of Primary Care* (New York: Rockefeller Foundation, 1978).

      i. Obesity
      j. Seizure disorder
      k. SLE (collagen diseases)
      l. Syncope
      m. Venereal disease
      n. Stress theory (psychological factors in all diseases)

   IV. Psychophysiologic Illnesses

    V. Common Psychological Problems

      a. Anxiety
      b. Depression
      c. Grief
      d. Hysteria
      e. Obsessiveness
      f. Phobia

D. *Psychological Responses to Life Change and Disease*

    I. Life Cycle—Specific Problems

      a. Pregnancy
      b. Childhood
      c. Adolescence
      d. Career choice
      e. Parenting
      f. Mid-life crisis
      g. Climacteric
      h. Retirement and aging
      i. Death

   II. General Issues

      a. Loss and life changes
      b. Malingering
      c. Chronic illness

E. *Psychopathology*

    I. Schizophrenia

   II. Suicide

  III. Neurosis/Psychosis

  IV. Delirium (Organic Brain Syndrome)

F. *Models of Health and Illness*

Skills

A. *Data Collection*

    I. Interview: Process

      a. Individual
      b. Family

      c. Group

   II. Communication Skills

      a. Staff (nurse, physician's assistants, social workers, etc.)

      b. Consultant specialists

      c. Community members

   III. Testing

      a. Mental status

      b. Psychological testing

B. *Data Recording*

   I. DSM III

C. *Helping Skills*

   I. Characteristics of a Helping Relationship

   II. Communication—Verbal and Nonverbal

   III. Specific Therapies

      a. Behavior modification

      b. Crisis intervention

      c. Existential therapy

      d. Family therapy

      e. Gestalt therapy

      f. Group therapy

      g. Humanistic therapy

      h. Humor

      i. Hypnosis, meditation, relaxation

      j. Jungian

      k. Marital therapy

      l. Paradoxical therapy

      m. Passivity

      n. Pain and placebo

      o. Psychoanalysis and psychotherapy

      p. Psychotropic medication

      q. Sexual counseling

      r. Short-term psychotherapy

      s. Single parenting

      t. Women

D. *Patient Education*

E. *Consultation Skills*

   I. The Family or Primary Care Resident as Medical-Psychiatric Liaison Consultant

   II. Use of Consultants

F. *Hindering Skills*

   I. False Reassurance

   II. Noninteraction

   III. Discussion of Fees First

IV. Explaining in Obtuse Language

V. Injecting Biases

VI. Nonverbal Communications of Disinterest, Business, and so on

VII. "There's Nothing Wrong—It's All in Your Head."

Attitudes (Personal Growth)

A. *Growth of Physician as a Person*

B. *Growth of a Person as a Physician*

C. *Inclusive Issues*

    I. Ethical Considerations

    II. Resident's Contextual Assessment, Goals, and the like

    III. Setting Limits

        a. When to let go of responsibility for a patient

        b. When not to be open

        c. How to be healthy in the midst of illness

APPENDIX B*

1: Psychiatric Disorders

2: Delirium and Dementia

3: The Adolescent Patient

4: The Chronically Ill Patient

5: The Patient with Pain

6: Drug Abuse and Alcoholism

7: Sleep Disorders

8: Sexual Disorders

9: The Myocardial Infarction Patient

10: The Dying Patient

11: The Psychotherapeutic Interview

12: Psychopharmacology

APPENDIX C†

Introduction

    1. Introduction to diagnostic and treatment models

    2. Gathering data

*Source: H. S. Abram, *Basic Psychiatry for the Primary Care Physician* (Boston: Little, Brown, 1976).

†Source: R. J. Cadoret, and L. J. King, *Psychiatry in Primary Care* (St. Louis: C. V. Mosby, 1974).

The Syndromes
   3. Affective disorders: depression and mania
   4. Schizophrenic and schizophreniform syndromes
   5. Anxiety neurosis
   6. Obsessive compulsive and phobic neuroses
   7. Hysteria
   8. Antisocial personality
   9. Alcoholism
   10. Drug dependency
   11. Mental retardation
   12. Organic brain syndrome
   13. Sexual variants
   14. Undiagnosed conditions

Treatment
   15. Psychotherapy: backgrounds of modern practice
   16. Psychotherapy: practical management
   17. Medication
   18. Electroconvulsive treatment
   19. Psychiatric emergencies

APPENDIX D*

Introduction   Psychosomatic Medicine: Current Trends and Clinical Applications

Current Trends in Psychosomatic Theory: The Mind-Body Complex and the External
    Environment

   Historical Perspective of Contemporary Psychosomatic Medicine
   Psychological Stress and Coping in Adaptation and Illness
   The Concept of "Stress" in the Biological and Social Sciences
   The Current Status of the Concepts of Physiological Response Specificity and Ac-
       tivation
   The Role of Developmental Factors in Susceptibility to Disease
   Operant Conditioning: A New Theoretical Approach in Psychomatic Medicine
   Determinants of Physiological Responses to Symbolic Stimuli: The Role of the So-
       cial Environment
   Biosocial Resonation: A Conceptual Model of the Links between Social Behavior
       and Physical Illness
   Family Process and Psychosomatic Disease
   Psychosomatic Knowledge and the Role of the Physician: A Sociological View
   Conversion: Fact or Chimera?
   The Role of Aggression in Somatic Symptom Formation

*Source: Z. J. Lipowski, D. R. Lipsitt, and P. C. Whybrow, *Psychosomatic Medicine* (London:
Oxford University Press, 1977).

Body Image and Its Disorders
The Current State of the Concept of a Psychosomatic Disorder
Physical Illness and Psychopathology
Observations of Psychosocial Factors and Their Relationship to Organic Disease

Intermediate Mechanisms: From Psychological Response to Physiological Reaction

From the Symbolic Stimulus to the Pathophysiological Response: Neurophysiological Mechanisms
Neuroendocrine Mediating Mechanisms: From the Symbolic Stimulus to the Physiological Response
From the Symbolic Stimulus to the Pathophysiologic Response: Immune Mechanisms

Current Trends and Methodological Approaches in Psychosomatic Research

A. Psychophysiological Approaches
Psychophysiological Research: Aims and Methods
Laboratory Studies of Psychological Stress
Quantification and Psychological Indicators of Emotions: The Content Analysis of Speech and Other Objective Measures of Psychological States
Electroencephalographic Correlates of Verbally Induced Stress in Man
Psychophysiological Responses to the Urban Environment

B. Clinical Approaches
Clinical Psychosomatic Research
Nocturnal Psychophysiological Correlates of Somatic Conditions and Sleep Disorders
Psychophysiology of Pain
Hypnosis as a Treatment Method in Psychosomatic Medicine
The Relaxation Response: Psychophysiologic Aspects and Clinical Applications
Therapy-Resistant Depressions: Biochemical and Pharmacological Applications
Psychosomatic Studies of Psychiatric Disorders: Schizophrenia

C. Epidemiological Approaches
Epidemiological Studies in Psychosomatic Medicine
Epidemiological Studies of Life Change and Illness

D. Animal Study Approaches
The Induction of Acute and Chronic Cardiovascular Disease in Animals by Psychosocial Stimulation
Psychosomatic Research Today: A Clinician's Overview

Psychosomatic Approach in the Practice of Medicine

The Psychosomatic Approach in the Practice of Medicine
The Doctor-Patient Relationship in the Practice of Medicine

Bodily Communication and Psychotherapy: A Psychosomatic Approach
Psychiatry and Medical Progress: Therapeutic Considerations
Psychophysiologic Disorders in Children and Adolescents
Management of the Persistent Somatizer
Operant Conditioning-Based Behavior Modification: One Approach to Treating Somatic Disorders
Biofeedback and Self-Control of Physiological Functions: Clinical Applications
Psychotropic Drugs in Somatic Disorders
Consultation-Liaison Psychiatry: A Psychosomatic Service in the General Hospital
Management and Care of the Dying Patient

Teaching Psychosomatic Medicine

Teaching Psychosomatic Medicine to Medical Students, Residents, and Postgraduate Fellows
Some Problems in the Teaching of Psychosomatic Medicine

APPENDIX E*

1. Psychosocial conditions disguised as physical illness
2. Anxiety and depression
3. Medical conditions in psychiatric disguise
4. Confusional states
5. Competency, refusal of treatment, and committability
6. Pain and addiction
7. Emotional aspects of major disease categories
8. Problem patients
9. Difficult hospital locations
10. Psychiatric emergencies in the hospital setting
11. Psychotherapeutic medications in the physically ill
12. The family: Whose patient is this?
13. Psychotherapy and counseling
14. Consultation and referral: Calling for help, resource number one: coping and occupational hazards of physicianhood
15. Appendix: Putting the patient's mind at rest

APPENDIX F†

General Considerations
1. Basic Principles of Management in Psychosomatic Medicine

*Source: M. R. Lipp, Respectful Treatment: The Human Side of Medical Care (New York: Harper & Row, 1977).

†Source: E. D. Wittkower and H. Warnes, Psychosomatic Medicine: Its Clinical Applications (New York: Harper & Row, 1977).

2. Crisis Intervention in Psychosomatic Medicine
3. The Process of Consultation

Models of Intervention
4. Therapeutic Consultation with the Surgical Patient
5. Evaluation and Management of Intractable Pain
6. Psychiatric Considerations in Chronic Pain States
7. Grief in General Practice
8. Hemodialysis and Renal Transplantation—Psychopathological Reactions and Their Management

Psychotherapies
9. Psychoanalytic Psychotherapy
10. Group Psychotherapy
11. Group Therapy for Specific Psychosomatic Problems
12. A Conceptual Model of Psychosomatic Illness in Children: Family Organization and Family Therapy
13. Hypnosis
14. The Behavior Therapies
15. Autogenic Therapy
16. Biofeedback and Biocybernetics
17. Pharmacotherapy
18. Marital Therapy
19. Yoga
20. A Social Ecological Perspective on Medical Disorders

Specific Disorders
21. Psychotherapeutic Management of Bronchial Asthma
22. Cardiovascular Disease
23. Anorexia Nervosa
24. Psychobiological Factors in Obesity
25. Gastrointestinal Disorders
26. Neurological Disorders
27. Obstetrics and Gynecology
28. Psychiatric Aspects of Endocrine and Metabolic Disorders
29. Musculoskeletal Disorders
30. Itching and Other Dermatoses
31. Psychosomatic Disorders in Children
32. Psychosomatic Problems in the Older Person

REFERENCES

1. D. Mechanic, "The Concept of Illness Behavior," *Journal of Chronic Diseases* 15(1962):189–94.
2. M. Lipkin, Jr., "Psychologic Aspects of Evaluation of Outcome," in *Resources for Health,* ed. H. D. Banta (New York: Praeger, 1982), pp. 90–98.

3. I. Kennedy, *Unmasking Medicine* (Reith Lectures, delivered on the BBC in 1980 and published in the *Listener* on November 6, 13, 20, 27 and December 4 and 11, 1980).

4. M. Lipkin, Jr., and S. Putnam, *On the Teaching of Interviewing: A Report of a Workshop* (New York: Society for Research and Education In Primary Care Internal Medicine, 1980).

5. E. Balint, *Six Minutes for the Patient: Interaction in General Practice Consultation* (New York: Harper & Row, 1973).

6. L. Green, "Educational Strategies to Improve Compliance with Therapeutic and Preventive Regiment: The Recent Evidence," in *Compliance in Health Care,* ed. R. B. Haynes, D. W. Taylor, and D. L. Sackett (Baltimore: Johns Hopkins University Press, 1979), pp. 157–93.

7. D. L. Sackett, "Evaluation of Health Services," in *Maxcy-Rosenau: Public Health and Preventive Medicine,* 11th ed., ed. J. M. Last (New York: Appleton-Century-Crofts, 1980), pp. 1800–23.

8. P. T. Rowley, L. Fisher, and M. Lipkin, Jr., "Screening and Genetic Counseling for B-Thalessemia Trait in a Population Unselected for Interest," *American Journal of Human Genetics* 31(1979):718–30.

9. M. Lipkin, Jr., J. Boufford, J. Froom, and K. L. White, *Primary Care Research in 1981* (New York: Rockefeller Foundation, 1981).

10. J. G. Carroll and J. Munroe, "Teaching Clinical Interviewing in the Health Professions," *Evaluation and the Health Professions* 3(1980):21–45.

11. M. Lipkin, Jr., "On the Teaching of Psychosocial Aspects of Primary Care," in *The Roles of Family Practice, Internal Medicine, Obstetrics and Gynecology, and Pediatrics in Providing Primary Care,* report of the 73rd Ross Conference in Pediatric Research, ed. D. M. Berwick (Columbus, Ohio: Ross, 1977), pp. 78–82.

21

Recommendations

¶ That the World Health Organization (WHO) promote understanding of the psychological and social dimensions of health and consequently support initiatives by member nations to structure their health services to promote and respond to such understanding.

¶ That papers prepared for this workshop revised as necessary in the light of the discussions, together with summary of the discussions, an editorial summary, and additional papers as appropriate be published as soon as possible under the joint auspices of WHO and The Rockefeller Foundation. There should be wide distribution of this publication preferably without charge to developing countries and at low cost to developed countries.*

¶ That WHO coordinate activities of member countries to implement the recording and use of psychological and social dimensions of health. The ultimate goal is to develop a classification of physical, psychological, and social problems that relate to health, to be included in future revisions of the *International Classification of Diseases (ICD)*.

¶ That the coordination of work on the development and use of an integrated triaxial classification of health problems should be a joint responsibility of the Divisions of Mental Health and Health Statistics and of the *ICD* Committee of WHO.

¶ The future work of the WHO Divisions of Health Statistics and Mental Health should include:

Pilot studies of the psychological and social classifications proposed in this volume.

These recommendations were drafted by Carol Buck, Mack Lipkin, Jr., and Kerr L. White and adopted by the working group convened at Bellagio, Italy, November 10, 1979.

Editor's note: The present volume meets the first portion of this recommendation.

Field trials in various member countries of these classifications revised on the basis of the pilot studies. The areas for field trials should be selected to represent and reflect the global diversity of primary care facilities in both developing and developed countries. Trials should be based upon existing routine health recording and reporting systems. Trials should utilize the United Nations Household Survey Capability as appropriate.

Thorough analysis of the field trials to insure valid and relevant methods for classifying data on psychological and social problems in health.

¶ That WHO accept as a high priority the creation and convening of a multinational steering committee to translate the principles developed in this volume into a comprehensive plan for pilot and field testing of a triaxial classification of health problems.

¶ That WHO stimulate more interest in the proposed work so as to obtain the funds necessary for implementing the foregoing proposals.

22

A Classification of Psychological Symptoms and Social Problems for Inclusion in a Triaxial Classification of Health Problems

The classification that follows was first compiled by a working group consisting of the authors of Chapter 11 of this volume in October, 1979. It was subsequently revised twice. The first revision occurred at the Bellagio meeting of November 1979. After comments by primary care workers from many nations, it was again revised at the Bellagio meeting of February 1981. This classification will be the subject of extensive field testing under the auspices of the Division of Mental Health of the World Health Organization. Norman Sartorius will direct the field tests.

The classification is to be used in conjunction with a third dimension or axis. This is the classification of physical problems and disorders used by the classifier presently. For example, it might be used in conjunction with the *International Classification of Diseases,* ninth revision (*ICD*-9); with the *International Classification of Health Problems in Primary Care,* second edition (*ICHPPC*-2); or with any other such classification. However, it would replace the portions of those classifications concerned with psychological symptoms or social problems.

CLASSIFICATION OF PSYCHOLOGICAL PROBLEMS

1. Feeling anxious or nervous
   Includes: apprehension
             bad nerves
             panicky feeling
             tension

upset
worried
fears

2. Feeling depressed
   Includes: crying excessively
             dejected
             feeling low
             hopelessness
             sadness
             unhappy
             low self-esteem
             guilt
             shame

3. Disturbances of sleep
   Includes: trouble sleeping
             sleeping too much
             nightmares

4. Sexual problems
   Includes: excessive concerns about masturbation
             concern with sexual performance (e.g., potency)
             concern with size and shape of sexual organs

5. Eating problems
   Includes: loss of appetite
             excessive appetite
             concern with weight

6. Ideas of suicide
   Includes: attempts

7. Feeling angry or irritable
   Includes: bitterness
             temper tantrums
             violence or homicidal

8. Psychomotor restlessness
   Includes: hyperactivity
             overactivity

9. Trouble with concentration or memory
   Includes: forgetfulness
             confusion
             distractibility

10. Problems with identity
    Includes: no confidence
              loss of identity

identity crisis

11. Social withdrawal
Includes: avoiding people
excessive shyness

12. Personality trait
Includes: dependence
oppositional or antisocial behavior
dominant behavior (e.g., provocative, negativistic)
cruelty to people or animals
destructiveness
fire setting
stealing
other behavior

13. Substance-related problems
Includes: alcohol problems
tobacco problems
other drug problems

14. Delusions, hallucinations, or incoherence
Includes: seeing things
hearing things
overly suspicious

15. Phase-of-life problems
Includes: problems adjusting to developmental stage such as adolescence or retirement

16. Age-specific developmental problems (excludes learning problems)
Includes: bedwetting
ancopresis
thumb sucking
delay in early development (e.g., acquisition of motor skills or language)

17. "Psychophysiological" problems (including any physical symptoms exacerbated by psychological factors)
Includes: skin problems
respiratory problems
gastrointestinal (GI) problems

18. Other psychological problems
Includes: "can't cope"
"going crazy"
"losing my mind"
rituals
stuttering

CLASSIFICATION OF SOCIAL PROBLEMS

1. Housing problems
   Includes: overcrowding
              lack of housing
              inadequate housing

2. Change in residence
   Includes: immigration
              moving out of parental home

3. Financial problems
   Includes: cannot pay bills or debts
              cannot afford food of sufficient quality or quantity

4. Problems within a family
   a. Conjugal (marital or nonmarital problems)
      Includes: marital discord
                 spouse abuse
                 sexual problems (not due to physical or mental disorder)

   b. Parent-child problems
      Includes: child abuse or neglect
                 excessive parental control
                 deficient parental control
                 child deprived of parental attention
                 conflict over rules

   c. Family disruption
      Includes: divorce
                 separation
                 death
                 family member leaves home

   d. Other problems of family relationships
      Includes: problems with relatives other than parent or children
                 problems with siblings

   e. Problems of caring for sick person (includes family members and
      friends)
      Includes: aged parent

5. Other nonfamily interpersonal problems
   Includes: problems with peers, neighbors
              social isolation
              death of a friend

6. Educational or learning problems
   a. Educational problems

Includes: school failure
school refusal
lack of schooling
absenteeism (truancy)
inadequate educational opportunities
cheating
quarrels with teachers

b. Learning problems
Includes: reading problems
arithmetic problems

7. Occupational problems (including problems as housewife)
Includes: problems with coworkers
role dissatisfaction
unemployment
difficulties at work or in adjusting to work situation

8. Legal problems
Includes: imprisonment
prosecution
litigation
legal investigation

9. Personal and environmental circumstances that impede access to health
care or are hazardous to physical health
Includes: lack of transportation
ignorance of significance of symptoms
rigid appointment schedules of health facility
advertising of a proprietary medicine for treating the patient's
symptoms
religious beliefs or cultural attitudes
air pollution
water pollution

10. Conflict with the practices or belief systems of a social or cultural institution
Includes: nonconformity with religious ritual
crisis of religious or political persecution
conscientious objection

11. Other social problems
Includes: unwanted pregnancy
persecution or discrimination (on the basis of politics, religion, sex, or race)
excommunication
hexing

Bibliography

Abiven, M. *Humaniser l'hopital.* Paris: Fayard, 1976.

Achenbach, T. M., and Edelbrock, C. S. "The Classification of Child Psychopathology: A Review and Analysis of Empirical Efforts," *Psychological Bulletin* 85:1275-1301, 1978.

Agbayani, B. F., et al., eds. *Proceedings and Selected Writings on Paraprofessional Health Workers Manpower Development.* Manila: University of the Philippines Post Graduate School of Medicine, 1975.

Aho, W. R., and Minott, K. "Creole and Doctor Medicine: Folk Beliefs, Practices and Orientations to Modern Medicine in Rural and Industrial Suburban Settings in Trinidad and Tobago, the West Indies." *Social Science and Medicine* 11:349-355, 1977.

American Hospital Association. *International Classification of Health Problems in Primary Care.* Chicago: Author, 1976.

American Psychiatric Association. *Diagnostic and Statistical Manual of Mental Disorders,* 3rd ed., draft. Washington, D.C.: Author, 1978.

American Psychiatric Association. *Diagnostic and Statistical Manual of Mental Disorders,* 3rd ed., micro-D, draft. Washington, D.C.: Author, 1979.

American Psychiatric Association. *Diagnostic and Statistical Manual of Mental Disorders,* 3rd ed. Washington, D.C.: Author, 1980.

American Psychiatric Association. *The Problem-Oriented System in Psychiatry: Task Force Report 12.* Washington, D.C.: Author, 1977.

Anderson, J., and Lees, R. "Optional Hierarchy Expansion of ICHPPC." *Journal of Family Practice* 6(6):1271-1275, 1978.

Anderson, J. A. D., Buck, C., Danaher, K., and Fry, J. "Users and Nonusers of Doctors: Implications for Self-Care." *Journal of the Royal College of General Practitioners,* March 1977.

Anderson, J. G. "Demographic Factors Affecting Health Utilization." *Medical Care* 11:104, 1973.

Anderson, R., Smedby, B., and Anderson, O. "Medical Care Use in Sweden and the United States: A Comparative Analysis of Systems of Behaviour." *Research Series No. 27.* Chicago: University of Chicago, Center for Health Administration Studies, 1970.

Andrews, G., Schonell, M., and Tennant, C. "The Relation Between Physical, Psychological, and Social Morbidity in a Suburban Community." *American Journal of Epidemiology* 105:324-329, 1977.

Apple, D., ed. *Sociological Studies of Health and Sickness.* New York: McGraw-Hill, 1960.

Ardoino, J. *Information et Communications dans les Entreprises et les Groupes de Travail.* Paris: Les Editions d'Organisation, 1964.

Argyris, C. "Diagnosing Human Relations in Organizations. A Case Study of a Hospital." New Haven: Yale University, Labor and Management Center, 1956. Document Polycopie.

_____. *Personality and Organization: The Conflict Between System and the Individual.* New York: Harper and Brothers, 1957.

Assises Nationales de l'Hôpitalisation Publique Française. "Evolution et Perspectives des Techniques de Lutte contre les Maladies Mentales: l'Hôpital dans la Sectorisation." *Revue Hospitalière de France,* No. 267 (I), pp. 175–206 (Rapport de la Commission); pp. 207–210 (note du Dr. P. Bonamour), 1974.

Augustine, J. C. "Personnel Turnover: What Is It?" In *Handbook of Modern Personnel Administration.* J. F. Formulare.

Australian Morbidity Study. Australian College of General Practitioners, 1965.

Bailey, V., Graham, P., and Boniface, D. "How Much Child Psychiatry Does a General Practitioner Do?" *Journal of the Royal College of General Practitioners* 28:621–626, 1978.

Bain, S. T., and Spaulding, W. B. "Importance of Coding Presenting Symptoms." *Canadian Medical Associaion Journal* 97:953, 1967.

Bakker, C. B., and Bakker Rabdau, M. K. *No Trespassing! Explorations in Human Territoriality.* San Francisco: Chandler and Sharp, 1973.

Balint, E. *Six Minutes for the Patient: Interaction in General Practice Consultation.* New York: Harper & Row, 1973.

Balint, M. "Le Medicine, son Malade et la Maladie." Paris: P.U.F., 1960.

Banks, M. H., Beresford, S. A. A., Morrell, D. C., et al. "Factors Influencing Demand for Primary Medical Care in Women Aged 20–44 Years: A Preliminary Report." *International Journal of Epidemiology* 4:189, 1975.

Barfield, O. "Poetic Diction and Legal Fiction." In M. Black, ed., *The Importance of Language.* Englewood Cliffs, N.J.: Prentice-Hall, 1962.

Barreto, Ramirez, y Delvasto. *Estudio de Comunidad del Barrio "El Diamante."* Cali, Colombia: PRIMOPS, 1977.

Barrot, J., and Alix, M. "Evolution de l'Expression et de la Satisfaction des Bésoins Sociaux en Milieu Hospitalier." *Revue Hospitalière de France,* No. 267 (II), 1974.

Beaglehole, R., et al. "Blood Pressure in Tokelauan Children in Two Contrasting Environments." *American Journal of Epidemiology* 108:283, 1978.

Berger, M., and Hortala, F., "Mourir a l'Hôpital." In *Coll. Infirmières d'Aujourd'hui,* No. 7. Paris: Le Centurion, 1974.

Berne, E. "Des Jeux et des Hommes." Paris: Stock, 1976.

Berrien, F. K. "Methodological and Related Problems in Cross-Cultural Research." *International Journal of Psychology* 2:33–44, 1967.

Berry, J. W. "On Cross-Cultural Comparability." *International Journal of Psychology* 4:119–128, 1969.

Blashfield, R. K., and Draguns, J. G. "Toward a Taxonomy of Psychopathology: The Purpose of Psychiatric Classification." *British Journal of Psychiatry* 129:574–583, 1976.

Bloom, S. W. *The Doctor and His Patient.* New York: Russell Sage, 1963.

Blumberg, P. J. "Implications of Presentation Trend for U.S. Corporations." *Harvard Business Review* January-February 1977, pp. 46–55.

Boesch, E. E. *Communication Between Doctors and Patients* (DHEW Pub. No. (OS) 74-50008). Washington, D.C.: Government Printing Office, 1974.

_____. *Communication Between Doctors and Patients in Thailand.* University of the Saar, Socio-Psychological Research Centre on Development Planning, 1972.

Bonifacio, M. F. "Family Physician: The Sociological Aspect of His Community Role." *Proceedings of the First Seminar-Workshop on Developing Standards in Family Medicine: An Overview* (Lake Caliraya Club, Lumban, Laguna, Philippines, December 7–9, 1978). Manila: The Philippine Academy of Family Physicians, 1978.

_____. *Rural Urban Doctors in Some Southern Tagalog Areas: A Social-Psychological Comparison,* 1979. (Mimeographed Research Report.)

_____. "The Transformative Nature of Social Work." *The SSWAP Exchange,* 1(5): 2, 5 (September-October), 1973.

Boom, W. H., Lamberts, H. E., Froom, J., and Blondell, R. *Patient and Family Doctor: Rochester, U.S.A. and Ommoad (Netherlands) Compared.* Huisarts en Wetenscharp, 1978.

Bowlby, J. M. *Child Care and the Growth of Love.* Harmondsworth, England: Penguin, 1953.

Brenner, M. H. "Mortality and the National Economy." *Lancet* (2):568, 1979.

Brislin, R. W. "Comparative Research Methodology: Cross-Cultural Studies." *International Journal of Psychology* 11:215–229, 1976.

British Medical Association, ed. Family doctor booklets (various topics).

Brody, E. B. "Psychiatric Implications of Industrialization and Rapid Social Change." *Journal of Nervous and Mental Disease* 156:295–296, 1973.

Brown, E. R. "Exporting Medical Education: Professionalism, Modernization and Imperialism." *Social Science and Medicine* 13A:585–596, 1979.

Brown, G. "Le Diagnostic d'Entreprise." Paris: Enterprise Moderne d'Edition.

Bruwer, J. "The Composition of a Cewa Village (Mudzi)." *African Studies* 8:191–98, 1949.

Bryant, J. H. "Community Health Workers: The Interface Between Communities and Health Care Systems." *WHO Chronicle* 32(4):114–144 (April), 1978.

_____. *Health and the Developing World.* Ithaca: Cornell University Press, 1969.

Burns, B. J., and Cromer, W. "The Evolving Role of the Psychologist in Primary Health Care Practitioner Training for Mental Health Services." *Journal of Clinical Psychology* 7:8–12, 1978.

Busnello, E. "A Integracao da Saude Mental num Sistema de Saude Comunitaria." Unpublished thesis for Associate Professorship in Psychiatry, Department of Psychiatry and Legal Medicine, School of Medicine, Federal University of Rio Grande do Sul, Porto Alegre, Brazil, 1977.

Busnello, E., Lewin, I., and Ruschel, S. "Estudo de um caso registrado num Prontuario de Familia Orientado para a Solucao de Problemas." Brazil: Revista da Associacao Medica do Rio Grande do Sul, in press.

Caimo, M. "Les Fonctions du Service Sociale Hospitalier." *Service Sociale dan le Monde,* No. 1, 1970.

Cantril, H. *The Pattern of Human Concerns.* New Brunswick, N.J.: Rutgers University Press, 1965.

Carraud, M. "Une Experience de Restructuration d' Entreprise en Vue d'Enrichir les Taches." *Sociologie du Travail,* No. 1, pp. 36–48, 1976.

Carroll, J. G., and Munroe, J. "Teaching Clinical Interviewing in the Health Professions." *Evaluation and the Health Professions* 3:21–45, 1980.

Cassell, J. "The Contribution of the Social Environment to Host Resistance." *American Journal of Epidemiology* 104(2):107–23, 1976.

Cassell, J. "Factors Involving Sociocultural Incongruity and Change." *Milbank Memorial Fund Quarterly* 45:41, 1967.

Centre Européenne de Formation et de Récherche en Action Sociale. *Proceedings of the Seminaire sur l'Interaction du Personnel d'Action Sociale et du Personnel de Santé: Incidence sur la Formation.* Vienna, Austria, November 17–21, 1975.

Chevalier, A. "Le Bilan Social de l'Entreprise." In *Institut de l'Entreprise.* Paris: Masson, 1976.

Chilivumbo, A. B. "The Social Basis of Illness." *Central African Journal of Medicine* 20:181–185, 1974.

Clare, A. W., and Cairns, V. E. "Design, Development and Use of a Standardized Interview to Assess Social Maladjustment and Dysfunction in Community Studies." *Psychological Medicine* 8:589–604, 1978.

Classification of Disease, Research Committee. *Journal of the Royal College of General Practitioners* 2:140–159, 1959.

Classification of Disease, Research Committee (amended version). *Journal of the Royal College of General Practitioners* 6:207–216, 1963.

Climent, C. E., and de Arango, M. V. *Development of an Alternative, Efficient, Low Cost Mental Health Delivery System in Cali, Colombia: II. The Health Center.* Manuscript in preparation, 1979.

Climent, C. E., de Arango, M. V., Plutchick, R., and Leon, C. A. "Development of an Alternative, Efficient, Low Cost Mental Health Delivery System in Cali, Colombia: I. The Auxiliary Nurse." *Social Psychiatry* 13:29–35, 1978.

Climent, C. E., and Guerrero, R. *Humanization of Medical Care: An Experimental Program at the University Hospital in Cali, Colombia.* Manuscript in preparation, 1979.

Climent, C. E., and Plutchick, R. "Confiabilidad y Validez de un Cuestionario de Autoreportaje de Sintomas de Enfermedad Mental (PASSR)." *Revista Colombiana de Psiquiatria* in press, 1979.

Cobb, S. "Physiological Changes in Men Whose Jobs Were Abolished." *Journal of Psychosomatic Research* 18:245, 1974.

———. "Social Support as a Moderator of Life Stress." *Psychosomatic Medicine* 38:300, 1976.

"Coded Classification of Disease." Richmond: Virginia Commonwealth University/Medical College of Virginia, Department of Family Practice, September 1972.

Cohn, H., and Schmidt, W. "The Practice of Family Health Care: A Descriptive Study." *American Journal of Psychiatry* 131:781–782 (July), 1975.

Colson, A. C. "The Differential Use of Medical Resources in Developing Countries." *Journal of Health and Social Behavior* 12:226–237, 1972.

Communautes Européennes. "Participation des travailleurs et structure des societies." *Bulletin,* suppl. 8/75, 1975.

Condon, T. B. "A Unit Management Evaluation." *Journal of the American Hospital Association,* 48(12):61–64, 1974.

Cooper, B., Fry, J., and Kalton, G. "A Longitudinal Study of Psychiatric Morbidity in a General Practice Population." *British Journal of Preventive and Social Medicine* 23:210–217, 1969.

Corbus, H., and Connell, R. W. "The Patient's Need: Does Anyone Care?" *Journal of the American Hospital Association* 48:46–49, 1974.

Council on Pediatric Practice. *Standards of Child Health Care.* Evanston, Ill.: American Academy of Pediatrics, 1972.

Countryside Development Conference Proceedings. Development Academy of the Philippines, Manila, 1979.

Crahay, S. "Des Lendemain de l'Acte Cherurgical les Suites Psychologiques et Pathologiques." June 6, 1974.

Cromwell, R. L., Blashfield, R. K., and Strauss, J. S. "Criteria for Classification Systems." In *Issues in the Classification of Children,* N. Hobbs, ed. San Francisco: Jossey-Bass, 1975.

Cruz, E. C. "A Comparative Study of Help-Seeking Behavior in an Urban Community." Unpublished master's thesis, University of the Philippines, 1978.

Cunningham, C. "Thai Injection Doctor: Antibiotic Mediator." *Social Science and Medicine* 4:1–24, 1970.

Damon, A. "The Residential Environment, Health and Behavior." In *The Effect of the Man-Made Environment on Health and Behavior,* L. E. Hinkle, and W. C. Loring, eds. Washington, D.C.: U.S. Department of Health, Education and Welfare, 1977.

Day, F. A., and Leoprapai, B. "Patterns of Health Utilization in Upcountry Thailand." Bangkok: Institute of Population and Social Research, Mahidol University, 1977.

Delbeke, B. "Synthèse et Etude Critique des Méthodologies de Dotation des Unites de Soins en Personnel Soignant." Brussels: U.C.L., Faculté de Médecine, 1975[–76]. Document Polycopie.

Deliege, D. "La Médecine Concertée, ses Buts, son Efficacité. *Médecins de Groupe* No. 60, pp. 633–643, 1973.

———. "Médecine Général, Place Actuelle et Critères de Satisfaction du Generaliste." *Louvain Medical* 95(1):33–48, 1976.

———. "Patients et Médecins, Aujourd'hui et Demain." *Journal International des Groupes Balint* No. 1, pp. 63–80, 1974.

———. "Le Role du Médecin, ses Relations avec le Milieu Social." *La Revue Nouvelle* No. 7–8, pp. 5–17, 1968.

———. "La Santé et les Soins, Aujourd'hui et Demain." Unpublished notes, 1975. Document Polycopie.

———. "The Sociological Framework Surrounding Inpatients." *International Nursing Review* 21(1):16–20, 1974.

Deliege, D., and Leroy, X. *Humanisons des Hôpitaux.* Paris: Maloine, 1978.

Deliege, D., and Lohle-Tart, L. "Faire Evaluer l'Hôpital par le Malade, Vademecum Methodologique." Brussels: Université de Louvain, 1979.

Dessainjean, N. "L'Accucil." *Psychologie Medicale* 5(2):305–306, 1973.

De Vogue, A., and Grasset, S. "S.O.S. Hôpitaux." Paris: Gallimard, 1975.

de Vries, M., Berg, R. L., and Lipkin, M., Jr. *Use and Abuse of Medicine.* New York: Praeger, 1982.

Diamond, L. K., and Fox, D. J. "Turnover Among Hospital Staff Nurses." *Nursing Outlook* No. 6, pp. 388–391, 1958.

Division of Mental Health. *WHO Project on Monitoring Health Needs.* Bangkok: Thailand Ministry of Public Health, 1979. Mimeographed.

Djudanovic, V., and Mach, E. P. *Alternative Approaches to Meeting Basic Health Needs in Developing Countries.* Geneva: World Health Organization, 1975.

Dohrenwend, B., and Dohrenwend, B. *Stressful Life Events: Their Nature and Effects.* New York: Wiley, 1974.

Donaldson, P. J. "Foreign Intervention in Medical Education: A Case Study of the Rockefeller's Intervention in a Thai Medical School." *International Journal of Health Services* 251–271, 1976.

Donoso, G. "Health Care and Community Action." *WHO Chronicle* 32(3):102–105 (March), 1978.

"Down With High Blood Pressure." *WHO Chronicle* 32:136–137, 1978.

"Draft Classification of the Reasons for Contact in Primary Care." WHO International Classification of Diseases Committee, 1978.

Drake, A. "Illness, Ritual and Social Relations Among the Chewa of Central Africa." Unpublished doctoral dissertation, Duke University, 1976.

Drossman, D. A. "The Problem Patient: Evaluation and Care of Medical Patients with Psychosocial Disturbances." *Annals of Internal Medicine* 88:366–372, 1978.

Dubos, R. *Men, Medicine and Environment.* Harmondsworth, England: Penguin, 1970.

———. *Mirage of Health.* New York: Harper & Row, 1971.

Ducamin, M. "L'Humanisation des Hôpitaux." *La Revue Hospitaliére de France* No. 236, pp. 1675–1789, 1970.

Duff, R. S., and Hollingshead, A. B. *Sickness and Society.* New York: Harper & Row, 1968.

Eastwood, M. R., and Trevelyan, M. H. "Relationship between Physical and Psychiatric Disorder." *Psychological Medicine* 2:363–372, 1972.

Editorial. "Behavioral Problems in General Practice." *Journal of the Royal College of General Practitioners* 29:323–327, 1979.

"Eighth Revision of the International Identification of Diseases, Adapted for Use in the United States, Vol. 1" (Public Health Service Pub. No. 1963). Washington, D.C.: U.S. Department of Health, Education and Welfare, 1968.

Eisenthal, S., Emery, R., Lazar, A., and Udin, H. "Adherence and the Negotiated Approach to Patienthood." *Archives of General Psychiatry* 36:393–398, 1979.

Elms, R. R., and Leonard, R. C. "Effect of Nursing Approaches During Admission." *Nursing Research* 15(1):39–48, 1966.

Engard, C. "Etude Psychologique d'Opères à Coeur Ouvert." *Psychologic Médicale* 5(2):417–429, 1973.

Engel, G. L. "The Need for a New Medical Model: A Challenge for Biomedicine." *Science* 196:129–136, 1977.

Epstein, R. Z., and Benson, D. J. "The Patient's Right to Know, the Patient's Right to Refuse." *Journal of the American Hospital Association* 47(August 1): 47–52; (August 16):38–41, 1973.

Escoffier-Lambiotte, C. "La Médecine et la Verité aux Malades." Paper presented at the conference à l'initiative du Conseille National des Femmes Belges, Brussels, May 1977.

Essen-Moller, E. "On Classification of Mental Disorders." *Acta Psychiatrica Scandinavia* 37:119–126, 1961.

Etzioni, A. *A Comparative Analysis of Complex Organizations on Power, Involvement and Their Correlates.* New York: Free Press, 1961.

Ever, J. "Hypertension as a Disease of Modern Society." *International Journal of Health Services* 5:539–558, 1975.

Eynikel, J. W. *Management by Group Objectives* (note 12E). Eindhoven-Turnhout: Philips, T. E. O. Informatiecentrum, 1975.

Ezzati, T. M. "Ambulatory Care Utilization Patterns of Children and Young Adults." *Vital and Health Statistics Series 13: Data from the National Health Survey, No. 39* (DHEW Pub. No. (PHS) 78-1790). Hyattsville, Md.: U.S. Department of Health, Education and Welfare, 1978.

Fabrega, H., Jr. "Group Differences in the Structure of Illness." *Cultural, Medicine, and Psychiatry* 1:379–394, 1977.

————. "Perceived Illness and its Treatment: A Nationalistic Study in Social Medicine." *British Journal of Preventive and Social Medicine* 31:213–219, 1977.

————. "On the Specificity of Folk Illnesses." *Southwestern Journal of Anthropology* 26:305–314, 1970.

Feinstein, A. R. *1967 Clinical Judgment.* Baltimore: Williams & Wilkins, 1967.

Feldman, A. "The Family Practitioner as Psychiatrist." *American Journal of Psychiatry* 135(6):728–731, 1978.

Feldstein, M., Piot, S. M. A., and Sundaresan, T. K. *Resource Allocation Model for Public Health Planning: A Case Study of Tuberculosis Control.* Geneva: World Health Organization, 1973.

Ferguson, V. "Nursing." *Journal of the American Hospital Association* 43:169–173, 1974.

Final Report of the Regional Conference on Primary Health Care (Manila, Philippines, November 21-24, 1977). Manila: World Health Organization, January 1978.

Fitzgerald, R. "The Classification and Recording of Social Problems." *Social Science and Medicine* 12:265–263, 1978.

Flahault, D. "The Relationship Between Community Health Workers, the Health Services and the Community." *WHO Chronicle* 32(4):149–153 (April), 1978.

Folta, J. R., and Deck, E. S., eds. *A Sociological Framework for Patient Care.* New York: Wiley, 1966.

Fontaine, G. "Hôpital, Malade et Société." *La Revue Nouvelle* 63(4):403–407, 1976.

Freidson, E. "Prepaid Group Practice and the New Demanding Patients." *Health and Society (Milbank Memorial Fund Quarterly)* 51(4):473–488, 1973.

Gaag, J. V. D., and Ven, W. V. D. "The Demand for Primary Health Care." *Medical Care* 16:229–312, 1978.

Garner, J. "Palliative Care: It's the Quality of Life Remaining That Matters." *CMA Journal* 115:179–180, 1976.

Gatmaitan, C. "Mental Health and the National Health Plan." *Philippine Journal of Mental Health* VIII(2):9–16 (July-December), 1977.

Geertsen, R., Klauber, M. R., Rindflesh, M., et al. "A Re-examination of Suchman's Views on Social Factors in Health Care Utilization." *Journal of Health and Social Behavior* 16:226, 1975.

Georgopoulos, B. S., and Mann, F. *The Community General Hospital.* New York: Macmillan, 1962.

G.E.R.M. "Creation d'une Poste 'Humanisation de l'Hôpital' " (lettre No. 52). Brussels, 1971. Document Polycopie.

———. "Hôpitaux Malades." *La Revue Nouvelle* 63(4):375–493, 1976.

———. "Humaniser l'Hôpital" (lettre No. 48). Brussels, 1971. Document Polycopie.

———. "L'Hôpital Technocratique et Inhospitalier: Ses Rites et son Ceremonial" (lettre No. 86). Brussels, 1975. Document Polycopie.

———. "Pour une Politique de la Santé." *La Revue Nouvelle* October 1971.

———. "Pour un rassemblement hospitalier" (lettre No. 108). Brussels, 1977. Document Polycopie.

Giel, R., and Van Luijk, J. N. "Psychiatric Morbidity in a Small Ethiopian Town." *British Journal of Psychiatry* 115:149–162, 1969.

Goffman, E. "Etudes sur la Condition Sociale des Malades Mentaux." Paris: Editions Minuit, 1968.

Goldberg, D. "Detection and Assessment of Emotional Disorders in a Primary Care Setting." *International Journal of Mental Health* 8:30–48, 1979.

Goldberg, D. P. "The Detection of Psychiatric Illness by Questionnaire." *Maudsley Monographs No. 21.* London: Oxford University Press, 1972.

Goldberg, D. P., and Blackwell, B. "Psychiatric Illness in General Practice: A Detailed Study Using a New Method of Case Identification." *British Medical Journal* 2:439–443, 1970.

Goldberg, I. D., and Reiger, D. A., eds. *Utilization of Health and Mental Health Outpatient Services in Four Organized Health Care Settings* (DHEW Pub. No. (ADM) 78-859). Washington, D.C.: Government Printing Office, 1980.

Goldberg, I. D., Regier, D. A., McInerny, T. K., et al. "The Roles of the Pediatrician in the Delivery of Mental Health Services to Children." *Pediatrics* 63:898–909, 1979.

Goldberg, S. "Infant Care in Zambia: Measuring Maternal Behavior" (HDRU Reports 13). Lusaka: University of Zambia, 1970.

Goldstein, M. S., and Donaldson, P. J. "Exporting Professionalism: A Case Study of Medical Education." *Journal of Health and Social Behavior* 20:322–327, 1979.

Gombrich, E. H. *Art and Illusion.* London: Phaidon, 1960.

Gorts, H., and Mues, E. *Management by Group Objectives—Theory and Practice.* Eindhoven-Turnhout: Philips, Departement du Personnel, 1974.

Gorts, H., and Van Goubergen, G. *Social Skills for Management.* Eindhoven-Turnhout: Philips, Technical Efficiency and Information Centre, 1976.

Gould, M. A. "The Implication of Technological Change for Folk and Scientific Medicine." *American Anthropologist* 59:507–513, 1957.

Government of the Republic of Zambia. *Decentralized Government: Proposals for Integrated Local Government Administration.* Lusaka: Zambia Information Services, 1978.

Graham, S., and Reeder, L. G. "Social Factors in the Chronic Illnesses." In *Handbook of Social Medicine,* 2nd ed., H. E. Freeman, S. Levine, and L. G. Reeder, eds. Englewood Cliffs, N.J.: Prentice-Hall, 1972.

Gray, M. "Au Nom de Tous les Miens" (propos recueillis par Max Gallo). Paris: Laffont, 1971.

Green, L. "Educational Strategies to Improve Compliance with Therapeutic and Preventive Regimen: The Recent Evidence." In *Compliance in Health Care,* R. B. Haynes, D. W. Taylor, and D. L. Sackett, eds. Baltimore: The Johns Hopkins University Press, 1979.

Greyhton, M. "Communication Between Peasants and Doctors in Tunisia." *Social Science and Medicine* 11:319–324, 1977.

Group for the Advancement of Psychiatry. *Psychopathological Disorders in Childhood: Theoretical Considerations and a Proposed Classification.* New York: Jason Aronson, 1966.

Grypdonck, M., and Van Der Schueren, Y. "Patient-Georienteerde Verpleging, een Opdracht voor Iedere Verpleegkundige." *Acta Hospitalia* 14(2):153–185, 1974.

Gumperz, J. J., and Blom, J. P. "Social Meaning in Linguistic Structures: Code Switching in Norway." In *Language in Social Groups* (selected and introduced by A. S. Dil), J. J. Gumperz, ed. Stanford: University of California Press, 1971.

Guyotat, J. "Médecin, Malade et More." *Psychologie Medicale* 2(3) 1970.

Haas, M. "Aspect Medico-Social des Problèmes des Patients Hospitalises." *Veska* (Suisse) 38(9):473 ff., 1974.

Hagberg, K. L., McNamara, E., Elledge, C. H., and Johnson, D. M. "Social Work Service." *Hospitals* 42(7):143–148, 1968.

Haggerty, R. J., Roghmann, K. J., and Pless, I. B. *Child Health and the Community.* New York: Wiley, 1975.

Haight, R. O., McKee, C. A., and Barkmeier, J. R. "Morbidity on the First Year of a Family Practice and its Comparison to the Virginia Study." *Journal of Family Practice* 9(2):295–299, 1979.

Haight, R. O., Marsland, D. W., and Mitchell, G. S. "Clinical and Educational Implications of a Longitudinal Audit for Asthma." *Journal of Family Practice* 5(3):481–485, 1976.

Hankin, J., and Oktay, J. S. *Mental Disorder and Primary Health Care* (HEW Pub. No. (ADM) 78–661). Washington, D.C.: Government Printing Office, 1979.

Hankiss, E. "Quality of Life Models." In *UNESCO. Indicators of Environmental Quality and Quality of Life* (Reports and Papers in Social Sciences, No. 38). New York: UNESCO, 1978.

Harding, T. W., de Arango, M. V., Baltazar, J., Climent, C. E., Ibrahim, H. A., Ladrido-Ignacio, L., Srinivasa Murthy, R., and Wig, N. N. "Mental Disorders in Primary Health Care: A Study of their Frequency in Four Developing Countries." *Psychological Medicine* 10:231–241, 1980.

Haworth, A. *Psychiatric Morbidity in Patients Attending a Lusaka Suburb Health Centre*. Unpublished manuscript, University of Zambia, Lusaka, Zambia, 1979.

Haworth, A., and Mwanalishi, M. *Report on the Pilot Survey Carried Out in George Compound, Lusaka*. Lusaka: University of Zambia, School of Medicine, 1978.

Haynes, R. D., et al., eds. *Compliance in Health Care*. Baltimore: The Johns Hopkins University Press, 1979.

"Health Myths and Realities." *Impact* 12(4), April 1977.

"Health, Nutrition and Housing." *CSC DEC JET Continuing Program Learning Package No. 6,* Manila, 1977.

Heggenhpugen, H. K. "The Utilization of Traditional Medicine: A Malaysian Example." *Social Science and Medicine* 14B:39–44, 1980.

Henry, J., and Cassel, J. C. "Psychosocial Factors in Essential Hypertension: Epidemiologic and Animal Experimental Evidence." *American Journal of Epidemiology* 90:171–200, 1969.

Hershey, J. C., Luft, H. S., and Gianaris, J. M. "Making Sense Out of Utilization Data." *Medical Care* 13:838, 1975.

Herzberg, F. *The Motivation to Work*. New York: Wiley, 1959.

Herzlich, C., ed. *Médicine, Maladie et Société*. Paris: Mouton, 1970.

Heuse, G. *Guide de la Mort*. Paris: Masson, 1975.

Hinkle, L. E., Jr., and Wolff, H. G. "Ecologic Investigation of the Relationship Between Illness, Life Experience and the Social Environment." *Annals of Internal Medicine* 49:1370–1373, 1958.

Hinkle, L. E., Jr., et al. "Studies in Human Ecology." *American Journal of Psychiatry* 114:212–220, 1957.

Hoeper, E. W., Nycz, G. R., Cleary, P. D., Regier, D. A., and Goldberg, I. D. "Prevalence of Psychiatric Disorder in Primary Care." Paper presented at the annual meeting of the American Psychiatric Association, Chicago, May 13–18, 1979.

Holmes, J. A., and Speight, A. N. "The Problem of Non-Organic Illness in Tanzanian Urban Medical Practice." *East Africa Medical Journal* 52:225–236, 1975.

Holmes, T., and Rahe, R. "The Social Readjustment Rating Scale." *Journal of Psychosomatic Research* 11:213–218, 1967.

Houghton, H. "Problems of Hospital Communication: An Experimental Study." In *Problems and Progress in Medical Care: Essays on Current Research,* G. McLachlan, ed. London: Oxford University Press, 1968.

Howard, J., and Strauss, A. *Humanizing Health Care*. New York: Wiley, 1975.

Hughes, C. C., and Hunter, J. M. "Development and Disease." In *Social Organiza-*

tion of Health, H. P. Dreitzel, ed. New York: Macmillan, 1971.

————. "Disease and Development in Africa." In *Social Organization of Health.* H. P. Dreitzel, ed. New York: Macmillan, 1971.

Hugues, E. W. *Human Relations in Management.* Oxford: Pergamon Press, 1970.

Humble, J. W. "Naar Betere Bedrijfsresultaten." Rijn: Samson, 1969.

Hungarian Academy of Sciences. "The Hungarian Quality of Life Research Project." *QOL Newsletter* May 2, 1978, and January 30, 1980.

Illich, L. *Nemesis Medicale.* Paris: Seuil, 1975.

International Classification of Diseases, 9th Rev. Geneva: World Health Organization, 1977.

International Classification of Diseases, 9th Rev.—Clinical Modification. Ann Arbor, Mich.: Commission on Hospital and Professional Activities, 1978.

International Classification of Health Problems in Primary Care. London: Oxford University Press, 1970.

International Classification of Health Problems in Primary Care, 2nd Ed. London: Oxford University Press, 1979.

Israel, R. A. "The International Classification of Diseases: Two Hundred Years of Development." *Public Health Reports* 93:2 (March-April), 1978.

Janzen, J. M. "Medicalization in Comparative Perspective." In *Use and Abuse of Medicine,* M. de Vries, R. L. Berg, and M. Lipkin, Jr., eds. New York: Praeger, 1982.

Jocano, F. L. *Folk Medicine in a Philippine Municipality.* Manila: National Museum, 1973.

————. *Slum As A Way of Life.* Quezon City, Philippines: University of the Philippines Press, 1975.

The Joint Commission on Mental Health of Children. *The Mental Health of Children: Services, Research, and Manpower.* New York: Harper & Row, 1973.

Joynson, R. B. *Psychology and Common Sense.* London: Routledge & Kegan Paul, 1974.

Jules-Rosette, B. *The New Religions of Africa.* New Jersey: Ablex, 1979.

Junod, J. P. "Prolongation de la vie et geriatrie." Paper presented at the Tenth International Congress of Gerontology, Jerusalem, Israel, 1975.

Kagan, A. R., and Levi, L. L. *Health and Environment—Psychosocial Stimuli: A Review.* Sweden: Karolinska Institut, 1971.

Kandler, H., et al. "A Study of Nurse-Patient Interaction in a Mental Hospital." *American Journal of Nursing* 52:1100–1103, 1952.

Kantor, M., ed. *Mobility and Mental Health.* Springfield, Ill.: Charles C Thomas, 1965.

Kaplan, H. B. "Social Psychology of Diseases." In *Handbook of Medical Sociology,* H. E. Freeman, S. Levine, and L. G. Reeder, eds. Englewood Cliffs, N.J.: Prentice-Hall, 1979.

Keirse, M., and Peers, J. Patienten-Begeleiding (Assistance du Patient: Fonction Inherente de l'Organisation Hospitalière). Leuven, Belgium: Accode Tijdstroom, 1976.

Kellert, S., et al. "Cultural Change and Stress in Rural Peru." *Milbank Memorial Fund Quarterly* 45:391–415, 1967.

Kelman, S. "The Social Nature of the Definition Problem in Health." *International*

Journal of Health Services 5(4):625–630, 1975.

Kennedy, Ian. "Unmasking Medicine" (Reith Lectures). *Listener,* November 6, 13, 20, 27; December 4, 11, 1980.

Kepner, C. H., and Tregoe, B. B. *The Rational Manager: A Systematic Approach to Problem-Solving and Decision-Making.* New York: McGraw-Hill, 1965.

Khan, A. A., Kaundra, W., and Maguire, J. M. *Traditional Healing Practices in Diseases of Childhood: Observations by Clinicians.* Lusaka: GRZ, Ministry of Health, 1977.

Kiev, A. "The Study of Folk Psychiatry." In *Magic, Faith and Healing,* A. Kiev, ed. New York: Macmillan, 1974.

King, S. H. "Social Psychological Factors in Illness." *Handbook of Medical Sociology,* 1972, p. 130.

Kleczkowski, B. M., and Pibouleau, R., eds. *Approaches to Planning and Design of Health Care Facilities in Developing Areas,* Vol. 3. Geneva: World Health Organization, 1979.

Klein, J. "Susto: The Anthropological Study of Diseases of Adaptation." *Social Science and Medicine* 12B:23–28, 1978.

Kleinman, A., Eisenberg, L., and Good, B. "Culture, Illness, and Care." *Annals of Internal Medicine* 88(2):251 (February), 1978.

Kohn, R., and White, K. *Health Care: An International Study.* London: Oxford University Press, 1976.

Kosa, J., Zola, I. K., and Antonavsky, A. "Health and Poverty Reconsidered." In *Poverty and Health: A Sociological Analysis,* J. Kosa, A. Antonovsky, and I. K. Zola, eds. Cambridge, Mass.: Harvard University Press, 1969.

Kraytman, M. "Le Cancer: Que Veut en Savoir le Malade?" *Le Soir,* September 18, 1976.

Kuan, L. G. "Concepts of Illness and Health Care Intervention in an Urban Community." *Graduate Seminar Journal* 1(2):61–72 (March-April), 1977.

Kübler-Ross, E. *On Death and Dying.* New York: Macmillan, 1969.

Kuhn, T. S. *The Structure of Scientific Revolutions.* Chicago: University of Chicago Press, 1962.

Kupka, K. *International Classification of Diseases,* 9th Rev. *WHO Chronicle* 32:219–225, 1978.

Lamberts, H. "De Morbiditeitsanalyse—1972 Door de Groepspraktijk Ommoord: Een Nieuwe Ordening van Ziekte-en Probleemgedrag voor de Huisartsgeneeskunde" (The 1972 Morbidity Analysis in the Ommond Group Practice: A New Classification of Illness and Problem Behaviour in General Practice). *Huisarts en Wetenschap* 17:455–473, 1974; 18:7–39, 1975; 18:61–73, 1975. (English summary available)

——. "Problem Behaviour in Primary Health Care." *Journal of the Royal College of General Practitioners* 29:331–335, 1979.

Lamberts, H., and Riphagen, F. E. "Working Together in a Team for Primary Health Care—A Guide to Dangerous Country." *Journal of the Royal College of General Practitioners* 25:745–752, 1975.

Lamberts, H., and Sloot, E. "Multidisciplinaire Probleemclassificatie" (Multidisciplinary Problem Classification). *Huisarts en Wetenschap* 21:53–59, 1978.

(English summary available)

Lambo, T. A. "A Form of Social Psychiatry in Africa." *World Mental Health* 13:190–203, 1961.

Lapassade, G., and Lourau, R. "Clef pour la Sociologie." Paris: Sehers. Coll. Clefs, 1974.

Larrieu, S. P. "Etude sur l'Accucil—Hôpital Pellegrin (Bordeaux)." *Proceedings of Reunion des Assistants Sociaux des Services Hospitaliers à Paris.* Paris: Ministère de la Santé Publique et de la Securité Sociale, 1971.

Laurell, A. C., Gil, J. B., Machetto, T., et al. "Disease and Rural Development: A Sociological Analysis of Morbidity in Two Mexican Villages." *International Journal of Health Services* 7:401–423, 1977.

Lawrence, D. W. "Sources of Patients in First Two Years of Solo Urban Family Practice." *Journal of Family Practice* 5:867–870, 1977.

Lazare, A., Esenthal, S., and Wasserman, L. "The Customer Approach to Patienthood: Attending to Patient Requests in a Walk-In Clinic." *Archives of General Psychiatry* 32:553–558, 1975.

Lee, S., and Butler, L. "The Three-Layered Cake: A Plan for Physician Compensation." *New England Journal of Medicine* 291:253–256, 1974.

Leeson, J., and Frankenberg, R. "The Patients of Traditional Doctors in Lusaka." *African Social Research* 23:217–234, 1977.

Leon, C. A., and Climent, C. E. "Anotaciones Sobre El Ojo en Cali." *Acta Psiquiatrica Psicologica y de America Latina* XIV (1):23–24, 1968.

Le Shan, L. "Psychological Status as Factors in the Development of Malignant Disease: A Critical Review." *Journal of National Cancer Institute* 21, 1959.

Levi, L. "Psycho-Social Factors in Preventive Medicine" (Report to the Surgeon General on Health Promotion and Disease Prevention). Report prepared for the Institute of Medicine, National Academy of Sciences, Washington, D.C., February 1979.

Levy-Leboyer, C., and Gadbois, C. "La Penurie d'Infirmières en France." *Cahiers de Sociologie et de Demographie Medicales* No. 3, pp. 152–159, 1968.

Lewin, I. "A Ficha Clinica e o Trabalho Medico; Papel na Assistencia, Educacao, Comunicacao e Avaliacao." *R. Med. ATM* 10:1–28, 1975.

Lewin, I., Busnello, E., and Ruschel, S. "O Prontuario de Familia Orientado para a Solucao de Problemas." *Rev. Associacao Medica Brasileira* 25(1):5–8, January 1979.

Lewin, K. *Psychologie Dynamique, les Relations Humaines.* Paris: P. U. F., 1959.

Likert, R. *New Patterns of Management.* New York: McGraw-Hill, 1961.

Lipkin, M., Jr. "Psychologic Aspect of Evaluations of Outcome." In *Resources for Health,* D. Banta, ed. New York: Praeger, 1982.

———. "On the Teaching of Psychosocial Aspects of Primary Care." In *The Roles of Family Practice, Internal Medicine, Obstetrics and Gynecology and Pediatrics in Providing Primary Care* (Report of the 73rd Ross Conference in Pediatric Research), D. M. Berwick, ed. Columbus, Ohio: Ross, 1977.

Lipkin, M., Jr., and Putnam, S. *On the Teaching of Interviewing: A Report of a Workshop.* New York: Society for Research and Education in Primary Care Internal Medicine, 1980.

Lipkin, M., Jr., and White, K. L. *Primary Care Research in 1980.* New York: The Rockefeller Foundation, 1981.

Lipowski, Z. J. "Psycho-Somatic Medicine in the Seventies: An Overview." *American Journal of Psychiatry* 134:3 (March), 1977.

Locke, B. Z., Finucane, D. L., and Hassler, F. "Emotionally Disturbed Patients Under Care of Private Non-Psychiatric Physicians." *Psychiatric Research Report 22.* Washington, D. C.: American Psychiatric Association, 1967.

Locke, B. Z., and Gardner, E. A. "Psychiatric Disorders Among the Patients of General Practitioners and Internists." *Public Health Reports* 84:167–173, 1969.

Looney, J. G., Lipp, M. R., and Spitzer, R. L. "New Method of Classification for Psycho-Physiologic Disorders." *American Journal of Psychiatry* 135(6): 304–308, 1978.

Mahler, H. "The Role of Health in Socio-Economic Development: WHO's Director General Makes an Appeal to the ECOSOC." *WHO Chronicle* 33(9):315–321 (September), 1979.

Malkin, S. "Care of the Terminally Ill at Home." *CMA Journal* 115:129–130, 1976.

Marks, J. N., Goldberg, D. P., and Hillier, V. F. "Determinants of the Ability of General Practitioners to Detect Psychiatric Illness." *Psychological Medicine* 9:337–353, 1979.

Marmot, M. G., et al. "Changing Social Class Distribution of Heart Disease." *British Medical Journal* 2:1109, 1978.

Marsland, D. W., Wood, M., and Mayo, F. "The Content of Family Practice." *Journal of Family Practice* 3:23, 1976.

_____. "A Data Bank for Patient Care, Curriculum, and Research in Family Practice: 526,196 Patient Problems." *Journal of Family Practice* 3:25–68, 1976.

Massion, J. "La Gestion des Hôpitaux." *Reflets et Perspectives de la Vie Economique* 15(6):425–442, 1976.

_____. "Le Management ou l'Art de Diriger et les Institutions de Soins." *Hospitalia,* pp. 25–30, January 1975.

_____. "La Participation et ses Instruments a l'Hôpital." Louvain: U. C. L., 1977. Document Polycopie.

Matsumoto, Y. S. "Social Stress and Coronary Heart Disease in Japan: A Hypothesis." *Milbank Memorial Fund Quarterly* 48:9–36, 1970.

Maurice, J. "Bruno Mon Fils. Une Mère et les Médecins." Paris: Stock, Coll. Temoigner, 1975.

Mayou, R. "The Nature of Bodily Symptoms." *British Journal of Psychiatry* 129: 5560, 1976.

McKeown, T. *The Role of Medicine.* Oxford: Basil Blackwell, 1979.

Meade, J. E. "Population Explosion, the Standard of Living and Social Conflict." *The Economic Journal* 77:233, 1967.

Meads, S., and McLemore, T. *The National Ambulatory Medical Care Survey: Symptom Classification* (DHEW Pub. No. (HRA) 751337). Washington, D. C.: Government Printing Office, 1974.

Mechanic, D. "The Concept of Illness Behavior." *Journal of Chronic Disease* 15:189–94, 1962.

_____. *Medical Sociology.* New York: Free Press, 1978.

_____. "Response Factors in Illness: The Study of Illness Behaviors." In *Patients, Physicians and Illness,* E. G. Jaco, ed. New York: Free Press, 1971.

_____. "Socioculture and Social-Psychological Factors Affecting Personal Responses to Psychological Disorder." *Journal of Health and Social Behavior* 16:393–404, 1975.

Melzack, R. *The Puzzle of Pain.* Harmondsworth, England: Penguin, 1973.

Mermot, C. G., and Syme, S. L. "Acculturation and Coronary Heart Disease in Japanese-Americans." *American Journal of Epidemiology* 104:225–247, 1976.

Metcalfe, D. H. H. "The Recognition of Family and Social Problems by General Practitioners: Towards Developing a Taxonomy." *Journal of the Royal College of General Practitioners* 28:46–52, 1978.

Micklin, M., and Leon, C. A. "Cultural Bases of Images of Causation in Psychological Disorder: A Colombian Survey." *Social Psychiatry* 24(2):79–94, 1978.

Mimura, G., et al. "A Study on Twins with Hypertension and Cerebrovascular Disease in Japan." In *Prophylactic Approach to Hypertensive Diseases,* Y. Yamori, et al., eds. New York: Raven Press, 1979.

Ministry of Health, Central Health Services Council. "Communication Between Doctors, Nurses and Patients: An Aspect of Human Relations in the Hospital Service" (Report of the Standing Medical Advisory Committee and Standing Nursing Advisory Committee). London: HMSO, 1963.

Ministry of Health, Republic of Zambia. *Priorities in Mental Health in Zambia.* Lusaka, Zambia: GRZ, Ministry of Health, 1979.

Minuchin, S. *Families and Family Therapy.* Cambridge, Mass.: Harvard University Press, 1974.

Moerman, F. "Etude de la participation dans l'entreprise hospitalier" (Memoire de Licence en Sciences Hospitalières). Louvain: 1971. Document Polycopie.

Monthly Vital Statistics Report Vol. 25, No. 2, Supp. 2 (DHEW Pub. No. (HRA) 76-1120). Rockville, Md.: Health Resources Administration, May 19, 1976.

"Morbidity, Continuing Observation and Recording of Research Committee." *Journal of Royal College of General Practitioners* 1:107–128, 1958.

Morley, D. "The Under-Five Clinics." In *Medical Care in Developing Countries.* N. King, ed. London: Oxford University Press, 1966.

Morrell, D. C. "Symptom Interpretation in General Practice." *Journal of the Royal College of General Practitioners* 22:297, 1972.

Morrell, D. C., Gage, H. G., and Robinson, N. A. "Symptoms in General Practice." *Journal of the Royal College of General Practitioners* 21:22, 1971.

Morrell, D. C., and Wale, C. J. "Symptoms Perceived and Recorded by Patients." *Journal of the Royal College of General Practitioners* 26:398–403, 1976.

Mount, B. "The Problem of Caring for the Dying in a General Hospital: The Palliative Care Unit as a Possible Solution." *CMA Journal* 115:119–121, 1976.

Mumford, E., and Skipper, J. K. *Sociology in Hospital Care.* New York: Harper & Row, 1967.

Murphy, M. B. "Social Change and Mental Illness." In *Causes of Mental Disorder:*

A Review of Epidemiological Knowledge. New York: Milbank Memorial Fund, 1961.

Mustafar, G. "Society in Relation to Mental Health in Kenya." *Journal of Nervous and Mental Disease* 156:300–305, 1973.

Mvunga, M. P. "A Call for Reform in the Law of Succession in Zambia." *ZANGO: Zambian Journal of Contemporary Issues* 4(5):18–23, 1978.

National Ambulatory Medical Care Survey of Visits to General Family Practitioners (Vital and Health Statistics of the National Center for Health Statistics) (Public Health Service pamphlet No. 15). Washington, D. C.: Government Printing Office, December 14, 1977.

National Center for Health Statistics. *Ambulatory Medical Care Rendered in Physicians' Offices, United States, 1975* (Advance Data from Vital and Health Statistics, No. 12) (DHEW Pub. No. (HRA) 771250). Hyattsville, Md.: Health Resources Administration, October 12, 1977.

National Center for Health Statistics. *The National Ambulatory Medical Care Survey: 1975 Summary, United States, January–December 1975* (Vital and Health Statistics, Series 13, No. 33) (DHEW Pub. No. (PHS) 78-1784). Washington, D. C.: DHEW, 1978.

National Center for Health Statistics: National Ambulatory Medical Care Survey, National Ambulatory Medical Care Survey of Visits to General and Family Physicians, January 1974-December. Washington, D.C.: DHEW, 1978.

Navarro, V. "The Underdevelopment of Health or the Health of Underdevelopment: An Analysis of the Distribution of Health Resources in Latin America." *International Journal of Health Services* 4:5–28, 1974.

Neuhauser, B. *The Relationship Between Administrative Activities and Hospital Performance* (Research Series 28). Chicago: University of Chicago Center for Health Administration Studies, 1971.

Office of Population Censuses and Surveys. *The General Household Survey* (Introductory Report). London: HMSO, 1973.

Office of Population Censuses and Surveys and the Royal College of General Practitioners. *Morbidity Statistics from General Practice.* London: HMSO, 1974.

Oliemans, A. P. *Morbiditeit in de Huisartspraktijk (Morbidity in General Practice).* Leiden, Netherlands: N. E. Stenfert Kroese, N. V., 1969.

Organisation for European Economic Cooperation. *Cost Reduction in Industry.* Paris: 1961.

"Organization of Mental Health Services in Developing Countries." *WHO Technical Report Series No. 564.* Geneva: World Health Organization, 1975.

Orr, D. "Employee Representation and Cooperation." *Harvard Business Review,* January-February 1977, pp. 36–46.

Ottosson, J. O., and Perris, C. "Multidimensional Classification of Mental Disorders." *Psychological Medicine* 3:238–243, 1973.

Pardes, H., and Daniels, R. S. "The Primary Care Dilemma." *Journal of Psychiatric Education* 1:123–134, 1977.

Patterson, E., and Stence, F. "Thinking Together to Solve Care Problems." *American Journal of Nursing* 70(8):1703–1706, 1970.

Paul, B., ed. *Health, Culture and Community: Case Studies of Public Reaction to*

Health Programme. New York: Russell Sage Foundation, 1976.

Peplau, H. E. *Interpersonal Relations in Nursing.* New York: G. P. Putnams Sons, 1952.

Pequignot, H., and Gatard, M. "Hôpital et Humanisation." Paris: E. S. F., 1976.

Perrow, C. "Hospitals: Technology, Structure and Goals." In *Handbook of Organizations,* J. G. March, ed. Chicago: Rand McNally, 1965.

Philips Technical Efficiency and Information Centre, ed. *The Organisation of Philips Turnhout.* Eindhoven-Turnhout:, 1975.

Phillips, L., Draguns, F. G., and Bartlett, D. P. "Classification of Behavior Disorders." In *Issues in the Classification of Children,* N. Hobbs, ed. San Francisco: Jossey-Bass, 1975.

Pike, K. L. *Language in Relation to a Unified Theory of the Structure of Human Behavior.* The Hague: Mouton, 1967.

Postel, G. *Gestion par Objectif et Participation: Un Case Concrèt de D. P. C.* Paris: Les Editions d'Organisation, 1971.

Poynter, N. *Medicine and Man.* Harmondsworth, England: Penguin, 1973.

Prevost, F. "Ma Vie en Plus." Paris: Stock, Coll. Elles-Mêmes, 1975.

Pride, L. P. "An Adrenal Stress Index as a Criterion Measure for Nursing." *Nursing Research* 19(4):292-303, 1968.

Primary Health Care (Report of the International Conference on Primary Health Care, Alma Ata, USSR, September 6-12, 1978). Geneva: World Health Organization, 1978.

Prugh, D. G. "Psychosocial Disorders in Childhood and Adolescence: Theoretical Considerations and an Attempt at Classification" (Appendix A). In *The Mental Health of Children: Services, Research and Manpower,* Joint Commission on Mental Health of Children, ed. New York: Harper & Row, 1973.

"Psychosocial Factors and Health." *WHO Chronicle* 30:337-339, 1976.

Puffer, R. R., and Serrano, C. V. *Caracteristicas de la Mortalidad en la Ninez.* Washington, D.C.: P.A.H.O., 1973.

Raimbault, E. "La formation psychologique de l'equipe hospitaliere en carcinologie." *Psychologie Medicale* 8(5):737-739, 1976.

Rawnsley, K. "Congruence of Independent Measures of Psychiatric Morbidity." *Journal of Psychosomatic Research* 10:84-93, 1966.

Reasons for Contact with Primary Care Services: A Model Classification. Geneva: WHO Working Group, 1979.

Records and Statistical Unit. "The Analysis of Routine Medical Records." *Journal of the Royal College of General Practitioners* 11:34-40, 1966.

Regier, D. A. "Psychiatry's Dilemma with Primary Care." *Journal of Psychiatric Education* 1:137-140, 1977.

Regier, D. A., Kessler, L. G., Burns, B. J., and Goldberg, I. D. "The Need for a Psychosocial Classification System in Primary Care Practice." *International Journal of Mental Health* 8:16-29, 1979.

Regier, D. A., Rosenfeld, A. H., Burns, B. J., and Goldberg, I. D. "The Nature and Scope of Mental Health Problems in Primary Care." Paper presented at the Institute of Medicine Conference on The Provision of Mental Health Services in Primary Care Settings, National Academy of Sciences, Washington, D. C., April 2-3, 1979.

Rescher, N. *Welfare: The Social Issues in Philosophical Perspective.* Pittsburgh: University of Pittsburgh Press, 1972.

Revans, R. W. "Standards for Morale." London: Oxford University Press, 1964.

Riessman, F., et al., eds. *The Mental Health of the Poor.* New York: Free Press, 1964.

Riley, J. N., and Sermsri, S. *The Variegated Thai Medical System as a Context for Birth Control Services.* Bangkok: Mahidol University, Institute of Population and Social Research, 1974.

Robbins, L. N. "Follow-Up Studies of Behavior Disorders in Children." In *Psychopathological Disorders of Childhood,* H. C. Quay, and J. S. Werry, eds. New York: Wiley, 1972.

————. "Mental Disorders in Children." Unpublished manuscript prepared for the President's Commission on Mental Health, February 1978.

Rojas-Aleba, I. "A Case Study on Community Health Development through Strengthening of the Health Care Delivery System and Research and Development." *Proceedings of the Interregional Workshop on the Development of Health Teams in Rural Work, Tacloban, Philippines.* Manila: World Health Organization, 1979.

Romanyshyn, J. M. *Social Welfare: Charity to Justice.* New York: Random House, 1971.

Rosen, B. M., Locke, B. Z., Goldberg, I. D., and Babigian, H. M. "Identification of Emotional Disturbance in Patients Seen in General Medical Clinics." *Hospital and Community Psychiatry* 23:364–370, 1972.

————. "The Mental Health Delivery System and Services to Children." In *Basic Handbook of Child Psychiatry,* J. D. Nospitz, ed. New York: Basic Books, 1979.

Rosen, G. "The Evolution of Social Medicine." In *Handbook of Medical Sociology,* H. E. Freeman, S. Levine, and L. S. Leeder, eds. Englewood Cliffs, N.J.: Prentice-Hall, 1979.

Rosenstock, I. "Prevention of Illness and Maintenance of Health." In *Poverty and Health: A Sociological Analysis,* J. Kosa, A. Antonovsky, and I. K. Zola, eds. Cambridge, Mass.: Harvard University Press, 1969.

Rosenthal, R., and Jacobson, L. *Pygmalion in the Classroom: Teachers' Expectations and Pupils' Intellectual Development.* New York: Holt, Rinehart & Winston, 1968.

Roth, J. "Information and the Control of Treatment in Tuberculosis Hospitals." In *The Hospital in Modern Society,* E. Freidson, ed. New York: Free Press, 1963.

Rowley, P. T., Fisher, L., and Lipkin, M., Jr. "Screening and Genetic Counseling for B-Thalessemia Trait in a Population Unselected for Interest." *American Journal of Human Genetics* 31:718–730, 1979.

Royal College of General Practitioners, Office of Population Censuses and Surveys and Department of Health and Social Security. *Morbidity Statistics from General Practice: Second National Study 1970–71.* London: HMSO, 1974.

Royal Commission on the Health and Safety of Workers in Mines. Ottawa: Government of Ontario, 1976.

Rubel, A. J. "The Epidemiology of a Folk Illness: Susto in Hispanic America." In *Culture, Disease, and Healing,* D. Landy, ed. New York: Macmillan, 1977.

Rutten, F. F. H., and Gaag, J. V. D. "Referrals and Demand for Specialist Care in the Netherlands." *Health Services Research* 12:233–249, 1977.

Rutter, M. "Classification and Categorization in Child Psychiatry." *Journal of Child Psychology and Psychiatry* 6:71–83, 1965.

_____. *Maternal Deprivation Reassessed.* Harmondsworth, England: Penguin, 1972.

Rutter, M., Lebovici, S., Eisenberg, L., et al. "A Tri-Axial Classification of Mental Disorders in Childhood: An International Study." *Journal of Child Psychology and Psychiatry* 10:41–61, 1969.

Rutter, M., Shaffer, D., and Shepher, M. *A Multi-Axial Classification of Child Psychiatric Disorders.* Geneva: World Health Organization, 1975.

Sackett, D. L. "Evaluation of Health Services." In *Public Health and Preventive Medicine,* 11th ed., J. M. Last, ed. New York: Appleton-Century-Crofts, 1980.

Saleh, S., et al. "Why Nurses Leave Their Jobs—An Analysis of Female Turnover." *Personnel Administration,* No. 27, pp. 25–28, 1965.

Samora, J., Saunders, L., and Larson, R. "Medical Vocabulary Knowledge Among Hospital Patients." In *Medical Care: Readings in the Sociology of Medical Institutions,* W. R. Scott, and E. Volkaert, eds. New York: Wiley, 1966.

Sandberg, C. G., and Nerell, G. "The Psycho-Social Working Environment—An Integrated View of Man and His Environment." Stockholm: Unpublished educational lecture material, Swedish Joint Industrial Safety Council, November 1979.

Sarda, F. "Le Droit de Vivre et le Droit de Mourir." Paris: Seuil, 1975.

Schneider, D., and Appleton, L. *Evaluation of NAMCS Symptom Classification: Final Report.* Chicago: American Medical Records Association, October 1976.

Schneider, D., Appleton, L., and McLemore, T. "A Reason-for-Visit Classification for Ambulatory Care." *National Center for Health Statistics,* Vital and Health Statistics, Series 2, No. 78 (DHEW Pub. No. (PHS) 78-1352). Hyattsville, Md.: Public Health Service, 1978.

Schneider, P. B. "Psychiatrie et Psychologie Medicale à l'Hôpital general." *Psychologie Medicale* 7(4):637–644, 1975.

Schottstaedt, W. W. "Sociologic, psychologic and metabolic observations of patients in the community of a metabolic ward." *American Journal of Medicine* (August): 248–257, 1958.

Schraml, W. J. *Pour un Hôpital Plus Humain: Guide à l'Usage des Infirmières, du Personnel Medical et Paramedical.* Mulhouse: Salvat, 1974.

Schwartz, L. R. "The Hierarchy of Resort in Curative Practices: The Admiralty Islands, Melanesia." *Journal of Health and Social Behavior* 10:201–209, 1969.

Scotch, N. "Sociocultural Factors in the Epidemiology of Zulu Hypertension." *American Journal of Public Health* 53:1205–1213, 1967.

Searle, J. "What Is a Speech Act?" In *Philosophy in America,* M. Black, ed. New

York: Allen & Unwin, 1965.

Sedes, J. M. *Efficacité et Rentabilité des Actions Medico-Sociales en Milieu Hospitalier.* Paris: Ministère de la Santé Publique et de la Prévoyance Sociale, 1974.

Sedes, J. M., and Sedes Sornay, I. "Evaluation des Besoins d'Assistance Medico-Sociale" (Documents de récherche du Ministère de la Santé Publique). Paris, 1974.

Seeman, M., and Evans, J. "Stratification and Hospital Care." *American Sociological Review* 26:6–80, 1961.

Serpell, R. "Context and Connotation: The Negotiation of Meaning in a Multiple Speech Repertoire." *Quarterly Newsletter of the Institute of Comparative Human Cognition* 1:10–15, 1977.

_____. "Cultural Validation in Psychological Research." In *Cross-Cultural Contributions to Psychology,* L. Eckensberger, Y. Poortinga, and W. J. Lonner eds. Amsterdam: Swets & Zeitlinger, 1979.

_____. "Learning to Say It Better: A Challenge for Zambian Education." In *Language and Education,* (Communication 14), L. N. Omondi and Y. T. Simukoko, eds. Lusaka, Zambia: Institute for African Studies, 1978.

Serpell, R., Anokhbonggo, W., Haworth, A., and Veno, A. *A Strategy of Increased Cooperation Between Traditional and Government Health Services in Zambia.* Lusaka: University of Zambia, 1979.

Shenkin, B., and Warner, D. "Giving the Patient His Medical Record; A Proposal to Improve the System." *New England Journal of Medicine* (September): 688-692, 1973.

Shepard, D. A. "Terminal Care: Towards an Ideal." *CMA Journal* 115:97–98, 1976.

Sheperd, M., Cooper, B., Brown, A. C., et al. *Psychiatric Illness in General Practice.* London: Oxford University Press, 1967.

Smith, J., and Cassell, J. "Factors Involving Sociocultural Incongruity and Change." *Milbank Memorial Fund Quarterly* 45:21–49, 1967.

Soljenitsyne, A. *L'Archipel du Goulag.* Paris: Seuil, 1976.

_____. *Le Pavillon des Cancereux.* Paris: Julliard, 1968.

Spitz, R. "Hospitalisme: Genese des Conditions Psychiatriques dan la Prime Enfance." *Etude Psychoanalytique de l'Enfant* I:53–74, 1945.

Spitzer, R. L., Endicott, J., and Robins, E. "Research Diagnostic Criteria." *Archives of General Psychiatry* 35:773–782, 1978.

Spitzer, R. L., and Forman, J. B. W. "DSM-III Field Trials: II. Initial Experience with the Multiaxial System." *American Journal of Psychiatry* 136:6, 1979.

Spitzer, R. L., Forman, J. B. W., and Nee, J. "DSM-III Field Trials: 1. Initial Interrater Diagnostic Reliability." *American Journal of Psychiatry* 136:815–817, 1979.

Starfield, B., et al. "Psychosocial and Psychosomatic Diagnoses in Primary Care of Children." *Pediatrics* 66:159–161, 1980.

Stewart, M. A., McWhinney, J. R., and Buck, C. W. "The Doctor/Patient Relationship and its Effect Upon Outcome." *Journal of the Royal College of General Practitioners* 29:77–82, 1979.

_____. "How Illness Presents: A Study of Patient Behavior." *Journal of Family Practice* 2:411–414, 1975.

Swift, J. K. "The Chaplain's Role in Care for the Dying: Toward a New Understanding." *CMA Journal* 115:181–185, 1976.

Szasz, T. S. "Psychiatric Classification as a Strategy of Social Constraint." In *Ideology and Insanity*, T. S. Szasz, ed. Garden City, N.Y.: Doubleday, 1969.

Tange, A. "Humaniser l'hôpital." *La Revue Nouvelle* 63(4):387–394, 1976.

Task Force on Pediatric Education. *The Future of Pediatric Education*. Evanston, Ill.: American Academy of Pediatrics, 1978.

Taylor, C. "Interpretations and the Sciences of Man." *Reviews of Metaphysics* 25:3–51, 1971.

Taylor, D. C. "The Components of Sickness: Diseases, Illnesses, and Predicaments." *Lancet* 2:1008–1010, 1979.

Tessler, R., Mechanic, D., and Diamond, M. "The Effect of Psychosocial Distress on Physician Utilization: A Prospective Study." *Journal of Health and Social Behavior* 17:353, 1976.

"Thai Injection Doctors; Antibiotic Mediator." *Social Science and Medicine* 4(1). 1–24, 1970.

The President's Commission on Mental Health. Washington, D. C.: Government Printing Office, 1978.

Thiadens, A. J. H. "The Patient as an Ally of the Doctor and the Nurse." Paper presented at an international seminar on Training programs in medical sociology, Leuven, August 1976. Document Polycopie.

Thiadens, A. J. H. *Ziekenhuis, menselijk en modern*. Kleventer: Kiliwer, 1972.

Thorne, M. Q., Jr. "PSRO—Future Impact on Community Mental Health Centers." *Community Mental Health Journal* 11(4):389.

Tryon, P. A., and Leonard, R. C. "A Clinical Test of Patient-Centered Nursing." *Journal of Health and Human Behaviour* No. 7, pp. 183–192, 1966.

United Nations International Children's Fund. *Children and Women in Zambia*. Lusaka, Zambia: UNICEF, 1979.

"Use of Health Care: An International Study." *WHO Chronicle*, Vol. 30, 1976.

Van Laethem, R. "La médecine psychosomatique va-t-elle remplacer la médecine générale." *Saint-Luc Medicale*, No. 3, 1971.

Verbond Der Christelijke Mutualiteiten. "Is uw ziekenhuis een goede gastheer?" (Projekt gezondheidsopvoeding). *Roeselaere*, 1976.

"The Virginia Family Practice Data System." Unpublished manuscript, Medical College of Virginia/Virginia Commonwealth University, Richmond, Virginia, 1979.

Weed, L. *Medical Records, Medical Education and Patient Care*. Cleveland, Ohio: The Press of Case Western Reserve University, 1969.

Weidman, H. H. "Falling Out: A Diagnostic and Treatment Problem Viewed from a Transcultural Perspective." *Social Science and Medicine* 13B:95–113, 1978.

Weil, R. "Formes Nouvelles d'Organisation du Travail dans l'Industrie Automobile Européenne." *Sociologie du Travail*, No. 1, pp. 15–35, 1976.

Weiner, H. *Psychobiology in Human Disease*. New York: Elsevier, 1977.

Westbury, R. C., and Taarant, M. "The Classification of Disease in General Practice." *Canadian Medical Association Journal* 101:82, 1969.

Westlander, G. *Summaries of Three Research Reports About Relations Between Working Conditions, Life Situation and Quality of Life*. Stockholm: The

Swedish Council of Personnel Administration, 1977.

White, C. H., and Maguire, M.-C. "Job Satisfaction and Dissatisfaction Among Hospital Nursing Supervisors: The Applicability of Herzberg's Theory." *Nursing Research* 22(1):25–30, 1973.

WHO Project on Monitoring Mental Health Needs. Bangkok: Ministry of Public Health, 1979. Mimeographed.

Williams, J. B. W. "Proposed Classification of Social Problems and Psychological Symptoms for Inclusion in a Classification of Health Problems." Rockville, Md.: National Institute of Mental Health, October 1979. Mimeo.

Williams, P. "Deciding How to Treat—The Relevance of Psychiatric Diagnosis." *Psychological Medicine* 9:179–186, 1979.

Wittgenstein, L. *The Blue and Brown Books.* New York: Harper & Row, 1958.

Wood, M., Mayo, F., and Marsland, D. "A Systems Approach to Patient Care, Curriculum, and Research in Family Practice." *Journal of Medical Education,* (50):1106–1112, 1975.

Woolley, P. O. *Syncrisis: The Dynamic of Health: Vol. XII, Thailand* (DHEW Pub. No. (OS) 74-50008). Washington, D.C.: Government Printing Office, 1974.

World Health Organization. *Basic Document,* 26th ed. Geneva: Author, 1946.

World Health Organization. *International Classification of Diseases, 1975,* 9th Rev. Vol. 1. Geneva: Author, 1977.

World Health Organization. *Manual of the International Statistical Classification of Diseases, Injuries, and Causes of Death,* 9th Rev., Vol. 1. Geneva: Author, 1977.

World Health Organization. *Medium-Term Programme for Mental Health, 1975–1982* (Report of the General Director). Geneva: Author, April 1978.

World Health Organization. *Primary Health Records: Report of a Working Group* (Rijeka, October 1977). (WHO Pub. No. WHO/HS/NAT.COM./78.357). Geneva: Author, 1978.

World Health Organization. *Psychiatry and Primary Medical Care: Report on a Working Group Convened by the Regional Office for Europe of the World Health Organization* (Lysebu, Oslo, April 10–13, 1973). Geneva: Author, 1973.

World Health Organization. *Psychosocial Factors and Health: Report of the Director-General* (WHO Pub. No. EB57/22). Geneva: Author, 1975.

World Health Organization. *Reporting, Processing and Using Data Generated from Nonhospital Health and Medical Records* (WHO Pub. No. WHO/HS/NAT.COM./79.364). Geneva: Author, 1979.

World Health Organization. *Strategies for Extending Mental Health Care: Report of the Second Meeting of Investigators* (Khartoum, October 10-14, 1977) (WHO Pub. No. MNH/78.7). Geneva: Author, 1978.

Zabarenko, L., Pittenger, R. A., and Zabarenko, R. *Primary Medical Practice: A Psychiatric Evaluation.* St. Louis: Warren Press, 1968.

Zigas, V., and van Delden, J. "New Guinea: Studies Relating the Medical and Behavioral Sciences, Part I." *Social Science and Medicine* 6:681–687, 1972.

Index

Recorder, definition of, 123
Recording health data, 58, 62, 134, 135,
    140, 142, 146, 147, 158, 161, 166,
    186, 187, 188, 190, 201, 219, 220,
    224, 312
Recording systems
    cross-cultural adaptation of, 243–274
    problem-oriented family records, 296–
    300
    values and value deficiencies in, 89–
    111
Referral in health care, 66, 154, 155, 156,
    158, 161, 188, 209, 252, 266, 271
Regression, 197
Reimbursement policies, 134, 148, 188
Reinforcement, 42, 315
Rejection, 6
Relationship problems, 162
Relatives, problems with, 332
Reliability of health data, 58, 116, 239,
    270, 303
Religion, 32, 264
Religious beliefs, 333
Religious persecution, 333
Reporting health data, 247–253, 258,
    270, 293–304
Reproduction problems, 3, 162
    see also Sexual problems
Research, 48, 91, 105, 111, 122, 142, 158,
    161, 162, 169, 203, 206, 219–220,
    232, 254, 255, 279, 286, 296, 298
    Netherlands, 57–66
Residential environment. See Housing
Residual, definition of, 123
Resistance
    to disease, 16, 41
    to psychosocial aspects in medical edu-
    cation, 315–316
    see also Susceptibility
Resource allocation, 87, 89, 157–158,
    169, 188, 220, 311
Resource sharing in medical education,
    317
Respiratory disease, 248, 287
Respiratory problems, 331
Response to illness. See Illness response
Restlessness, psychomotor, 330

Retirement problems, 331
RFC, 132–133, 136–137
Rigid appointment schedules of health
    facility, 333
Risk factors, 224, 235
    see also High-risk clients
Rituals, 331
    religious, nonconformity with, 333
Rockefeller Foundation, 327
Role dissatisfaction, 233, 333
Role models in medical education, 310,
    316
Roles
    medical profession, 294
    patient, 56
    plurality of, 223
    sex, 223
    social, 92, 106
    work, 45
Rubrics, classification, 67–68, 121, 125,
    126–133, 134, 160, 164, 165, 167,
    168–169, 170–183, 194, 198–199,
    202–203, 211, 212–213, 216–217,
    226–231, 329–333
    definition of, 122
Rules, conflict over, 332
Rural society, 22, 30, 32, 37, 156, 235,
    245, 246, 257, 261
RVC, 141–142, 144, 161, 172–176

Sadness, 330
Sanitation, 20, 41, 244, 245, 301
Satisfaction, 42, 97, 101, 102, 106, 162,
    233, 306
Scandinavian countries, 44
Schizophrenia, childhood, 189
School, health and, 189, 194, 205, 222
School failure and refusal, 333
Science and technology, 3, 255
Scientific medicine, 84, 278, 285, 296
    see also Western medicine
Screening, 142, 147–148, 154, 161, 308
Sects and cults, 235, 280
Seeing things, 331
Seizures, 18, 278
Self-care, 5, 10, 35, 57, 86, 142, 308
Self-esteem, 45, 92, 330

List of Contributors

MANUEL FLORES BONIFACIO, Ph.D., Sociologist, College of Arts and Sciences, University of Philippines, Quezon City, Philippines

CAROL BUCK, M.D., Ph.D., D.P.H., President, International Epidemiological Association; Professor of Epidemiology and Preventive Medicine, Faculty of Medicine, University of Western Ontario, London, Ontario, Canada

JACK D. BURKE, JR., M.D., M.P.H., Research Psychiatrist, Division of Biometry and Epidemiology, National Institute of Mental Health, Rockville, Maryland

BARBARA J. BURNS, Ph.D., Chief of Primary Care Section, Applied Biometry Research Branch, Division of Biometry and Epidemiology, National Institute of Mental Health, Rockville, Maryland

BURTON G. BURTON-BRADLEY, M.D., F.R.C.P., Professor of Psychiatry, Division of Mental Health, Department of Public Health, Konedobu, Papua, New Guinea

E. D'ARRIGO BUSNELLO, M.D., Chief Medical Officer, U. la Sao do Murialdo Health Center; Associate Professor of Psychiatry, Universidade Federal do Rio Grande do Sul, Porto Alegre, Brazil

ANTHONY W. CLARE, M.D., Senior Lecturer and Honorary Consultant Psychiatrist, Deputy Director of the General Practice Research Unit, Institute of Psychiatry, London, England

CARLOS E. CLIMENT, M.D., Professor and Chairman, Department of Psychiatry, Universidad del Valle, Cali, Colombia

DENISE DELIEGE, Ph.D., Professor of Social Sciences, Ecole de Santé Publique, Faculté de Médicine, Université de Louvain, Brussels, Belgium

LASZLO FUSTOS, B.A., M.A., Senior Associate, Center for Value Sociology, Hungarian Academy of Science, Budapest, Hungary

IRVING D. GOLDBERG, Ph.D., M.P.H., Chief, Applied Biometrics Research Branch, National Institute of Mental Health, Rockville, Maryland

WALTER GULBINAT, Statistician, Division of Mental Health, World Health Organization, Geneva, Switzerland

ELEMER HANKISS, Ph.D., Programme Director, Center for Value Sociology, Hungarian Academy of Sciences, Budapest, Hungary

THAVITONG HONGVIVATANA, Ph.D., Director of Medical Social Science Graduate Programme, Mahidol University, Bangkok, Thailand

LARRY KESSLER, Ph.D., Statistician, Division of Biometry and Epidemiology, National Institute of Mental Health, Rockville, Maryland

KAREL KUPKA, M.D., Chief Medical Officer, International Classification of Diseases, World Health Organization, Geneva, Switzerland

HENK LAMBERTS, M.D., Ph.D., Gemeentelijke Gen-eskundige en Gezondheidsdienst, Groepspraktijk Ommoord, Rotterdam, Netherlands

MACK LIPKIN, JR., M.D., Co-chairman, Task Force on Medical Interviewing, Society for Research and Education in Primary Care Internal Medicine; Clinical Associate Professor of Medicine, New York University; The Rockefeller Foundation, New York, New York

ROBERT MANCHIN, M.A., Senior Associate, Center for Value Sociology, Hungarian Academy of Sciences, Budapest, Hungary

DARREL A. REGIER, M.D., M.P.H., Director, Division of Biometry and Epidemiology, National Institute of Mental Health, Rockville, Maryland

ROBERT SERPELL, Ph.D., Director and Professor, Institute for African Studies, University of Zambia, Lusaka, Zambia

ROBERT L. SPITZER, M.D., Professor of Psychiatry, Columbia University; Chairman, Task Force on Nomenclature and Statistics, American Psychiatric Association, New York, New York

PETER WESTERHOLM, M.D., Consultant Epidemiologist, The National Board of Welfare, Stockholm, Sweden

JANET B. W. WILLIAMS, M.S.W., D.S.W., Assistant Director, Department of Social Service, New York State Psychiatric Institute, New York, New York

MAURICE WOOD, M.D., Professor and Director of Research, Department of Family Practice, Medical College of Virginia, Virginia Commonwealth University, Richmond, Virginia

The contributors listed above participated in one or more of the following meetings:

1. Primary Health Care: Triaxial Recording of Physical, Psychological, and Social Components
   Bellagio, Italy, February 9–13, 1981

2. Recording Health Problems Triaxially: WHO Consultation on an International Collaborative Study
   Rockefeller Foundation, New York, February 19–21, 1980

3. Workshop on Psychosocial Factors Affecting Health: Assessment Classification and Utilization
   Bellagio, Italy, November 6–10, 1979

About the Editors

Mack Lipkin, Jr. is Clinical Associate Professor of Medicine at New York University. He is a consultant to the Rockefeller Foundation where he was formerly Visiting Research Fellow. Prior to that he was Assistant Professor of Medicine and Psychiatry at the University of Rochester. Dr. Lipkin has published widely on psychosocial aspects of primary care internal medicine and on integrated approaches to medicine. Most recently he has published *Population-Based Medicine: The Use and Abuse of Medicine* and *Primary Care Research in 1982*. He is the author of numerous articles, has edited eight books, and presently co-chairs a task force on the medical interview and related skills for the Society for Research and Education in Primary Care Internal Medicine. Dr. Lipkin holds an A.B. from Harvard College, an M.D. from Harvard Medical School, did internal medicine residency at the University of North Carolina, and was a United States Public Health Service Fellow in Medicine and Psychiatry at the University of Rochester.

Karel Kupka is Chief Medical Officer, International Classification of Diseases, World Health Organization, Geneva. He has held this position since 1967. Prior to that he was WHO Medical Officer and Advisor to the Moroccan government in epidemiology and health statistics. From 1958 to 1961, he was Assistant Professor of Epidemiology at the University of Pittsburgh. Dr. Kupka has written a series of articles on epidemiology. As well, he has written widely on the classification of diseases and is responsible for the *International Classification of Diseases*. Dr. Kupka holds an M.D. degree from the Faculty of Medicine in Paris and a doctorate in Public Health and Epidemiology from the University of Pittsburgh.

49305